The Catholic Church and Politics in Brazil, 1916-1985

The Catholic Church and Politics in Brazil, 1916-1985

Scott Mainwaring

Stanford University Press   Stanford, California   1986

Stanford University Press
Stanford, California

©1986 by the Board of Trustees of the
Leland Stanford Junior University
Printed in the United States of America
CIP data appear at the end of the book

Published with the assistance of a special grant
from the Stanford University Faculty
Publication Fund to help support nonfaculty work
originating at Stanford.

For my parents

Acknowledgments

DURING THE RESEARCH and writing of this book, I incurred a large number of intellectual and personal debts. I began the book as a dissertation at Stanford University, and I am especially grateful to my reading committee, Robert Packenham, Richard Fagen, and John Wirth, for their excellent comments and criticisms, their encouragement, and the time they invested in helping give the work the degree of cohesion and clarity it now possesses. All three were careful and challenging readers.

From August 1980 until June 1982 I lived in Brazil, where I did most of the research and began the writing, and I made follow-up trips in October 1983 and January 1985. To all the people who shared in the intellectual and personal journey of my years in Brazil I feel a deep gratitude. Here I can acknowledge only a few of the many friends and acquaintances—bishops, priests, and nuns; theologians and social scientists; workers and peasants—who encouraged my work. Special thanks go to Vanilda Paiva, Luiz Alberto Gómez de Souza, and Estrella Bohadana, excellent colleagues and friends. J. B. Libânio, Luiz Gonzaga de Souza Lima, Cristiano Camerman, and Marina Bandeira provided many helpful suggestions. I had a rich experience getting to know workers and priests who participated in the Catholic Youth Workers movement, and I would particularly like to acknowledge the help and encouragement of Agostinho Pretto, José Domingos Cardoso, Maria Angelina de Oliveira, Maria Irony Bezerra Cardoso, Manoel de Jesus Soares, Tibor Sulik, and Wilson Farias. Equally rich were my experiences in Nova Iguaçu, where I especially appreciated the help of Azuleika Rodrigues Sampaio, Ivo Antônio de Carvalho, Hugo Paiva, and Frei Luiz Thomas. I appreciated the encouragement of many other individuals, including Wanderley Guilherme dos Santos, Eli Diniz, Diane Grosklaus, Cândido Procópio Ferreira de Camargo, Júlia Adão Bernardes, Jether Pereira Ramalho, Ivo Lesbaupin, Rubem César Fernandes, Paulo Krischke, Rosane Costa de Alves, and Leda Lúcia Queiroz. Maria Luiza Amarante generously donated her time to do an excellent translation of an expanded version of Chapter 6. The institutional support of IBRADES, IUPERJ, where I worked for several months, and ISER was helpful.

I finished the book as a Fellow of the Kellogg Institute and member of the Government Department at the University of Notre Dame. Many friends and colleagues at Notre Dame, Stanford, and elsewhere in the United States contributed to the book. I am particularly grateful to Guillermo O'Donnell, Alfred Stepan, and Ralph Della Cava. Alexander Wilde, Thomas Bruneau, Daniel Levine, Juan J. Linz, Donald Share, and Eduardo Viola made invaluable contributions. I appreciated the help of Renato Boschi, Charles Drekmeier, Lisa Fuentes, Eric O. Hanson, Edson Nunes, Madeleine Adriance, Susan Elfin, and Claude Pomerleau. John Ziemer, John Feneron, and Norris Pope provided many helpful suggestions for revisions.

An earlier version of Chapter 9 appeared as "The Catholic Church, Popular Education, and Political Change in Brazil," in the *Journal of Inter-American Studies and World Affairs*, 26 (Feb. 1984): 97–124, copyright ©1984 by Sage Publications, Inc. I am grateful to Sage Publications, Inc., for permission to reuse this material.

The research for this book would not have been possible without grants from the Fulbright-Hayes Commission, the Social Science Research Council, the Whiting Foundation, and Soroptimist International of the Americas. The Kellogg Institute offered a singularly stimulating environment for finishing this book and starting new projects. The Department of Political Science and the Center for Latin American Studies at Stanford provided institutional and financial support. Although acknowledging the support received from these institutions, I bear sole responsibility for the ideas.

My greatest source of support and inspiration during many years, including those in Brazil, was Mary Elene Wood. Her easygoing nature, fine sense of humor and fairness, and intelligence greatly enriched my life.

S. M.

Contents

Preface

MANY OF THE GREATEST social theorists of the past 150 years saw the death of God or religion as imminent and desirable. Writing in the 1830's, Ludwig Feuerbach dismissed religion as a projection, a response to a perceived need for protection against nature. For Feuerbach, religion diverts attention from real problems and is one of the most alienating elements in society. Marx agreed with Feuerbach that religion is a projection, but he was even more severe in his assessment, perceiving religion as an ideological mystification that bolsters domination by the bourgeoisie and serves as an opiate for the masses. Nietzsche saw religion as a projection that creates psychological torture and unhappiness. In his most famous statement, Nietzsche proclaimed and applauded the death of God. Freud saw religion as an illusion that grows out of the individual's need for protection and society's need to impose moral guidelines to maintain the social order. He believed that making our world more rational would lead to a healthy displacement of this illusion. Weber was more reluctant to write an obituary for religion or God, but he believed that as society became more "rationalized," religion would become a distinctive realm of the nonrational. Implicitly for Weber, as well as for the majority of subsequent sociologists of religion, religion would become a less central force in the world, perhaps even a completely atavistic practice.[1]

These obituaries seem strikingly premature today. God may have died at Nietzsche's hands, but He has been born again and again. Religion may be, as Feuerbach, Marx, and Freud agreed, an illusion, but contrary to their predictions it has been an illusion with a strong future.

For the North American public, nothing so sharply called attention to the tremendous motivating power of religion as the Iranian revolution. However dramatic it was, the Iranian revolution was not the only recent incident to show the continuing importance of religion in the lives of much of the world's population. In Poland, the Catholic Church has been a prominent force in legitimating the struggles of the opponents of the Soviet-backed regime. Throughout Europe and the United States, religion remains a major determinant of voting behavior and other social practices. Large segments of the Latin American Church have played an important role in combating authoritarian abuses, in defending human rights, and, in Central America, in working toward revolution.

This book examines the history from 1916 to 1985 of one of the most important religious institutions in the world, the Brazilian Catholic Church. Beginning with the meeting of the Latin American Bishops Conference at Medellín, Colombia, in 1968, the Latin American Church has strongly influenced the development of Catholicism. Since the early 1970's, the most significant impetus for change in Catholicism—and the biggest headaches for the cautious Vatican bureaucracy—has come from Latin America; within Latin America, the Brazilian Church is particularly important as the largest and most progressive national Church. The Brazilian Catholic Church has more adherents than any other church in the Western world, and since the mid-1970's it has probably been the most progressive Catholic Church in the world. It has been at the forefront of some of the most significant changes the Church has undergone in recent centuries.

In addition, the Brazilian Church has established an important presence in national politics. Closely linked to the state and the dominant classes until 1964, the Church came into serious conflict with the state during the two decades of military rule. During the most repressive period (1968-74) the Church was often the only institution with sufficient political autonomy to criticize the authoritarian regime and defend human rights. As Brazil moved toward liberal democracy in the mid-1980's, it continued to be politically important.

In examining the Church's transformation, we should emphasize that this process is open-ended. The Church remains a highly complex and heterogeneous institution, and conservative forces have reasserted themselves in recent years. Beginning with the papacy of John XXIII (1958-63), Catholicism moved to become more relevant to the modern world. Yet it continued to retain many traditional customs, beliefs, and practices. As new ideas have emerged within the Church, the old ones have displayed a remarkable resilience, leading to a curious admixture of traditional and new, of radical, liberal, conservative, and reactionary.

My study focuses on how and why the Church has changed and on some of the consequences of these changes. Chapter 1 discusses some theoretical considerations concerning the study of the Church. The remainder of the book is divided into three parts. Part I examines the neo-Christendom Church, 1916-55 (Chapter 2), and the Church during the late populist period, 1955-64 (Chapters 3-4). Part II analyzes the Church under the authoritarian military regime, 1964-73 (Chapters 5-6), and Part III discusses the Church during the liberalization of the authoritarian regime, 1974-85 (Chapters 7-11).

The book begins with a famous pastoral letter written by Dom Sebastião Leme in 1916 and ends with the return to liberal democracy in March 1985. Chapter 2 provides background information essential to understanding the transformation of the 1955-85 period. The rest of the book divides the recent transformation into three periods: 1955-64, 1964-73, and 1974-85. Chapters 3, 5, and 7 provide overviews of Church developments during these periods, focusing primarily on the bishops. Chapters 4, 6, and 8 analyze lay and grass-roots movements in the Church. The last three chapters discuss major questions in the contemporary Church: the contributions grass-roots Catholic organizations can make to the democratization process, the political vision of the popular Church, and the decline of the popular Church after 1982.

The heart of the book focuses on the origins, development, and dilemmas of the "popular" or "progressive" (the terms are used synonymously) Church. By popular Church, I mean those sectors that have a progressive political vision of the Church's mission. This political vision is expressed in theological conceptions and in pastoral work with the popular classes (peasants, workers, and poor urban residents). In general, the intellectuals of the popular Church are committed to radical social transformation. In Brazil, in contrast to some Latin American countries, the popular Church does not consist of local-level pastoral agents who are in conflict with the institutional Church. The fundamental cleavage in the Brazilian Church does not pit the base against the hierarchy, but rather involves dif-

ferent conceptions of the Church's mission, crossing boundaries between lay groups, priests and nuns, and bishops. Except for the
1916-55 period, the book focuses principally on movements for reform or radical change. Less attention is paid to conservative movements and groups, but throughout I am concerned with assessing
the relative strengths and views of different factions.

The book discusses four different models of the Church, each of
which understands its mission and relationship to politics differently. These are the neo-Christendom, the modernizing (and later
the neo-conservative), the reformist, and the popular models of the
Church. I compare the way these four models perceive the Church's
mission and its relationship to the society (state, dominant and middle sectors, popular classes). These four models of the Church are
"ideal types" in the Weberian sense. Any particular individual or
movement could embrace elements of at least two of the models.
Also, the emergence of a new model does not preclude the continuing existence of models that arose earlier. In the contemporary
Church, the neo-conservatives are close to the modernizers of the
1950's, and the reformists are still vital elements. The typology is
not exhaustive; other categories could be added.

All of these models have a political impact. The question is not
whether the Church is involved in politics, but *how* it is involved.
Despite conservative arguments calling for a return to a traditional
Church aloof from politics, the neo-Christendom Church and its
predecessors in Brazil were more overtly involved in politics than
the contemporary activist Church. Many important historical figures of the nineteenth century were priests, and during the years of
neo-Christendom dominance, leading clerics cultivated friendships
with politicians to extract favors from the state, formed an electoral
league to tell Catholics how to vote, and participated in the right-
wing Integralist movement. Conservative Catholics frequently criticize the activists on the grounds that their actions are political and
not religious. In reality, however, all religious practices, symbols,
and discourse either reinforce or challenge (or both, in different
combinations) dominant values and ultimately the mode of domination. To assert that the Church necessarily has a political impact,
however, does not resolve what that impact should be or how close
the linkages between politics and religion should be. The proper relation between politics and religion is the great question within the
contemporary Brazilian and Latin American churches.

Over the past fifteen years, the Catholic Church in Latin America has become the object of study by social scientists and historians. My analysis builds on their work, but it also differs on some theoretical questions, as Chapter 1 makes clear. I spend more time analyzing Church–civil society relations (as opposed to Church-state relations) than most previous works have. Specifically, I analyze in some depth the relationship between the Church and the popular classes. I also devote considerably more attention to lay movements (Chapters 4 and 6) and grass-roots movements (Chapters 8 and 9). It is impossible to understand the Church's role in contemporary Latin America without considering grass-roots organizations, especially the ecclesial base communities. Finally, whereas most previous analysis has focused on institutional strategy for responding to change, I pay more attention to the unintended consequences of social movements and conflicts in changing the Church.

One of the difficulties in studying the contemporary popular Church is obtaining access to information. Relying exclusively on written documents is inadequate, both because of the gap between ideology and practice and because documents indicate little about how religious ideas motivate people to participate in politics. Consequently, it is important to study actual Church practices—yet doing so is difficult. Years of repression against popular organizations and activist Church leaders, coupled with a widespread Church tendency to reject "outsiders," create access problems. I was fortunate enough to win the trust of a group of insiders, who opened many doors for me. Particularly significant in this regard was my opportunity to work at the Brazilian Institute of Economic and Social Development (IBRADES), a Jesuit center in Rio de Janeiro. I spent considerable time talking with people in the popular Church, and an indispensable part of the ideas for Chapters 7-11 came from such conversations.

I also had contact with political and Church leaders critical of radical Catholics. My view of the Brazilian Church therefore reflects contact with a wide range of people, even though I concentrated on progressive Church participants and leaders. I spent most of my time in Rio de Janeiro, a relatively conservative archdiocese, but I also interviewed pastoral agents in the archdioceses and dioceses of Nova Iguaçu, Duque de Caxias, Volta Redonda, São Paulo, Santo André, Goiás Velho, Brasília, Goiânia, João Pessoa, Recife, Pesqueira, Petrópolis, and Belo Horizonte.

The Catholic Church and Politics in Brazil, 1916-1985

CHAPTER 1

The Church and Politics:
Theoretical Considerations

OVER A PERIOD of time, new religious experiences emerge and old religious institutions change, and it becomes necessary to rethink past arguments about the relationship between churches and politics. This is the case with even an established institution like the Roman Catholic Church. My purpose in this chapter is to outline the general theoretical perspective of the book, calling particular attention to the ways in which the changes of the past three decades challenge some conventional social science theorizing about the Church and politics. The chapter draws upon—but also questions aspects of—three main lines of interpretation of the relationship between the Church and politics: institutional analysis, which has prevailed in most North American works on the subject; a neo-Marxian approach, which has been formulated primarily by Latin Americans; and the classical line of analysis established by Max Weber, Ernst Troeltsch, H. Richard Niebuhr, and others.

The Church as an Institution

A basic postulate—well established by both contemporary institutional analysis and classical sociological studies of the Church—is that any analysis of the Church and politics must consider the institutional character of the former. Faith is a suprarational phenomenon that claims to be above everything else. The Church starts from this faith, but like all institutions it develops interests and then attempts to defend them. The foremost objective of any church is to propagate its religious message, but depending on its perception of that message, it may become concerned with defending interests such as its unity, its position vis-à-vis other religions, its influence in society and on the state, the number of its adherents, and its financial situation. Almost all institutions are concerned with their own preservation; many are concerned with expansion. These concerns easily lead to adopting means inconsistent with the initial goals.[1]

Despite its transcendent character, the Church is subject to this same process. Given a belief that it offers the sole path to salvation, a church easily becomes concerned with such issues as its position with respect to other religions or the number of priests available to disseminate its message. These instrumental interests can acquire a dynamic of their own and help to determine the church's actions. In competing with other religions, a church may engage in practices inconsistent with its own creed. In this sense, protection of its interests can conflict with the initial religious message. "Christendom," H. Richard Niebuhr argued,

has often achieved apparent success by ignoring the precepts of its founder. The Church, as an organization interested in self-preservation and in the gain of power, has sometimes found the counsel of the Cross quite as inexpedient as have national and economic groups. In dealing with such major social evils as war, slavery, and social inequality, it has discovered convenient ambiguities in the letter of the Gospels which enabled it to violate their spirit and to ally itself with the prestige and power those evils had gained in their corporate organization.[2]

Defending organizational interests is not necessarily counter to pursuing a sincere faith; nor does pure faith occur only outside the institutional Church. In some conceptions of religion, defending conventional organizational interests is essential to promoting the faith. In this view, since salvation can come only through the institution, the church needs these resources to fulfill its mission effectively.

The tendency to protect organizational interests has been a key element of the Catholic Church's involvement in politics, and it will remain so. Today this is especially true of the Church's need to maintain a degree of unity and coherence. The Church's traditional commitment to universal salvation (as opposed to salvation for the chosen few) is critical in its attempt to appeal to all social classes and to people of widely different political beliefs. This effort to appeal to all imposes a cautious character upon the Vatican and national bishops conferences—cautious not necessarily in the sense of being politically conservative, but rather of avoiding extremes and radical changes.[3] The Church has consistently marginalized those movements that threatened its ability to appeal to people from different classes and to people with a wide range of religious and political beliefs.[4] In the contemporary Latin American Church, radical movements that the hierarchy perceived as constituting a parallel magisterium have been consistently undermined.[5]

Many leaders within the radical Catholic movement have ignored the implications of the Church's attempt to protect its identity and other interests. Historically, the Church has co-opted or undermined sectarian movements within Catholicism, and we can expect such treatment to continue. From this observation stem two conclusions. First, progressive Catholics who wish to contribute to changing the whole institution will have to make concessions to avoid becoming a sectarian movement. Second, the pace of innovation and change that the popular Church has stimulated during the past decade will almost certainly be difficult to sustain. As part of a larger institution committed to retaining universal appeal, the popular Church will have to accept some limitations. Indeed, as my concluding chapter argues, Rome and the Latin American Bishops Conference (CELAM) began to increase pressure on the Brazilian Church about 1982.

Church Interests and Models of the Church

Though agreeing with institutional analysts and the classical sociologists of religion that we must consider the Church's institutional character, I differ in the way I conceive of Church interests. The basic idea of institutional analysis is that we can understand change in institutions as an attempt to defend their interests and expand their influence. The organization changes principally because its interests oblige it to change in accord with transformations in the society at large. This mode of analysis emphasizes the study of the institution itself, although it does not overlook the social conditions that affect the institution.

The pioneer study of the Latin American Church to employ institutional analysis was Ivan Vallier's *Catholicism, Social Control, and Modernization in Latin America*. As does Thomas Bruneau, author of two important books on the Brazilian Church, Vallier suggests studying the Church principally in regard to its attempts to maximize its influence in society. He sees the transformation of the Latin American Church as the institution's means of maximizing its influence in a changed society. Despite significant differences in approach, a number of Brazilians also suggest that change in the Church resulted from its attempts to defend its interests, increase the number of practicants, and preserve the institution.[6]

Organizational analysis that emphasizes the unique character of the Church as an organization and the conflict between different institutional objectives can offer important insights. Unfortunately, studies of the Latin American Church have tended to reify the notion of institutional interests and failed to perceive that different models of the Church result in different conceptions of its interests.[7] If institutional interests were consistently conceived broadly as the Church's efforts to promote a certain vision of faith, institutional analysts would be correct in asserting that the Church functions according to different understandings of its interests. But institutional analysts waver between this broader conception and a narrower one, often reducing the Church's motivations to a mere defense of its influence. For example, though recognizing that the Church's foremost goal is transcendental, Bruneau measures influence in terms of "mass attendance, ability to stimulate vocations, number of schools, money received, and percentage of the population formally declared members of the religion."[8] The Church's transformation, then, would be an attempt to maximize these goals.

Bruneau's explanation begins to falter when confronted by groups within the Church who consciously seek to live on less money, who are less concerned with attendance at mass, or who sever ties with elites. Most organizational analysts have understated the conflicts between different conceptions of institutional objectives—different models of the Church. Defending the Church's interests includes such potentially contradictory goals as encouraging high mass attendance, fighting Communism, fighting for social justice, and having a close relationship with the elite.

The Church has a hierarchy of goals, ranging from its ultimate objective (saving people and teaching the religious message) to instrumental concerns. Goals such as institutional expansion, a strong financial position, influence among the state or elite are *instrumental* objectives that the Church need not pursue. Most organizational approaches tend to confuse these instrumental goals with the Church's ultimate objective, ignoring the possibility that some models of the Church could opt not to defend certain of these interests.

The Church's actions reflect value choices and political struggles within it. Any particular model of the Church protects some interests—but at the expense of others. Church goals as articulated by one vision of faith may be downplayed or rejected by another. For example, a close relationship with ruling elites was part of the neo-Christendom model of the Church, but the contemporary popular Church sees this as impeding its mission in fighting for social justice. There are no objective interests that a church is compelled to pursue.[9] Within the Church there are many conflicting views of the institution's true interests and how to pursue them. Depending on one's model of the Church, pursuing a given interest can be seen as absolutely essential or as wrong.

As is the case with institutional interests, the notion of exercising influence is not politically neutral or objectifiable. The Church's influence is as much a question of *what* groups it chooses (consciously or not) to favor as it is of *how much* influence it exercises. It is possible to attempt to maximize certain kinds of influence or to maximize influence among some social groups and classes. But increased influence among some classes and groups can lead—and has led in the Brazilian case—to decreased influence among other classes and groups. Similarly, influence of one kind (for example, ability to organize the popular classes) can conflict with other kinds of influence (influence among the ruling elite, access to mass media, financial resources).

Although the sphere of the Church's influence has clearly changed, it is difficult to tell whether it has more influence than before, or whether a different strategy would have proved more successful. The Church's choices during the past two decades strengthened its alliance with the popular classes, but they also led to a distancing from the dominant classes and the state. In regions where the class structure is more complex and where political alliances do not follow clear class lines, the popular Church has successfully incorporated large numbers of the middle classes. In the Amazon, the Northeast, and the most conflictual agricultural regions, however, this proved impossible. The dominant classes and the state could not accept the Church's new message, which they perceived as "political" at best and subversive at worst. Nothing underscores this fact so clearly as the many cases of imprisonment, torture, destruction of Church property, and other instances of state and private repression against Church leaders.

Many traditional Catholics found the style and message of the new Church difficult to understand or accept. Many left the Church, unable to agree with the changes. Reports from the diocese of Goiás Velho, Goiás, note some of these conflicts: "At first, the people who had most trouble understanding were those linked to the traditional Church. They didn't accept the renovation and they didn't tolerate our words." "The traditional dominators express resentment, as if they were victims of an expropriation. They threaten to break with the Church or they just leave."[10]

Serious tensions emerged between traditional groups and progressive ones, particularly between the early 1960's and the early 1970's, and again after 1982. Thus although the changes in the Church defended some institutional interests, they came at the expense of other problems: conflict with the state and the dominant classes or with traditional attenders, internal tensions, and even repression against Church members.

In addition, realizing institutional objectives in a complex society is not easy, particularly when the interests are diffuse and often contradictory. Even in the most rational institutions, discerning final objectives and means of realizing those objectives can be difficult.[11] This problem is even more pronounced in an institution like the Church, where objectives and means are less clear. Even if there were, for example, a consensus that the Church should develop pastoral practices to save the working class, this consensus would indicate neither the means nor the goals.

A concern with the working class could have led to politically conservative practices such as those found among Pentecostals, who have expanded rapidly among the popular classes. Pentecostalism addresses some of the same human problems as the Catholic Church's work with the poor, creating community around a sense of faith, giving people at the margins of society something to believe in, and supplying an ordered conception of the universe in a society undergoing rapid changes. The growth of Pentecostal groups suggests that a more intense religious experience, whatever its political content, could have helped revive the Catholic Church's presence among the working class. As the Pentecostals' experience has shown, in addition to standing a good chance of success, this kind of change would not have alienated the dominant classes.[12] Conversely, nothing guaranteed that the changes the Church promoted would effectively deepen its presence among the popular classes. In fact, during the initial reformist phases of the Church's transformation, the progressives' campaign against some traditional religious symbols and customs widened the chasm between the institution and the popular classes.

The different sectors within the Church do have implicit models for influencing society, but the institution's actions do not always depend on an evaluation of which strategy will prove most effective. The hegemonic sector within an institution such as the Roman Church cannot be oblivious to interests and influence, but interests do not determine all its actions. Change within the Church results from the struggles of groups with different conceptions of faith, not from the institution's attempts to protect interests agreed on by the conflicting factions.* In the Brazilian Church, the crucial debate is not how to further the Church's interests, but rather what its mission should be. Among the politically significant sectors, the key questions are the meaning of the "preferential option for the poor" espoused by the Latin American bishops at Puebla (1979) and what the limits of the Church's political involvement should be.

Throughout this book, I interchangeably use the notions of the Church's institutional identity, different models of the Church, or the Church's conception of its mission.[13] The notion of models of the Church suggests that the starting point for understanding the Church's politics must be its conception of its mission. The way the Church intervenes in politics depends fundamentally on the way it perceives its religious mission. This approach dictates attention to Church goals as understood by the leaders, and hence also to doctrine and theology.[14]

The Church and Institutional Change

One of the fundamental questions in this book regards the ability of churches to promote internal change and develop new links to the society at large, including the political system. This question has

---

*These struggles are usually not articulated in directly antagonistic fashion, as often happens in the society at large. Nor is the search for hegemony within the Church generally conscious. But the less antagonistic and less conscious nature of these attempts to establish hegemony does not mean that the process does not take place. It occurs largely through the attempts of different sectors to establish their vision of the Church's mission as the most appropriate.

interested some of the greatest social theorists of this century; yet
the recent changes in the Catholic Church raise the possibility that
they may have exaggerated the inflexibility and conservative character of religious institutions.

Religious organizations present complex problems for the social
scientist, for they spring from nonrational inspirations yet generally
develop a concern for institutionalized practices and roles, self-preservation, and expansion. To become stable, religious movements
usually develop many institutional mechanisms that were not present in the initial phases of their history. The transformation from
charismatic leadership to institution building was one of Max Weber's major concerns. Weber argues that if charismatic authority

is not to remain a purely transitory phenomenon, but to take on the character of a permanent relationship forming a stable community of disciples
or a band of followers or a party organization or any sort of political or
hierocratic organization, it is necessary for the character of the charismatic
authority to become radically changed. Indeed, in its pure form charismatic
authority may be said to exist only in the process of originating. It cannot
remain stable, but becomes either traditionalized or rationalized, or a combination of both.[15]

For Weber, although a charismatic leader or prophet is responsible for starting a religion, charisma becomes institutionalized within an established church. As the institution expands, the scope for
prophecy and charismatic leadership narrows, and a caste of func-
tionaries—the priests—emerges; their role is to administer sacraments and teach the new dogma. In contrast to the prophet, who
creates a new institution, the priest acts upon a set of established religious norms and practices. Very few priests become prophets: the
great majority of prophets arise outside institutional church structures.[16] At the same time, the institution develops routines for ensuring the allegiance of practicants, who initially participated in response to the prophet's personal appeal. Religious rituals routinize
practices in a way that remains meaningful to the participants.

As religious organizations become institutionalized, they tend to
become more concerned with self-preservation and expansion, and
they also become less flexible. This is particularly true of churches,
which (as opposed to sects) attempt to be inclusive and offer salvation to all. Sects are restrictive voluntary associations of the religiously qualified; churches are less selective, hence less rigid in their

demands, but also less able to incorporate the kind of radical messages characteristic of charismatic leaders.[17]

Within Christianity, Roman Catholicism has traditionally been the most institutionalized—and the least flexible—church. Catholicism traditionally emphasized unity and authority, a belief in universal salvation rather than salvation for the select, and a vast organizational structure to minister to the wide range of practicants. Ernst Troeltsch wrote that "Roman Catholicism . . . has to an ever-increasing degree sacrificed the inwardness, individuality, and plasticity of religion to the fixed determination to make religion objective."[18]

In the transformation from sect to church, religious organizations usually develop alliances with the state and elites as a means of ensuring their institutional position.[19] Simultaneously, the class basis of the religion often changes, either through the ascension of the social classes that originally created the religious movements or through the displacement of the lower-income sectors by wealthier ones.[20] This change accentuates the tendency of religious organizations to be politically conservative. In this regard, the strong correlation between political conservatism and strong religious involvement in many countries is significant.[21]

It is within this historical context of relative rigidity and political conservatism that the Roman Church's recent changes must be understood. On the one hand, Roman Catholicism has undergone significant change, and the Brazilian Church has played a leading role in this process. In few periods since the merging of Church and state under Constantine has the Church experienced such widespread changes. After more than a century of combating modernization, since World War II and especially since the papacy of John XXIII, the Church has opened itself to the modern world. The traditional images of the Church (Church as institution and Church as perfect society) have in recent years been challenged by a rapid succession of new images of the Church: as people of God, as servant, and as a sign of salvation in the world.[22]

From the sixteenth century until recent times, the Church, with few exceptions, identified God's will with institutional forms of authority; obedience was a fundamental virtue. By contrast, Vatican II theology stressed the very different notion of the Church as the people of God, assigned a more important role to the laity, and re-

defined the authority of the pope over the whole church and the
bishop over the diocese.[23] Since the papacy of John XXIII, there
have been attempts, especially in Latin America, to merge Catholic
faith and radical political change. Even papal declarations have
changed remarkably. Paul VI's major encyclical on development,
Populorum Progressio, argued that rich nations are partially responsible for the problems of the Third World, sharply criticized colonialism and the tendency of capitalism to promote profit as a supreme value, and subordinated the right to property to the need for
social justice.[24]

On the other hand, the institutional character of the Church and
its desire to appeal to all impose constraints upon the future direction of the Church as a whole, including the Brazilian Church. It remains committed to appealing to people of all nations and all political beliefs, and it avoids radical change in ecclesial practices or in
politics. Paul VI's refusal to change the Church's position on the
questions of clerical celibacy and birth control, the Vatican's control
of lay movements, the reprisals against Hans Küng for his dissenting
theological positions, the underlying threat of actions against liberation theologians, and the measures against the Dutch Church
(which was the most progressive in the world from the time of Vatican II until at least 1972) call attention to the limits and constraints
that Church leaders continue to impose.[25]

Despite these tensions, the Church's transformation calls into
question traditional arguments about the objectives, inflexibility,
and political conservatism of religious institutions. When an institution's fundamental end is nonrational, it may be willing to sacrifice some interests if it is convinced it has a calling to do so. A
church will renounce financial benefits, prestige, institutional expansion, and other interests if it feels that its religious mission com-
pels it to do so.[26] Forgetting this point is tantamount to eliminating
the religious element from the study of the Church.

A second point concerns the supposed institutional inflexibility of
churches. Here it is again helpful to recall Weber's writings. He understands change within all institutions as the result of nonrational
and rational processes, of the interaction between charismatic
forces and institutional interests. Although Weber sees rationaliza-
tion as the outstanding characteristic of the contemporary world, he
argues that all institutions continue to be marked by nonrational,

charismatic elements.[27] This nonrationality is particularly strong in religious institutions. Even ascetic Protestantism, which contributed to rationalizing the Western world, contains traces of nonrationality. Furthermore, in the contemporary world, as society becomes increasingly rationalized, religion becomes a distinctive sphere of nonrationality.[28]

Even though Weber primarily emphasizes the conservative character of religion, his writings suggest that churches are never completely closed to charismatic influences. Even the most universal and institutionalized churches can contain some charismatic elements. All churches suffer tension between charismatic impulses and more routine practices. The history of Catholicism reflects this tension, with some periods of remarkable ferment and others of conservatism.

The transformation of the Church, particularly in countries such as Brazil, El Salvador, and Nicaragua, also calls into question the belief that institutionalized religion is a conservative force that palliates the suffering of the masses and bolsters the domination of elites. Marx, Nietzsche, and Durkheim all argued that religion has a fundamentally conservative impact. Weber, Troeltsch, and Niebuhr qualified this argument but still concluded that even though sects frequently challenge the political order and dominant values, churches are conservative. In general this observation was true in the past.[29] But the fact that Catholicism has inspired millions of people to work toward radical change in Latin America, either as a short-term project (as in Nicaragua and El Salvador) or a long-term one (as in Brazil) underscores that political conservatism is not intrinsic to churches. Though it is too early to tell, some modification may be occurring in the old linkage between political conservatism and the Catholic Church, which originated as a radical, lower-middle-class movement.[30]

The Church and the Broader Social Process

A key argument throughout this book is that like all other institutions, a church is influenced by changes in the society at large. More specifically, I argue that political ideologies in Brazil have influenced the Church's vision of faith. In turn, social conflicts and the way the state has attempted to resolve or suppress them have largely determined these ideologies and visions of politics. The political struggle can cause social identities and ideologies to be rethought, creating new ones. Most social practices and institutional identities change not because new ideas arise but rather because the social struggle leads to a new way of understanding reality.[31]

If a religious organization or movement believes that its mission dictates political involvement, the political struggle will affect its vision of faith. Then the analysis of institutional change requires focusing on the political struggle.

This is what happened to the Catholic Church in Brazil. As the Church became more concerned about its social mission, social change and political conflict affected it in new ways. Different social forces developed new visions of politics, and the resultant debates were mirrored in the Church's discussion of its mission.[32] The Church's conception of faith and of its mission did not change only as the result of debates about what it should be or about how it should protect its institutional interests. Rather, its identity changed principally—though not exclusively—because the political struggle generated new conceptions about the society and the Church's role within it.

The impact of political change on institutions depends on how they define themselves and on the level of politicization in society. The Brazilian Catholic Church was relatively impermeable to change through class conflict for much of this century. But as the Church increasingly opened itself to the society, and as the society became more polarized, drawing major institutions into the conflicts of the times, the Church was more affected by political changes.

Although social and political changes helped reshape the Church's conception of its mission, we should avoid reducing analysis of a church or a church movement to a class issue. In this sense, I again differ from most of the Latin American neo-Marxian analysts, who tend to understate the autonomy of religion and the Church vis-à-vis class. Religion can be a powerful force in determining political orientation, frequently even more powerful than class.[33] Furthermore, political change does not inevitably change the way institutions or movements view themselves. All institutions have a specific way of responding to social changes, and they can insulate themselves from conflicts in society at large, especially when they participate only peripherally in the political struggle. If a church or a religious movement remains outside political debates and defines its mission as being above politics,* it is possible that the political process will not directly affect the way it perceives its mission. For example, in the United States the Amish have retained many eighteenth-century customs despite the dramatic changes in the society and polity around them. Their understanding of faith has been relatively impermeable to social change and conflict.

Thus analysis of the Church or a Church movement should neither see its transformations as direct, inevitable results of broader historical change nor neglect the impact of these broader changes. We must understand the institution's self-identity as expressed through its discourse and practices as well as the social changes that can alter that identity.

Much of this book addresses the question of how the Church is shaped by broader processes of change. It is also important, however, to consider the ways in which the Church helps to shape the political changes. The Church is not only an object of change; as an important institution, it also influences the political process as it forms the consciousness of the various social classes, as it mobilizes political forces to act, and as it makes alliances with political elites or criticizes them.

My work shares with Marxist writings on the sociology of religion (Althusser, Gramsci, Portelli, Maduro) a concern with (1) the way the Church responds to changes in class structures, conflicts, and ideologies, and (2) the way religious practices and discourse affect the consciousness of the social classes. In other respects, however, it differs from most Marxist perspectives. Because their principal concern is with social classes and class conflict, most Marxists de-emphasize the importance of institutions or see them as representing class interests.† By contrast, I insist on the importance of in-

---

*No church is ever really above politics. Religious practices and discourse necessarily either reinforce or challenge the predominant values and ultimately the system of domination. Levine (*Religion and Politics*, pp. 18-55) argues that all religions have a political content. Nevertheless, a church can believe it is above politics and remain aloof from political discussions. In this case, it is usually less directly affected by the political struggle.

†For example, Althusser (*Lenin and Philosophy*, pp. 127-86) regards religion as an "ideological apparatus of the state," which he sees in turn as the means for "ensuring the reproduction of the social order." This vision obscures the distinction between state and civil society; in the post-medieval world, the Church has not been part of the state apparatus. In this confusion, Althusser reduces religion to a tool of domination, assumes that religion always has a stabilizing function, and denies that

stitutions as major political actors and on their relative autonomy with respect to the class struggle. I pay more attention to the specific ways religious institutions respond to political conflict and social changes. Furthermore, the Church and other institutions help shape Brazilian society, and they cannot be reduced to class analysis. The way an institution reacts at a given moment reinforces or challenges patterns of domination, as Marxists correctly underscore, and in doing so bolsters the interests of some classes at the expense of others. But to see complex institutions like the Church or the military as expressions of a given class oversimplifies reality. This reductionist vision fails to perceive how fluid institutions can be in the long run, defending (consciously or not) the interests of a given class during one period only to develop an institutional ideology that challenges the interests of that class in another.[34] An institution's needs and values, not class interests, determine its interests, identities, and ideologies.

Grass-roots Movements and Popular Religiosity

Most studies of the Catholic Church have focused principally on the hierarchy, often for good reason. The Church has been very hierarchical, and in general grass-roots organizations and lay movements have had limited autonomy and impact within the institution.[35] In studying the Church, however, we should remember that it comprises more than the hierarchy. The Church also includes ecclesial institutes, grass-roots pastoral agents (priests, nuns, and laity), organized lay movements, Catholic universities and schools, and lay people who do not participate in lay movements. Although they are formally under the control of the hierarchy, these other levels can acquire some autonomy, influence the Church, and have an independent effect on politics.

One of my principal arguments is that since the early 1960's, lay

---

it can contest the social order. Marx's statement that religion is the opiate of the masses also encourages this understanding by suggesting that religious organizations always serve the interests of the dominant classes. Of course, not all Marxists reduce the Church to an element of class domination. Maduro (*Religião*, pp. 113-23) emphasizes the Church's autonomy and institutional specificity. Along with such Brazilian social scientists as Luiz Alberto Gómez de Souza, Luiz Gonzaga de Souza Lima, and Carlos Rodrigues Brandão, Maduro has opened new horizons in the Marxian sociology of religion. Gramsci inspired this line of analysis even though his own writings on religion were inchoate; see, for example, *Prison Notebooks*, pp. 408-9.

and grass-roots movements have played an important role in the transformation of the Brazilian Church. Well before liberation theology appeared, Brazilian lay movements and progressive pastoral agents at the grass roots had already reflected on the major themes that would be systematized by the new theology and had introduced a conception of faith linked to radical politics. Several of the most famous Latin American liberation theologians, including Leonardo Boff (Brazilian) and Gustavo Gutiérrez (Peruvian) have recognized that these grass-roots and lay movements shaped their theological reflection.[36] Later, after repression had destroyed the radical lay movements of the early 1960's in Brazil, pastoral agents in the communities continued to innovate. The first base communities, the early discussions about pedagogy among the popular classes, the early work with the Indians, and most of the other major innovations in the Brazilian Church started at the grass roots. Furthermore, it was usually the actions and statements of lay groups and pastoral agents working with the popular classes that, after the 1964 coup, led to repression against the Church. This repression was a key factor in the institution's transformation.

Grass-roots movements alone were not, however, responsible for the Church's transformation. On the contrary, without support from the hierarchy these movements could not have transformed the Church. The transformation process was dialectical. Only because of institutional receptivity could radical lay movements emerge, and it was only when the hierarchy actively supported change that the Church strongly defended human rights. Given the hierarchical structure of the Catholic Church, movements not supported by the bishops remain relatively isolated and are incapable of changing the thrust of the institution's weight.

Even though the groundswell of change met some resistance and even reprisals within the Church, grass-roots innovations were important in promoting change. To see the transformation of the Brazilian Church as a process initiated exclusively from above, in response to the Church's attempts to defend its corporate interests, overlooks how these movements introduced new conceptions of faith, new theologies, and new pastoral practices; "converted" nuns, priests, and bishops to a new understanding of the Church; and involved the Church in a repressive cycle that helped transform the institution as a whole.[37]

Neglect of grass-roots Catholic organizations can also lead to a failure to comprehend one of the Church's most important sources of political influence. Catholicism has moved toward a more lay-oriented Church, particularly in several Latin American countries, where neighborhood Catholic groups called Christian or ecclesial base communities have proliferated and become active politically. We cannot understand the Church's role in politics in societies such as El Salvador, Nicaragua, or Brazil without analyzing the way communities of poor Catholics have bolstered the struggles of peasants and workers to change their societies. In contrast to most European Catholic Action movements, Latin American base communities are often somewhat autonomous of the hierarchy. This autonomy has been especially pronounced in El Salvador and Nicaragua, where serious tension exists between, on one hand, tens of thousands of organized Catholics committed to revolutionary change and the priests and nuns who support them and, on the other, the conservative-to-moderate bishops worried about excessive Church involvement in politics and about maintaining obedience within ecclesiastical structures.

The situation in Brazil is very different from that in Nicaragua and El Salvador. The political involvement of the progressive Church in Brazil has been more cautious, and there is less tension between the base communities and the hierarchy. In Brazil, too, however, the base communities and other organizations such as the Pastoral Land Commission and the Workers Pastoral Commission have reinforced popular struggles and significantly influenced political life.

Another reason for expanding the analysis beyond the hierarchy is the importance of popular Catholicism, a set of traditional religious beliefs and practices developed outside the institutional Church and widely practiced throughout Latin America. In Brazil, the gap between the institutional Church and popular practices has always been significant. Among the popular classes, the institutional Church has been relatively weak, but religious beliefs still shape the world view of a majority of the people. It is important to understand the nature of these popular beliefs. In past decades, popular religious beliefs and customs gave rise to messianic movements that challenged the political system, and they continue to influence the way most Brazilians (especially peasants) understand politics.[38]

Most studies of the Church and politics have focused on the

Church's relationship to the state, but it is also important to consider its linkages to different social classes. The way religious ideology and symbols legitimate or challenge aspects of the dominant values has a significant impact on political life. The Brazilian Church has always been an important institution. Its symbols and discourse help shape the identity of different social classes and institutions and help define social and political practices.

During much of the history of Brazil, popular religious practices and beliefs led to *basically* fatalistic attitudes toward poverty.* Most religious practices also encouraged acceptance of one's position in the class structure, thereby legitimating relationships of power and dominance. Such a role in shaping the world view of the popular classes probably was more important in legitimating the social order than were the Church's alliances with the state.

In more recent years, factions in the Church have developed a vision of faith that challenges the social order. The base communities in particular have encouraged a vision of faith that emphasizes the institution's preferential option for the poor and that stimulates political *conscientização* (consciousness raising).[39] The Church's encouragement of a new political and social consciousness is particularly significant in light of its institutional legitimacy and the religious world view of the popular classes.[40] They understand not only politics and social position, but also the family, the success or failure of a harvest, health and illness, with reference to religious symbols and practices.[41] The institutional Church does not completely control the formation of popular religious beliefs, but strong popular religiosity could enhance the Church's prestige and political importance. We cannot understand the implications of the Church's transformation without examining it.

The International Church and Ecclesiastical Change in Brazil

Throughout this book I explain change in the Brazilian Church as resulting from two kinds of factors: changes in Brazilian society and politics, and changes in the international Church. Enough has been

---

*I italicize *basically* because of the complexity of this issue. Recent studies have argued that popular religious practices reject some of the dominant religious values and hence contain the seed of resistance.

said already about the first by way of introduction; here I introduce
the theme of the international Church's influence, to which I return
repeatedly.

To say that the Church is an international institution is to state
the obvious, yet frequently the importance of this statement is
underestimated. Particularly since the reassertion of Vatican authority over national churches in the nineteenth century, Rome has determined the parameters of permissible Church development. The
Vatican can promote, discourage, or prohibit different theologies
and pastoral practices.

The pope's role as head of the Church is far more than titular; despite changes in authority relations, papal authority remains supreme. Often the most important Vatican means of influencing the
development of national churches is episcopal nominations. The
bishops are the formal leaders of their local dioceses, and they are
the most important agenda setters for their national churches. The
Vatican and its representatives to different countries, known as papal nuncios, largely determine the process of choosing bishops.

Through selective encouragement and discouragement of change,
Rome greatly influenced the development of the Brazilian Church
during the 1916-85 period. In Brazil, the neo-Christendom model of
the Church was directly encouraged by Rome, as were the cautious
reforms of the 1950's. The innovations between the late 1950's and
the late 1970's would have been unthinkable outside the context of
the most progressive papacies in recent Church history. And finally,
the decline of the popular Church after 1982 has been largely a consequence of Vatican pressures.

Although the Vatican is the most important international influence, it is not the only one. Since the Medellín meeting of 1968, CE-
LAM has exercised considerable influence over the Latin American
church, first by encouraging reform, and after 1972 by attempting
to limit it. The Brazilian Church itself has influenced other national
churches in Latin America by serving as a model for progressive ecclesiastical change. Finally, theological developments in one part of
the world can influence Church thought and practices elsewhere. In
the 1950's, for example, the reformists in the Brazilian Church extensively read leading European theologians.

In emphasizing the international character of the institution, I do
not downplay the differences among the churches in different countries. Indeed, a key objective of this book is precisely to call atten-

tion to the distinctive character of the Brazilian Church. These national differences coexist within a single institution largely because
Rome has always allowed some autonomy for national churches.
This autonomy has itself varied considerably over time. Until the
second half of the nineteenth century, the Brazilian Church did not
have particularly strong ties with the Vatican, so it developed in
somewhat more autonomous ways. Later, popes John XXIII and
Paul VI encouraged greater national autonomy, a factor of considerable importance in understanding the evolution of the Brazilian
Church during the 1960's and 1970's. Conversely, under the papacy
of John Paul II the Vatican has perceived such autonomy as a threat,
precisely because of the way the Church evolved in Brazil and a few
other Latin American countries.

Furthermore, Rome's impact on different national churches has
not been uniform. From 1952 to 1964, the papal nuncio to Brazil
was a reformist who encouraged Church innovation. Elsewhere in
Latin America, the Church did not undergo comparable changes
during those years.

Simultaneously emphasizing the capacity of local innovations to
change the Church and the capacity of Rome to shape Church developments in the most remote parts of Brazil may seem contradictory. In fact, this apparent contradiction reflects the enormous complexity and multidimensionality of this institution. Church leaders
at different levels respond to different issues and set their agendas in
correspondingly different ways. The pope and the Vatican bureaucracy are necessarily deeply concerned with the multinational character of the Church, its need to appeal to all nations and social
classes, and consequently its need to avoid political extremes. Conversely, working with exploited Indians in the depths of the Amazon
jungle provides little occasion to reflect about the spiritual needs of
wealthy businessmen and considerable stimulus to believe that the
Church must undergo radical change. To return to a critical theme,
this remarkable diversity in institutional situations stimulates very
different visions of what the Church should be.

Church Interests and the Popular Church

Analysis of the relationship between Catholicism and politics
must recognize that the Church is an institution. The question
is how to understand the institution. It is essential to remember

that serious conflict can arise between different objectives; that these objectives have a subjective and political component; that the Church's ultimate goals are diffuse; and that the institution can have a charismatic element.

The crisis in the Brazilian Church started after World War II and resulted from the rapid transformation of the society without an accompanying transformation of the Church. Its manifestations included a resistance to secularization, the dramatic growth of Protestantism and Spiritism, declining mass attendance, a vocation crisis, growth of the Left, and a loss of influence among the dominant classes and the urban working class. The dominant groups within the Church felt that these changes threatened the institution.[42] The crisis promoted change by making the hierarchy aware that the Church needed to rethink its mission. But although the institutional crisis explains why the Church began to open, it does not explain the direction or magnitude of the change. The Church could have responded to the crisis in a variety of ways. In fact, different groups within the Church developed different answers, each of which represented a different conception of the Church, its role in society, and its "interests." It is not clear that the actual response was the one that most furthered Church interests; alongside the gains there have been many losses.

It is true that the Church changed partly to protect traditional interests when its influence was declining. But equally important, it changed because the political struggle led some people and movements to a new vision of faith deeply concerned about social justice and the poor. These groups had a new vision of the Church's mission and were willing to forsake many traditional interests in the name of their new conception.

The popular sectors of the Church have questioned some of the institution's interests and have renounced some kinds of influence. They care less about the expansion of Protestantism and are more interested in ecumenism. They do not care about having influence among the dominant classes; on the contrary, they call for a "poor Church, of the poor people."[43] They are concerned more with being a sign in the world than with the number of people who attend mass. As Peruvian theologian Gustavo Gutiérrez says, the popular Church has become concerned more with the qualitative and less with the quantitative aspects of salvation.[44] And it is concerned more about fighting authoritarianism than about fighting Communism, although there are marked political differences between the popular Church and most of the Marxian Left.[45]

Throughout the popular Church appears the vision that the Church's fundamental mission is to serve the world, not to serve itself. Leonardo Boff writes, "The Church is comprehended as a sign of salvation present in all dimensions of life. . . . The emphasis is placed on a liberating praxis. As the sign of salvation, what should the Church do to help people overcome sin? . . . As the city above the wilderness, the model among the nations, and the light burning in the house, the Church cannot live in a narcissistic fashion."[46]

From the Weberian viewpoint, the changes of the past decades had strong charismatic elements. Certain leaders broke with the established order, sought legitimation on the basis of personal revelation, and inaugurated a new model of the Church. Yet in the Weberian framework, the transformation of the past twenty years was also legitimated by many traditional elements. Even while it was undergoing deep changes, the Brazilian Church has respected many traditional values of the popular classes, including aspects of popular religiosity. It has used its traditional prestige and image to help implant a new vision of faith. Without understanding this combination of old and new, of traditional and charismatic legitimacy, one cannot comprehend these changes.

The popular Church has assumed some characteristics of a sect, with greater emphasis on quality rather than quantity of salvation and higher demands on the participants. Yet it is impossible to understand the strength or importance of the popular Church by adhering to the sect analogy because the popular Church functions within a larger institution and is committed to working with it. The popular Church has been far from oblivious to institutional questions. The distinctive feature that has made the Brazilian Church one of the most important in the world is the popular Church's ability to work within the whole institution. In other Churches, the tensions between the base and the institution dissipated or enervated the impulse for change. The Brazilian Church, however, struck a balance between change and continuity, between community and institution, between the base and the hierarchy. Without the deep concern the progressive groups have displayed for institutional questions, especially for working within the whole institution, they would probably have suffered the same marginalization that radical priests' organizations did elsewhere in Latin America.

Because of the Church's institutional character, its identity as a specifically religious organization and concern about ecclesiastical unity will continue to affect the Brazilian Church.[47] Although the need to maintain cohesion and unity may not directly affect pastoral work at the base, at the top it will undoubtedly lead to compromises that limit the popular Church. The institution's weight will assert itself as Rome and CELAM press the Brazilian Church toward more cautious positions. Much of the popular Church has underestimated the importance of this constraining force. By 1982, nominations of conservative bishops, pressure against progressive theologians, bishops, and pastoral practices, and favoring of the moderates and conservatives, coupled with pressure for the Church to curtail and modify its political involvement because civil society had developed its own political channels, began to impede the radical Catholics from expanding their niche within the Church. Nevertheless, the Brazilian Church had already established itself as one of the most innovative and important actors within the international Church and Brazilian politics in recent decades.

Part I

The Church from 1916 to 1964

CHAPTER 2

The Neo-Christendom Church, 1916-1955

IN 1916, THE NEWLY named archbishop of Recife and Olinda, Dom Sebastião Leme, published a famous pastoral letter that marked the beginning of a new period in the Church's history (Leme was archbishop of Rio de Janeiro and the outstanding leader of the Brazilian Church from 1921 until his death in 1942). He called attention to the weakness of the institutional Church, the deficiencies of popular religious practices, the shortage of priests, the poor state of religious education, the absence of Catholic intellectuals, the Church's limited political influence, and its poor financial situation. Leme argued that Brazil was a Catholic nation and that the Church should take advantage of that fact and develop a much stronger presence in the society. The Church needed to Christianize the major social institutions, develop a cadre of Catholic intellectuals, and bring popular religious practices in line with orthodox procedures.[1]

To set Leme's argument in perspective, it is necessary to describe briefly the traditional problems of the Brazilian Church. During most of its history, the Catholic Church was weaker in Brazil than in Spanish America; the Brazilian Church never had the financial resources or the zeal of its counterparts. Its weakness reached a nadir in the nineteenth century. A significant part of the clergy had families and spent little time on ecclesiastical activities; the seminaries were lacking in number and quality; the titular head of the Church was the Brazilian emperor, who in the case of Dom Pedro II (1840-89) was a lukewarm Catholic; links to the Vatican were weak; and the number of priests and nuns declined after 1855, when the state prohibited new admissions to religious orders.[2]

This institutional decline continued well into the second half of the nineteenth century, but as early as the 1850's some leading Church figures attempted to impart a new direction. During the second half of the nineteenth century, Rome pushed for greater control over national churches. In Brazil it pressed for a more official, "acceptable" Catholicism. Out of a sense of being threatened, the Vatican began to promote a more vigorous Catholic presence in society. The leaders of the reform movement in Brazil were politically conservative, consistent with the teachings of Pope Pius IX (1846-78). They were closely linked to Rome, intolerant of Freemasonry and competing religious groups, and insistent upon hierarchical obedience, celibacy, and the wearing of clerical vestments. This new orientation led to conflicts within the Church, and between 1872 and 1875 it also led to one of the most serious Church-state conflicts in Brazil's history.[3] Encouraged by Rome to develop more acceptable pastoral practices, parts of the Brazilian Church began to assert their autonomy vis-à-vis the state. Pedro II, influenced by the anticlericalism of liberal nineteenth-century circles, refused to comply with the activist bishops. The resultant tensions eventually led to the imprisonment of two bishops in 1874 and the severing of official ties between Church and state in 1890, which was embodied in the constitution of 1891. After 1891, however, the Church began unofficially to restore the links to the state that had officially been severed. Despite these tensions, the more Romanized Catholicism won a decisive victory, especially after the legal separation.[4]

Even though the Vatican's official position was that legal separation between Church and state was a modernist heresy, in Brazil the legal disestablishment freed the Church from a subservient relationship to the state. Its sense of being threatened led to internal reforms that helped improve its image. Aided by a new influx of foreign clergy, the Church began to reverse the institutional decay of the preceding decades. The religious orders, which had been debilitated by the 1855 decree, began to recruit and import new members. New dioceses were created, and episcopal control over clerical activities grew in most regions.

Although the primary thrust of Church efforts between 1890 and 1916 was toward consolidating internal changes, some leaders began to promote a more vigorous presence in the society, anticipating the neo-Christendom model. The beginning of the neo-Christendom model can be dated to 1916, but the preceding 25 years had been marked by institutional adaptations to the challenges of existing in a secular republic. By accepting rather than fighting legal disestablishment, Church leaders avoided contentious anticlericalism. In Mexico and Spain, anticlericalism created lingering hostilities that made institutional adaptation more difficult. By contrast, the Brazilian Church has a century-long history of institutional development and adaptation to challenges and social changes.[5]

Although Leme's vision had precedents, it was not until the 1920's that his new model of the Church, the neo-Christendom model, flourished. It reached its apogee from 1930 to 1945, while Getúlio Vargas was president. The Church remained politically conservative, opposed to secularization and to other religions, and in favor of hierarchy and order. But in its insistence on a more rigorous Catholicism that would penetrate the society's major institutions, especially the state, the neo-Christendom model differed significantly from previous pastoral practices and attitudes. It successfully protected what it perceived as indispensable Church interests: Catholic influence over the education system, Catholic morality, anti-Communism, and anti-Protestantism. Through the neo-Christendom model, the Church revitalized its presence in the society. In brief, the neo-Christendom model was a means of dealing with institutional weakness without significantly changing the institution's conservative nature. By the 1930's, the institution had halted its decay.

The Vatican encouraged the Brazilian Church's efforts to develop a stronger presence in society, especially during the papacy of Pius XI (1922-39), whose approach to Church development and politics was close to Dom Sebastião Leme's. Under Pius XI, Catholic Action movements became central to Church activity. Pius dismissed political parties as too divisive, but he still sought alliances with the state to defend Catholic interests. He directly supported and encouraged Dom Leme in his efforts to foster a Catholic revival.[6]

The Church began to formulate a more progressive social doctrine during the papacy of Leo XIII (1878-1903), especially with the publication of *Rerum Novarum* in 1891. This encyclical marked the Church's belated acceptance of the modern world after its open combat with modernization during much of the nineteenth century. But although it called for a juster social order and a balance between labor and capital, the Church's social doctrine continued to have conservative elements. Pope Pius X (1903-14) repudiated efforts to adapt to the modern world, and Benedict XV (1914-22) and Pius XI (1922-39) were fundamentally conservative. In an important encyclical issued in 1937, Pius XI condemned Communism as intrinsically wrong,[7] and throughout Europe, the Church aligned with conservative forces in the 1920's and 1930's. Only after the Fascists attempted to suppress the Church did the institution begin to criticize Mussolini and Hitler. In Spain the bishops insisted that Catholics support Franco's forces.* The revolutionary upheavals of Pius's reign, especially the violent anticlerical movements in the Soviet Union, Spain, and Mexico and other Latin American countries, reinforced the pontiff's conservative nature.[8]

The Church, Faith, and the Secular Society

The Church's conception of its overall mission directly determines its involvement in political life. When religious leaders argue that the Church should fight Communism, that it should remain above politics, or that it has a special commitment to the poor, these beliefs derive from the religious system. This means that we must understand the institution's goals and the conception of faith that motivated it, which have been relatively neglected aspects of studies on the Church during the 1916-55 period.

Beginning with the Romanization of the Brazilian Church and lasting until the 1950's, the Church saw faith as an inward process of having close personal contact with Jesus Christ in a devotional sense. Even the external manifestations of faith were narrowly religious—attending mass, praying, observing the sacraments, contributing money to the Church, and observing a Catholic moral ethic in family life and personal relations. The Church perceived the modern world as essentially evil because it eroded this devotional faith and

---

*Pius XI attempted to use the Fascist state to further Church goals, and Mussolini made strong overtures to the Church. At times, relations were cordial; the Concordat of 1929, by which Mussolini recognized Vatican City as a sovereign state, was the high point. But the totalitarian tendencies of Fascism led to conflicts over the Church's autonomy. Significant conflict also developed between Hitler and the Vatican. See Rhodes; Holmes, pp. 33-170; and Delzell. In Spain, partly because the Church had been the victim of virulent anticlericalism during the Republic and the Civil War (1931-39), and partly because Franco made no similar attempts to control it, the Church fully endorsed the regime. In 1937, the bishops issued a pastoral letter exhorting all Catholics to support Franco, and relations with the regime remained warm until the early 1960's. On the 1931-36 period, see Sánchez. On 1936-39, see Montero Moreno. For an overview of 1936-75, see Cooper.

encouraged the cult of self, prestige, money, and power. As one priest wrote, "Charity, devotion, and generous cooperation are absent in this world. The world is self-centered; people pay attention to the earth, to their stomachs, to money, to comfort, to prestige, to sensuality."[9] Modern society had also eroded a number of religious-related values, such as the traditional family and respect for authority.

There was a fundamental antagonism in this perception between faith and participation in secular society. Most Catholics saw salvation as the result of rising above the world rather than acting in it. The priestly mission was "to be of God and the Spirit in a world divorced from God and inimical to the Spirit, to live in continuous contact with the world without being of the world, without being contaminated by its seductive maxims."[10] There was an "incompatibility between the world and service to God."[11] The priest had to rise above the world, rejecting the secular tendencies that were undermining Catholic morality and faith. The good Catholic would manifest his or her relationship to God in action, but salvation came only through faith. The acts that accompany faith were meaningless without the faith, and they were not as important as personal devotion.[12]

There was almost no sense that faith could require a political commitment or that political action could be a major component of faith. Most priests did not see faith as closely linked to attempts to create a juster world. Even those who felt the Church should seek a social mission generally limited its nature to charity and palliative measures. The Church did not view transformation of the society as part of its mission; on the contrary, most clergy vigorously opposed far-reaching social change as undermining the traditional Christian order.

In emphasizing the Church's separation from the world, the neo-Christendom conception of faith differed from that of the nineteenth-century Church, in which priests were actively involved in politics, wore secular clothes, and even had concubines. Concerted efforts to develop a more vigorous Catholicism and penetrate the major social institutions were also relatively new.[13] The Church's new mission was to Christianize the society by developing greater influence within the major institutions and by imbuing all social institutions and private practices with the Catholic spirit. As one lay leader wrote, "Returning to Christ means returning to public, social, functional, and domestic life. [We cannot] reduce religion to mass, confession, communion, ribbons, medals, processions."[14] If the Church did not fulfill this mission, these institutions would march down the path to perdition. The neo-Christendom model for influencing society contained triumphal overtones. The Church wanted to "conquer" the world. Catholic Actions's mission was to "regain for Our Lord Jesus Christ the modern world."[15] "Gaining Catholics" and competing with other religions assumed considerable importance.

The process of re-Christianizing the society began in the waning years of the nineteenth century, but it was not until the 1920's that the new Church model blossomed. In the 1910's in Minas Gerais, known as Brazil's most Catholic state, the efforts to affirm a stronger presence in the society had their first success. After 1906, when the governor abolished religious education in the public schools, Catholic leaders in Minas mobilized the laity to exert pressure to reverse the measure. They did not succeed until 1928, but in the meantime they had organized strong Catholic Action movements, organized petitions with hundreds of thousands of signatures to defend Catholic interests; turned the tide against the rationalist, positivist thought of the previous generation of elites; encouraged internal institution building; and regenerated the image, prestige, and influence of the institution. In all these respects, the Minas Church anticipated changes that would occur at a national level, principally under the leadership of Dom Sebastião Leme and the lay leaders of the Centro Dom Vital.[16]

One Church accomplishment during the neo-Christendom period was mobilizing the middle-class laity. One of the most impressive generations of Catholic lay leaders in Latin American history emerged in the 1920's around the Centro Dom Vital, a small but highly influential Catholic center that was critical in the Church's development and in national politics. The Centro was created in 1922 by Jackson de Figueiredo, a close collaborator of Cardinal Leme's. Jackson, known for his antidemocratic nationalism, was an outstanding figure of the Catholic revival from the time of his conversion in 1918 until his death in 1928.

From 1928 until the early 1940's, Alceu Amoroso Lima became the outstanding figure at the Centro. Also a close collaborator of Leme's, Amoroso Lima, like Father Helder Câmara, was closely associated with the Catholic Right during the 1930's, only to become one of the leaders of progressive Church reforms in later decades. During the 1930's, Amoroso Lima was lay head of Catholic Action and helped form the Catholic Electoral League. Later, inspired by French theologians Jacques Maritain and Emmanuel Mounier, he left behind his authoritarian past and became a leading exponent of the Church's social doctrine.

Besides Jackson and Amoroso Lima, many other intellectual luminaries of the period participated in the Centro Dom Vital, including Hamilton Nogueira, Gustavo Corção, Plínio Correia de Oliveira, Sobral Pinto, Perilo Gomes, Allindo Vieira, and Jonatas Serrano. Most of them played important roles in the Church and Brazilian politics for several decades. Some followed Amoroso Lima and Helder Câmara in a more progressive direction beginning in the 1940's; others, most notably Gustavo Corção and Plínio Correia de Oliveira, became leading Catholic reactionaries.[17]

Although the intellectuals associated with the Centro Dom Vital were the outstanding lay people in the Catholic revival, the neo-Christendom Church mobilized hundreds of thousands of people into organized lay movements, particularly among the urban middle class. The Popular Union (Minas, 1909), the League of Brazilian Catholic Women (1910's), the Feminine Alliance (1919), the Marian Congregation (1924), the Workers' Circles (1930's), the Catholic University Youth (1930's), the Catholic Youth Workers (1930's), and Brazilian Catholic Action (1935) were important movements created during this period. Tightly controlled by the hierarchy, these movements affirmed a stronger Catholic presence in institutions and the state.[18]

The contrast between the neo-Christendom model and the earlier model was also apparent in the relationship between Church and state. From legal disestablishment in 1890 until the mid 1910's, the Church concentrated on internal institution building and paid less attention to influencing ruling elites. By contrast, from 1916 until 1945, Catholic leaders became deeply involved in politics, attempting to use an alliance with the state to influence society. The Church wanted the state to reinstitute informally the favored relationship that disestablishment had legally ended. The state, realizing it had much to gain through an alliance with the Church, grasped the opportunity to trade some privileges in return for religious sanction.

Church leaders worked closely with and supported the administrations of Epitácio Pessôa (1918-22) and Artur Bernardes (1922-

26),[19] but relations with Vargas were exceptionally close. The hierarchy never officially endorsed Vargas, but most bishops, priests, and active lay people supported the government.[20] A 1942 statement by five prominent archbishops, "Discipline and Obedience to the Head of the Government,"[21] succinctly summarized the Church's attitude. The Church supported Vargas not only because of the privileges it had won, but also because of the political affinity most of its leaders felt for his regime. The Church's emphasis on order, nationalism, patriotism, and anti-Communism coincided with Vargas's orientation. Leading clerics believed that Vargas's legislation embodied the Church's social doctrine and that the corporatist labor structures of the *Estado Novo* answered the need to develop a state that superseded the ills of liberalism and Communism.

Leme's actions exemplified the neo-Christendom political strategy and unequivocally refute the claims of those who argue that the traditional Church was above politics. Leme attempted to influence critical issues through his personal friendship with Vargas. He obtained state concessions on funds for Catholic schools, a prohibition of divorce, religious education during school hours, and other measures.[22]

Leme's activities and his ability to establish close relationships with high circles were notable for their political success. Following Leme and Pope Pius XI (1922-39),[23] most Catholic leaders in Brazil believed that it was the Church's duty to Catholicize other institutions to safeguard the Christian character of social life. An episcopal document issued near the end of World War II expressed the sense that the Church should seek to influence other social institutions. "Without the Church's collaboration, any effort, inspired in false principles, will be frustrated, if not imprudent. In reforming institutions and in regenerating customs, the Church's intervention is a necessary condition of success."[24]

Father Agnelo Rossi, later to become archbishop of São Paulo, wrote in 1942, "Let us always defend the Catholic Church, and we will be defending Brazil."[25] This identification of the Church with the nation was common throughout the 1920's, 1930's, and 1940's. In the Church's view, the state should follow the Church's social doctrine and protect its interests, and the education system and news media should reflect Catholic principles and doctrine. Any institution that promoted secularization or failed to follow the Church's guidelines came under Church attack. The radio, the press, movies—all seen as voices of the modern world—merited occasional condemnations.[26]

One of the outstanding examples of the neo-Christendom model for influencing society was the Catholic Electoral League (LEC), created by Leme in 1932 to advise Catholics how to vote. LEC was not linked to any particular political party, but it was avidly anti-Communist. It generally encouraged Catholics to vote in conservative ways and promoted candidates who took favorable stands on the major Catholic issues of the day. Until 1937, when the authoritarian regime eliminated parties and elections, LEC realized many of its goals. Most of its favored candidates for the 1933 Constituent Assembly were elected. The 1934 Constitution met LEC's principal demands, including state financial support for the Church, prohibition of divorce and recognition of religious marriage, religious education during school hours, and state subsidies for Catholic schools.[27]

The Church remained a conservative force despite the Vatican's formulation of a social doctrine that attempted to address the concerns of the modern world. Beginning in the early 1930's, the Church paid inordinate attention to combating Communism, reproducing Rome's attitudes even though the Communist threat was not very strong in Brazil. Brazilian clerics portrayed Communists as devious moral degenerates, "a modern plague," "modern barbarians, armed with sickle and hammer."[28] Shortly after Pius XI's 1937 encyclical on Communism, the Brazilian bishops issued a pastoral letter warning against Marxism, which would destroy Christian morals and bring material penury.[29] Later documents condemned class struggle "because it divides people in the name of hate, violence, and death."[30] In practice, this generally meant critical attitudes toward strikes and other expressions of popular dissent.

Most Catholics were silent about the authoritarian aspects of the Vargas regime, and many adhered to the rightist Integralist movement between 1932 and 1937.[31] The Church formed relatively conservative, clerical movements to compete with the more progressive trade unions, creating the Bible Circles (Círculos Operários) and Catholic Youth Workers (Juventude Operária Catolica) in the 1930's. The hierarchy encouraged Catholic workers to participate in unions as "witnesses of their Christian social formation,"[32] which meant in opposition to the Communists.

The bishops perceived social problems in moralistic ways and ignored structural causes. Characteristic of this moralistic idealism was a 1937 statement that "in the true reform of consciences lies the secret of great social reforms."[33] Even statements on the Church's social doctrine were timid and depoliticized social problems. For example, a 1946 episcopal statement affirmed that Church charity "constitutes, when well organized, an element of relief for millions of children who otherwise would not find a way of meeting their urgent life needs."[34] This response revealed an unrealistic assessment of what charity could accomplish, a dependence on the dominant classes and the state (for financial resources to implement charity programs), and paternalism toward the popular classes. In the document's discussion of infant mortality, the bishops ignored issues like unequal distribution of income and basic services and espoused preventive medical care. They overlooked the fact that a widespread system of preventive medicine would require major political change. In the absence of reforms dealing with the causes of poverty, any solution that treated only symptoms was bound to be limited.

The Church and the Popular Classes

All social relations reinforce or challenge existing patterns of domination. An emphasis on obedience to the hierarchy and paternalistic pastoral practices can reinforce patterns of domination as much as episcopal support for the government does. The latter action is more directly related to the state, but both practices are *political* in the broad sense.[35] Consequently, pastoral practices and attitudes are as important in understanding the Church's political impact as is the Church's relation to the state.

During the papacy of Leo XIII, especially with the encyclical *Rerum Novarum*, the Church started to develop a social doctrine that emphasized workers' rights. In Brazil, however, this social doctrine did not significantly alter pastoral practices among the popular classes until much later. During the nineteenth century, the Church worked mostly with elites; it provided only scanty religious education for peasants and workers. Even Romanization, which attempted to institute greater uniformity in religious practices and led to attempts to control popular religiosity, failed to strengthen the Church's presence among the masses.

It was only in the 1920's and 1930's, when Spiritism and Protestantism started to make inroads among Catholics, that the Church became more concerned with popular religious practices, which it saw as manifestations of "religious ignorance." Popular religious practices that the Church previously ignored or even tacitly condoned began to encounter clerical disapproval. The predominant view was that the Church needed to fight this "primitive" religion and implant a more mature faith. An increasing number of priests expressed their dismay that the masses "live in ignorance or at the margin of the Bible."[36] There was a widespread feeling that "religious ignorance continues to be the great obstacle to the spreading of the Kingdom of Jesus Christ."[37]

One of the most important changes the Church undertook during the 1940's and 1950's was reforming catechism and religious education. Religious leaders felt they needed to "raise the depressed level of customs, purify religious ceremony from the embarrassing mixture of empty and superstitious practices, establish piety on a solid base."[38] Religious education had to be ongoing, rather than directed exclusively toward children preparing for their first communion.

In theory, the solution to the problem of religious education appeared simple. But in practice this solution encountered some barriers, the most important of which, from the Church's point of view, was the shortage of priests. Since a large part of the country's relatively few priests were engaged in teaching or administrative activities, many pastoral functions were inadequately fulfilled. Many clerics considered the shortage of priests the Church's most serious problem.[39]

In a less clerical institution, the shortage of priests would not have mattered so much, but neither nuns nor the laity exercised autonomous leadership. One priest succinctly captured the centrality of the priest within the institution and the society: "The salvation of Brazil depends on the clergy."[40] Although isolated clerics started to emphasize the laity's role, priests held all formal authority and largely determined the orientation of lay movements. Even during mass, the laity barely participated.

Clergy concerned about popular religious ignorance traditionally believed that the people, not the institution, had to change. The institution could help the masses overcome their religious deficiencies, but to be mature, the people's faith had to be clericalized. There was little respect for popular religiosity, which was seen as inferior.

The pedagogical principles behind this attitude are interesting be-

cause of their dramatic contrast to the attitudes of the popular
Church of the 1970's. The underlying belief was that the common
people had nothing to teach; the priest's mission was to elevate the
people's faith nearer his own. The learning process was as hierarchical as the Church structures: the priest imparted knowledge to
the flock. Paternalism was explicit in the religious language of the
period. Priests were called to assume the role of fathers who would
guide the flock, "redirect people to the path of the good, guide them
to Heaven, and save them."[41]

The ideal priest was a virtuous man, superior in manners, moral
conduct, education, and religious spirit. The priest fulfilled a divine
mission in a world that had fallen from grace. The priest was, as one
person put it, "Minister of the Highest, chosen by God to sanctify
souls. . . . Salt of the earth, he will, as Jesus prophesied, be crushed
by people if he is not full of divine grace."[42]

As a reading of Weber's observations on religious castes would
lead one to expect, priests generally see themselves as a special
group within the Church. Indeed, throughout the 1960's and 1970's
priests engaged in the popular Church continued to see special
qualities in the work they did. In later years, however, the priest became a special figure because of his proximity to the people, not because of his superiority.

Priests maintained distance from the masses through an emphasis
on lay respect and obedience to the clergy. One priest wrote, "We
must teach the faithful, as is our duty, the sublimity and greatness
of the Catholic priesthood. We must inculcate, in the light of the
revelation, the respect due to the priest. . . . We must teach discipline and obedience, the obedience of rational and supernatural
beings."[43]

Probably more than the hierarchy's statements, these paternalistic
practices reinforced a world view that supported traditional forms
of political domination. Religious practices reinforced authoritarianism in other social institutions. In addition, the Church helped
sustain the perception that ordinary people were incapable. La-
ments about the "mediocrity of the souls we deal with" or "natural
naïveté" and "religious ignorance" expressed attitudes about the
popular sectors that could hardly go unnoticed.[44]

Ironically, the campaign to improve popular religious education,
intended as a means of creating greater contact between the Church
and the people, may have had the opposite effect. The disapproval

of popular religion prevented the clergy from realizing their goal of "conquering more souls." The masses, as distant as ever from the institutional Church, continued to search for religious expressions outside the Church.

The Decline of the Neo-Christendom Model

For two or three decades, the neo-Christendom model effectively defended the Church's most significant interests. Despite its relatively weak presence among vast segments of the population, the Church was able to attain many important goals. It had a virtual religious monopoly; it had developed a strong Catholic presence among the ruling elites and dominant classes; it had the major voice in education; some of its outstanding moral concerns, such as the status of the family, were respected; the society was stable and well ordered; and Vargas's legislation satisfied many aspects of the Church's social doctrine.

The Brazilian Church has always been somewhat heterogeneous, and throughout its history some leaders have believed that the Church should forgo privilege and align with the poor. Writing in 1899, Father Júlio Maria, a prominent and prescient figure, argued: "As in the rest of the world, there are only two forces in Brazil: the Church and the masses. . . . The clergy cannot, nor should they, shut themselves in sanctuaries and contemplate the people from a distance. . . . Their mission should be to show the weak, the poor, the proletarians, that they are the preferred people of the Divine Master."[45]

Over the following decades, a handful of other leaders and movements challenged some aspects of the neo-Christendom model. Nevertheless, it was only when the Church's influence within the state was threatened, when its influence in the educational system started to decline, when religious competition began to expand, when some traditional Catholic values started to erode, that the Church became more deeply concerned about its pastoral work. It took a crisis in the neo-Christendom model to cause the institution to modify its practices and beliefs.

By 1945, the Brazilian Church had furthered many objectives, but at the expense of effecting deeper changes in ecclesiology and political orientation. In a society undergoing rapid modernization, the Church's efforts to halt secularization were atavistic. The neo-

Christendom model modernized the institution's structures, deepened its influence, and shifted its primary political allegiance from
landowners to the urban bourgeoisie and middle class, but without
really changing its contents.

The success of the neo-Christendom model depended on its ability to fight secularization, use the state to influence society, and
maintain a religious monopoly. By the postwar period, it could not
meet these conditions. Brazil's society was changing rapidly, and no
action by the Church could prevent that. Any institution that resisted irreversible trends doomed itself to gradual decay, as a number of Catholic leaders began to realize. By 1945, antimodernism
had become unsustainable for an institution that had pretensions of
universality and that was especially concerned with influencing the
state and elites. In opposing secularization, the Church was casting
its lot with groups of declining importance.

The expansion of Protestantism and Spiritism made apparent
what had been true for some time: the Church was not effectively
reaching the masses.[46] Even though an overwhelming percentage of
the population declared itself Catholic, only a minority participated
actively in the Church. Protestants, although a small minority of the
population, were growing rapidly in number. The 1940 census registered slightly more than a million Protestants, a number that increased 150 percent by 1964. Growth was especially rapid in urban
areas and among the popular classes, further eroding Catholicism's
weak base among the masses.[47] Spiritism and other Afro-Brazilian
sects were also making inroads, especially in the cities, and many
declared Catholics practiced Afro-Brazilian religions.[48]

The decline of religious monopoly alarmed the hierarchy. Excor-
iating Protestants and Spiritists became commonplace. A leading
theologian accused the Protestants of "active, unctuous, and whee-
dling proselytism" and argued that the appeal of Protestantism was
the result of "superstitious curiosity, the sick sentimentalism of our
people, and the need to find cheaper, more guaranteed cures for
health problems."[49] To some clerics, Protestantism was part of a
North American plot to dominate Latin America and destroy Catholicism,[50] and Spiritism was an expression of popular religious ignorance. The battle against Spiritism was especially fierce because
many Catholics combined the two religions.

Characteristic of the measures taken to combat Protestantism and Spiritism was the creation of the National Secretariat for the Defense of Faith and Morality in 1953. Its goals were to watch over "the march of false religions, condemned movements, and false ideas" and "the expansion of immorality and amorality in public and private life." The movement initiated a campaign against Spiritism because, according to the bishops, "Spiritism denies not a few of the truths of our Holy Religion, but all of them."[51]

The leaders of the neo-Christendom Church professed a concern with popular religiosity, but they did little to change pastoral practices among the popular sectors. They were too busy dealing with elites to develop closer ties to the masses. As a result, the problem of "popular religious ignorance" was no less acute in the 1950's than it had been in 1916. Writing in 1955, nearly four decades after Dom Leme had announced his hope of revitalizing Brazilian Catholicism and elevating popular religious practices, sociologist Thales de Azevedo affirmed that the Church's influence in the society was still weak, that the institution was still underdeveloped, and that popular religious practices had not changed.[52] Religious leaders shared this perception. The editor of the country's leading theological journal lamented the prevalence of "extreme religious confusion and religious ignorance."[53]

When an institution opens itself to change, sometimes the change differs significantly from that originally imagined. The campaign against Protestants, Spiritists, and Masons, in itself a defensive response, began to make the Church more aware of its need to reformulate pastoral practices. More priests became concerned with popular needs and values. Although efforts to retain a virtual religious monopoly were doomed to fail in an increasingly heterogeneous society, the concomitant reformulation of pastoral practices eventually forged a new relationship between the institution and the poor.

The neo-Christendom model also depended on an increasingly unreliable alliance with the state. Through its arrangement with Vargas, the Church had maintained its dominance in the school system and its status as the privileged religious institution in the society. The democratic governments of the 1945-64 interlude attempted to win the Church's support and provided some favors in return, but the trade was neither as favorable nor as stable as it had been under Vargas.

Following its traditional strategy of accommodating itself to the
state whenever possible,* the Church had to change to maintain a
good relationship with the democratic governments. It had to tone
down its emphasis on authority, order, and discipline in order to
keep pace with the changes in national politics. The society was becoming more participatory and democratic, and it became more difficult for an institution that hoped to represent all social classes to
remain as hierarchical and authoritarian as before.

The strengthening of popular movements also caused some religious leaders to reassess the Church's mission. Despite a lengthy history of less organized forms of popular protest, it was only after
1945 that popular movements established a continuous, organized
presence in national politics. The growth of popular movements
underscored the efforts of the popular classes to change their position in the society. These classes were, in T. H. Marshall's sense,
fighting for citizenship.[54] This fight sometimes led them to reject paternalism and authoritarianism in other social spheres, including
religion.

For the traditionalists, the popular movements constituted a
threat. To the extent that they acquired progressive, anti-Catholic
overtones and questioned the hierarchical character of the society,
they challenged the basic world view of traditional Catholics. The
peasant movements of the 1950's, for example, supported agrarian
reform, which traditional Catholics saw as undermining the Christian right to private property.[55]

Institutional analysts have argued that the Church changed largely because of external threats, but it was not only by threatening the
traditional Church that the popular movements encouraged ecclesiastical change. They also helped generate a new awareness of the
fundamental problems in Brazilian society, changing the way many
leaders and institutions perceived the society. They politicized social problems that had existed for generations, making the progressive clergy more aware of social injustices and the Church's need to
address them. As an important 1962 document of the National
Conference of Brazilian Bishops stated, "Nobody can overlook the
cry of the masses, who, victimized by the specter of hunger, are
reaching the depths of desperation."[56]

*This does not mean that relations between the Church and state were always
harmonious. On occasion, religious leaders opposed the state's attempts to restrict
the Church. The most famous such case occurred in the Church-state crisis of 1872-
75.

It is no coincidence that the Church's most progressive pastoral practices during the 1950's involved peasants and students, for both groups were highly politicized. Nor is it a coincidence that the Church in the poverty-stricken Northeast was the first to address social problems seriously. Peasants had lived in dismal conditions for decades, and the Church had remained silent, but when the peasants organized, this changed. It was not the existence of poverty, but rather the politicization of that poverty, that made some sectors of the Church rethink their political conservatism.

The expansion of the Communist party after World War II also encouraged the Church to rethink its mission. The Communists were the third strongest party in the country in 1946 and were especially strong in Rio de Janeiro. Given the Church's anti-Communism, their success prompted considerable concern. The expansion of Communism was seen as a sign of the decay of Catholic culture and traditional values. It also indicated the need for the Church to implant itself in the society more firmly.

Between 1930 and 1964, the Communist threat was one of the outstanding concerns within the Church. In 1937, the bishops issued a document on Communism, and during the following decades most episcopal documents on social and political questions addressed the issue. Yet it would be erroneous to suggest that the emphasis on the Church's social doctrine was simply a response to the growing threat from the Left. The Church could have responded to the Left in a variety of ways, and it did. The traditionalists, who felt most strongly threatened by the Left, were the least enthusiastic supporters of the Church's social doctrine. Their solution was to repress the Left and avoid making social change. Conversely, the clergy most favorable toward the Church's social doctrine were the least hostile to the Communists. For them the Left demanded a response not because they were implacable anti-Communists, but rather because they agreed with the Left's perception of the need for major social change.

By 1955 there were three principal factions in the Church, with markedly different responses to social change. Those who continued to endorse the neo-Christendom strategy became the traditionalists even though the model would not have been classified as traditional before the 1950's. This group believed that the Church should continue to combat secularization and to strengthen the institution's presence in the society. For example, the Church should

organize campaigns against the secularized media, public education, and progressive political parties. It should operate as an interest group, using the state to ensure as many privileges as possible
and employing these privileges as a means of Catholicizing the
society.

The conservative modernizers believed the Church needed to
change to fulfill its mission in the modern world more effectively.
They shared the concern about secularization, the expansion of
Protestantism, and the Communist threat, but their response was
more open to the modern world. Although they rejected radical
change and had a limited conception of how to effect justice, they
were more concerned with social justice than were the neo-Christendom leaders. Although still hierarchical in Church practices, the
modernizers were more concerned with developing effective lay organizations and means of reaching the common people.

Finally, there was a nucleus of reformists.[57] This faction shared
the concern of the conservative modernizers about more intensive
pastoral work and more effective religious education, but its social
positions were more progressive. Whereas the conservative modernizers emphasized the need to fight Communism, the renovators were
more concerned about social change as an end in itself. During the
1950's, this group launched some experiments that gave rise to
more innovations later on.

CHAPTER 3

The Reformist Church, 1955-1964

THE DECADE 1955-65 saw significant changes in the Roman Catholic Church, both internationally and in Brazil. The relatively cautious and conservative Pius XII died in 1958, and his replacement, John XXIII, promoted significant changes. John's encyclicals, such as *Mater et Magistra* (1961) and *Pacem in Terris* (1963), changed official Catholic thought. Both developed a new conception of the Church, more in tune with the modern secular world, more committed to improving the lot of human beings on earth and to promoting social justice.[1] The Second Vatican Council began in 1962 under John's guidance; bringing the world's bishops to Rome to discuss a more open vision of the Church had a resounding effect. When John died in 1963, Paul VI assumed the papacy and, despite some oscillations, provided continuity to the process of Church renewal until his death in 1978.

For both its critics and its supporters, the Second Vatican Council (1962-65) marked one of the most important events in the history of Roman Catholicism. Despite the contradictions, tensions, and limits that surrounded the changes, the Vatican Council emphasized the Church's social mission, affirmed the importance of the laity in the Church, encouraged greater coresponsibility (for example, the sharing of responsibility between the pope and bishops or between priests and laity) within the Church, developed the notion of the Church as the people of God, called for ecumenical dialogue, changed the liturgy to make it more accessible, and introduced a host of other changes.[2] Conciliar documents emphasized the hierarchical character of the Church and insisted that its mission is above politics, but the new doctrine significantly revised patterns of authority in the Church and the relationship between faith and the world.

Before Vatican II and the papacy of John XXIII, many theologians, bishops, and movements had worked for change in the Church.[3] In this sense, the progressive papal encyclicals and Vatican II incorporated and legitimated existing trends rather than creating something new. But in a hierarchical institution like the Roman Church, legitimation from above is very important. Even though the Vatican may never create radical new programs or theologies, its positions help determine what conceptions of the Church's mission become hegemonic; hence, they help determine pastoral practices throughout the world. Despite the increased autonomy of national churches in the past two decades, Rome continues to exercise a profound authority over national churches, lay movements, and theological developments through both persuasion and coercion. In this sense, the Second Vatican Council reproduced a pattern that reappears throughout the Catholic Church. Change was initiated from below, but it took hold only when it was legitimated from above.

Vatican II was a European event, dominated by European bishops and theologians and aimed principally at the European Church. Curiously, however, the Council reforms led to more significant changes in some Latin American countries than in Europe. Greater lay participation, social justice, greater sense of community, greater coresponsibility in the Church, and closer relations between the clergy and the people demanded greater change in Latin America than in Europe. With the notable exception of Colombia, the weakness of Church structures was glaring. Equally glaring were the egregious social injustices. The terrible living conditions of the poor, the increasing wealth of the elites, social discrimination against the poor, and repression of popular movements made ecclesial support of the extant system more difficult.

Dom José Maria Pires, archbishop of João Pessoa and one of the outstanding leaders in the popular Church, commented on Vatican II's impact on the Brazilian Church: "Vatican II was the motor of all this change; it systematized things. There were always theologians, pastors, and lay people in the Church who assumed a dialectical position in favor of the oppressed, but it was only with Vatican II that this position became official and the attitudes were systematized. . . . What made me opt for the poor was Vatican II."[4]

Changes in the national society and polity also helped stimulate

Church reform. The increasingly democratic, participatory character of the society and polity encouraged the Church to become more democratic too, both in internal governance and in political orientation.

During the last years of the period, popular movements acquired new strength. These movements affected many Church leaders, either by calling attention to the importance of supporting reforms or, in the case of conservatives, by creating an awareness of the rapid growth of the Left. Innovations in popular education, including the Movement for Grass-roots Education (Movimento de Educação de Base; MEB), the work of Paulo Freire, and the Centers for Popular Culture, generated new reflections on the role of the masses in the society.[5] These movements helped create an atmosphere of questioning that indirectly encouraged innovation in pastoral work among the popular classes.

After 1961, however, the country experienced intense polarization and conflict. A reaction against progressive movements began to grow among the military, the Church, and the middle and dominant classes. These conservative movements, which became stronger in the years leading up to the coup, were concerned about economic stagnation, social disorder, and the growth of the Left. The incipient political crisis became apparent in 1961 when President Jânio Quadros resigned and serious tensions concerning João Goulart's assumption of the presidency emerged.[6]

The Cuban Revolution also had a profound impact on the Church throughout Latin America. The events in Cuba created the awareness that revolution was a possibility in Latin America; indeed, throughout most of the 1960's, both the Left and the Right significantly overestimated the continent's revolutionary potential. Cuba inspired some people to intensify their efforts to promote radical change, others to adopt more intransigent defenses of the existing order, and still others to promote social reform as a way of aborting revolution. Within the Brazilian Church, all three reactions were present; among practicing Catholics, the first was the weakest, and the reformist impulse the strongest. The strident conflict between the Church and the Castro regime reinforced the defensive tendencies within some sectors.[7]

My discussion of the 1955-64 period focuses principally on the forces for change within the Church, but it is important to analyze the resistance to change as well as the pressures for change. By 1964 the Brazilian Church had changed significantly, but the Church was fraught with internal conflicts. At one extreme was the Catholic Left, committed to major social transformation. At the other were the traditionalists, from whose ranks the Catholic Right sprang. Many people remained faithful to a traditional conception of Catholic faith. Out of this sector arose a Catholic Right, which helped to bring about President Goulart's fall in 1964 and to create pressures against the Catholic Left and the progressive bishops. The military coup of 1964 meant that the Right had temporarily prevailed over the Left, both in the Church and in the broader political struggle. The government supported the anti-Communist positions of the Catholic Right, and the Right retained its prominence within the Church for several more years.[8]

The core of the institutional Church favored neither the Left nor the traditionalists. Rather, it was divided between the reformists and the conservative modernizers. The conservative modernizers were the dominant faction in the Church during the early and middle 1950's, and until the late 1960's they shared hegemony with the reformists. Like the reformists, they believed the Church had to change, but they promoted a stronger Catholicism through more intensive religious education. They were more concerned about social justice than were the traditionalists, but less prone than the reformists to see social problems as the result of the social structure. Concerned with making the Church more effective and relevant to its adherents, they launched programs such as the Christian Family Movement and the Christian mini-courses (*Cursilhos de Cristandade*). Like the reformists, the conservative modernizers believed the Church needed to promote greater lay participation, but they were more concerned about maintaining hierarchical obedience than were the reformists, who emphasized the notion of the Church as God's people.

Both groups considered the Church's social mission important, but they perceived this mission differently. The conservative modernizers shied away from overt political involvement, arguing that the Church should be above politics. They focused principally on individual development (through education, for example) rather than on changing social structures.

Despite substantial change, at the end of this decade the Church remained relatively conservative. A majority of the bishops were conservative modernizers, but the reformists occupied many central positions in the National Conference of Brazilian Bishops (CNBB), giving them a power that went beyond sheer numbers. The major CNBB documents of the period represented a compromise between the two groups. The conservatives, though not actively resisting the Church's renovation, were hardly enthusiastic about enacting the changes implied by the new vision of the Church's mission. In 1964, paralleling the fears of the bourgeoisie and the middle class, the conservative modernizers responded to a perceived threat to themselves from the religious and political changes and defeated the progressives in the CNBB elections.

The Reformists

In Chapter 2 I argued that the Church's desire to remain a universal institution in an increasingly secular, participatory, and democratic society encouraged the emergence of new conceptions of the Church's mission. The reformist model of the Church was one of the responses. Some expressions of it emerged during the early 1950's. From the late 1950's until about 1970, the reformists shared leadership with the modernizers; they then had sole hegemony until around 1976. From 1976 to 1982 they shared hegemony with the popular Church; after 1982, with the international strengthening of the conservatives, the reformists once again became the dominant sector.

The reformists accepted secularization as inevitable and believed it had some positive consequences. They were less anti-Protestant and anti-Communist than their predecessors and more concerned with social justice and community. The reformists believed that political change was needed to create a juster society, but they eschewed radical politics. They were more democratic in ecclesial practices and gave more autonomy to lay groups. They pushed for change on many other issues, including liturgy and catechism, and paid more attention than their predecessors to working with the masses.[9]

The most significant reforms echoed those taking place internationally: increasing emphasis on the laity and on coresponsibility, an understanding of the Church that challenged the separation between faith and earthly matters, and a greater emphasis on the Church's social mission. These changes were encouraged by the Vatican, but they also resulted from movements within the Brazilian

Church and from the political and social changes taking place in
Brazil.*

Between 1955 and 1964, the CNBB was the most important force
for reform in the Brazilian Church. The CNBB was created in 1952
through the initiative of Dom Helder Câmara, at the time auxiliary
bishop of Rio de Janeiro, with strong support from the reformists in
the Vatican.† It was one of the first national episcopal conferences
in the world and the first one in Latin America. Since its inception,
the CNBB has been very important in the Brazilian Church. It has
legitimated some practices, discouraged and even prohibited others,
facilitated communication within the Church, and created pressures
for change or impeded it.[10]

During these years, the reformists also started a number of grass-
roots programs that promoted ecclesiastical change. The liturgical
movement, the Catholic Bible Movement, the program in popular
catechism in Barra do Piraí, and innovations in Nízia Floresta in
Rio Grande do Norte, where the shortage of priests led to greater
authority for nuns, increased lay participation and reduced clerical
control. These movements were politically conservative, but they
paved the way for a conception of the Church as the people of God
rather than as the hierarchy and clergy. Other movements, such as
the Christian Family Movement, attempted to develop a deeper
Christianity and make the laity more active in the Church.[11]

More significant were the innovations in implementing the
Church's social doctrine. Among the most important programs were
the Natal Movement for adult education in the Archdiocese of Natal; the Foundation Leo XIII and the São Sebastião Crusade, both
of which were active in the *favelas* (slums) of Rio de Janeiro; and
the Movement for a Better World (MMM). These programs meant
accepting rather than fighting secularization, criticizing rather than
tolerating the inegalitarian nature of the society, and working with

---

*Any conception (theological, political, literary) can develop a different meaning
according to cultural context. An idea that has one meaning in a developed Western
nation can acquire a different meaning in a Third World country. For this reason, it
is not surprising that Roman Catholicism has always had some transcultural differences, even during periods when the central authority attempted to impose uniformity. Conversely, the Church's own need for adaptability has almost always led the
Vatican to accept some national and local differences.

†A national council of bishops was set up in the late 1890's, and the bishops occasionally issued collective pastoral letters. Nevertheless, there was no organized, ongoing structure until 1952.

the poor as well as the elites. Inspired in part by anti-Communism, these innovations broke sharply with traditional practices. Rather than teaching acceptance of poverty, they promoted solutions aimed at overcoming or alleviating misery.[12]

The New Ecclesiology: Faith and Human History

One of the fundamental postulates of the reformists was that the Church is part of the world and must participate in it. They no longer perceived the world as an evil that corrupts the Church or as a force that must be overcome. The radical theological separation between the heavenly Kingdom and earth disappeared. Concomitantly, the idea that the Church should Christianize a fundamentally evil world started to erode. One priest criticized the "pastoral work of the clerical monopoly, legacy of a distant past in which the culture and the entire physiognomy of the society had a sacred character. . . . The Church cannot and should not dominate temporal structures and institutions."[13]

The reformists believed that the Church neither could nor should be wholly above the world, but rather should act as a sign that helps transform the world. To them, Christ's message included creating a just social order. This meant working toward constructing the world that God Himself would envision, even though humans could not complete the task. An influential theologian succinctly summarized this new conception of the relationship between faith and action in the world: "It is the responsibility of human beings, of Christians of this generation, to construct a world in accordance with divine will. This cannot be done by escaping the world; it is necessary to work effectively in institutions."[14]

The Church had traditionally seen secularization as an evil to be combated, but the reformists believed that secularization was inevitable and had some positive consequences. One priest, in summarizing the new attitude toward secularization, argued that "the progress that is transforming the world in such radical and profound ways is not a rebellion against God, but rather the fulfillment of His will."[15]

The new attitudes challenged the triumphal views that had characterized the 1940's. In the neo-Christendom model the Church was a perfect society; for the reformists it was not free of shortcomings. Characteristic of the reformist spirit was Aloísio Lorscheider, later to be secretary general of the CNBB, who in 1963 wrote that "the Church is far from being the leaven that works on the masses of humanity; it is far from being, as Christ's spouse, the light of the nations."[16] Rather than perceiving the Church as an institution above the world, the reformists believed that the Church had to become a servant to the world.[17] Some priests argued that the Church should divest itself of its power and its wealth.[18] Others criticized its alliance with the bourgeoisie and the state, feeling that this impeded a closer connection with the working masses.[19] The progressive clergy and laity insisted that the Church do more for the masses.[20]

An increasing number of priests criticized social structures and practices, including elitism, the concentration of power and economic resources in the hands of a small minority, the poverty of millions of Brazilians, the limited opportunities for education and social mobility for the poor, the land tenure system, and the conditions in urban slums. Many prominent priests became critical of liberal capitalism, and by 1961-64, a number of priests and bishops showed an interest in socialism.[21]

Considering the great heterogeneity among the bishops, it is not surprising that the CNBB was not as progressive as reformist priests. Yet although the reformists were a minority within the CNBB, they managed to articulate a view of the Church's mission that went far beyond episcopal attitudes of the 1940's. This new vision was particularly apparent in the CNBB's Emergency Plan (Plano de Emergência) of 1962, which was the first national-level pastoral plan for the Brazilian Church, and General Pastoral Plan (Plano de Pastoral de Conjunto; PPC), approved by the Seventh General Assembly of the CNBB, which met in Rome in 1965 during the last session of Vatican II. In both plans, the bishops made an explicit break with the neo-Christendom conception of the Church's mission and called for many innovations, including better pastoral planning and coordination, a more active role for the laity, parish renewal, a stronger sense of community, and less authoritarian episcopal practices. Despite a markedly anti-Communist bent, they called for major socioeconomic reforms.

The PPC, which advocated further reform, argued that though above the world, the Church must still take part in that world and inform human society; and that although the Church is not a political force, it must promote communion among people. Written at a time when the CNBB was retreating from political involvement, the

PPC still stressed that salvation and terrestrial matters are not antagonistic. "The Church consists of more than the community of people and their history, but it lives in this community. This presence in the temporal world and the Church's relation to human history are part of its mystery. . . . Pastoral action should, in light of the Concilium [Vatican II], rethink and renew the Church's relationship to the human family and its presence in human history."[22] Despite many limits, both plans encouraged change in the Church and contained the outline of a reformist consciousness that shaped the early and mid-1960's innovations in pastoral work. The new conception of the relationship between faith and social justice had profound consequences in a society that after 1964 suffered from repression, highly inegalitarian development, social elitism, and authoritarianism.

The Role of the Laity and Parish Renewal

The theological reforms culminating in Vatican II challenged the traditional lay role in the Catholic Church. For centuries, the Church had downplayed the role of the laity. Pius XI and Pius XII argued for expanding the laity's role, but they were not willing to grant lay groups the autonomy and responsibility needed to effect this change. Lay movements that threatened to become more autonomous were often disbanded by the hierarchy and the Vatican.[23] Not surprisingly, the hope that lay movements would become more dynamic was not fully realized, notwithstanding the emergence and growth of movements such as the Workers' Circles and Catholic Action.

Following in the footsteps of reformist French theologians,[24] the encyclicals of John XXIII and Paul VI modified this traditional conception of the Church. The Vatican Council stressed that the Church is the people of God, emphasizing coresponsibility more than hierarchy. Throughout the world, this helped change authority patterns in the Church.[25] In Brazil the role of the laity started to change during the 1950's and early 1960's. Some lay movements, especially the Catholic University Youth (JUC), criticized the institution's failure to reach out more actively to the laity.[26] Father José Marins voiced the opinion of many priests working for pastoral renewal when he wrote that "without a doubt, the most negative point [of past ecclesial practices] was our unilateral concept of a

Church restricted to priests, bishops, and the pope. The laity did not have the responsibilities they should have had."[27] Such priests realized that the laity needed more autonomy and responsibility, if they were to participate more meaningfully in the Church's life, and sharply criticized the clericalism and paternalism of the Church's past.

Some rural areas tried a new experience in lay responsibility: a Sunday religious celebration without a priest. Initially conceived by some progressive priests as a response to their inability to celebrate Mass every Sunday in the large territories they served, these new experiences were the first examples of what later came to be known as ecclesial base communities.*

Although reformist lay groups and priests were instrumental in pushing the Church to open itself, even conservative modernizers agreed that it should do so. The laity generally understood Catholicism poorly, and the Church needed to evangelize more effectively to compete with other religious groups. For the modernizers, the desire to encourage more active lay participation emerged from attempts to enhance the Church's ability to influence temporal affairs and to develop a laity that would help evangelize the masses; in this sense, the goals were traditional, even though they led to new forms of action. The modernizers also hoped that a well-informed laity would help resolve the problems created by the shortage of priests.[28]

Conservative clerics thought of the bolstering of lay groups as a means of extending rather than changing traditional Church domination of the society.[29] To them, lay groups were an extension of the hierarchy and a means of exercising deeper influence in temporal affairs and of developing a cadre of lay leaders to help defend Catholicism against its religious competitors. If the conservatives had been

---

*The earliest references to such experiences were two 1963 articles by priests who played midwife to the birth of base communities: Leers, "Estrutura do Culto Dominical"; and A. Rolim, "Culto Dominical." Almir Ribeiro Guimarães and José Marins have argued that the base communities date to the late 1950's, with D. Agnelo Rossi's experiment with popular catechism, popular Bible Circles in Volta Redonda, and the radio schools in Natal; see Guimarães; and Marins, "Comunidades Eclesiais de Base." I disagree with this perspective for two reasons. First, these early experiences differed markedly from the base communities. They involved significant clerical control and were not very concerned about the social implications of the Gospel. Second, no existing base communities trace their history back farther than about 1963. The CNBB's nationwide study of 101 base communities, Comunidades, did not find any CEBs that began before 1964, and none of the communities' reports to the national meetings mention pre-1964 activities.

consistently successful in their design, the strengthening of lay movements would have reinforced rather than challenged the traditional relationship between the Church and politics. Movements such as the Marian Movement, the Bible Circles, and the Christian mini-courses reinforced the Church's traditional political involvement.[30]

The concern with more active lay participation was also expressed in the Emergency Plan and the PPC. The Emergency Plan recognized that "rarely do we give the laity the role they should have; we reduce their collaboration to limited, unexpressive proportions."[31] The PPC introduced the notion of the Church as the people of God and emphasized "a new attempt to recognize not only the specific role of all members of the Church, but also their complementarity and integration as members of the people of God."[32]

Despite these advances, the bishops' view of the Church was still hierarchical compared to that of the popular model. Although they called for greater lay involvement, they did not relegate much responsibility or autonomy to lay groups. In the Emergency Plan, the laity were "precious helpers who collaborate with us" and who should "collaborate effectively in all parish activities." The bishops noted that "the initiative and responsibility of the laity are determined by the orientation of the Church, represented by the parish priest."[33] Equally significant, the hierarchy was at the time suppressing one of the most important lay movements, JUC (see Chapter 4).

Connected to the new emphasis on the laity was parish renewal, which became one of the major themes within the Brazilian Church during the early 1960's. It was championed by both the modernizers and the reformists. The modernizers saw parish renewal as a means of deepening the Church's influence and developing a more mature faith. Because the limited number of priests could not attend to the large numbers of people in urban areas or to the vast rural regions, the traditional parish was an obstacle to developing adequate clerical contact among the people.[34] The priest's contacts with his parishioners were superficial, and he could not ensure adequate religious instruction. More effective Church structures would allow for better teaching of the fundamentals of Catholic faith and practice and would compensate for the shortage of priests.

The progressive clergy emphasized parish renewal as a means of developing a sense of community, greater lay responsibility, and the Church's social mission. They considered the present parishes too dispersed and too large to encourage a true sense of community.[35] They also perceived parish renewal as a way to give the laity a stronger voice in religious life. Rather than directly controlling activities, the priest would help lay groups assume control of such tasks as catechism, social work, and community activities. Strengthening the local religious community was also a way of encouraging the Church's mission as a witness. These local communities would act as solidarity groups, developing a sense of concern for their sisters and brothers.

The Agrarian Question

Between 1950 and 1964, rural problems came to the fore, largely because the strengthening of peasant movements created tensions and helped politicize the plight of the poorest part of the Brazilian population. From a relatively early date, the Church was concerned about the rural question, and it became more socially active in rural areas than elsewhere. The Church's social reforms in rural areas, especially the Northeast, included the Natal program, increased responsibilities for nuns in Nízia Floresta, the first ecclesial base communities, and MEB. The reformist bishops' perception of the agrarian question illuminates their political ideology.

Although most of the Church was still conservative in the early 1950's, some leaders had begun to support social reforms in rural areas. A talk by Dom Inocêncio Engelke, bishop of Campanha, Minas Gerais, in September 1950 was the first important statement by a member of the Brazilian hierarchy calling for agrarian reform. Engelke criticized the existing order in rural Brazil, focusing on the plight of the peasants. "The situation of the rural worker is generally subhuman. Should the shacks they live in be called houses? Can the food they eat be considered nutrition? Can the rags they wear be called clothing? Can their vegetative existence be called life when they have no health, no hopes, no visions, no ideals? . . . We must establish a minimum program of social action to benefit these workers. . . . Reforms in the structures and bases are needed."[36]

Engelke was not alone in his denunciations. In 1951, three Northeast bishops issued a statement on the land problem. That same year, the assembled archbishops and bishops of Brazil published a statement supporting limited agrarian reform. In August 1952, sev

eral other prelates from the Northeast made a stronger call for
agrarian reform. This document, "The Church and the São Francisco Valley," criticized the large landowners and denounced the situation of the rural workers.

Large rural estates fail to fulfill their social function when they lead to rigid
monopolies that favor a small minority, to insufficient utilization of the
land, to impoverishment through the exploitation of the work force, or to
demographic pressures that sharply increase land value. In these cases, the
public authorities should take the necessary steps, which may include partial or complete redistribution of the land with reasonable indemnifica-
tion. . . . Cattle farm workers, rice sharecroppers, and sugarcane sharecroppers frequently live in virtual slavery.[37]

In 1954, in its first statement on agrarian reform, the CNBB stated
that "the demands of social justice and those of development require a 'reform in the base and methods' of the current system of
rural life."[38]

Despite the clamor for change, until the late 1950's even the most
progressive episcopal statements expressed the belief that economic
development would resolve the peasantry's problems. The issue was
modernization, not land tenure. Cooperation between peasants and
owners would solve the peasants' problems.[39] There was an unques-
tioned belief that the landowners would willingly implement juster
labor policies; the answer was "economic, professional, intellectual,
moral, and religious solidarity" among the social classes.[40]

The early reformist documents consistently eschewed major land
redistribution as unnecessary and undesirable. Even though ecclesiastical discourse emphasized that private property had to serve a
social function, it essentially consecrated the right of property.[41] The
early statements on agrarian reform generally said that only unused
land should be redistributed; even then, the state should reimburse
the owner. The CNBB's 1954 document stated, "What really matters is the partial or full utilization of land. Dividing or subdividing
private property should not be part of the agrarian reform. Property
should be respected and should not be divided up except when the
common good so dictates."[42] Agrarian reform, then, was virtually
limited to promoting faster rural development. The reformists believed that peasants should have access to land, but they felt that
they should settle unclaimed lands.

The early reformist documents had elitist overtones and implied that peasants were incapable of developing a critical perception of reality. One statement, for example, criticized the "superficiality of popular sense" and the peasants' "mental confusion."[43]

At the end of the 1950's and especially between 1961 and 1964, the Church's involvement in agrarian reform intensified. This is hardly surprising, given the international Church's concern with elaborating a modern social doctrine and the increasing prominence of the land question in Brazilian politics. The bishops' reflections on the agrarian question became more critical and more insistent upon reform. Whereas previously the bishops had urged the modernization of Brazilian capitalism, in the early 1960's they began to call for more significant reforms to help modernize Brazilian capitalism and to promote social justice.

By the late 1950's, the bishops had begun to question whether economic development alone would resolve the problems of the peasants. The reformist perspective changed from encouraging modernization without land redistribution to encouraging modernization *and* redistribution. Although the real turning point on these issues came in the early 1960's, a 1956 document by the northeastern bishops, the most progressive in the country, anticipated the changes. While still within a nationalist-developmentalist perspective, it suggested that without land distribution, economic growth would not resolve the plight of the rural indigent.[44]

In 1963, the Central Commission of the CNBB issued a stronger statement. The document was pessimistic about the ability of economic growth and modernization of the countryside to resolve the plight of the rural poor. It recognized that millions of people did not share in the "benefits of our development" and lived in conditions that "affront human dignity." Access to the land was "indispensable for the realization of people's natural right to property. So that this imperative can be realized, [we affirm that] land expropriation not only does not contradict the Church's social doctrine, it is one of the means of realizing the social function of rural property."[45]

The bishops began to perceive that some forms of modernization could have adverse effects on peasants and subsistence farmers. Beginning with the 1956 document by the northeastern bishops, Church leaders emphasized the wants and the contributions of small farmers and peasants and said that the state had not met small farmers' needs.[46] By 1961, even a fairly conservative document by the bishops of the Rio Doce Valley emphasized the need for special attention to small farmers.[47] Some documents began to question the dominance of export crops at the expense of consumption crops, which are generally grown by small property owners.[48] Other statements showed an awareness of the problems created by capital-intensive rural modernization oriented toward exports. The 1956 declaration of the northeastern bishops indicated concern over the tendency of capital-intensive rural development to expel workers from the land.[49] This was the first sign of awareness of a problem extensively discussed by the Church during the 1970's.

The calls for agrarian reform conformed to the bishops' thinking on other social questions. By the late 1950's, the CNBB supported the reformist governments except on educational issues.[50] The bishops called for a reformed capitalist system that would offer greater opportunities and better material conditions for the masses. Said a 1958 document signed by all the bishops, "We feel anguish when we see that the socioeconomic structures often continue to be the source of injustice, suffering, and oppression. . . . We must speak out against the social injustices that are all too evident in the shocking living conditions of the working class and the popular sectors."[51] By 1962, the bishops were criticizing "the egoism and profit generated by economic liberalism."[52]

Although the statements of the early 1960's were more progressive than those of a decade earlier, they contained some of the same limitations. The prelates continued to believe that economic development would *eventually* resolve the major problems of the peasants. Modernization of the large farms would improve the living standards of peasants on those farms. A 1961 statement by the Central Commission of the CNBB is particularly illuminating. It stated that the "integration of Brazilian agriculture in the pace of national development" was crucial and recommended classic developmentalist measures: infrastructure development, fiscal incentives, technical improvements, and agricultural modernization.[53]

The reformists continued to believe in class harmony. They thought cooperation between the landowners and peasants would improve living conditions. On this score, the reformists clashed with the Peasant Leagues established by Francisco Julião and the *sindicatos* founded by the Communist party, both of which saw pressure from below as the best way to promote social change in rural areas. Only in the 1960's, after the Peasant Leagues and the Communist party had been organizing the peasantry for several years, did the

Church become actively involved in organizing; even then, the Church-created unions were more conservative.[54]

In retrospect, episcopal documents of the period seem somewhat naive in their faith that the landowners would be willing to support the reforms called for by the Church. Dom Inocêncio Engelke's 1950 speech made clear his belief that the owners had the responsibility for making the necessary changes and would be willing to do so.[55] "The Church and the São Francisco Valley" (1952) suggested that the Church should work principally with the owners rather than the peasants, and it failed to question the assumption that the landowners would willingly make significant reforms without pressure from below. A similar faith in the good intentions of the landowners is apparent in the "Declaration of the Northeastern Bishops" (1956), which envisioned sugarcane plantations donating plots to workers and making other efforts to improve their living conditions. In a particularly ingenuous statement, the CNBB suggested in 1954 that landowners could implement local agrarian reform in a spontaneous contribution to help make landownership feasible for as many rural workers as possible.[56] This belief in class harmony and the beneficence of Brazilian elites also characterized pre-1964 episcopal documents on other questions.[57]

Until 1964, the progressive bishops' views were compatible with those of the reformist, populist governments. In striking contrast to the post-1964 period, relations between the Church and state were generally cordial until the last months before the coup. The bishops perceived the state as the instrument for social change, and throughout the late populist years (1956-63), the CNBB supported the government. Several important social projects of the Church were undertaken in collaboration with the state. The state, for example, financed the Movement for Grass-roots Education. The Superintendency for Development of the Northeast (SUDENE), created in the late 1950's, was a product of Church-state cooperation. The CNBB supported a nationalism similar to that of the Kubitschek-Quadros-Goulart governments.[58] In most cases of conflict, the problem arose between the government and the conservative or Integralist sectors of the Church.

The Communist "threat" was very much on the minds of the bishops, especially during the last few years before the coup. The bishops were extremely critical of Communism. In 1961, the Central Commission of the CNBB charged that "the Communists are not really interested in solutions. On the contrary, for them, the worse things are, the better."[59]

As a collective body, the bishops believed that the most effective way to deal with the Communist threat was to effect reforms that would satisfy the aspirations of the masses, making them less susceptible to Communist ideas. For example, Engelke's 1950 speech exhorted landowners to "anticipate the revolution." Only if social change were effected could "the man of the countryside defend himself against the dangerous seductions of those who see in the agrarian question a source of fertile culture for the bacillus of disturbances and violent revolutions."[60] Ten years later the bishops of the state of São Paulo affirmed that "the choice is between a balanced, reasonable reform and a rural revolution led by Communists, exploiting the precarious and sometimes explosive situation in the rural areas."[61]

The Communist threat clearly changed the perspectives of the Brazilian hierarchy regarding land questions. Yet it would be a mistake to exaggerate its importance. Existence of a Communist threat need not have made the Church adopt more progressive attitudes. The bishops could have seen strengthening the traditional social order rather than social reform as the antidote to Communism. Indeed, a number of Catholic lay groups and a significant group of bishops did precisely that, becoming some of the most vocal anti-Communist forces in the society.

CHAPTER 4

The Catholic Left,
1958-1964

IN CHAPTER 1, I argued that despite the Catholic Church's hierarchical character and historical tendency to smother lay movements
that threaten the institution's interests as its leaders perceive them,
it has from time to time allowed some progressive movements to develop. Even if these movements are eventually stifled or co-opted,
they can affect the institution. Institutions, even highly bureaucratic
ones like the Roman Church, do not always change because of initiative from above; they can also change because their bases innovate and create effective pressures for change.

Grass-roots and lay movements have been a significant force for
change in the Brazilian Church since 1958. An important example
is the Catholic Left of the 1958-64 period. Even though it was nu-
merically small, and was ultimately undermined by the hierarchy
and then repressed by the military regime, it introduced new concepts of faith and showed the potential dynamism of the laity within
the Church.

Because the history of the Catholic Left has already been told in
a number of fine accounts, there is no need to go into great narrative
detail in this chapter. It is, however, essential to analyze its impact
in changing the Brazilian Church.

Lay Movements, Society, and Church

It is impossible to understand the development of Catholic lay
movements only in reference to the institutional Church. The polit-

ical orientation of Catholic lay activists is not determined solely by
their ties to the Church. Catholics are also part of the social structure, and as such they participate in politics as university students,
peasants, workers, medical doctors. They interact with the society
and are influenced by trends in the society at large and particularly
by social movements within their own class.

Even when the hierarchy is responsible for creating lay movements, it does not always rigidly control them. In recent decades, as
the Church has promoted greater lay responsibility and participation, there has been a tension between hierarchical control, which
reduces the possibility of effective lay participation, and lay autonomy, which increases the possibility of conflict with the hierarchy.
The lay movements studied in this chapter fall at one end of this
spectrum: they developed considerable autonomy with respect to
the hierarchy. Catholic lay leaders did not act in certain ways because the bishops commissioned them to do so. They came into frequent conflict with the hierarchy precisely because they had enough
autonomy to develop independently.

There were, however, limits to this autonomy. Although Catholic
lay movements respond to changes in the society at large, they are
always part of the institutional Church. And even though lay movements can acquire some autonomy vis-à-vis the hierarchy, the
boundaries of this autonomy depend principally on the hierarchy. In
Brazil, during the late 1950's and early 1960's, the deepening participation of Catholics in the labor, peasant, and student movements
was contingent upon the hierarchy's acquiescence. At a different
historical moment, the hierarchy could have proscribed participation, foreclosing the possibility that the laity could participate as
Catholics in progressive politics.

Catholic University Youth

Catholic Action, one of the most important lay movements in the
contemporary Church, was created in Italy in the late nineteenth
century as an instrument for influencing society after the Church
had lost political power as a result of the unification of Italy in
1870.[1] Brazilian Catholic Action (ACB) was created in the 1920's
under the auspices of Dom Sebastião Leme, who was encouraged by
Pope Pius XI. During its first decades, Catholic Action in Brazil

closely paralleled the European movements in its dependence on the hierarchy. The conclusions of the First National Congress of ACB in 1946 highlighted lay subordination to the hierarchy. Catholic Action professed "the most filial submission to all members of the Hierarchy."[2] The hierarchy called for "the discipline of prompt and filial obedience to your hierarchical superiors."[3]

The Catholic University Youth movement (JUC) was created in the 1930's as part of ACB.[4] It began as a conservative, clerical means of helping Christianize the future elite. But after the reorganization of ACB between 1946 and 1950, the movement became more autonomous. JUC became increasingly involved in and affected by the student movement and the Left. By the end of the 1950's, JUC began a rapid radicalization that led it into sharp conflict with the hierarchy. The turning point came at JUC's national conference in 1959, when it assumed explicit responsibility for political action as part of its evangelical commitment.

In 1960, the Central-Western Regional Committee, headed by social science students at Belo Horizonte, published an important document, *Algumas Diretrizes de um Ideal Histórico Cristão para o Povo Brasileiro* ("Some considerations on a Christian historical ideal for the Brazilian people"). The paper criticized capitalism, portrayed as the cause of underdevelopment. Capitalism was "a monstrous structure, sustained by all kinds of abuses, exploitation, and crimes against the dignity of the human person. . . . Capitalism deserves the condemnation of the Christian conscience."[5]

By 1960, JUC was actively involved in the Brazilian Left. Progressive Catholics reacted to the same events as the rest of the Left, and despite their criticisms of Leninist groups, they were in constant contact with leftist organizations and influenced by them. Catholics were influential in the student movement and many movements for popular education and culture. They were also important in organizing peasants, communities, and, to some extent, workers. By 1964, the Catholic Left competed with the two Communist parties—the Brazilian Communist Party (PCB) and the Communist Party of Brazil (PC do B)—as the major force in the organized Left.[6]

As JUC sought to follow its new vision of faith, the movement became very involved in student and national politics. Starting in 1960, it became active in the National Union of Students (UNE). That year, JUC supported the successful candidacy of Oliveiros

Guanais, a leftist, for UNE president. In 1961, Aldo Arantes, an active JUC participant, was elected president, beginning a period of Catholic domination of the UNE that lasted until after the 1964 coup.

JUC's 1960 statement, "A Christian Historical Ideal for Brazil," provoked sharp criticisms by the Catholic Right, which included some bishops. By 1961 the ideological gap between the bishops and JUC had become significant. JUC leaders played a visible role at the UNE congress on university reform, causing concern among Church leaders that the movement was becoming too political. Later that year, students at the Catholic University in Rio published a manifesto. Although the document was not formally a JUC publication, it reaffirmed a vision of faith similar to JUC's and was largely written by JUC participants.[7] Its affirmation of the links between faith and progressive politics caused a wave of conservative protest, followed by a widely publicized response by leading Jesuit philosopher Father Henrique Vaz defending the movement.[8]

More serious problems erupted in 1961, when Dom Eugênio Sales, apostolic administrator of the diocese of Natal and an articulate spokesperson for the prelates concerned with challenges to episcopal authority, assumed the leadership of the increasing opposition to JUC. As the Catholic Right attacked JUC, moderate bishops became more concerned with the movement's radicalization. The result was an episcopal document issued in late 1961, forbidding the movement to make radical pronouncements and "undesirable" political commitments. In response to JUC's discussions of socialism, the document affirmed that "Christians cannot consider socialism a solution to socioeconomic and political problems, much less *the* solution. In discussing the Brazilian revolution, JUC cannot consider a doctrine that espouses violence as valid and acceptable." Other sanctions were imposed, including a decision to expel Aldo Arantes from JUC because of his role in UNE.[9]

This was only the beginning of pressure against JUC. Between 1961, when reprisals against JUC commenced, and 1966, when the movement finally disbanded, disgruntled with the hierarchy, JUC gradually declined. No longer content with being a subordinate lay movement, JUC felt that it had no compelling reason to follow the dictates of bishops who had not contributed to the movement. After 1961 the primary thrusts for progressive Catholic participation in politics became Popular Action, the Movement for Grass-roots Education, and Paulo Freire's movement (as well as other movements not discussed in this chapter).

Popular Action

After its creation in 1961, one of the main channels for radical Catholic political activity was Popular Action (Ação Popular; AP).[10] Popular Action was a result of the search by Catholics to create a juster society after it had become difficult for such a search to occur within existing Church structures. As the rifts opened in 1961, many JUC leaders wanted to create a new Christian-inspired movement because they felt constrained by the Church. They believed that they would be more effective politically if they acted as an autonomous movement. AP quickly became one of three major leftist organizations in Brazilian politics, along with the PCB and PC do B. A small organization of about 3,000 members,[11] it was nevertheless very influential. AP members were leaders in popular education, union work, and peasant organizing.

The conflict between the hierarchy and the Catholic radicals carried over into AP. The bishops attempted to restrict JUC participation.[12] Yet neither the bishops' attitude toward AP nor its lack of a formal connection to the institutional Church should obscure its Catholic origin and imprint.[13] Although AP was not a denominational movement, the impulse for its creation came from JUC participants. Father Henrique Vaz strongly influenced the philosophical foundations of its ideology, and until the coup AP remained heavily influenced by its Christian humanist origins.

Free of the restrictions the bishops placed on JUC, Popular Action developed more radical political positions than JUC. Whereas JUC was relatively optimistic about the Goulart government's ability to bring about major social changes, AP was critical of its populist "developmentalist nationalism." Popular Action saw revolution as the only means of resolving the society's problems.

In contrast to JUC, which never made an unequivocal socialist commitment, AP's "Statement of Principles" affirmed the necessity of superseding capitalism and establishing a socialist regime. Socialism would be "a victory for humanity as subject of the socialization process" and would end the servitude created by the market economy.[14] Despite its vague understanding of how to effect a revolution, AP believed the revolution required a vanguard to lead the process of formulating ideas and enlightening the masses. AP saw itself in this role; it would help prepare an effective mass movement and would assume responsibility for educating the masses and turning their struggle into a revolutionary one. Nevertheless, Popular Action, though predominantly Catholic in orientation, differed from earlier Catholic movements in its affinities with Marxist thought.[15]

AP repeatedly emphasized the importance of freedom and pluralism. AP's final end, to "guarantee the freedom of the development of people, the possibility of their expression, and the expression of their will,"[16] required a democratic political order. AP criticized the Soviet Union for "the hypertrophy of political power, the mythical consecration of the party apparatus, [and] ideological fetishism."[17] AP's humanism, its emphasis on freedom and participation, and its criticisms of stultifying bureaucratic socialism constitute a significant link to the popular Church of the 1970's.

These early philosophical and political views changed quickly after 1964, as most AP leaders embraced various Marxist positions. The history of AP's development after the coup was tragic, as was the history of most of the Brazilian Left. The movement went underground almost immediately in response to repression. It underwent rapid radicalization that ultimately led to Maoism and participation in armed struggle. Like the rest of the Left, AP suffered a series of internal struggles and divisions. Reduced to a small Maoist party, in 1973 AP decided to dissolve itself and join the PC do B. Along the way, it abandoned its Christian origins and, in doing so, lost its influence within the Church. The progressive movement within the Church passed to new channels, even though it drew on the legacy of the young Catholic radicals.[18]

Despite the differences between Popular Action and the progressive Catholics of the 1970's, and despite AP's eventual separation from its Catholic background, it left an important mark on the Church. At a time when the bishops had started to close other channels for radical Catholic participation in politics, Popular Action created a new possibility that was no longer dependent on the hierarchy. It is noteworthy that out of a fairly conservative and hierarchical institution had emerged a movement with positions as radical as Popular Action's. Equally remarkable is Popular Action's prescience on a large number of issues, ranging from a commitment to radical social transformation to a critical perspective on Leninism and bureaucratic socialism. In these regards, Popular Action anticipated the ideology of popular Church intellectuals during the 1970's and 1980's. There was not a direct causal relation between AP and the popular Church, but AP did establish a tradition of radical humanism within Brazilian Catholicism that continued after the movement itself had abandoned its Catholic origins.

The Movement for Grass-roots Education

During the early 1960's, Catholics also participated in and created a number of new types of "popular education,"* efforts to organize and develop a critical political sense in the popular classes. Whether created by the state, universities, or the Church, the movements for popular education tried to respect popular culture and values and to overcome the paternalistic bent of most previous work with these classes.

The most significant popular education programs in terms of impact on the Church were the Paulo Freire Method and the Movement for Grass-roots Education (MEB). Freire and MEB were as influential in transforming the Brazilian Church as JUC and AP, although for somewhat different reasons. Freire and MEB were concerned less with theoretical formulations about faith and more with working with the poor. Both Freire and MEB were committed to transforming the society, but neither dealt at length with theological considerations as JUC had or with humanist socialism as AP had. Their contribution to change in the Church lay rather in developing a new means of working with the popular classes.

MEB was created in 1961 through an agreement between President Jânio Quadros and the progressive bishop of Aracaju, Dom José Távora, an associate of Dom Helder Câmara's.[19] The state would provide the financing, and the Church would carry out a program of basic education, principally through radio schools in the country's least developed regions, the Northeast and the Amazon.

Many MEB participants came from ACB ranks. They were seek-

*The closest equivalent to "popular education" would be "community organizing," but there are some differences. "Popular education" refers to efforts to provide a politically relevant education to the masses. These efforts generally involve community organizing, but there is a greater emphasis on consciousness raising than in many community-organizing efforts in the United States.

ing concrete ways to express their religious and political commitments.[20] By mid-1962 MEB declared itself in favor of radical social transformation. Education was to be a means to accomplish this transformation rather than an end in itself. MEB focused on *conscientização*, an educational approach that encouraged the people to see their problems as part of larger social ills.

The guiding idea behind MEB's approach to popular education was that the people must be the agent of their own history. They, and not some external force (whether vanguardist leftists or the traditional politicians), must make the major decisions concerning their lives. As one document stated, "To do honest, meaningful, and coherent work, it is necessary that the common person be the agent of the necessary transformations."[21] This philosophy assigned greater responsibility to the popular sectors than the Church ever had, and it questioned the traditional view that the masses are incapable of changing their situation and uninterested in doing so. MEB also emphasized the need for popular participation in the movement's major decisions and criticized paternalistic practices.

MEB anticipated the popular Church's pedagogical practices in underscoring the need to work from concrete problems. This meant starting from immediate needs as the people perceived them rather than beginning from more abstract considerations or attempting to impart a revolutionary consciousness. It also meant respect for popular culture and values and for the individual, regardless of level of education or financial situation. "A total respect for the people and their decisions, and for the communities and their way of doing things, is fundamental."[22]

MEB, like Paulo Freire, developed an ideal of education as an exchange between teacher and learner, anticipating the philosophy developed later by the popular Church. The good pedagogue should start from the popular world view, which the teacher must learn from the masses. "Education, as we understand it, must be realized through dialogue."[23] Finally, MEB helped introduce the belief that a fundamental goal of Christian faith is the full realization of all people. The movement emphasized the importance of encouraging greater self-respect among the poor. The notion of self-discovery, so prominent in the contemporary popular Church, became a key feature of MEB's pedagogy.

By the time of the coup, MEB was one of the most important experiences in popular education and popular culture. It played a major role in the peasant struggles in the Northeast, where it was more closely allied with the Communists than with the moderate Church peasant organizations. After the coup, MEB came under pressure from the state, which repressed the most political aspects of the movement's activities.

MEB also came under increasing pressure from the bishops, who were caught between the movement and the state and between their own efforts to encourage lay participation while maintaining hierarchical discipline. This situation furthered the position of the bishops concerned with strengthening ecclesiastical controls over the movement. They curtailed MEB's autonomy and tried to give the movement a more religious orientation. Thanks to the Church's protection, MEB became the only major experiment in popular education to survive. Survival had a price, however; MEB was forced to tone down some of its statements. The combination of state repression, diminished financing, and ambivalence of the hierarchy gradually made the movement less central to the push to transform the Church. But MEB was able to continue its progressive practices among the popular classes at a time when this was extremely difficult.

MEB's pedagogical innovations ensured it a special influence in the development of the Brazilian Church. MEB was the first major Catholic attempt to develop radical pastoral practices with the popular classes. Its practices reversed the traditional exclusion of the masses from decision-making within the Church and were a precursor to the popular diocesan assemblies that progressive bishops started during the late 1960's and 1970's. The emphasis on learning from the people challenged the Church's more conventional elitist conception of the popular classes.

Popular Education: Paulo Freire

Born in Recife in 1921, Paulo Freire was the most important of the intellectuals who stimulated new methods of popular education between 1958 and 1964. Freire started to develop his thinking about popular education in the middle and late 1950's, when he taught at the University of Recife. During the early 1960's, when MEB and other experiences in popular education emerged, Freire introduced new adult literacy programs as director of the Cultural Extension Service of the University of Recife. Today his ideas and

his techniques for teaching writing and reading have become world
famous.[24]

Freire's "pedagogy of the oppressed" stressed respect for the popular classes and their abilities. Criticizing elitists who denied that
the masses possessed critical qualities, he wrote, "It is enough to be
human to be able to understand social reality."[25] As part of this effort to respect the dignity of all people, Freire insisted that the
teacher engage in a dialogue rather than simply imparting knowledge. The educator's primary purpose is to have a "dialogue with
the illiterate person about concrete situations, simply offering the instruments with which he/she can become literate. Literacy work
should not be done from above to below, like a donation or an im-
position, but from inside toward the outside, by the illiterate person, with the simple collaboration of the educator."[26] Freire argued
that to engage in a dialogue, the teacher must understand and em-
pathize with the world view of the people. The beginning point of
the education process was their concrete living situation. Literacy
efforts should use the everyday words of common people, not an inaccessible, intellectual language.

Linked to Freire's emphasis on the dignity of all humans was the
notion that the poor should control their own destiny. He believed
that the goal of education should be to help people "reflect on their
own capacity to reflect."[27] To Freire, these objectives were not fully
realizable within the confines of the extant society. He pronounced
himself in favor of "a new society that would make the individual
and the people the agents of their history."[28]

Freire encouraged the common people to participate as much as
possible in the learning process. Learning should be an active process, not a simple absorption of concepts. Consequently, the masses
should participate in major decisions concerning how this process
occurs. The pedagogical process should also be democratic. If the
objective is to enable individuals to establish greater control over
their lives, the method should reflect this goal by letting the students
have a central role in the process.

Although Freire did not believe that popular education could resolve the structural problems of society, he considered it important
for creating a democratic "space" in a nondemocratic society and
for its potential to mobilize the popular sectors to work for social
transformation. He saw education as having a political end because
it can help construct a new society that facilitates the realization of

a new human being. Although convinced that radical political change was important, Freire rejected the view that it inherently resolves major social problems. In this sense, Freire rejected Leninism. His emphasis on liberty, the abilities of all people, and respect for the popular classes conflicted with the Leninist emphasis on the need for a centralized party that makes the key decisions.

On all these scores, Freire's thought was a precursor to the popular Church of the 1970's and 1980's. The popular Church developed a similar emphasis on respecting the individual, seeing teaching as a dialogue, and using concrete situations to teach the popular classes. It is similarly committed to popular participation in the learning process and to non-Leninist social transformation.

Today Freire is one of the most highly regarded theorists in the entire Latin American Church. An American who worked for many years in the Church in Central America wrote, "It is impossible to overstate the importance of Freire for the Christian left,"[29] and Peruvian Gustavo Gutiérrez praised Freire's work as "one of the most creative and fertile efforts in Latin America."[30] Throughout Brazil, his work has influenced pastoral agents, theologians, and social scientists.

Although Freire was strongly influenced by Catholicism and still considers himself a Catholic, he never worked extensively with the Church in Brazil until he returned from exile in the late 1970's. Freire's method became so influential in religious circles not because he directly acted to change the Church but because he developed new ways of working with the popular classes that resonated with those developing within progressive Catholicism. Freire is an important example of how individuals and movements outside the Church can affect it.

The Catholic Left and the Transformation of the Church

Like all hierarchical institutions, the Roman Church allows some space for pluralism and differences at the base, so long as these differences do not threaten its fundamental identity. Autonomy at the grass roots can allow some groups to develop conceptions of faith that differ markedly from the predominant institutional view. On some occasions, even though the movements have been undermined or co-opted, some of the changes they hoped to realize have been incorporated. In these cases, the base has helped transform a hierarchical and seemingly unresponsive institution.

This is not to suggest that lay and grass-roots movements have uniformly challenged the institution. Many conservative and reactionary lay movements have impeded change in the Church, just as the progressive ones have furthered it. On some occasions, reactionary movements have threatened the Church's identity by narrowing the institution's ability to appeal to all social classes.*

The movements of the Catholic Left in Brazil were an outstanding example of change coming from below. They began as sponsored groups, effectively controlled by the hierarchy. Yet several Catholic Action movements developed increasing autonomy vis-à-vis the hierarchy and had serious conflicts with Church authorities. Driven out of the mainstream by the military regime and the ecclesiastical conservatives, the Catholic Left nevertheless played a significant role in the Church's transformation.

How did lay movements that began as sponsored organizations develop such radically different views from the bishops'? The Brazilian Church allowed lay movements considerable autonomy. The hierarchy never encouraged JUC's radicalization, but some important priests and bishops aligned themselves with the young Catholic radicals, and the moderates in the hierarchy tolerated the movement until late 1961. A number of dynamic leaders in the CNBB, including Dom Helder Câmara, Dom Luis Fernandes, Dom Cândido Padim, and Dom José Távora, consistently defended JUC and MEB. JUC had the full support of the clerical assistants, who encouraged the movement's increasing involvement in politics. The support of some key bishops and the clerical assistants was essential in pre-

---

*An apposite example would be the reactionary movement called Tradition, Family, and Property (TFP), which originated in Brazil and was influential in creating the pressures leading up to the coup in 1964. TFP was also important in generating the pressures that led to Institutional Act V in December 1968, the military decree that institutionalized the sharp increase in repression. The movement spread to other countries and, in some cases, such as Chile and Argentina, also buttressed the far Right. In Brazil, TFP was never an official Church movement, but it had the active support of the leading representatives of the reactionary bishops, Dom Antônio de Castro Mayer and Dom Geraldo de Proença Sigaud. The hierarchy tolerated the movement's attempts to identify itself as a Church group until the early 1970's, when its reactionary positions had become incompatible with the way most bishops perceived the Church's mission. The most comprehensive work on the Catholic Right is Antoine, *Integrismo Brasileiro*.

venting the hierarchy from taking reprisals against JUC earlier and more forcefully.

Furthermore, in contrast to Catholic Action movements in some European countries, which were intraclass movements organized by sex and age, after 1947, ACB was organized on the French model, based principally on occupational—hence class—lines. Therefore Catholic Action in Brazil was more susceptible to identification with class issues.[31] The movements had competing commitments to the Church and to the world, or more specifically to their class or occupational group. The ecclesiastical allegiance had greater weight during the early stages, but as the Church opened up and as social conflicts polarized and politicized the entire society, JUC and MEB (and later the Catholic Student Youth, Youth Workers, and Agrarian workers organizations) became deeply involved in politics.

The experience of the Catholic Left also reveals the limits to the new autonomy permitted to lay groups. Ultimately the hierarchy forced JUC and MEB to choose between a more cautious orientation and leaving the Church. But by this time, the Catholic Left had profoundly influenced a generation of young Catholics.

A major contribution of the Catholic Left was changing the traditional conception of the laity. No experience contributed as much to indicating the laity's competency as ACB. The Catholic Left of the early 1960's paved important ground in lay experiences with the popular sectors in the 1970's.[32]

The Catholic Left also helped introduce a new understanding of the relationship between faith and politics. JUC's new vision of faith linked religion to radical social transformation; AP extended it into the first major expression of a synthesis of Christian humanism and socialism; and MEB and Paulo Freire made the vision concrete by educating the society's least fortunate members. This new vision of faith reflected a renovation of Catholic thought throughout the world, which culminated in the Second Vatican Council. European progressive theologians (such as Maritain, Lebret, Congar, Mounier) were influential early in this process, but the Catholic Left did far more than introduce European social thought to the Brazilian Church. It applied European ideas to Brazilian conditions and developed a new conception of the Church's mission.

The Catholic Left began to develop one of the first uniquely Latin American theologies.[33] It was one of the earliest reflections on the specificity of Catholic faith in the Third World. This role as precursor to liberation theology was an important and generally over-looked contribution of Brazil's Catholic Left. The young radical Catholics did not reduce faith to political action or put Marx ahead of Christ, but they did believe that faith requires striving toward a juster world. The Catholic Left insisted that as children of God, all people deserve respect and the right to decent living conditions. They felt that Christians are called to help transform social structures that prevent the realization of God's temporal designs. They belived in participating actively in the construction of a juster, more humane society, which they were convinced required radical social change.

The generation of young Catholic radicals also affected the understanding many priests, pastoral workers, and bishops had of their faith. It is no coincidence that many of the progressive bishops of the 1960's worked with ACB. A partial list would include Dom Helder Câmara, Dom José Maria Pires, Dom José Távora, Dom Antônio Fragoso, Dom Waldir Calheiros, Dom Marcelo Cavalheira, Dom Fernando Gomes, Dom Cândido Padim, and Dom David Picão. Many of these men acknowledge that their vision of the Church was deeply affected by working with ACB.[34] Many lay leaders and priests who helped shape the popular Church were also products of the Catholic Left.

The fact that the Catholic Left of this period helped change the Brazilian Church does not of course mean that it is above criticism. At the time, Church moderates and conservatives were incensed by the radicals' unwillingness to abide by episcopal mandates. Retrospectively, many ex-participants feel that the movements were excessively romantic and that there was a gap between their (democratic) discourse and (less than democratic) practices.

In any case, the emergence of an important Catholic Left in the early 1960's constitutes one of the unique factors in the development of the Brazilian Church and helps explain why it became more progressive than other Latin American Churches. The pioneer movements left an important legacy even after they disappeared. Yet for two reasons, we should qualify the importance of leftist groups in the Church's transformation. First, progressive bishops and pastoral agents at the base were also working to change the Church. It would be misleading to overlook these other initiatives and suggest that change came exclusively from below, especially be cause, with isolated exceptions, the base communities and other innovations of the post-1964 period were creations of the clergy, not of the leftist lay movements.

Second, there are significant differences between the Catholic Left of the early 1960's and the popular Church. In contrast to the popular Church, the Catholic Left was an elite movement that directly involved only a limited number of people. The movements for popular education developed new connections to the masses, but their leadership was in upper-middle-class hands. The Catholic Left was committed to the common folk, but it did not emphasize popular leadership as much as later movements did. Whereas Catholic Action was directed toward forming a limited number of leaders, the popular Church of the 1970's involved millions of people, often the poorest, least formally educated members of the society. In contrast to the Catholic Left of the early 1960's, the popular Church of the 1970's and 1980's was deeply critical of vanguardism. And the Catholic Left of the early 1960's was more optimistic about the imminence of the revolution than is the popular Church.

These differences showed up clearly in attitudes toward popular religion. The faith practiced by the student youth movements in ACB was Europeanized and secularized, profoundly different from and often antagonistic to popular religiosity. Faith in the base communities is not at all Europeanized or secularized. Despite their linkage of faith to politics, the religiosity of the base communities involves many traditional elements. Mary, Jesus, the Bible, and the saints are at the center of the base communities. That was not the case with the Catholic Left. The contemporary popular Church has made strong efforts to respect popular religiosity, whereas ACB was generally critical of it.

Finally, the relationship between the Catholic Left and the hierarchy differed dramatically from the relationship between the base communities and the hierarchy. The Catholic Left was in conflict with the hierarchy; there have been few cases of conflict between base communities and the hierarchy. The clash of the Catholic Left with the bishops was probably inevitable, given the significant religious and political differences, but it was also a significant limitation because all formal authority in the Church rests with the bishops. The only movement that survived within the Church, MEB, was the only one willing to make concessions. The combative character of these movements enabled them to grow in their own direction, but when they severed their links with the hierarchy, their abil-

ity to change the Church also diminished. This highlights one of my
central arguments: only when the hierarchy accepts and legitimates
change can it become successfully institutionalized, and only when
the base is able to maintain a dialogue with the hierarchy can it successfully exert pressures for change.*

In an ironic sense, this need to work with the hierarchy to effect
change may underscore a final contribution of the Catholic Left in
Brazil. The Catholic Left provided the Church with an important
example of a movement marginalized from the institution because
of its inability to work with the hierarchy. Its fate may have helped
the radical clergy avoid a similar mistake later, when, in contrast
to what happened in some other Latin American countries, they
worked with the hierarchy rather than challenging it. It was this dialogue between base and hierarchy that transformed the whole institution.

*Of course, under some conditions it is extremely difficult for radical movements
to work within an institution. This presupposes an institutional flexibility that does
not always exist. It would be unfair to place all the blame for the tensions between
the Catholic Left and the hierarchy on the former. The Left was often unwilling to
make any concessions, but the hierarchy's intransigence made it difficult for the Left
to continue working with the institution.

Part II

The Church and the Military Regime,
1964-1973

CHAPTER 5

The Emergence of the Popular Church, 1964-1973

> We are the people of a Nation;
> We are the people of God.
> We want land on earth;
> We already have it in heaven.
>
> Dom Pedro Casaldáliga
> Bishop of São Féliz do Araguaia

The military coup of March 31, 1964, ended "Brazil's experiment in democracy."[1] The new military regime quickly repressed peasant and labor organizations and the Left. In 1965, it abolished the political parties and created two new parties: the National Renovative Allliance (Aliança Renovadora Nacional; ARENA), the government party; and the Brazilian Democratic Movement (Movimento Democrático Brasileiro; MDB), a somewhat tenuous opposition party. During its early years, the regime attempted to build legitimacy principally by establishing order and defeating the subversive threat. It also undertook measures that significantly altered the course of the country's economic development. In response to the economic problems of the Goulart years, the government attempted to reduce the fiscal deficit, correct the balance of payments deficit, curtail inflation, and restore economic stability.

During its first four years in power, the military vacillated between relaxing the repression in preparation for a return to civilian government and attempting to institutionalize long-term military rule. In 1968 the latter option won. The actions of the far Left were the occasion for intensifying repression in the second half of 1968; between 1964 and 1968, a significant part of the Brazilian Left became more radical, opting, in many cases, for clandestine political activity and even armed struggle. The most important repressive measure was Institutional Act V, decreed in December 1968, which strengthened the executive, eliminated the right of habeas corpus, and in effect declared war on the entire Left. The most repressive years of authoritarian rule, 1968-74, were marked by hundreds of political murders and thousands of cases of torture. Nonetheless, the regime enjoyed considerable support in civil society.

Beginning in 1967, after three years of recession, the economy began a period of sustained growth that became known as the Brazilian miracle. Until 1974, the gross domestic product (GDP) expanded at an annual rate of about 10 percent, one of the highest growth rates in the world. Among the outstanding features of the new growth were increasing inflows of foreign capital, rapid expansion of state corporations, industrial concentration, rapid export growth and diversification, and a particularly strong performance in the durable consumer goods sector (automobiles were the notable example). The growth led to substantial income redistribution toward the wealthier sectors of the society. Nonetheless, economic success gave the regime a new basis for legitimacy: efficiency, national prestige, and national power. Anti-Communism remained strong, but the regime had created some positive symbols of legitimation.[2]

On June 2, 1964, two months after the coup, the CNBB issued an important, albeit contradictory, statement, part of which gave thanks for the military takeover.

Responding to the widespread and deeply felt desires of the Brazilian people, who saw Communism knocking at the door, the armed forces arrived in time and prevented the implementation of a Bolshevik regime in our country. . . . Immediately after the victorious revolution, a sensation of relief and hope was felt. In the face of the climate of uncertainty and virtual desperation that the different classes and social groups felt, the divine protection made its presence known. . . . Upon giving thanks to God, who answered the prayers of millions of Brazilians and saved us from the Communist threat, we thank the military leaders who acted in the name of the nation's supreme interests.[3]

On May 6, 1973, only nine years later, seventeen bishops from northeastern Brazil and six from the Amazon signed the two most radical episcopal documents ever issued until that time. Both documents denounced the military regime for systematic violations of human rights, repression, and widespread social marginalization. They asserted that the regime's economic policies and violations of human rights countered all major tenets of the Church's social doctrine and its emphasis on human dignity.

What was behind this dramatic transformation? In part, the changes were encouraged by the international Church, especially Rome and the Latin American Bishops Conference (CELAM). In addition, as I have been concerned with showing throughout this book, social and political changes caused the Church to change its identity. Although institutions respond in unique and complex ways to political change, the political struggle is one of the most important factors conditioning changes in their perception of their own function and of politics. Following this line of argument, this chapter shows how the post-1964 political changes caused a growing number of bishops to move toward radical political views. The widespread violations of human rights, the marginalization of the popular classes, the repression against the Church, and the closing of other channels of political dissent caused many bishops to become more progressive.

The CNBB, 1964-1968

The Catholic Church, long an active combatant of Communism, was strongly affected by the growth of the Left after 1960. Groups within the Church, concerned about a threat of Communism or of social disintegration and disorder, allied themselves with the anti-Left forces. Within the Church, the sharpest anti-Left reaction was in the Catholic Right, which between 1963 and 1968 enjoyed a high profile in Brazilian politics. Closely linked to the military movement that deposed Goulart, with a reactionary ideology and morality, the Catholic Right thrived during the first years of military rule and lent its support to the authoritarian regime. But it was not only the far Right that joined in the anti-Left struggle. A large number of persons and movements, committed in principle to the Church's social doctrine, supported the same cause. The archbishop of Rio de Janeiro, Dom Jaime de Barros Câmara, was not alone in affirming that "the threat is knocking at the door; it is inevitable, perhaps even imminent."[4]

After having supported the reform program of the Goulart regime, the CNBB moved into opposition to it and eventually supported the coup.[5] In this sense, the CNBB paralleled moderate sectors of the society, which, fearing social disorder or a communist takeover, initially supported the coup, only eventually to oppose the military.[6] Although the CNBB thanked the military for saving the country, its June 1964 document included some more critical statements, which revealed the profoundly contradictory positions within the episcopacy at that time. The declaration anticipated the hierarchy's later criticisms of repression. It warned that the search to "purge the causes of disorder" could not justify violence or tyranny and insisted that the accused have a right to self-defense. The bishops stated their disagreement with the repressive measures taken against the Church. "We cannot agree with the attitude of certain groups that have encouraged cheap hostilities against the Church, in the person of bishops, priests, lay leaders, and faithful. . . . We do not accept the malicious accusation that bishops, priests, the laity, or organizations such as Catholic Action and the Movement for Base Education (MEB) are Communist or sympathetic to Communists."[7]

The declaration also referred to a point that was to become a serious source of tension between Church progressives and the regime: the Church's emphasis on social justice. Thus, even though the CNBB's declaration supported the new regime, it conditioned this support upon respect for the Church, observance of basic human rights, and (especially for the progressives) social justice. Implicit in the CNBB's initial statement of support was a kernel of future conflict.

From the time of the CNBB's creation in 1952, progressive bishops had occupied the leadership positions.[8] In October 1964, however, a conservative slate defeated the progressive bishops who had dominated the CNBB since its inception. The most important position, secretary general, was transferred from Dom Helder Câmara to Dom José Gonçalves, a conservative, and the new president was Dom Agnelo Rossi, archbishop of São Paulo, also a conservative. The archbishop of Pôrto Alegre, Dom Vicente Scherer, was named head of lay affairs. In this position, he implemented the ecclesiastical sanctions against JUC that culminated in the dismantling of that movement in 1966. The CNBB's Central Commission was expanded from 7 to 37 members, temporarily weakening the position of the progressive bishops who had been its leaders.

During the next several years the CNBB became more conservative and bureaucratized. Yet although the 1964 changes represented a defeat for the progressive bishops, they retained control of several important positions. Dom Helder was elected secretary of social action, Dom Fernando Gomes became secretary of special pastoral concerns, and Dom Cândido Padim was the new secretary of education.

Between 1964 and 1968, the CNBB was concerned more about internal housekeeping than about politics and social action. Even the Second Vatican Council, the emergence of a more specifically Latin American theology, and a wide range of pastoral innovations at the grass roots did little to focus the CNBB's concern on promoting social justice. In contrast to the pre-coup years, the CNBB had nothing to say about social conditions. Episcopal documents were limited to abstract theoretical formulations that did not even refer to events of the time, much less prescribe changes. Although documents criticized "unjust and oppressive capitalism,"[9] the bishops said nothing about the military government, the repression, or the regime's economic model.

At its 1967 General Assembly, the CNBB presented a conception of faith that was conservative compared to the theology that had emerged in some Latin American circles, to mainline European theology, and to pre-coup CNBB statements. The bishops declared a Year of Faith, but neither social reform nor the necessity for political change entered into their conception of faith. Even after the Medellín conference in 1968, at which Brazilian lay leaders and the progressive bishops played integral roles, the CNBB continued to produce conservative statements. On paper, it supported social change, but it refrained from criticism of the regime's repressive policies or political economy. In its first meeting after Medellín, the Central Commission issued a cautious statement. "The Church recognizes the autonomy of the civil authority and expresses the support that this authority deserves from us. Furthermore, with its authority, the Church hopes to collaborate with those responsible for the common good."[10]

A 1969 internal memorandum, written for the secretary general and not intended for publication, was even more cautious, criticizing "conventional democracy" in a fashion reminiscent of the military's justifications for authoritarian rule. The bishops' counterposing of democracy and political efficiency paralleled the military's. "The model of conventional democracy . . . becomes increasingly incompatible with the administrative speed and efficiency needed to accompany a process of rapid change."[11] The document criticized the Goulart government in a fashion that legitimated authoritarian intervention; it accused the popular leaders of taking radical positions and aggravating tensions rather than attempting to resolve problems. Even though this document cannot be taken to reflect the secretary general's official position, it reveals a tendency to support the regime despite all that had happened since 1964 and despite the progressive positions espoused by Vatican II and CELAM.

Capitalism and the Church in the Amazon

Because the CNBB is the ultimate authority of the Catholic Church in Brazil, its positions deserve special emphasis in any evaluation of the Church's view of politics. Nevertheless, the CNBB is not the only expression of Catholicism in Brazil, even among the bishops. The CNBB was relatively cautious between 1964 and 1970, but a number of dioceses and regional conferences were undergoing changes that eventually caused the Brazilian Church to become the most important institution defending the poor and human rights. It is impossible to understand the post-1970 changes in the CNBB without being aware of the prior changes at other levels in the Church.

In 1964, the CNBB created thirteen regional divisions, which acquired significant influence. While the CNBB was having trouble providing dynamic leadership, several of the regionals advanced far beyond the CNBB's pre-1964 positions. Because they were more responsive to local differences, the regionals were more appropriate forums for encouraging discussion of social issues and pastoral responses to them.

The most remarkable transformation of a regional Church between 1964 and 1973 occurred in the Amazon. Before 1964, the Amazon bishops were fairly traditional, especially in comparison to their counterparts in the Northeast. Some missionaries were trying new approaches to peasants and Indians, but on the whole, pastoral work was oriented toward celebrating the sacraments, expanding the institution, and providing many of the region's limited services (schools, health posts, hospitals). By 1973, the Amazon and the northeastern bishops were the most progressive in the country. Although other factors contributed to the evolution of the Amazon

Church, the most significant was the rapid transformation of capitalism after 1964, which unleashed violence against the peasants and pushed the Church into a greater commitment to the poor.

In July 1965, President Humberto Castello Branco expressed a strong commitment to developing the vast Amazon region, and the following year the government inaugurated Operation Amazon, which marked the beginning of rapid changes in what had been a largely unpopulated region. Although the Amazon was occasionally used for resettlement of peasants expelled from the Northeast, state subsidies to agribusiness and massive infrastructural investments (especially highway construction) have been the major development tools in the region.[12] The government's agricultural policies have prompted the modernization of the traditional latifundia and encouraged rapid growth of nontraditional primary exports. But alongside the successes have come numerous problems.

To the Church, the most significant problem caused by these policies was the rapid expansion of agribusiness and expulsion of peasants from the land. In response to large fiscal incentives, investors from other countries and from the South acquired huge tracts of land beginning in 1966. In the state of Pará, where investors flocked, the number of farms with 10,000 or more hectares increased from 33 in 1960 to 81 in 1970 to 142 in 1975. The amount of land these farms owned increased more than sixfold in this fifteen-year period.[13]

The rapid expansion of large farms has made it more difficult for peasants to own land. In 1950, 19.2 percent of rural establishments were run by farmers who did not own their land. By 1975, this figure had doubled, to 38.1 percent. In 1950, there were 4.2 owners to every nonowner; by 1975, there were only 1.6.[14]

Contrary to the government's claims, the agribusiness projects were not pioneers in these frontier areas, which were already occupied by *posseiros*, or peasant squatters, who occupied the land without holding title to it. The large agribusiness projects represented *re*settlement of the frontier, with large cattle farms displacing subsistence agriculture. Beginning in the late 1960's, this government-sanctioned settlement on previously occupied land generated violent conflict throughout the Amazon.[15]

As the Amazon suffered increasing conflict, many pastoral agents felt the need to re-evaluate the Church's role there. Many priests and bishops who went to the Amazon changed their pastoral orientation because of the population's extreme penury and the level of private and state violence against the peasants. The lack of legal assistance, unions, schools, and hospitals led the Church to assume a broader range of functions than under other circumstances it might have done.

In about 1967, shortly after Operation Amazon began, priests and religious workers from various parts of the region began to organize to discuss responses to the increasing violence. Three important meetings took place in 1968. The first major regional gathering on pastoral work with the Indians was held in February. Its concern for the Indians was not completely new, but it took a combination of new pastoral perspectives and violent expulsions of Indians from their land for it to become a significant issue.[16] The participants denounced the government's Indian policies and reached many of the conclusions that the Indian Missionary Council (CIMI) adopted during the 1970's. They called for respecting the Indians and argued that the Church must serve the Indians rather than impose the institution's values on them. They emphasized the Indians' creativity and abilities and insisted that to be effective, missionaries must learn the Indians' way of life.[17]

At about the same time, priests from various parts of the Amazon expressed concern with what was happening to the peasants. In March 1968, after a regional meeting, 36 priests from Regional North I of the CNBB called for the Church to defend the poor more energetically. They urged the bishops to become "creative, imaginative, and courageous leaders in search of new paths, new methods, and new perspectives."[18]

As often happened in the early years of the popular Church, the bishops responded only after pastoral agents at the grass roots had taken the initiative. At their meeting, the bishops of the same regional responded to the priests' challenge. They criticized the government's wage, health, and education policies and its repression of unions. They also made an early statement on the violence caused by land development. "The problem of land settlement and ownership requires clear criteria that would avoid both minifundia and latifundia and would, above all, prevent the speculation and violence that have been occurring."[19] But the bishops still believed that underpopulation and lack of economic integration were major problems and assumed that increased population and stronger links to the national and international economy would help resolve them.

They thought that the state and the dominant classes would be open to the Church's vision of justice. In contrast to later documents, which criticized the devastating effects of the regime's fiscal incentives, this early statement praised these incentives.

In 1969, the progressive Amazon bishops started to hold meetings to discuss pastoral practices. By this time, the effects of the government's Amazon policies were becoming clear. Equally clear was the decision of some Amazon bishops to support the peasants and the Indians. Dom Giocondo Grotti (Acre), Dom Tomás Balduino (Goiás Velho), Dom José Maritano (Macapá), Dom Estevão Cardoso (Marabá), and (after 1971) Dom Pedro Casaldáliga (São Félix do Araguaia) were prominent examples.

Radical episcopal criticisms of developmental policies in the Amazon started in 1970, coinciding with one of the most repressive periods of military rule. Along with three priests, Dom Estevão Cardoso, bishop of an especially violence-prone region in the south of Pará, issued a statement on November 20, 1970, denouncing the government's policies, the private violence employed by entrepreneurs, the terrible living conditions among the peasantry, and a widespread practice resembling debt peonage in the region.[20]

Four days later, under Dom Estevão's leadership, the bishops of Regional North II issued the most radical episcopal statement published to that date in Brazil. In a complete break with *desenvolvimentista* perspectives, they proclaimed that certain paths to development could exacerbate poverty and result in violence. Widespread land redistribution was the only means of addressing the problem.

We feel compelled to express our pastoral concern about the serious problems the peasants of our region face. . . . The installation of agribusiness firms in the south of Pará, a result of the fiscal incentives, is causing problems that affect a large segment of the poor population of our rural areas and forests. . . . The development of the Amazon cannot become a reality if it is not directly oriented toward the people. We believe this can be attained only through an authentic reform of the structures and of rural policies.[21]

In 1971, the Amazon bishops began to speak in chorus, denouncing the military rulers and the large investors. In July the diocese of Goiás denounced "the striking injustices that especially affect the poorest and the marginalized."[22] The situation exploded in October when Dom Pedro Casaldáliga, newly named prelate of São Félix do

Araguaia, Mato Grosso, another area of conflict, issued one of the
strongest denunciations of the authoritarian regime during the most
repressive years. His first pastoral letter, "A Church in the Amazon
in Conflict with the Latifundia and with Social Marginalization,"
issued days after his consecration as bishop, was a lengthy (120
pages), detailed denunciation of the regime's policies, private violence, and local living conditions. As Dom Pedro described São Félix, violence and repression were omnipresent. One large company
had burned down the houses and public buildings of a village where
500 people lived. Landowners had hired two men to kill one of the
region's priests, but the men denounced the company instead, then
fled the region. Health conditions were terrible; most people working for the large companies had serious diseases, and a high percentage died within a few years of coming to the region. Private ar-
mies prevented the workers from leaving company jobs, and the
local police terrorized the peasants. In one case, when peasants
complained of contract violations and constant abuse to the local
police chief, he denounced them to the farm owner.[23]

Two months later, as Dom Estevão, Dom Tomás, and Dom Pedro
were suffering threats of death and imprisonment, the Central Western Regional joined the campaign. As early as 1970, these bishops
had sharply criticized the systematic violation of human rights, especially the use of torture.[24] On December 2, 1971, the regional's
executive officers issued a statement condemning repression in rural
areas, particularly violence against peasants. "We have heard the silent cry of some families, concerned about how their loved ones
have been imprisoned. . . . The terror is increasing."[25] Months later,
the Far West Regional (Mato Grosso), echoing problems already
discussed by CIMI, addressed the Indian issue. "In the whole country we are witnessing the invasion and gradual dispossession of the
Indians' lands. Their human rights are not recognized, and they are
gradually being driven to death."[26] All four regional bishops' groups
from the Amazon (North I, North II, Central Western, Far West)
had now issued strong denunciations of the regime's policies.

In July 1972, at the general assembly of the Central Western Regional, the bishops issued a statement that reiterated many points
raised by Dom Pedro.

In rural areas, we are concerned about the abandonment of our brothers,
the peasants, who are subjected to chronic injustice and permanent exploitation. The rapid economic growth of our region coincides with the in-

creasing marginalization of rural workers, *posseiros*, and small landowners, victims of the latifundia's voracity. Those who educate the people about their legal rights are misunderstood and even denounced and imprisoned.[27]

Efforts to coordinate pastoral work more effectively throughout the vast region continued. The Amazon bishops began to elaborate pastoral plans that emphasized Indian communities, the base communities, and the explosive frontier areas. In May 1972, the seed for the Pastoral Land Commission (CPT) was planted at the Fourth Pastoral Encounter of Bishops and Pastoral Agents of the Amazon Region. The participants agreed on the need for technical and juridical assistance to help the Church defend the peasants and Indians.[28]

As the Church denounced government policies and violence, Church-state conflict in the Amazon became chronic. Priests risked police intimidation, beatings, imprisonment, and torture. Private violence against religious workers was common.

One of the most embattled dioceses was São Félix, a prelature that covers 150,000 square kilometers in northwestern Mato Grosso,[29] an area of heavy agribusiness investment. Conflicts between the local Church and the latifundia and state began in 1966, coinciding with the stepped-up investment. The conflicts escalated after the publication of Dom Pedro's pastoral letter in October 1971. Shortly thereafter, Dom Pedro was briefly detained by the police. A peasant lay leader was imprisoned on December 16, 1971, and the same day Dom Pedro was questioned again. In January 1972, the bishop had to fly to Brasília with the CNBB's secretary general, Dom Aloísio Lorscheider, for interrogation by the minister of justice.

A widely reported incident in February 1972 culminated in the imprisonment and expulsion of a French missionary. The conflict dated back to 1966, when the Codeara Company purchased 196,-492 hectares. Part of the land that had been sold to Codeara as virgin jungle was occupied by a village, Santa Terezinha, which had a population of about 500. This village had been settled since 1910, and the prelature had built a church and school there in 1931. By 1966, when the company arrived, it had been a stable residence for decades.

The company tried to intimidate the villagers into leaving, prompting the local priest, French missionary Francisco Jentel, who had lived there since 1954, to take action. The conflict between Codeara and the local peasants continued over the years, with Father Jentel defending the peasants. Then in February 1972, Codeara used one of its tractors, accompanied by a private army of 25 men, to destroy the village's health post and service center. A local police chief who protested against the company's actions was immediately beaten up and, when he continued to protest, was assassinated. No investigation of the first assault or the murder was ever made.

On March 3, the peasants attempted to rebuild the health post, but the company returned to destroy it, aided by the state military police. This time the peasants were armed with shotguns, and an exchange of fire ensued. Several peasants were shot in the confrontation. Five *posseiros* were arrested and tortured; 40 others fled and hid in the jungle for two months, living off the land. Father Jentel was accused of directing an attack against the company, even though he was not present at the confrontation. The governor of Mato Grosso charged that Jentel and Casaldáliga "are leftists who are agitating the people. They are probably directed by agents of other countries."[30]

On May 22, 1973, Jentel was tried for violating the National Security Law and was condemned by a military court to ten years in prison. The only nonmilitary judge dissented, averring that Jentel deserved a medal and not a prison sentence. In an act of Church solidarity, the secretary general of the CNBB, the bishops of the Central Western Regional, and Catholics from all over the country protested the verdict.*

Catholic solidarity did nothing to diminish the attacks on the Church. In June and July 1972, shortly after the confrontation between the peasants and the military, the prelature was occupied by a hundred soldiers trained in anti-guerrilla methods. Searching for the 40 peasants who had fled, the battalion terrorized the population and intimidated pastoral agents. Two months after the shootout, on June 5, 1972, police invaded Dom Pedro's house and confiscated his papers. Then in July, the police imprisoned and tortured eight lay leaders, invaded the house of four priests and imprisoned and tortured them, and barricaded Dom Pedro's house, placing him under house arrest and prohibiting visitors.

---

*In 1974, after serving one year of his sentence, Jentel was retried and absolved. He went to France for a visit and, on December 1, 1975, returned to Brazil. Eleven days later, while visiting the archbishop of Fortaleza, Jentel was arrested, to be deported three days later under a decree signed by President Geisel, prompting another display of solidarity from bishops all over the country.

The violence against the Church came from private circles as well as the state. In 1971, the Association of Entrepreneurs of the Amazon (AEAA) attempted to impede Dom Pedro's consecration as a bishop by appealing to the papal nuncio. Having failed in their attempt, they tried to direct the state security agencies against him. In February 1972, the AEAA officially declared that the Church was a focus of agitation and responsible for directing the peasants to rebel.[31] In early 1973, a large landowner, notorious for using violence against the peasants, began a defamatory campaign against the Church. On March 13, 1973, he visited a priest, demanded an explanation of the priest's support for the peasants, physically assaulted him in front of several people, then pulled a revolver and threatened to kill him and the bishop. Similar incidents recurred over the years, including the assassination of priests on two different occasions and at least one attempted assassination of the bishop.

The Araguaia region in southern Pará was another area of severe conflict. The construction of the Trans-Amazon Highway and the massive investments of large agribusinesses led to constant friction between large landowners and peasants. The Superintendency for the Development of the Amazon (SUDAM) approved more projects in Araguaia than in any other region, and the changes in social structure, land tenure patterns, and production were dramatic. Between 1960 and 1970 the population more than quadrupled, from 9,085 to 38,038. By 1970 only 34.5 percent of the population of Pará had been born in the state. In 1950 peasants without titles held 91 percent of the land in the region, a figure that declined to 44 percent by 1970.[32]

Exacerbating the situation was the fact that a small group from the Communist Party of Brazil settled in the region to plan guerrilla warfare. This group was ineffectual; it had not yet done anything concrete when its existence was discovered through a party member's confession under torture in São Paulo.[33] The presence of would-be guerrillas created a nightmare—any resistance to the state or the dominant classes was labeled subversion. The military terrorized the local population and anyone who challenged private or public authority.

The violence pushed the Church into more progressive positions and constant conflicts with the state. One of the worst periods of conflict was mid-1972. On June 2, two priests and a nun were imprisoned, and one of the priests was tortured. Only after Dom Es-

tevão intervened were the three released. On June 10, the police attempted to detain another priest, but he fled; Dom Estevão again
intervened, causing the police to give up their search. On August 30,
the residence of one of the priests who had been imprisoned in June
was invaded. Then on September 27, at the official opening of a segment of the Trans-Amazon Highway to which Dom Estevão had
been invited, a government official harassed the bishop and demanded to see his identification papers.

The repression against the Church caused so much concern that
the prelature called a special meeting. The pastoral workers decided
that two priests and two nuns should leave the region indefinitely.
Not only would the four risk further imprisonment and torture if
they stayed, but their work would entail a risk to lay leaders associated with them. At the same time, the Church decided that "the
bishop and clergy of Marabá no longer believe in the possibility of
a sincere dialogue with the military officials or in the solutions that
these authorities may offer."[34]

Throughout the country, the repression solidified resistance
among progressive clergy. One leader of the CPT stated:

There was a need to respond to the problem of violence against the peasants. This violence increasingly affected the Church itself. The exacerbation
of social tensions, caused by the penetration of agribusiness, created a conflict for the Church. When the pastoral agents assumed the defense of human rights, they also started to be persecuted. The agents started to feel the
necessity for a land institute. How should we deal with the repression?
How could we help the peasants? Above all else, it was the repression
against the Church that led to the creation of the CPT. We felt that by joining forces we could do better. The repression forced us to work together.[35]

The actions against the Church called attention to the gravity of
the problems in the Amazon, and concern about the Church-state
crisis in the region spread. In late January 1972, the secretary general, president, and vice-president of the CNBB visited the region
to see for themselves what was happening. Amid government attempts to discredit the Amazon Church, the CNBB's support for the
region's most progressive bishops gave the radicals a needed legitimacy.

In June 1973, a week after Jentel's sentencing, Dom Avelar Brandão, archbishop of Salvador, primate of Brazil, and vice-president of
the CNBB, made another trip to the Amazon. Dom Avelar held
(and still holds) an important position within the Brazilian Church

and was one of the leading spokesmen for the sectors that attempted to maintain a cordial relationship with the state. Rather than denouncing the radicals, as the military expected, Dom Avelar reinforced earlier statements of support for the Amazon Church. He stated that it was important for the Church to defend human rights, especially in a region where those rights were frequently violated. He also insisted that the Church must promote a social ethic that would prevail above the private interests of the wealthy. He concluded that it was essential "that there be discipline in occupying lands so that everyone has real opportunities."[36]

The Amazon, where before the coup the Church had been politically moderate, had become the arena of greatest conflict between Church and state. Even though there were still many conservative bishops in the region, it had become, along with the northeastern Church, the most progressive regional Church. In a short time, the Amazon bishops had developed an impressive network. In 1973, this culminated in two documents by the Amazon bishops that had international repercussions. The first, "Marginalization of a People," was published on May 6, 1973, along with a similar document from the northeastern bishops, on the twenty-fifth anniversary of the United Nations Declaration of Human Rights. At the time, these two documents were probably the most radical statements ever issued by a group of bishops anywhere in the world.

"Marginalization of a People" denounced the high level of unemployment and underemployment in the Amazon region, the terrible housing conditions, the lack of health care and education facilities, and the masses' lack of means to defend their interests because of private and public repression. The bishops stated that the root of the problem was the land tenure system and called for radical alterations. The necessary reforms could not be effected within a capitalist system, especially one with such uneven land distribution. "What is really needed is to change the structure of rural production. . . . If we want a change, we must overcome private ownership of land and have socialized use of the land."[37]

The bishops criticized the state: "Any form of protest is repressed, the people are put in prison, and they remain there with no opportunity of having a fair trial, or they are simply killed."[38] They also criticized the government's encouragement of exports at the expense of subsistence farming. The document called for the construction of a different society, "where we are all brothers and sisters, a

world without dominant classes and without marginalized people."[39] The concluding section proclaimed, "We must overcome capitalism. It is the great evil, the rotten root, the tree that produces
those fruits we all know: poverty, hunger, sickness, death of the majority. . . . A few people own the land and the means of production,
while the great majority of the people are used and have no chance.
The vast majority work to enrich the few, who become wealthier at
the expense of the masses."[40]

On December 25, 1973, many of the same bishops signed another
controversial document, "Y Juca-Pirama. The Indians: A People
Doomed to Die." "The 'Brazilian model' means a 'development'
that enriches only a small minority. . . . For the poor, the system offers a future of increasing marginalization. For the Indians, it offers
a future of death."[41] Like "Marginalization of a People," "Y Juca-
Pirama" strongly criticized capitalism. It also expressed the faith in
and respect for the Indians that was characteristic of the pastoral
agents most active in working with the indigenous population. Because the Médici government considered the Church's work with
the Indians subversive, on December 21, 1973, it prohibited clergy
from working with the Indians. This decree was never enforced, but
it underscored how threatening the government considered work to
defend human rights during that period.

Repression and the Northeast Church

Ever since the 1950's, the Northeast Church has been prominent
in the transformation of the Brazilian Church. Throughout the
1950's, the northeastern bishops championed agrarian reform, and
they were responsible for the most important Church innovations in
popular education, the Natal Movement and the Movement for
Grass-roots Education (MEB). They were the best-organized group
of Brazilian bishops; they held regional episcopal conferences at
Campina Grande, Paraíba, in 1956 and in Natal, Rio Grande do
Norte, in 1959. After the coup, they continued their progressive tradition. During the first four years of military rule, the Northeast
Church was more critical of the government than any other regional
Church.

Northeastern Brazil is by far the poorest region in the country. In
1975 it had 30 percent of the country's population and only 10.2
percent of its income. Its per capita income was only 27.4 percent

that of the rest of the country. The per capita income of the poorest state, Piauí, was less than 15 percent that of the state of São Paulo; it was similar to that of India, Pakistan, or Haiti.[42]

Poverty pushed the Northeast Church toward change; as the Church's social doctrine developed, it was more likely to be implemented in areas of greater injustice. But poverty alone does not explain the Church's new vision of faith. The Northeast has been poor ever since the second half of the nineteenth century, but only in the 1950's did the Church display concern about the problem. More important to the change than poverty were the region's social struggles, which made the Church become more aware of the reality the popular classes faced.

From 1955 to 1964, the Northeast experienced considerable conflict. Various institutions and factions of the Left competed to organize the peasants and direct their political actions. Peasant movements called attention to problems that had existed for generations. It was this politicization of poverty rather than its mere existence that led to new forms of intervention by both the state and the Church.[43]

The mobilization of the peasantry and the involvement of so many political actors in the region helped sensitize the Church to the people's problems. Some Churchmen tried to prevent radical peasant mobilization, while others supported independent peasant organization, especially after the creation of MEB. In any case, the creation of Church unions and MEB were clear responses—favorable in some cases, defensive in others—to this mobilization.[44]

The coup put a quick end to the popular mobilization. The first wave of repression, in 1964, affected the peasant movements in the Northeast more than any other sector of the society. The state tacitly permitted private violence, whose sadistic character was notorious. The peasant movement quickly fell apart. Despite occasional, isolated resistance, it lacked the level of organization and the ability to confront the landowners that it had in the pre-coup years.[45]

The violence against the peasants and the deterioration in their standard of living offended the religious sensibilities of a large number of northeastern clergy. In the post-1964 period, the popular movements that had encouraged the Church to change no longer existed—but the Church no longer needed their direct stimulus. In the absence of other institutions able to defend the peasants, the clergy assumed this task, and in the process they gradually developed a stronger commitment to the poor. After the coup, the Northeast Church not only extended its progressive tradition, but went far beyond its earlier positions.

From 1964 until the mid-1970's, the most noteworthy leader of the Northeast Church was Dom Helder Câmara. A diminutive man who was born in Ceará in 1909, Dom Helder supported the right-wing Integralist movement during the 1930's. In the 1940's, his understanding of faith became more progressive. As general assistant for Catholic Action, he became convinced of the importance of the laity, and his concern with the ties between faith and social justice deepened. In 1952 Dom Helder created the CNBB, which he served as secretary general until 1964. He was named auxiliary bishop of Rio in 1952. On March 12, 1964, Dom Helder was transferred to Recife. Although his removal from Rio was an attempt to quiet him, it had the opposite effect, for it freed him from dependence on the conservative Cardinal, Dom Jaime de Barros Câmara.

From the beginning, Dom Helder and the new government clashed. Shortly after his arrival in Recife, his papers were searched —the start of continuing attempts to harass and intimidate him. Yet Dom Helder refused to give ground. Throughout the 1960's and 1970's, Dom Helder continued to defend the poor and the repressed and to call for social justice. He criticized the regime's conception of order—order based on "preserving structures we all know should not and cannot be preserved."[46] As fewer people had the courage to criticize the military regime, Dom Helder continued to denounce capitalism, call for agrarian reform, espouse consideration of socialism, criticize North-South relations, condemn internal colonialism, and criticize the widespread impoverishment and repression. Equally important, he defended lay movements and pastoral agents harassed by the state. His message, dynamic leadership, and charisma made Dom Helder one of the most famous leaders of the Third World Church.[47]

Although Dom Helder was the best known of the northeastern bishops, there were a number committed to a new understanding of faith. The government once identified seventeen northeastern bishops as subversives. Dom Antônio Fragoso, bishop of the extremely poor Crateús diocese in Ceará; Dom José Távora, archbishop of Aracaju, Sergipe, and national advisor of MEB; and Dom José Maria Pires, archbishop of João Pessoa, Paraíba, the second black bishop in Brazil's history, were particularly strong leaders.[48]

In March 1965, at a time when other regional episcopal groups were quiet about social issues, the northeastern bishops reiterated progressive statements of the pre-coup years, claiming that "the social structures do not afford real opportunities for the masses." Although efforts to work with the poor carried personal risks, the bishops reaffirmed their commitment and insisted on "human and Christian opportunities for rural and urban workers."[49]

Progressive initiatives were not limited to the clergy. Lay groups continued to play an important role in the development of the Northeast Church, especially until 1968, when repression made it difficult for them to continue functioning. Catholic Workers Action (ACO), Catholic Youth Workers (JOC), Catholic Agrarian Youth (JAC), and Christian Rural Support (ACR) were stronger in the Northeast than elsewhere, and MEB retained some strength in the region, even though after 1964 the repression forced it to concentrate primarily on the Amazon.

Often led by the activist lay groups, especially JOC and ACO, the Church in the Northeast was the first to launch radical critiques against the regime. The most significant state/Church conflict since the nineteenth century erupted in 1966 in response to a document published by ACO. ACO and JOC had become important political voices for the urban masses. They had also supplanted Catholic University Youth (JUC) as the most important lay movements working for a more progressive faith. On May 13, 1966, ACO published a denunciation of the regime and the working class's situation. It said, "The situation of the working class in the Northeast is marked by disrespect for the worker. This disrespect translates into a climate of persecution. . . . It seems that there is a plan to destroy people by destroying their dignity and their rights. The person who suffers this injustice is without freedom, without a future, without hope, without faith, without love."[50]

At the bishops' request, ACO followed this statement with a shorter one that reiterated its major conclusions. The bishops responded with a nationally publicized manifesto on July 14, 1966, that was the most progressive episcopal document issued until that time. "There can be," they stated, "no real development where the people are not given first consideration. Wherever the individual is not respected, wherever the common good is neglected, wherever the fundamental equality of all people is not defended, there is neither development nor Christianity." The bishops also called for a preferential option for the poor. "The Church has to favor those who suffer; those who cannot earn their daily bread, even with the abundant sweat of their labor; those who seem condemned to stagnation, in subhuman living conditions."[51]

The police confiscated the manuscript and prohibited the bishops from publishing it. Military authorities in Recife accused Dom Helder of being a Communist subversive and threatened him with imprisonment. The commander of the Fourth Army distributed a circular throughout Recife condemning Dom Helder, and the Catholic Right took advantage of the incident to excoriate the archbishop.

The attacks by the military and the Catholic Right generated sympathy with the victims and criticism of the regime. Without necessarily changing their understanding of the Church's mission, some conservatives and moderates condemned the attacks on the progressives; some leading conservative prelates, including Dom Agnelo Rossi (São Paulo), Dom Alberto Ramos (Belém), and Dom Vicente Scherer (Pôrto Alegre), criticized the measures against Dom Helder. The repression against the Church, intended to silence the progressives, instead strengthened them. Dom Scherer's reaction to the repression typified that of many conservatives. Although he fundamentally supported the regime, Dom Scherer criticized the military for attacking legitimate ecclesiastical authority and interfering with the Church's autonomy. He noted that the bishops' document closely followed the Church's international social doctrine, stated his full support for it, and announced that he would have signed it had he been asked.

A long series of clashes ensued between the Church and the state in the Northeast, leading to increasing state repression against the Church and increasing Church determination to fight the government and defend human rights. The next confrontation occurred in September 1967, shortly before Brazil's independence day. The radio station of the Archdiocese of São Luís (capital of Maranhão, in Regional Northeast I) broadcast a text questioning whether Brazil was truly independent, and what that independence meant for the masses. "Is the independence we celebrate real? Is Brazil really independent? . . . Brazil continues to be exploited by other countries and by some Brazilians who are traitors."[52] The radio station was suspended for subversion. When the reprisals came, both the auxiliary bishop and the archbishop criticized the military. The archbishop of Fortaleza, Dom José Delgado, accused the military of attempting to silence one of the last living forces in the society. He stated that the repression, not the Church, was subversive because it was responsible for social unrest. The repression against the Church, far from silencing the bishops, inflamed them to more vocal criticism.

The most volatile region was Northeast II, where Dom Helder exercised his charismatic leadership. But the bishops of Maranhão, Piauí, and Ceará did not lag far behind in their denunciations of northeastern society and the military regime. "The Northeast is victimized by profound injustice," they said, "yet driven by a strong desire for development. In some areas, this development is benefiting a small minority, but the majority of our fellow people remain marginalized, condemned to an increasingly inhuman misery."[53]

After the declaration of Institutional Act V in December 1968, the conflicts grew worse. In the Northeast, the military ceased making concessions to avoid conflict with the Church. As the Church became virtually the only institution able to contest the government, it also became a victim of the repression. On December 15, two North American priests working in Recife were imprisoned. In January 1969, a priest in Fortaleza was arrested for a sermon considered subversive; he was sentenced to a year's imprisonment. As often happened, this repression against local priests pushed higher-level churchmen into denouncing the regime. The archbishop of Fortaleza closed the city's churches on Penitent Sunday and filed a strong public protest: "If the Church were to remain silent when it witnesses the violation of human rights, it would be a deplorable omission or a flagrant confession of its lack of confidence in Christ."[54]

It became more difficult for lay leaders to act because of the repression, and priests and nuns assumed more responsibility in defending the rights of the poor. As a result, they increasingly became the targets of repression. In an escalating spiral, the bishops again spoke out against the injustices. In late 1970, they stated, "We have witnessed the tragic situation in which most of the population lives, especially in the interior, the countryside, and the periphery of the large cities, because of the absurd wage levels."[55]

On May 25, 1969, security forces assassinated Father Antônio Henrique Pereira Neto, a 28-year-old JOC assistant. This was the first assassination of a clergyman in Brazil. Despite protests, his assassins were not tried, nor was a serious investigation made. Two and a half months after the assassination, the bishops of Regional Northeast II issued an energetic condemnation of torture.

The Church's criticisms had no effect on the government's policy. On the contrary, the regime viewed any institution that criticized the military as threatening the social order and saw all the more reason to persecute the Church. In August 1970, two priests in Rio Preto, Maranhão, were imprisoned, and one of them was tortured until he signed a confession that he was a subversive. Both were held incommunicado for a week, and then they were tried for subversion.

Once again, repression against local clergy resulted in nationwide repercussions. In all the churches of São Luís, a statement was read on August 9, explaining the imprisonment and the Church's condemnation of it. On August 22 and 23 all the churches in the state preached sermons criticizing torture, and Archbishop Dom João José de Motta Albuquerque issued a statement defending the Church's work with the poor. The auxiliary bishop read Dom João's statement over the archdiocesan radio station; subsequently the police prohibited further communication on the case. On August 25 the bishops of Regional Northeast I issued a condemnation of the widespread terrorism and torture, saying, "Priests and laity work to inform and help the people. In many places, landowners and politicians call this work subversion, agitation, or Communism. They attempt to prevent it directly through threats and persecutions, or indirectly through defamatory campaigns."[56]

In 1970 a defamatory campaign emerged against Dom Helder as he was being considered for the Nobel Peace Prize.[57] Not only Dom Helder's progressive colleagues, but also such moderates as Dom Avelar Brandão and Dom Rossi (who, along with Dom Scherer and Dom Eugênio Sales, were the outstanding churchmen trying to maintain a dialogue with the military) issued statements in favor of the fiery northeastern bishop.[58]

The incident in Maranhão, another smear campaign against Dom Helder, and some particularly strong repression against JOC (see Chapter 6) prompted Regional Northeast I to issue a statement of solidarity on October 8, 1970.[59] Later that month the Central Commission of the CNBB also issued a statement of solidarity.

In July 1971 a JAC assistant from Crateús was jailed and sentenced to a year in prison, and another JAC assistant was imprisoned in Paraíba. Days later, military police invaded the headquarters of Regional Northeast I in Recife. In August another priest was imprisoned in Fortaleza, prompting the archbishop to state that teaching the population its rights and responsibilities should not be confused with subversion.[60] In October 1971 another priest from Crateús was imprisoned, to be expelled from the country ten days later. This triggered a smear campaign against Dom Fragoso, and rumors of the bishop's imprisonment were again heard.[61]

In March 1972, a more important churchman was expelled. Joseph Comblin, a close associate of Dom Helder's and head of the Northeastern Regional Seminary, was a noteworthy theologian during the early phases of the popular Church in Brazil. He had been attacked before, especially in connection with a paper he wrote in 1968 in preparation for the Medellín conference.[62] Returning from his native Belgium, Comblin was detained at the Recife airport, transported to Rio, held incommunicado, and told he had to leave the country. His crime was having associated with Dom Fragoso and his use of the term *conscientização* (considered subversive). A note from Dom Helder to the CNBB asked, "Does anyone fail to perceive that the Comblin episode is another chapter in what is happening throughout the whole country with the Church, whenever it refuses to continue supporting oppressive structures and commits itself, in peaceful but meaningful ways, to the people and their liberation?"[63]

Most conflicts between the Church and the state during the years 1964-73 involved little-known lay leaders and local priests and nuns. The hierarchy became involved because of the actions of lower-level Catholics. Attention focused on the bishops, who are the visible leaders of the Church, but the conflict usually arose at the local level.

The foregoing discussion of a handful of conflicts between the Church and the state in the Northeast suffices to show some general patterns. Bureaucratic-authoritarian regimes are not disposed to allow significant political criticism. They attempt to create political stability by politically excluding large parts of the nation. In their more repressive phases, they seek to suppress all opposition. As Guillermo O'Donnell writes, bureaucratic-authoritarianism "entails a drastic contraction of the nation, the suppression of the citizenship, and the prohibition of the appeals to the pueblo and to social class as a basis for making demands for substantive justice. . . .

Such exclusion appears as a necessary condition for healing the body of the nation."[64]

Under these circumstances, the Church lost its invulnerability and became subject to attack. But whereas the repression effectively forced other institutions and movements into silence, in the case of the Church it was a catalyst for change within the institution. Countless acts of repression against the Church led to strong defenses of its own institutional integrity and autonomy; even conservative bishops perceived attempts to neutralize the progressive clergy as an illegitimate intrusion. The conservative bishops may have disagreed with the kind of pastoral work that led to problems with the state, but they resisted interference with the Church's work. Ironically, then, the attempts to silence the progressives actually helped strengthen their position. Especially after 1968, the Church spoke out more critically against capitalism and more pessimistically about realizing social change through capitalism.

Efforts to repress progressives within the Church have not always strengthened their position, however. In Paraguay, Argentina, and Uruguay, authoritarian regimes have weakened the progressives through repression, sometimes more extreme than that in Brazil. In Argentina and Chile, perceived revolutionary situations were coupled with serious political and economic problems; the moderates and conservatives in the Church there were not willing or able to defend radical clerics. Furthermore, in these cases the progressives were not as well established within the Church as they were in Brazil, and when state repression came, the hierarchy was less willing to support them.

The commitment of the northeastern bishops to a new vision of the Church led to the publication of "I Heard the Cry of My People" on May 6, 1973. This document was similar in style and content to "Marginalization of a People," issued by the Amazon bishops on the same day. The two groups had worked together in writing the documents and in developing the view of faith behind them. Like the Amazon document, "I Heard the Cry of My People" was one of the most radical episcopal documents ever issued.

At a time when political leaders were afraid to criticize the regime, the bishops condemned "official terrorism," "espionage," "increasing domination by the state over the private lives of the citizens," and the "widespread use of torture and assassination."

Repression is increasingly needed to guarantee the functioning and security of the associated capitalist system. The legislature has no authority; urban and rural unions are forcefully depoliticized; the leaders are persecuted; censorship has gotten worse; workers, peasants, and intellectuals are persecuted; priests and activists in the Christian Churches suffer persecution. The regime has used various forms of imprisonment, torture, mutilations, and assassinations.[65]

The criticisms of the economic model were equally strong. The bishops condemned the Brazilian miracle for exacerbating income inequalities, for enriching those who had enough, and for causing the relative and absolute impoverishment of the majority of the region's poorest people. The document stated that dependent capitalism was the root cause of this unjust system and called for "a global historical project for transforming the society" and a new society with "socialized means of production."[66] It was a far cry from the 1965 statement that expressed confidence in capitalism. In a remarkably short time, the northeastern bishops' vision had changed from a politically reformist, liberal one to one committed to radical social transformation.

Political Vacuum and Church Transformation: São Paulo

Throughout this work I have emphasized that the transformation of the Brazilian Church resulted from dialectical interactions between pastoral agents, lay movements, and bishops. The base developed important pastoral innovations that helped transform the whole Church. But this does not detract from the centrality of the bishop. In dioceses where the bishop has opposed pastoral change, it has been almost impossible to implement. Conversely, formerly conservative dioceses have been transformed under the leadership of a progressive bishop.

Throughout the 1960's, there was significant grass-roots activism in the São Paulo Church. The archbishop who departed in 1964, Dom Carmelo Vasconcellos, had promoted some important pastoral reforms. After he departed, a strong contingent of priests and nuns continued pastoral work with the working class. They started the city's first base communities in the late 1960's and began the first discussions on forming the Workers Pastoral Commission.[67] Until 1968, the São Paulo Church supported the student movement.

São Paulo priests led in composing letters demanding that the bishops be more decisive in moving toward a new Church. In addition, the archdiocese had strong Catholic Action movements, especially JUC before 1964 and JOC and ACO until 1970. These movements were active in the creation of the Workers Pastoral Commission and after 1973 contributed to many popular movements throughout greater São Paulo, including the auto workers' movement in the heavily industrialized ABC area (Santo André, São Bernardo, and São Caetano).

Despite these progressive activities, the archdiocese as a whole did little to defend human rights or to voice the needs of the poor until 1970. The new archbishop, Agnelo Rossi, helped legitimate the authoritarian regime, neutralizing the work done by the progressives. In May 1965, Rossi stated that the Castello Branco administration had accomplished the social reforms the Church had desired for many years. Although he noted the difficulties that high unemployment caused the working class, he stated that the bourgeoisie was also adversely affected by the economic crisis and praised the government's efforts and intentions.[68]

Rossi criticized repressive measures and defended the victims of repression, especially in the case of Church people. On one occasion, he even refused a decoration offered by the military on the grounds that "any member of the Church who receives a government decoration could be seen as cultivating relations with a regime that many priests consider detrimental to the people's interests."[69] Yet when non-Catholic people or movements were affected, Dom Agnelo was less willing to respond. His entire tenure as archbishop of São Paulo (1964-70) was marked by a reluctance to criticize the regime, by efforts to deny the existence of Church-state conflict, and by continual attempts to negotiate with the regime. He was among the few prominent archbishops who continued to say mass to commemorate the coup, and on several trips abroad he argued that reports of torture in Brazil were exaggerated.

Because the highest Church leadership remained in conservative hands, it was not until 1970, when Dom Paulo Evaristo Arns replaced Rossi, that the archdiocese as a whole galvanized the development of the Brazilian Church. Dom Paulo himself has indicated that he personally created very little that was new in the São Paulo Church.[70] All the major changes that have pushed the archdiocese to prominence had already been started at the grass roots. There

were already some base communities, many priests and religious
workers were committed to a new vision of the Church, and some
important innovations had been made in pastoral practices. But
these trends did not come together in a cohesive whole until Dom
Paulo became archbishop. Under his leadership, the base communities, the defense of human rights, and the rights of the poor became archdiocesan priorities.[71]

During the Médici years, nowhere was repression worse than in
São Paulo. In part, this was because guerrilla organizations and
other clandestine groups were stronger there than elsewhere (opposition in general, ranging from the universities to the labor movement, was especially strong in São Paulo). As a result, the government had more reason to use repression. Hard-line right-wing
military leaders were in charge of the Second Army, whose headquarters were in São Paulo, and the paramilitary Death Squad was
active there.[72]

In the midst of the repression and difficult economic situation,
there was a political vacuum in the society. The opposition was
forced into silence. The popular movements were reduced to ineffective voices, and the only legal opposition party, the Brazilian
Democratic Movement, presented only ineffectual opposition between 1969 and 1974. The Church, with a powerful international
structure and great moral legitimacy, was the only institution that
retained sufficient autonomy to defend human rights. It assumed
this task partially in response to the inability of other institutions to
do so. As Dom Paulo stated, "The society needed a voice, and because of the repression, no other institution could provide that
voice. The Church became the voice of all those sectors that had no
voice."[73]

Because of the repression against other institutions and the
Church's transformation, the Church became the most important
opposition force during much of the 1970's. It was the only institution that could criticize the economic model and the repression,
defend human rights, and organize the popular classes. In this
sense, the political vacuum encouraged the transformation of the
Church.

In late January 1971, shortly after being named archbishop, Dom
Paulo was faced with a difficult case involving the imprisonment
and torture of a priest and a woman lay worker. He intervened personally and attempted to see the two prisoners. He was stunned at

how badly the police treated him and at what they had done to the imprisoned pair. He published a note denouncing the tortures, insisted that it be posted in all the city's churches, and sent a copy to the CNBB, which circulated it nationally.

Bishops like Dom Helder, the victim of an ongoing smear campaign and threats, had long been dismissed by the regime and the tightly censored middle-class press as subversives. But Dom Paulo was a careful man, not known for his radical views, head of the most populous archdiocese in the world, and religious leader of the country's largest, most developed city. His denunciations publicized the widespread practice of torture, and he quickly won the respect and support of his fellow prelates. In February 1971 the CNBB sent Dom Paulo a letter openly supporting his actions. Two months later, he traveled to Rome, where Paul VI supported him and expressed concern about torture in Brazil. In 1973 the pope named Dom Paulo a cardinal.

Dom Paulo continued to issue strong denunciations. He demonstrated particular interest in the problem of torture and personally spent scores of hours visiting prisoners, but he was unable to handle the work alone. After a member of the Workers Pastoral Commission was tortured to death in late 1971, Dom Paulo called a meeting and proposed the creation of the Justice and Peace Commission, which led the archdiocese's endeavors to protect human rights.[74] In July 1972, in the midst of a hunger strike by political prisoners, he sent a note to the press, saying, "The Church of São Paulo has repeatedly and clearly supported the basic postulates of justice and of respect for the rights of the prisoner. It has condemned torture, delays in trials, and arbitrary injustices against prisoners. We will do anything to promote a just and humanitarian solution of this problem."[75]

Dom Paulo quickly became the nationwide leader—inside and outside the Church—of the campaign to protect human rights. The popular classes and the liberals requested that the Church assume their cause, and this became another factor in encouraging the Church's transformation. The Church became known as "the voice of those who have no voice," which for several years meant the voice of large segments of the society. Particularly visible was the Church's role in protesting the deaths by torture of student Alexandre Vanucchi Leme (1973), journalist Vladimir Herzog (1975), and metalworker Manoel Fiel Filho (1976). Meanwhile, the archdiocese was also creating a large network of pastoral organizations, ranging from hundreds of base communities to the Workers Pastoral Commission.

The São Paulo Church not only helped introduce the defense of human rights as a national-level Church priority, it also linked this issue to poverty. Living in the country's most developed city, the clergy of São Paulo were exposed to the extreme contradictions of development of the Médici period. At the same time that middle- and upper-income groups were rapidly increasing their real income, others were doing worse in relative terms and perhaps even in absolute terms. Between 1960 and 1975, the infant mortality rate in São Paulo increased 45 percent; the incidence of malnutrition rose; real wages for industrial workers fell; and urban services for the working class (transportation, sewers, electricity) deteriorated.[76] These contradictions and inequalities helped sensitize many clergy, including Dom Paulo, to the needs of the popular classes. In 1976, Dom Paulo wrote in the preface to a major study on São Paulo's development commissioned by the archdiocese, "The rapid development of São Paulo has been accompanied by an increase in poverty. The gap between the opulence of the few and the difficulties of the masses has grown. The bishop, and with him the entire Church, cannot remain silent, given the diffuse violence that affects the people."[77]

Under Dom Paulo's dynamic leadership, the bishops of the state of São Paulo denounced torture. In their 1972 meeting, the state's bishops issued a major denunciation that had nationwide repercussions.

It is not just to imprison people in this fashion: without identifying who ordered the imprisonment and who is carrying it out, without communicating to the judge in charge of the case within the legal period of time. . . . It is not permissible to torture people to obtain confessions, revelations, or identities of other people, especially when these tortures cause physical mutilation, destroy the person's health, and even result in death. Yet this has happened. . . . It is not permissible to deny the accused their right of free trial, to determine trial results by using threats, or to determine the prisoner's guilt before the trial.[78]

Thus, in São Paulo, as in other parts of the country, the post-1964 changes caused the Church to open itself. Although it was not as politically active as the Church in some parts of the Northeast or the Amazon, the São Paulo Church can influence the rest of the country as no other diocese can. By linking human rights to the worsening plight of the poor, the São Paulo Church identified the issue around which the bishops as a collective body first reached consensus in their criticism of the government.

Ecclesial Base Communities

The years 1964-70 witnessed dynamism at the grass roots, as all the trademarks of the popular Church started to develop.[79] Among the most important innovations was the emergence of ecclesial base communities (CEBs). A base community is a small (average of 15-25 people) group that usually meets once a week, generally to discuss the Bible and its relevance to contemporary issues. The members are responsible for the group's religious observances as well as for many decisions. In Brazil—in contrast to some Central American countries—priests or nuns have almost always created the communities. From the outset the Brazilian CEBs were closely linked to the institutional Church. Through religious educational materials and occasional but important participation of the clergy in CEB meetings, the Brazilian Church has maintained close links to them.[80] The base communities have become one of the Brazilian Church's outstanding contributions to Catholicism. There are an estimated 80,000 of them, with two million participants. Based on their reading of the Bible, many CEB participants have become involved in popular movements, though there is a remarkable (and generally understated) heterogeneity in political activity.[81]

Considering their present importance in international Catholicism and in the Brazilian political struggle, CEBs had an inauspicious beginning. The bishops, priests, and nuns who started CEBs were concerned with constructing a new Church that would develop closer human relations,[82] but lacked a clear idea of what they should be. In the words of an important theologian who works with CEBs, "The weakness of the early history of the communities is noteworthy. They did not spring from a premeditated plan. . . . The planning that exists today came from developments that occurred almost randomly."[83] According to the General Pastoral Plan (PPC), the base communities would enrich human relationships, facilitate more effective evangelization, develop better religious education, and promote more active lay participation. The PPC's discussion of ecclesial base communities was the earliest use of the term, but the

PPC certainly did not envision the base communities as they ultimately evolved. It did not define the base communities beyond stating that they would become the lowest-level organization within the
Church. The writers revealed no vision that the base communities
would become as politically relevant as they did or that they would
be primarily for the popular classes.

The PPC and early advocates of CEBs saw the base communities
as a means of developing more effective Church structures,[84] but not
as groups that would find a great response among the poor or that
would be politically significant. Even two progressive priests whose
writings encouraged the creation of CEBs saw them principally as a
means of promoting a richer experience of faith and community.[85]
The base communities were originally intended as a means of strengthening the Church's traditional presence, not as a new form of the
Church. They were intended to encourage faith in a secular society,
not to change the society.[86]

A large number of CEBs started because giving the laity a greater
role was the only means of developing an effective Church, given the
shortage of priests and religious. In explaining the impulse behind
starting base communities in his parish in Recife, one priest re-
marked: "I can celebrate Sunday mass in the parish only every two
weeks. This created in the [community's] leaders a consciousness of
the precarious and fleeting character of clerical help and stimulated
the beginning of a reflection about the relativity of the clerical structures in the Church."[87]

Another stated, "In 1966, I was working on Marajó Island. Dom
Ângelo had begun some work with the CEBs, not for political reasons, but simply because it was good sense. There was a shortage of
priests, poor transportation, the terrible situation of the population.
From this concrete situation to the CEBs was a very small step."[88]

Like many innovations in the Brazilian Church, the base communities generally sprang from grass-roots pastoral agents. The hierarchy issued documents calling for creation of CEBs, but local-
level priests and nuns committed to the ideals of community and
greater lay participation actually started them. In São Paulo, according to Archbishop Paulo Evaristo Arns, "The base communities
came from the base. All I did was support the pastoral agents who
had already started something new."[89]

Until after Medellín, the most important innovations in the CEBs
had more to do with their religious mission in the narrow sense—

developing greater lay participation, developing a sense of community, changing the relationship between pastoral agents and the
people—than with politics. Over the next few years, however, the
CEBs became more political.

The emergence of CEBs reflected the changing nature of the leading actors in promoting ecclesiastical innovation. The transformation of the Brazilian Church had started in the 1950's and culminated in the development of the Catholic Left. There were three
principal actors: the young radicals, the progressive bishops, and
progressive agents at the grass roots.

During the emergence of the popular Church, the young radicals
ceased to be significant.[90] The innovations, including the CEBs,
sprang from the institutional Church, under the inspiration of progressive bishops, priests, and nuns. The popular Church, which
started to emerge in the late 1960's, was a direct descendant of the
reformist Church of the early and mid-1960's, despite significant
differences between the two.

The CNBB, 1968-1973

The CNBB was virtually silent about repression between the June
1964 statement by the Central Commission and 1968. At the Ninth
General Assembly, held in July 1968 on the eve of the Medellín conference and during a period of intensified repression, the bishops began to address the issue. The assembly's pronouncement was cautious and moderate, but it contained seeds of the more forceful
criticisms the CNBB published some years later. The document re-
captured the spirit of developmentalist nationalism that had characterized episcopal thinking in the pre-coup years, calling for "urgent and courageous reforms of mentality and structures" and for
real popular participation. Although the bishops criticized the violence of the far Left, they also protested violations of human rights.
"We do not agree with the disrespect of the fundamental rights of
people, principally the right to free expression and meetings, the
right to just remuneration, and the right of defense." The bishops
called for a more participatory economic system with better income
distribution.[91]

The 1968-69 period witnessed several important events for the
CNBB: the Medellín conference, the intensification of repression,
the exacerbation of income inequalities, the expansion of new eccle-

sial innovations at the base. Also in 1968, Dom Aloísio Lorscheider was elected secretary general of the CNBB. He restored the kind of dynamic leadership the CNBB had lacked since Dom Helder's defeat in 1964. His administrative competence, theological talents, and leadership abilities made the CNBB more dynamic. Although he himself is a reformist, Dom Aloísio supported the progressives on a wide range of issues. At the same time, his moderation enhanced his position among the conservatives, who would not have easily accepted the leadership of a more progressive bishop.

These institutional changes and the recrudescence of the repression pushed the CNBB into more critical positions toward the state. On February 18, 1969, in response to Institutional Act V and the wave of repression against the Church, the CNBB took a step forward on the issue of human rights. The bishops criticized Institutional Act V for permitting arbitrary violations of human rights, including its curtailment of the right to self-defense in court, the right to legitimate expressions of beliefs, and the right to information. They criticized the military government for threatening the physical and moral dignity of the individual and for encouraging further radicalization of the political situation. The document expressed a concern about the highly inegalitarian nature of development policies, criticizing any system where "profit is the supreme value of economic progress, competition is the only law of the economy, private property is an absolute right."[92]

The bishops affirmed that the individual, not technical criteria, should be the focus of development. They also began to question whether development would resolve the problems of most of the population. Some paths of economic growth seemed to harm rather than benefit large sectors of the population.

At the Eleventh General Assembly in May 1970, the CNBB issued a statement that went beyond previous documents. It included a strong denunciation of the military regime's authoritarian abuses and explicitly addressed the question of torture.

We cannot accept the lamentable manifestations of violence in the form of physical beatings, kidnappings, deaths, or other forms of terror. . . . The postulates of justice are frequently violated by trials of a delayed and dubious nature, by imprisonments realized on the basis of suspicion or precipitous accusations, by interrogations that last for months, during which the person is held incommunicado in poor conditions, frequently without any right to defense. . . . We would be remiss if we did not emphasize our firm position against any and all kinds of torture.[93]

This strong denunciation of torture contrasted with the document's cautious statements on economics. The CNBB expressed concern about the "tragic situation in which much of our population lives," but the bishops were reluctant to criticize economic policy. They even praised the government for its "palpable results in the economic, financial, and administrative fields, transportation, energy, communication, and housing."[94] In 1970 (as was still the case in 1985), most of the Brazilian bishops were liberals or social democrats. Only the progressives took active stands on socioeconomic issues, but moderates and conservatives began to combat the violation of human rights.

The next major step in the CNBB's political development came in 1973, the year of the twenty-fifth anniversary of the United Nations Declaration of Human Rights. The popular sectors of the Church, which were establishing a major presence in the society and in the Church as a whole, took what could have been a reformist campaign and turned it into a more comprehensive, progressive one. They postulated that situations of extreme poverty and oppression are also violations of human rights.[95] Even with some conciliatory passages and caveats, the declaration of the Thirteenth General Assembly, held in February 1973, was by far the most progressive in CNBB history until that point. It said, "The situation that above all causes us sorrow is the impoverishment of millions of our brothers and sisters, who are not even aware of, much less in a position to enjoy, the benefits that their human rights should guarantee. . . . We lament the high human price the Brazilian people have paid for economic development."[96]

The CNBB still lagged behind the most progressive regional bishops' groups, but it had come a long way. After virtually supporting the military regime (1964-68), it raised a timid voice against the repressive excesses (1968-72) and finally a much stronger voice against violations of human rights and authoritarian excesses (1973-82).

In 1973 it also linked human rights issues to the material needs of the popular classes. In April, only months after the General Assembly, the Central Commission issued a stronger statement that eliminated the equivocal passages of the February document. The bishops stated their desire to "help the poorest conquer their human rights. . . . The Church needs to open itself to the marginalized classes."[97]

Conclusion: Explaining Church Change, 1964-1973

The rapid changes of the 1964-73 period resulted from a combination of changes in Brazilian politics and society and from changes
in the international Church. Whether as a result of torture, the egregious inequalities in São Paulo, violence against peasants in frontier
areas in the Amazon, or repression against the Church in the Northeast, the first decade of military rule affected the Church significantly. Nevertheless, religious institutions do not always become
more progressive if a society becomes more inegalitarian or repressive. Political and economic changes do not automatically cause institutions to change their identity or their perceptions of politics.
Some regional churches in Brazil (especially in the South) and some
other denominations did not undergo the same transformation. The
Catholic Church in other Latin American societies has experienced
repressive and elitist authoritarian regimes without undergoing similar change. In other historical periods, including as recently as
1937-45, the Brazilian Church supported an authoritarian regime.
The Spanish Church supported the Franco regime until the 1960's
despite its highly repressive nature.[98]

On balance, the international Church also continued to encourage progressive ecclesial change. Although the Brazilian bishops initially retreated from some pre-1964 positions, the young popular
Church received encouragement from the international Church, especially from Rome and the Medellín conference of Latin American
bishops in 1968. The papacy of Paul VI was marked by some vac-
illations and pressures against progressive Catholicism in Europe,
but Pope Paul issued his most progressive statements in relation to
the Third World. *Populorum Progressio*, published in 1967 and labeled by the *Wall Street Journal* "warmed-over Marxism," inspired
progressive Catholics throughout Latin America. The encyclical
criticized the wealthy nations for their dealings with the South and
called for more equal development among countries. It argued that
the right to live decently, with dignity, and to participate in the political process are just aspirations of all people. The encyclical subordinated private property rights to rights that it claimed were more
essential and called for bold transformations to create juster societies.[99]

Another important event in the papacy of Paul VI was the 1971
Bishops' Synod on Justice in Rome. This gathering of representative

bishops from around the world affirmed the Church's need to support justice. The bishops expressed their concern about "the domination, oppression, and abuses which stifle freedom and which keep the greater part of humanity from sharing in the building up and enjoyment of a more just and more fraternal world."[100] They also stated particular concern about the Third World.

The Medellín gathering of CELAM, held in 1968, was the watershed of the popular Church in Latin America. Medellín began as an attempt, inspired by Vatican II, to understand the Church's role in the midst of change in Latin American societies. Yet this attempt to adapt Vatican II to Latin America ended by reaching conclusions well beyond the Council's.

Medellín represented a surprising success for the emerging popular Church. Despite the numerical inferiority of the popular bishops, CELAM approved a document that represented pastoral positions more progressive than those found in any Latin American country at the time. The document was particularly emphatic about the Church's need to see salvation as a process that starts on earth, the connections between faith and justice, the need for structural change in Latin America, the importance of encouraging base communities, the Church's special concern for the poor, the sinfulness of unjust social structures, the necessity of seeing the good aspects of secularization, and the importance of having a poor Church.[101] Characteristic of Medellín was the final document's discussion of ecclesial base communities. At the time, there were few base communities on the continent, but the bishops voted to make them one of the top priorities of the Latin American Church. Compared with the Brazilian bishops' discussion in the PPC of 1965, Medellín had a decidedly more progressive conception of the CEBs. The conference stated that CEBs were especially appropriate for the poor, and more than the PPC, it recognized the potential of CEBs as a means of testifying to faith through social and political stands.[102]

Like Vatican II, Medellín profoundly affected the way a large number of Church leaders perceived their faith. At a time when much of the Brazilian Church was still closely linked to the state, Medellín helped legitimate the progressives. Ironically, the Brazilian Church helped make the conference what it was. Lay participants in Catholic Action, priests involved in the innovations, and the progressive bishops played a major role in Medellín's deliberations.

Medellín provided a great stimulus to what came to be called liberation theology. The early landmarks in liberation theology appeared between 1969 and 1973, including such works as *Opresión–Liberación: Desafío a los Cristianos* by Brazilian Hugo Assmann (1971), *A Theology of Liberation* by Peruvian Gustavo Gutiérrez (1971), and *Jesus Cristo, Libertador* by Brazilian Leonardo Boff (1971). The new theology encouraged innovations throughout the continent.

If political change in itself does not necessarily cause churches to change, neither does doctrinal change. The introduction of new theologies that emphasized social justice did not necessarily affect the way national churches acted. Throughout the world, the Catholic Church preaches the same basic social doctrine; yet it is particularly in the repressive situation of some Latin American countries (Brazil, Chile, El Salvador, Nicaragua before 1980) that the Church has become most progressive. There are some exceptions (Argentina and Uruguay), but generally, the Latin American Church has become more progressive in repressive situations since the 1960's.

Thus, it was neither a conscious design to protect institutional interests nor the political process itself that caused the Church to change. Rather, a combination of a new institutional identity with new social, political, and economic conditions explains Church change. To see either the political and social conditions or the new institutional ideology as the sole factor of change would miss the dialectical character of this process.

CHAPTER 6

The Catholic Youth Workers Movement, 1947-1970

THIS CHAPTER traces the history of the Catholic Youth Workers movement (JOC) of Brazil from 1947 to 1970.[1] Part of Brazilian Catholic Action, JOC was and is a movement for the urban working class. During the period under consideration, it was one of the most important lay movements in Brazil. It was also one of the most important precursors to the popular Church of the 1970's. JOC virtually died out in 1970, a victim of brutal repression from the state and insufficient support from the bishops. But the movement testified to a kind of faith that would gain increasing importance within the Brazilian Church. At a time when most of the Church was still closely linked to the state and dominant classes, JOC helped the institution understand the needs and values of the working class and the importance of developing more adequate pastoral practices for workers. In this regard, JOC helped transform an institution noted for being hierarchical, authoritarian, and unresponsive to grassroots or lay movements.

The JOC experience was particularly interesting because of the rapidity of change within the movement. Before 1958, JOC was politically moderate, seldom involved in popular movements, and concerned more about youth activities and the Church's sacramental life than about politics. By 1970, it had become one of the military regime's primary targets of repression because of its leadership in popular movements, its radical critiques of the regime, and its commitment to socialism. It had also lost its concern with youth activities and had become distanced from the institutional Church.

Throughout this chapter I examine changes in JOC with respect to the political vision of the Catholic Church as a whole and the political struggle in society at large. As a Church movement, JOC's development was conditioned by changes in the hierarchy; in other lay movements, especially Catholic Action; in JOC movements in other countries; and in Church doctrine and theology. Even during the late 1960's, when its conception of faith was far more progressive than the dominant thinking within the Brazilian Church, JOC was marked by a religious character. Nowhere was this more evident than in JOC's pedagogy, which retained a Christian humanist emphasis on respecting the individual, especially the masses' values and abilities. Its religious ties also appeared in JOC's critical attitude toward clandestine groups and in its maintenance of ties with the institutional Church despite profound differences.

The second major reference point for understanding JOC's evolution is social, political, and economic change in Brazilian society. JOC's vision of faith was strongly influenced by political ideologies in Brazilian society. After 1958, JOC became increasingly open to political questions and more directly affected by the political struggle. Not only were *Jocistas* participants in a Church movement, they also were workers. As such, they were affected by the same changes and policies that affected other workers. As the Jocistas' political commitment deepened, political events affected them just as they affected others active in popular movements or on the Left. As wage earners and as participants in popular movements and in the debate about Brazil's political future, they were affected by the regime's economic and political policies. The changes in the political climate during the 1958-70 period—the nationalistic optimism of the 1958-64 period; the repression, declining real wages, and growing disillusionment with capitalism after 1964—strongly influenced JOC's development.

We should, however, avoid reducing analysis of a church or a church movement to the class constituency of its participants. Even though societal and political changes influenced JOC, these changes in themselves do not adequately explain JOC's transformation; other working-class religious movements remained relatively conservative. It was the combination of JOC's religious views (which emphasized social justice, political participation, decent wages, and a special concern with the poor) and political changes (which closed channels for participation, reduced wages, and adversely affected the working class) that was crucial. Analysis of a church or a church movement should neither see its transformations as direct, inevitable results of broader historical change nor neglect the impact of these broader changes.

JOC's Development, 1947-1957

The Catholic Youth Workers movement was founded by Father Joseph Cardijn, a Belgian priest from a working-class family, in 1923.[2] From the beginning the movement was aimed at the urban working class, both in Europe and in Brazil, where the first JOC groups were created in the mid-1930's. It was not until the second half of the 1940's, when Catholic Action was reorganized, that JOC started to become an important movement. From the institutional Church's viewpoint, JOC was part of an overall effort of cautious modernization by developing more effective pastoral work among the working class. Pope Pius XI had lamented that the greatest scandal of the nineteenth century was that the Church had lost the working class, and both Pius XI and Pius XII saw recapturing that class as an important goal.

In Brazil, the process of secularization, the erosion of the Catholic religious monopoly, and declining Church attendance in rural areas brought an awareness of the need to develop more effective pastoral practices, especially among the urban working class. One of the principal expressions of this was a belief that the working class was religiously ignorant and that the Church needed to implant a more mature faith. This concern is clearly expressed in JOC documents of the late 1940's and early 1950's. "Most workers don't know what baptism is; they baptize their children simply because everyone always was baptized. . . . Few young workers go to mass. . . . There is great religious ignorance. . . . As a result, Spiritism has penetrated many places. . . . The cinema, the press, and the radio are also a grave danger, breaking youth away from the Church as they develop the cult of sensuality and immorality."[3] To the Church, JOC was a way of "Christianizing" the working class. There was a widespread view that "the need for a working-class Christian movement is urgent. . . . The Church gave JOC the mission of re-Christianizing the young workers."[4]

JOC was not the only attempt to Christianize the Brazilian working class. Another movement, the Bible Circles, predated JOC by a few years and, until the 1950's, was more prominent. Organized in the early 1930's, the Circles expanded rapidly and became a national movement in 1937. Like JOC, they incorporated a concern with the Church's social doctrine, but from the outset they were more conservative and clerically dominated than JOC.[5]

Until the mid-1950's, JOC had strong triumphal overtones. Its mission was to "conquer and convert young workers."[6] Along with this conception went a strong concern for the movement's numerical expansion. By 1956, JOC had 8,500 activists and several regular publications (the most significant were the monthly newspapers *Construir* and *Juventude Trabalhadora*).

Although JOC was structured on a parish basis, there were some tensions between the parish structure, usually self-contained, and JOC, with its concerns about the world at large. The laity already played a more significant role than in the Bible Circles, and by 1957, the movement had hired some full-time workers. JOC also gradually acquired more full-time priestly advisors who worked with the movement rather than in a parish, thereby creating more autonomy from the parish structure.

Until about 1950, JOC had a relatively traditional, individualistic conception of faith. One advisor defined the movement's goals as "the glory of God and the salvation of souls."[7] There was little sense that salvation could imply working for a juster society. JOC was not oblivious to social problems, but generally proposed religious solutions to these problems. Political and social action was secondary to religious concerns and was usually seen in moralistic ways.

During this period, JOC was more a Church youth movement than a working-class organization. It was closely linked to the Church's sacramental life and celebrations. Jocistas held lengthy discussions of the family (relations with parents, dating, marriage, parenthood) and personal problems (finding jobs, career hopes). The movement also organized recreational activities, ranging from picnics and dances to assemblies and short excursions.

JOC did, however, have some interest in political and social issues. An early (1948) document stated, "Contrary to some associations exclusively concerned with religious activities, JOC has a social mission."[8] JOC's pedagogy—"See, evaluate, act"—always expressed a concern for social reality. Starting with the concrete facts in their lives, Jocistas were to analyze these facts and then act upon the analysis. Analysis and action were limited until the late 1950's, but the method always lent itself to involvement in social questions.

JOC held educational campaigns on health, housing, child labor, and other social questions.

As early as 1950, the movement had a peripheral interest in the working-class struggle. A document from that year states, "JOC was always interested in the labor struggle. Through study groups and its newspaper, it has insisted that young workers, especially the Jocistas, join the unions."[9] A 1956 document noted the importance of participating in popular movements as a means of responding to the material problems most young workers faced. "JOC teaches young workers to be authentic leaders of working-class organizations in addition to being good fathers and mothers."[10]

But there were limits to JOC's political participation and vision. During its first decade, the movement became more concerned with *discussing* questions such as factory safety, work hours, adequate lunch breaks, and wages, but few Jocistas were leaders in the labor movement. JOC's lay leaders were fairly politicized, but the membership as a whole was far less so. Its publications frequently criticized "Communist agitators" and insisted that a good Catholic would not vote for a Communist.

1958-1961

During the late 1950's JOC became more involved in political questions, beginning a rapid and profound transformation of one of the more important lay groups in the Brazilian Church. JOC's belief that its religious mission required some attention to social and political questions meant that it was open to influence by conflicts in society at large. The politicization of the society during the late populist period led JOC to become increasingly identified with the working-class struggle and to participate more actively in politics.

This tendency was reinforced by changes in the Church. During the late 1950's, although most of the institution was still conservative, more thrusts for change, supported by the CNBB and by Pope John XXIII, emerged. This situation helped stimulate pastoral innovations among the popular classes, providing support for progressive activities.

In addition, in the late 1950's, other movements within Brazilian Catholic Action, particularly Catholic University Youth (JUC), began the process of radicalization out of which emerged the Catholic Left. The Catholic Left exercised a deep influence on JOC by helping to create a new vision of faith linked to a commitment to radical social change. JOC had some interactions with other movements in Brazilian Catholic Action, especially at the national leadership level. JUC militants encouraged Jocistas toward a more progressive vision of faith and, on some occasions, gave courses to help Jocistas develop a deeper understanding of Brazilian reality. The Movement for Grass-roots Education (MEB) helped stimulate thinking about pedagogical practices, even though there was limited direct exchange between the two movements.

During the 1958-61 period, JOC continued to be concerned about the expansion and structure of the movement. Through its publications and more frequent contact among leaders of different geographic regions, JOC became better organized and developed a centralized national leadership. It paid more attention to preparing lay leaders. By 1961, JOC's monthly newspaper had a circulation of 40,000, and the movement had 25,943 members.[11] Brazil's JOC had become one of the most active Catholic Youth Workers movements in the world and one of the most important lay groups in the Brazilian Church.

During this period, the movement became less triumphal, more oriented toward working-class questions, and more progressive politically. By the late 1950's, influenced by the dynamism of the labor movement, JOC spent more time discussing professional training, wages, working conditions, unions, and neighborhood associations. Concern with material problems in working-class life replaced the earlier concern with traditional moral issues. JOC no longer saw the principal problems of young workers as moral questions in a narrow sense but rather as political and economic issues. It opened itself to the working class as a whole rather than focusing on young Catholic workers. As one document stated, there was "an awakening of young workers to their value as workers, as poor people, and the importance of their work, their social group, and the responsibilities they have."[12]

Nineteen sixty-one was a turning point. The year was marked by three important conferences in Rio de Janeiro: the Second World Congress of JOC, the First National Congress of Young Workers, and the Congress of Young Domestic Workers, organized by JOC. In addition, the movement launched the Campaign of Working-class Consciousness to "alert the workers, especially the youth, to the gravity of the problems they face: inadequate wages, cheating on

the minimum wage, unemployment, exploitation in their work . . .
[and to] call attention to working-class organizations: unions, cooperatives, neighborhood associations, etc."[13]

The conclusions of the Congress of Young Workers (November
1961) reveal JOC's political positions at this time. The document
contains strong traces of the political optimism that marked most
progressive groups within the populist pact, specifically the view
that the "base reforms" of the Goulart government would resolve
the country's major problems. But for the first time JOC criticized
capitalism. "Because of its failure to respect the human individual,
capitalism is as much an evil as socialism." The movement also expressed sharp criticisms of Brazil's model of development. "The development race does not necessarily benefit the working class. In
Brazil, it has made the poor poorer, and the rich richer."[14]

These changes were significant, but we should not exaggerate
how deeply JOC had changed by 1961. In terms of its political vision, the movement still expressed optimism in the populist system.
The document from the First National Congress of Young Workers,
for example, the most progressive document of the period, falls
within the progressive nationalistic-developmentalist perspective. It
argues that the necessary reforms can be realized through the capitalist system and, more specifically, through having better politicians direct the development process.

The faith that the state and dominant classes could solve working-class problems appeared more clearly in other documents. In
1959, JOC advisors called for "the intelligent and disinterested collaboration of all the classes."[15] The annual queries for group discussion for 1960-61 expressed a belief in class harmony. "The working
class, along with other classes, wants to participate in human progress."[16] The responses of JOC members I interviewed reveal the limits of JOC's political consciousness during the period. "At that time,
our concern was to evaluate the situation, denounce injustices and
hope that the authorities would resolve the situation. . . . We demanded that the government make the changes. We believed that by
putting a good person, a conscientious Christian, in office, everything would be OK. We didn't understand that there were structural
problems. We didn't question the structures."[17] "It was a movement
that still made a lot of effort to talk with the owners, with the government, with authorities, even while it maintained a critical line."[18]

At the same time, JOC remained strongly religious. Its reading of social reality was marked by its vision of faith, and it continued to be deeply involved in the Church's sacramental life. A religious moralism pervaded some texts. "The depraved, skeptical, and nonreligious ambience of the work place, with its bad examples, scandals, pornography, obsession with sex, solicitations, revolts, injustices, hatred and plots, corrupts the working youth."[19]

Although JOC was still closely linked to the parish and relatively moderate politically, the first tensions between the movement and the Church surfaced. JOC's practices and vision of faith were already more advanced than the general position of the Church. One document stated that "a large part of the clergy is completely oblivious to the problems and aspirations of the working class and is more concerned with other social classes. The Church's pastoral work is almost completely out of touch with the reality of the working class."[20] Some of those I interviewed also noted the emergence of conflict. "At that time, JOC was as advanced as anything in the Church. Often we weren't accepted because the bishops didn't understand." And, "The JOC World Congress was held at the Metalworkers Union's headquarters. A lot of bishops frowned on this. How could JOC have a congress at a union headquarters? They felt this was going too far. JOC was always doing things that were in advance of most of the Church."[21]

1962–1964

Between 1962 and 1964, the political effervescence and the dynamism of the popular movements strongly influenced JOC's development. The new experiences in popular education stimulated thinking about work with the popular classes that affected progressive pastoral work. As citizens and workers, Jocistas participated in the political discussions of the society, and a large number of Jocistas participated in the popular movements that were central actors in the political arena. JOC's opening to a vision of faith that emphasized political involvement meant that its development would be more directly shaped by political change.

The changes within the Church also favored JOC's deeper and more progressive political involvement. It was not that the Church as a whole opted to favor the popular classes; on the contrary, the bulk of the institution remained allied with the state and the dominant classes. But the Second Vatican Council promoted a more pro-

gressive vision of faith, and an increasing number of persons within
the Brazilian Church chose progressive pastoral stances. The hierarchy, while divided, issued its most progressive documents. In
1962, the CNBB, under the leadership of Dom Helder Câmara, criticized the "social imbalances produced by the egotism and profit
promoted by economic liberalism."[22] In 1963, the bishops issued a
document calling for land reform and insisting that all people
should have access to land.[23] Progressive pastoral innovations
among the popular classes multiplied. The political commitment of
the Catholic Left continued to deepen. Although JOC generally
maintained some distance from the Catholic Left, a few Jocistas
also participated in these movements.

The 1962-64 period marked a decisive turning point in JOC's history. JOC entered the period already in a transition to increasing
political involvement and away from a more sacramental conception of faith. It was leaning toward greater involvement in working-
class questions and away from personal issues such as dating and
marriage. Many Jocistas had a strong political awareness and participated in popular movements. These choices were consolidated
during the 1962-64 period. The 1963 national conference brought
a break with the past.

Like JUC earlier and like the Church as a whole later, JOC was
faced with different conceptions of its proper mission. With more
participants than it had ever had, the movement began to suffer serious internal divisions. A clear split emerged at the 1963 National
Council (the annual gathering) over how far JOC's political commitment should go. The groups from São Paulo and Recife pushed
for more radical positions, were more critical of capitalism, and
were more inclined to propose structural solutions to social problems. The National Committee (the movement's lay leaders) and the
national advisor felt that the Church had to work within the capitalist system, albeit a reformed one. The former position won out,
and the National Committee and advisor resigned. The incident
had many important consequences for the movement, including a
decline in participation and deeper and increasingly radical political
participation. Concomitantly, concern with traditional spirituality
waned. A 1964 document noted, "Many leaders are concerned
more about their personal political involvement than about developing new leaders. There is an absence of spiritual discussion. The

activists aren't receiving enough support. At the grass roots, JOC is weaker."[24]

During these years JOC's commitment to the working-class struggle deepened. Whereas during the early 1950's JOC principally reflected its Church affiliation, during the years prior to the coup it more strongly reflected its working-class character.

The working-class character of the movement is felt more strongly. . . . JOC is more open to the world. The activists are more oriented toward the realities of life and work. There is a greater concern with reaching and supporting the factory struggle. . . . There is a stronger working-class consciousness among the activists, who are more committed to an integral pro motion of the workers. There is greater involvement in the unions, in politics, and in the labor movement.[25]

The optimism that pervaded most of the Brazilian Left was felt in JOC. "There is an awareness of the misery of the workers. There is a desire to change things, to transform mentalities and structures, a desire for justice, for a better distribution of wealth and better living conditions for all. We are in a revolutionary moment of demanding the reforms desired especially by the oppressed."[26]

In 1962, ex-Jocistas created Catholic Workers Action (ACO) to continue JOC's work among older workers. ACO defined itself as

a movement of Christians engaged in the life and movements of the working class, acting with all other activists; an apostolic movement that reveals to the working class the presence and message of Jesus, not so much through words as through friendship, courage, and fidelity; a movement that represents the working class within the Church, with the right to demand from the Church that it be faithful to the working class.[27]

From 1962, ACO would play an important role in the Church and in popular movements, complementing JOC's efforts. Many ACO activists were former members of JOC.

Despite its political awakening, JOC continued to be reformist. It felt that the "base reforms" would successfully transform the country. Some publications noted that not enough Jocistas participated in popular movements, and an anti-Communist ideology was still pervasive. A pre-election edition of the publication for JOC leaders stated, "Catholics should not vote for Communist candidates or people who preach class struggle or hateful or violent revolution."[28] Several of those I interviewed expressed the idea that JOC still was reformist. "We didn't have any consciousness about the capitalist system or about political tactics. The only thing that existed was an awareness that we were being exploited."[29]

1964-1970

During the second half of the 1960's, JOC's political vision changed at a remarkably rapid pace. During this period, JOC abandoned reformism and became a staunchly anticapitalist movement. Although JOC's views still differed sharply from those of the Marxist Left, it became committed to radical social change as an element of Christian faith. This vision of faith and the pedagogical practices developed in JOC would make it one of the most important precursors of the popular Church.

In the post-1964 period, two political and economic changes had a particularly significant impact on JOC. First, the military regime pursued a highly inegalitarian model of development, leading to a decline in real wages that exacerbated already difficult living conditions. Between 1958 and 1969, real wages for industrial workers fell 36.5 percent in São Paulo,[30] and between 1960 and 1976, the share of the bottom 50 percent in total national income decreased 17.4-13.5 percent and the share of the top 5 percent increased 28.3-37.9 percent.[31] Second, the regime strongly repressed the most significant popular movements, leading to the imprisonment of many Jocistas.

This changing reality and the new ways in which other groups and movements perceived that reality affected JOC's development. The Left as a whole was increasingly critical of capitalism, and new theological conceptions were legitimating progressive visions of faith. Many leftist groups were gradually losing their belief that the needed reforms could happen within the capitalist system. Although JOC never followed the most radical movements, a large part of the Left went underground and saw clandestine struggle as the only solution.[32] Because of its concerns and its links to other groups interested in transforming the society, JOC came into contact with new methods of analyzing reality. At the time, Marxism and dependency analysis were becoming important intellectual tools in Latin America. Like other Church movements interested in transforming social reality,[33] JOC was influenced by these analyses, especially after 1968.

Changes in the Church as a whole also help explain JOC's evo-

lution during the 1964-70 period. Although the Brazilian episcopacy essentially retreated during the 1964-68 period, other changes
within the Church were move favorable to the positions that JOC
started to adopt. The Vatican Council, which ended in 1965, encouraged progressive Catholic thought and pastoral practices. At
the grass roots, an increasing number of pastoral workers became
concerned with the popular classes and social justice. The first base
communities sprang up, and the first systematic reflections about
pastoral work among the working class occurred. A new Latin
American theology emerged, developing many themes discussed in
JOC: faith and politics, faith and liberation, Jesus's preferential option for the poor, and pastoral practices and pedagogy among the
popular classes. The gathering of the Latin American Bishops Conference in Medellín in 1968 captured much of the richness of this
new theology and grass-roots pastoral innovations.

Immediately after the coup, several Jocistas were detained or imprisoned for their leadership of popular movements, and the 1964
and 1965 National Councils had to be canceled for political reasons. In September 1964, the National Committee issued a major
document defining JOC's position on the coup. "For the workers
who are more involved in the labor movement and politics, the military government is an attempt not to satisfy the workers' aspirations but, on the contrary, to block the labor movement, prevent the
advance of new ideas, and remove from circulation the principal labor and popular leaders."[34]

JOC's position showed not only how far the movement had gone
politically, but also how much its vision differed from that of the
other major working-class movement within the Church, the Bible
Circles. Conservative and dominated by the clergy, the Bible Circles
supported the coup in the name of anti-Communism. From the outset, the Circles had a predominantly middle-class leadership, sepa-
rated faith and social reality, and lacked a pedagogical method that
raised questions about social reality. Hence they were more closed
to the influences that helped transform JOC. In addition, they
lacked the links to progressive sectors in the Church (especially
other movements in Catholic Action) that played an important role
in JOC's transformation.

The rapid destruction of the pre-coup ideals and optimism posed
new questions for the popular movements and the Left. Along with
other movements, JOC became concerned with theoretical analysis

of past mistakes and future actions. The feeling that previous political practices had been flawed, the disillusionment with capitalism, and the difficulty of acting because of the repression led to a desire for a better understanding of Brazilian reality. As one ex-Jocista stated, "The repression forced the movement to turn inward. It could no longer be a mass movement. It became a movement for leaders, for activists. When the possibility for mass action was eliminated, we spent more time studying, and this led to greater political sophistication. The activists began to understand the working-class problem at large—the social, political, and economic system."[35]

The movement's earliest criticisms of the regime were somewhat timid, focusing on specific issues such as jobs and wages. It had little sense of the futility of asking the military government for concessions. A 1965 document requested the government leaders to make the needed reforms. "What we request from the government and firms are new opportunities to work and urgent measures so that the nation is not built with the hunger and sufferings of the poor."[36]

But as more Jocistas were persecuted or had factory colleagues persecuted for their involvement in popular movements and as the regime's authoritarian nature became clearer, JOC critiques became more radical. A first step in this direction had come at the 1963 National Council, when the movement started to criticize "neo-capitalism," previously defended by JOC's documents. But in 1963 only the leaders had argued for this position. A second step came in 1965 in Nova Friburgo, Rio de Janeiro, at the First Week of Studies, when the bulk of the movement started to question capitalism.

This process culminated at the April 1968 National Council, held in conjunction with ACO, in Recife. Here the leaders, with the full support of the regional and local movements, broke with capitalism, which they now considered the root of the problems of the Brazilian working class. The council concluded that it was necessary to overcome capitalism and fight for a socialist system.[37]

The conclusions of the Recife council were the most radical any Church movement had adopted and caused JOC to come under fire from the bishops and the military. The bishops asked JOC to write a report defining its positions. The "Yellow Document," finished in July 1969, reaffirmed JOC's condemnation of capitalism. "The fundamental cause of working-class problems is an economic system based on profit, which does not take into account the needs of the people. . . . We denounce capitalism as an intrinsically bad system."

JOC committed itself to radical social transformation. "JOC should contribute to radically changing the current society through the formation of Christian activists, genuinely involved in this process. The movement wants to contribute to all those organizations fighting for the construction of a new humanity and a new society, where the fundamental rights of all people will be respected."[38]

JOC's attitude toward Marxism had changed dramatically since 1964. Another important document stated, "Marxism, for us, is a doctrine like any other. Communism does not frighten us. If Marxism helps the workers get what they need and allows them to realize their humanity, we will not oppose it. . . . We are not Communists, but we do not fear Communism; rather, we fear poverty, hunger, alienation."[39]

The Recife National Council marked more than the culmination of JOC's turn toward more radical political analysis and solutions. It also initiated a period of violent repression against the movement, and, to a slightly lesser extent, against ACO. Several Jocistas had been imprisoned in 1964 and during the ensuing years, but these imprisonments had been a result of participation in other movements. In fact, participation in JOC had sometimes helped a popular leader avoid repression. As JOC became more radical, however, it also became a target of state repression. Between 1966 and 1970, many of the most serious conflicts between the Church and state involved JOC or ACO. The first arose in July 1966 when the northeastern bishops issued a statement supporting an ACO document that was highly critical of the regime. The regime initially prohibited the circulation of the statement and launched several attacks against Dom Helder Câmara. As would happen repeatedly, these attacks against the Church created greater cohesion within it.[40]

The state also repressed JOC and ACO because they were part of the embryonic efforts to challenge the corporatist labor structures. Both movements played an important role in the efforts to create a stronger, more autonomous labor movement, particularly during strikes at Contagem, Minas Gerais, and Osasco, São Paulo, in 1968. Even though the labor movement had challenged some aspects of the corporatist system before 1964, these strikes were marked by stronger factory-level organization of the kind that would characterize the "new labor movement" of the late 1970's. In both cases, the strikes were repressed, and several JOC and ACO participants were imprisoned. At Osasco the regime imprisoned and later expelled Pierre Wauthier, a French worker-priest who served as a JOC advisor, leading to one of the most publicized Church-state conflicts of the period.[41]

Wauthier was punished because of his alleged role in the strike, not because of his link to JOC. Direct repression against JOC came only after the Recife Council. The government confiscated the council documents and distributed them to several conservative bishops, hoping that the hierarchy would take reprisals against JOC just as it had done earlier with JUC.

But before the CNBB could deal with the question, the repression fell. The repressive wave started with the imprisonment and torture of three priests and a deacon associated with JOC in Belo Horizonte, November 28, 1968, two weeks before Institutional Act V was decreed on December 13. The military alleged that the four had, among other subversive activities, helped instigate the strikes at Contagem. This incident precipitated another of the most controversial Church-state conflicts of the period. The torturing of the four was widely publicized. Even relatively conservative Church leaders, many of whom had hitherto dismissed reports of torture as apocryphal, denounced the state's actions. The case not only generated a greater consciousness within ecclesial ranks about the nature of the regime, it also created a greater sense of cohesion within the Church at a time when the institution was still profoundly divided over its response to the regime. After the imprisonments, several leading conservative prelates, including the president of the CNBB, Dom Agnelo Rossi; the archbishop of Rio de Janeiro, Dom Jaime Barros de Câmara; and the archbishop of Pôrto Alegre, Dom Vicente Scherer, wrote letters protesting the government's actions. On December 4, the Central Commission of the CNBB issued a note denouncing the incarcerations, one of the CNBB's earliest protests against a violation of human rights.[42]

Immediately after Institutional Act V was decreed, the regime started to search for many JOC advisors and leaders. In early 1969, JOC advisors were imprisoned in Recife, Pôrto Alegre, Rio, São Paulo, and Nova Hamburgo. The police invaded JOC's local headquarters in São Paulo in January; other invasions of JOC offices occurred in Rio, Terezina, Crateús, and elsewhere. A large number of activists were imprisoned and tortured.

On May 25, 1969, a JOC advisor in Recife, Father Antônio Henrique Pereira Neto, became the first priest to be assassinated by the regime.[43] One general told a JOC leader that as long as there was a single Jocista left, his work was unfinished; he wanted to wipe out the movement.[44] JOC had become one of the regime's primary targets on the spurious pretext that it was working with clandestine groups. Although there were isolated cases of Jocistas' joining clandestine groups, the relationship between JOC and the underground parties was hostile. These parties considered JOC reformist; JOC's Christian humanist perspectives, its decision to remain in the Church, its commitment not to go underground, and its sharp criticisms of the authoritarian methods of the clandestine parties established strong differences.

In addition to the problems caused by the repression, JOC faced difficulties with the institutional Church. One ex–JOC advisor noted that "JOC lost some of its support. It was well supported when it was concerned with youth questions. But when it began to take positions, when it began to discuss class issues, that changed."[45] Isolated bishops risked their own security to defend JOC, but on the whole the hierarchy did little to protect the movement. The majority of bishops had reservations about JOC's political choices and decreasing involvement in the Church's sacramental life. The movement had equally serious reservations about the hierarchy, which, far from reaching out to defend the working class, remained silent until the end of the decade. Many Jocistas left the Church, disgruntled with its silence about the military regime and its closeness to the elite. The groups that continued to function became increasingly distant from parish life, and contact between JOC and the institution was reduced to a minimum.

Faced with severe repression from the state and a relative lack of support from the bishops, JOC turned to the International Catholic Youth Workers for help—and received it. Throughout the world, Youth Worker groups demonstrated on its behalf. The international advisor, Australian priest Brian Burke, went to Brazil to help defend JOC vis-à-vis the hierarchy. Burke supported JOC, but the CNBB granted him only fifteen minutes at its annual session to state the movement's case.[46]

A second repressive wave, which almost silenced JOC for a few years, occurred in October 1970. The police raided the national headquarters in Rio and imprisoned and tortured the National Committee and four advisors. This began another series of incarcerations of Jocista activists and priests. Most JOC groups in São

Paulo, Belo Horizonte, and Volta Redonda were wiped out. By this time, the CNBB was beginning to respond to the regime's violations of human rights. The torturing of Jocistas in Volta Redonda led to a serious conflict between the bishop, Dom Waldir Calheiros, and the regime, with a number of conservative bishops coming to the defense of Dom Waldir and those who had been tortured.[47]

In Rio the search for Jocistas caused one of the most dramatic conflicts between Church and state during the two decades of military rule. The military invaded a Jesuit study center and detained the secretary general of the CNBB, Dom Aloísio Lorscheider; the head of the Catholic University of Rio; and the head of the Jesuits in the southeastern region. The torturing of so many Church people and the violation of Church property caused such an uproar that Dom Eugênio Sales (then archbishop of Salvador) and Dom Vicente Scherer (Pôrto Alegre) flew to Rio to speak with government officials. Again, repression against the Church started at the grass roots and ultimately affected the highest levels of the institution.

Faced with this frontal attack against the Church, the Central Commission of the CNBB issued one of its most energetic protests to date. "The promotion of the individual should be sought by all levels of political and administrative organizations. This objective will not be attained when, to eliminate terrorist subversion, the concern for national security generates a climate of increasing insecurity. Terrorism by the repressive apparatus is not a legitimate response to terrorism by subversives."[48]

The case even received international attention. Vatican Radio denounced the imprisonments, and *Osservatore Romano*, the official organ of the Holy See, published the Central Commission's statement on its front page and expressed editorial support. All over Europe, Catholic Youth Workers bombarded Brazilian consulates and embassies with calls protesting the tortures. Pope Paul VI also announced his solidarity with the Brazilian Church, helping to legitimate those clergy committed to denouncing the regime's abuses.

JOC was unprepared for repression. One ex-Jocista stated, "We never imagined we could be imprisoned. We didn't believe that they would get people who were Christians. It didn't make any sense. We thought we were doing the most beautiful thing in the world. There was a pureness in our actions. . . . We were acting as Church people, and nobody was going to touch the Church."[49]

The fierce repression of the Médici years (1969-74), coupled with the crisis within JOC and the bishops' lack of support, virtually destroyed the movement, both in terms of numbers and of efficacy in stimulating popular movements. From 26,000 members in 1961, participation declined to 654 by 1968.[50] At one point, over a hundred Jocistas were in prison, and in many places the movement was wiped out. At best, small groups continued to meet irregularly and semiclandestinely. The repression was so bad that it was difficult to find lay people and priests willing to continue. One person stated, "Everyone wanted me to join the National Committee. No way! I had a girl friend. I was planning to get married. How could I join the National Committee? Most of the people were terrified when they left prison. They were really tortured badly."[51]

The repression forced the movement to abandon attempts at popular organizing. It is hard to exaggerate the extreme difficulties of popular organizing between 1969 and 1974. The state viewed even rudimentary popular discussions as subversive, and efforts to organize the popular classes were almost suicidal.[52] The most Jocistas could do was to maintain contact with their colleagues and friends.

As a consequence of the repression, JOC virtually lost its character as a movement concerned with youth problems. Political discussion replaced recreational activities and personal questions. Though not completely by choice, this deep politicization transformed JOC from a mass organization into a group for leaders of the popular movement. Jocistas attained a more sophisticated and radical understanding of the capitalist system, but had few possibilities for political action. The emphasis on study generated a certain elitism, which often led to a distancing from the average worker. One person said, "You can never get out of touch with your fellow workers. When this happens, you start to intellectualize. There was a time when this happened in JOC. We began to study and see things in such a way that we didn't know how to talk with other workers at the grass roots. We discussed capitalism, socialism, Marxism, and the worker doesn't have any of that stuff in his head."[53]

By the late 1960's, JOC was so involved in political work that it had no time for colleagues whose political vision was "backward." Today many ex-participants criticize this elitist character; even at the time there was some awareness of the problem. One 1970 document stated, "JOC is not reaching the mass of young workers. The groups are small, closed, and disconnected from the masses. The groups are gradually disappearing; so the movement lives in permanent instability."[54] But given the repression and the hierarchy's lack of support, the movement had trouble overcoming these problems. Because of the repression, JOC closed its publications, which had been one of the principal means of recruitment. In any case, the risks of participating were so high that few were willing.

Surprisingly, JOC rarely criticized the institutional Church. Even though the institutional Church neither identified with the working class nor supported JOC, the movement remained committed to the Church, and religion pervaded its vision of politics. JOC saw its activities as part of a testimony of faith. Faith required a commitment to working for a juster world as a way of realizing God's design. This religious vision and the desire to work within the Church were clear in the Yellow Document, one of the most radical JOC ever produced.

JOC remains faithful to its apostolic mission as a Church movement present among young workers. It wants to help young workers find Christ in their lives and help them discover the power of the Bible. . . . JOC of Brazil wants to remain part of the Church. However, it wants to be faithful to young workers and therefore to the working class. For us this fidelity is the only way of being faithful to the Church of Christ.[55]

This religious vision, the insistence upon staying in the Church, the rejection of clandestine political struggle, and the relative quietness of JOC's work helped keep the movement immune from attack by the hierarchy at a time when its positions were more radical than anything JUC had ever adopted. There was no official Church action against JOC, even though in some cities JOC met the resistance of the bishop. The hierarchy reacted by refusing to support the movement, not by repressing it. JOC escaped attack at the two moments when it was most likely, in 1966 when the hierarchy closed down other branches of Catholic Action and in 1969 when the regime tried to pressure the bishops into taking reprisals against it.

JOC and the Transformation of the Church

One of my principal arguments is that the transformation of the Brazilian Church was realized through a dialectical process. Many innovations were initiated at the grass roots but became significant only after the hierarchy adopted them. JOC's contributions to and limitations in encouraging change in the Church illustrate this point.

The repressive wave of 1970 effectively silenced JOC just as the popular Church was making itself heard and as the institution started defending human rights. During the Médici years, other Church groups acquired a dynamism that surpassed that of JOC and ACO. The base communities flourished, and the newly formed Workers Pastoral Commission and Pastoral Land Commission became the active centers of Church innovation.

JOC never fully recovered, even though the movement started to expand again after 1972. As other Church movements were born, JOC remained eclipsed, a victim of many years of repression and of internal problems. Today the movement continues to face the identity crisis that first appeared at the 1963 National Council, was greatly exacerbated by the repression, and was complicated by the emergence of the base communities, the Workers Pastoral Commission, and parish youth groups. The crux of this problem is whether JOC should be oriented toward the common worker or toward a politically aware minority.

Despite internal divisions and problems, JOC filled an important historical role in the Brazilian Church. Perhaps its most important contribution was to develop a conception of faith, a commitment to popular struggle, and pedagogical practices that served as a model for other movements. Even though JOC's level of political militancy and rejection of popular religiosity differentiate it from the Church movements of the 1970's, JOC influenced their theological reflections and pastoral practices.

JOC and ACO carried on a tradition, begun by JUC, MEB, Popular Action, and other movements, of a faith linked to radical politics. But JOC and ACO also made a unique contribution. Whereas the earlier movements had been led by middle-class intellectuals, JOC and ACO articulated their vision of faith from a working-class perspective. The starting point in JOC, and in the popular Church more generally, was the material situation, faith, and values of the masses. An integral part of this new faith was seeing Christ as a poor person who chose other poor people and workers for disciples, who came to save the poor above all others, and who attacked the wealthy and powerful in calling for social justice. This concern for the popular classes would become central to the popular Church.

JOC was originally a means of bringing the Church to the working class, of Christianizing the working class. But its historical significance resides in doing the opposite, in helping the Church understand the working class. JOC and ACO were part of a number of progressive pastoral activities in the early 1960's among the popular classes. JOC and ACO were particularly important, both because of the development of their vision of faith and because of their status as major national movements. Through its publications and congresses, JOC promoted an exchange of ideas between people throughout Brazil and gained an influence that few local innovations had.

JOC helped the Church reassess its traditional paternalism and elitism in working with the popular classes. In the period before the coup, JOC advisors were already reflecting on the working-class world and its values. Along with the Jocistas, the advisors started to reject the traditional belief that the working class had left the Church because of religious ignorance. In a 1961 document, a group of JOC advisors concluded that the workers had left the Church because the institution did not understand the workers' world, because they lived in subhuman conditions that prevented a strong religious life, because they identified the Church as an oppressive force, and because the Church was not active in the labor struggle. "The Church has committed sins of omission: its absence in working-class matters and problems. The workers are completely oblivious of the existence of a Church social doctrine capable of resolving their problems."[56]

Another early (1964) reflection on pastoral work with the popular classes was even more critical of the Church.

For the workers, the priest represents knowledge and authority, but is distant and belongs to a different milieu. There is often a contradictory attitude; in front of the priest, the worker is very respectful, but in discussions in the factory or at home, his attitude is different. In our contact with workers in the factory or the neighborhood, many people start off by affirming their religiosity. Later, when there is an atmosphere of trust, they start to mention their prejudices about the Church. Probably the most common idea is that priests are connected to the wealthy. . . . The problem is not that some priests have weaknesses; they understand that. It is the bourgeois attitudes of the priests that scandalize the workers.[57]

As early as 1964, JOC advisors criticized the Church for "its compromises with capitalism, its neglect of the temporal order, its moralizing attitudes."[58] They were pioneers in calling for popular liturgy, popular catechism, and accessible language in working with the poor, and in emphasizing popular values and abilities. They were also among the first to call for a preferential option for the poor. A 1963 document stated, "If the Church does not become concerned with the workers' problems and attempt to overcome the chasm that separates it from the workers, it will be failing in its mission: evangelizing the poor."[59]

Influenced by other experiences in popular education and popular culture, JOC advisors were among the first priests to reflect deeply on pedagogical principles for pastoral work with the popular classes. JOC advisors came to feel that the priest must listen to and learn from the workers. They affirmed that the workers have something to teach and that they are complete human beings, worthy of as much respect as any others. This emphasis on the fundamental human worth of all and the importance of respecting the masses, characteristic of the contemporary popular Church, surfaced in JOC around 1963.

Respect for the human worth of the working class required sensitivity. "A fundamental characteristic of our commitment is sensitivity to working-class values. We should value their work and their solutions and respect their capacity to receive and give. We should believe that they can and do help us." A major objective was to "gain acceptance among the workers, have a normal and spontaneous life among them, identify with them, become one resident among others."[60] Anticipating the pedagogy of the base communities, JOC advisors, at their national meeting in 1964, expressed the importance of "living with the workers, participating in all their manifestations of sorrow and joy; combating the bourgeois habits and attitudes that divide our world from theirs; not considering ourselves superior because of our background, but a brother among them. . . . Our mission is not to resolve problems in a paternalistic manner, but to encourage, awaken, motivate."[61]

Ex-participants in JOC see this emphasis on pedagogy as one of the movement's most important contributions. JOC helped invert pedagogical practices within the Church, which, like the rest of society, had traditionally been elitist. Workers assumed the leadership of JOC and were encouraged to do so in other popular movements. This was an important step in a society where the popular classes have historically had limited opportunities to participate.

JOC's pedagogy was not above criticism. At times, advisors excessively dominated discussions. At other times, the reverse problem appeared—a naïve veneration of popular values, abilities, and consciousness. By the late 1960's, a glorification of the working class and a rejection of elements not from that class had developed. Found throughout many parts of the contemporary popular Church (see Chapter 9), this *obreirista* or *basista* tendency dismissed the contribution that nonworkers could make and apotheosized popular consciousness and practices. As one ex-advisor commented, "There were elements in JOC convinced of the self-sufficiency of the labor movement as a means of transforming reality. This position was predominant in the Brazilian JOC during the 1960's, and even today many people have that attitude. This creates an isolation, a feeling that the truth is in the working class. Anyone outside the working class is bourgeois and doesn't understand."[62]

In addition to living a new model of faith and developing the kind of pastoral practices that would later emerge in the popular Church, JOC helped transform the Church by sensitizing many priests to the problems of working-class life. Many individuals who participated are still important figures in the Church. Among those who note their personal indebtedness to JOC is Dom Antônio Fragoso, bishop of Crateús, Ceará, one of the outstanding figures of the popular Church. Dom Fragoso, who worked with JOC for ten years, stated that the experience changed his vision of faith and helped him to "see that the weak are the great."[63] JOC and ACO also created a new cadre of lay leaders who continue to hold leadership positions in Church and popular movements and in political parties. The Workers Pastoral Commission in most major cities in Brazil is largely a product of ex–JOC and ex–ACO participants, and in some cases, JOC advisors and participants helped create early base communities.[64]

Tragically, JOC also helped transform the Church by forcing the institution to face the repressive nature of the authoritarian regime. Initially the repression affected only the Jocistas who were leaders in popular movements, but eventually it encompassed the movement as a whole. In some cases—most notably those of Father Wauthier in Osasco, the three priests and the deacon in Belo Horizonte, the assassination of Father Henrique Pereira in 1969, and the systematic imprisonments and tortures in 1969 and 1970—conflicts between JOC and the regime provoked major Church criticisms of the military, with even relatively conservative bishops coming to the defense of the victims.

This repression against the Church was one of the outstanding factors that produced its transformation, and it was principally the actions of lay leaders and pastoral agents working at the grass roots that brought on the repression. Until around 1970, the main conflict was not between the dominant group in the Church and the state, but rather between the state and popular organizations or student groups and the pastoral agents working with or defending them. During the first four years of military rule, most high-ranking ecclesiastics and the military government worked to maintain a good relationship. The regime's anti-Communism and its claim to defend Western, Christian civilization impelled it to seek a good relationship with the Church.[65] On the basis of this appeal, many bishops supported the 1964 coup and the regime during its first years. From the Church's side, the efforts to maintain a good relationship with the state marked the continuation of the strategy that Dom Leme had employed half a century earlier. The mutual efforts to construct a harmonious relationship were manifest in the declarations of both sides about their good relations. Often, in the aftermath of conflict between the regime and the Church, leaders from both sides would express the view that the conflict was an isolated incident that did not alter the fundamental understanding between the two institutions.[66]

These declarations did nothing to alter the military's attempts to silence the opposition, however, and Catholic activists played a central role in that opposition. Progressive Catholics were such an important part of the Left by 1964 that a regime determined to eliminate the Left could not avoid repressing Catholic leaders and organizations. The regime's strategy was to isolate radical Catholics from the rest of the Church so as to avoid conflict with the whole institution. Until 1968, this strategy was partially successful; the hierarchy generally did not aid the victims of the repression. However, as the repression stiffened, as more grass-roots agents became committed to the popular cause, and as more bishops defended these agents, the Church became caught in a repressive spiral. Even relatively conservative bishops considered the repression against the Church an unjust intrusion upon ecclesial autonomy. Thus, even bishops who did not support JOC's religious views ultimately protested the imprisonments and tortures of Jocistas and JOC advisors. Ironically, the process that almost led to JOC's extinction simultaneously awakened the Church to JOC's message. Although the repression almost destroyed JOC, it also caused changes within the Church that would lead the institution closer to positions that JOC, among other groups, had introduced.

JOC was, in many ways, a precursor of the popular Church of the 1970's. Yet it would be misleading to see the Church's transformation simply as a result of grass-roots movements or to overlook some differences between JOC and the most significant expressions of the popular Church of the 1970's.

Even though JOC's political vision was always informed by its faith, by the late 1960's it had developed a faith based almost exclusively on testimony through action. Political practice was the primary expression of JOC's religious convictions. The movement had become distanced from the Church's sacramental life, and many members had little contact with the hierarchy or even with active Catholics outside of JOC. JOC spent little time on spirituality; prayer, for example, was not cultivated.

Most Jocistas saw traditional forms of popular Catholicism as alienating. The rejection of traditional religiosity increased the distance between the common worker and the Jocistas, reinforcing elitist tendencies created by JOC's political positions. "JOC never really dealt with the question of popular religiosity. On the contrary, we considered popular religiosity a form of alienation. . . . JOC is still indifferent to popular religiosity. That is one of its problems; it is elitist."[67]

Perhaps more clearly than anything else, this negative attitude sharply distinguishes the kind of faith practiced by JOC from that practiced in the base communities (CEBs). Although influenced by MEB, JOC, and ACO, the CEBs combine traditional religious practices and a politically progressive message. Even though the communities have given prayer and Bible discussion a new content, they are the core of these religious communities.

The base communities also continue to participate actively in the Church's sacramental and parish life. Their relations with the institutional Church are far closer than those of JOC in the late 1960's. Serious tensions between CEBs and the hierarchy have been unusual. And whereas JOC became an elite movement for leaders in the popular movement, the CEBs have become a mass movement with perhaps as many as two million people. The level of political involvement varies greatly in CEBs, but a developed political awareness is no prerequisite for participating. Despite their importance in popular movements and sharp regional and individual differences, most CEBs continue to be politically cautious. The observation made in 1976 by J. B. Libânio, an important CEB advisor, that "the political level of the CEBs is very weak" is still true.[68]

JOC's elitist character, its negative attitude toward popular religion, and its tenuous links to the bishops ultimately became liabilities. Whereas JOC and the other elite movements of the 1960's ultimately became fringe groups within the institution, until 1982 the base communities and other expressions of the popular Church gained increasing importance, helping the Church to become a major political force in the society and one of the most significant expressions of contemporary Catholicism.

Part III

The Church and Political Liberalization,
1974-1985

CHAPTER 7

The Development of the Popular Church, 1974-1982

IT WAS DURING the 1974-82 period that the Brazilian Church assumed such importance in international Catholicism and became the most progressive Church in the world. Even though the two preceding decades had witnessed considerable change, the years between 1974 and 1982 were the period of ascendancy of the popular Church. By 1976, the progressives shared leadership with the reformists, and the Brazilian Church had gone further than any Catholic Church in the world in linking faith to a commitment to social justice and to the poor. Brazilian theology matured considerably, becoming more systematized. The innovations at the grass roots continued and were consolidated in new ecclesial structures, pastoral practices, and political involvement. The base communities (CEBs), which had been limited to two or three dozen dioceses in 1973, multiplied rapidly. The Church continued to evolve in a progressive direction until 1982, when the combination of political developments and pressures from Rome changed the tide. After 1982, the progressive sectors faced an uphill struggle to retain the position conquered during the previous fifteen years.

The popular Church can be distinguished from the reformist Church in several ways. Like the reformist Church, the popular Church is concerned with social justice and community, but it postulates that true justice requires radical political change. The popular Church also takes coresponsibility further than the reformists. The laity participates more effectively and more significantly, both in religious ceremonies and in diocesan decision-making. Both the reformist and the popular Church use the image of the Church as the "people of God," but the popular Church is more inclined to speak of the Church as a sacrament of salvation in the world. Both the reformists and the progressives verbally support the preferential option for the poor, but the progressives are more apt to create ecclesial structures to support popular movements. The popular sectors are largely responsible for creating the ecclesial base communities and are supportive of what has been called liberation theology.[1]

Liberation theology and the pastoral practices associated with it are the most significant original contribution in the history of the Latin American Church. For the first time, Latin Americans have produced some of the most important theological works in contemporary Christianity.[2] More than any other national Church, the Brazilian Church has been responsible for translating this theology into new pastoral approaches.

In some ways, the fact that the Brazilian Church became more progressive during this period seems unusual. Both Rome and the Latin American Bishops Conference (CELAM) have been under moderate leadership concerned about the perceived excesses of the Latin American Church's involvement in politics. They have attempted to limit further progressive change in the Brazilian Church. The gradual easing of the repression after 1973 created another potential motive for decreasing Church involvement in politics. As other political channels opened up, there were pressures for the progressive sectors to get out of politics.

By the second half of 1973, a number of conditions favorable to political liberalization existed. Most important was the military's perception that high levels of repression were no longer necessary. The guerrilla Left had been decimated, there were no important popular movements, and the opposition in general had been reduced to timid criticisms. High levels of repression would only erode the regime's support in civil society and increase the friction between military hard-liners and soft-liners. The economic situation enhanced the military's confidence that the repression could be relaxed. Since 1968, gross domestic product had grown at an average of 10 percent a year, and inflation had been limited to an annual rate of about 20 percent. The high level of economic and political stability gave the regime greater flexibility and control in introducing changes.

Within this context, the regime started to promote a "slow and gradual" liberalization in 1974. This liberalization coexisted with attempts to continue key elements in the system of domination—limited popular participation, tight control over major economic decisions, a strong executive, and an inegalitarian economic model. The liberalization was initially more an elite attempt to secure a continuation of the most important features of the system than a fundamental alteration in the regime. It enabled the military to defuse some problems created by direct control of the state while still controlling many elements of political change.[3]

At the beginning of the liberalization, popular movements were as silent as they had ever been; so it would be fallacious to suggest (as some Church leaders have) that they had much to do with the initial decision to liberalize. Yet even though the *abertura* ("the opening") did not start as a result of popular pressures, popular movements became an important factor in the national political struggle by 1978. During the initial period (1974-78), the liberal sectors of the society benefited the most, but by 1978, popular movements were also in a period of ascension. In 1978, the first major strike in a decade occurred among auto workers in the ABC region of greater São Paulo, and the urban, working-class Cost of Living Movement grew to national proportions.[4] These movements pressured the regime into making more concessions than it otherwise would have.

Although the use of repression declined, it did not completely end, particularly with respect to the popular movements and popular Church. Yet as the electoral process became more important, even though the regime continued to limit popular movements, it made some gestures toward the popular classes. The blatant repression of the Médici years by and large gave way to more subtle attempts to control and co-opt.

Another important phase in the *abertura* began with the reform of the party system in 1979. In 1965, the government abolished the existing parties and created the National Renovative Alliance (ARENA) and the Brazilian Democratic Movement (MDB). In 1979, it dissolved these parties and established regulations for the creation of new ones. Party reform had been a fundamental demand of the opposition, but the government skillfully managed the reform to maximize divisions within the opposition. Six new parties emerged. The new government party, the Democratic Social Party (Partido Democrático Social; PDS), largely replaced ARENA. The op-

position forces split into five parties: the Party of the Brazilian Dem-
ocratic Movement (Partido do Movimento Democrático Brasileiro;
PMDB), the largest of the five; the Popular Party (Partido Popular;
PP), a relatively conservative opposition party that merged with the
PMDB in December 1982; the Brazilian Labor Party (Partido Trabalhista Brasileiro; PTB), also conservative but smaller than the
PP; the Democratic Labor Party (Partido Democrático Trabalhista;
PDT), a party with a social-democratic orientation that won the
1982 elections in the state of Rio but was otherwise generally small;
and the Workers Party (Partido dos Trabalhadores; PT), a small
party that won the support of a significant faction of the Left.

Within the popular Church, the party reform created new dilemmas. Some leaders felt that the Church should have nothing to do
with political parties; others considered the issue so important that
they felt the base communities needed to discuss it. Furthermore,
among popular Church activists there were divisions over which
party to support. Most lay leaders who actively participated in parties chose the PMDB or the PT. The PMDB, by far the largest opposition party, favored working to consolidate a democratic regime.
It covers a wide spectrum, ranging from moderate liberals to the
most important Leninist parties, which entered the PMDB because
they were convinced of the importance of forming as broad an alliance as possible to work against the military regime. The PT is more
concerned with grass-roots organizing and educating the lower
classes politically. It is less concerned about institutional politics
since it believes that unless the masses are well organized, a more
democratic system will not fundamentally alter their lot. The PT
sees its project as a long-term one and is relatively unconcerned with
its short-term prospects.

In 1982, during a worsening economic crisis, the most competitive elections since the coup took place. The strengthening of political parties caused some Church leaders to favor less involvement in
politics. After 1983, as the economic crisis became severe, the military government, which had successfully managed earlier phases of
the liberalization, finally lost part of its legitimacy and credibility,
leading to the return to democracy in March 1985.

In Chapter 1, I argued that it is important to analyze both the effect of broader social and political changes on the Church and the
contribution of the Church to these changes. Part III examines both
of these problems. The political liberalization had a major impact
on the Church and on Church-state relations, just as the evolution

of the military regime between 1964 and 1973 did. Political liberalization pushed the Church toward a more cautious, yet in many ways more dynamic, conception of its mission and its relationship to politics. The relaxation of the repression alleviated Church-state conflicts, let the Church focus more on evangelizing, and consequently facilitated the consolidation of new ecclesial structures, new attitudes toward popular religiosity, and a greater sense of internal harmony and cohesion. Especially after 1978, with the strengthening of the opposition parties and the efforts of the Order of Brazilian Lawyers (OAB) and the Brazilian Press Association (ABI), the Church became less involved in defending middle-class civil liberties. As it did with other opposition forces in the society, the party reform created some new tensions and dilemmas for the popular Church. The *abertura* also changed the relationship between the Church and popular movements.

In addition to examining the effect of political liberalization on the Church, in Part III I consider how the Church contributed to the pressures that led to the *abertura*. I discuss three principal contributions. First, grass-roots ecclesial organizations helped reinvigorate popular movements. Though it would be a mistake to see the initial relaxation of repression as a result of popular pressures, by 1978 the popular movements were an important factor in politics, in part because of Catholic organizations. Second, the Church helped bring together opposition forces during the most repressive years, providing these forces with legitimacy and protection. Finally, along with the opposition political parties, the Church was an important defender of human rights and a source of alternative conceptions of development. The impact of this role as a moral force is indirect and immeasurable, but any institution that plays an important role in shaping and expressing the moral consensus of a society influences other actors. This is not to say that the Church was responsible for political liberalization, but within the context of a military divided over liberalization and a civil society anxious for it, the Church's capacity to empower civil society, its moral legitimacy, and its sharp criticisms of abuses of human rights were significant.

The Consolidation of Progressive Positions in the CNBB

During the second half of the 1970's and the early 1980's, the bishops as a collective body developed an understanding of the Church's mission that contrasted sharply with models of the Church prevalent earlier in the century. The neo-Christendom Church had relied on alliances with the state and dominant sectors; during the 1970's episcopal documents criticized reliance "on the influence of certain groups to further some ecclesiastic objectives. . . . In a Church of this kind, it would be hard to recognize the profile of Christ, who freed because He was completely free."[5]

In earlier years the Church had perceived secularization as a great enemy; the contemporary Church accepts secularization and tries to be a sign of salvation in secular society. It repudiates ecclesial efforts to control society. The Church does not see itself as "a transcendent arbitrator, above the plane of human history with its temporal problems. The Church does not accept the image of a 'helicopter-Church,' hovering above human affairs, dictating from above the path to follow. . . . Whether we like it or not, the era of the Christian republic, in which the spiritual power was the supreme arbiter and the agent of cultural and religious unity, is past."[6] The bishops reject Dom Leme's traditional strategy of building alliances to ensure the Church's power. "The Church should not be one power among others. It should not trust in power or attempt to use the same means as the powerful."[7]

The Church believes it should continue to be an institution that inspires morality and evaluates all phases of social life, including politics. The Church can give up some of its old functions (in elite education and social welfare, for example) because in doing so it becomes free to perform a new role. One CNBB document affirmed, "When it is poor and less compromised with certain social structures, the Church becomes free to assume with greater vigor its critical and prophetic mission of denouncing injustice and promoting the solidarity and legitimate hopes of people."[8]

The perception of the relationship between salvation and the secular society also changed profoundly. For the popular Church, salvation is complete only in the after-life, but it must begin on earth with the effort to construct better human relations and societies. In 1980, at the CNBB's Eighteenth General Assembly, the bishops stated, "The evangelical goal to realize, the prefiguration on earth of the Kingdom of God, is the construction of a fraternal society, based on justice and love."[9] Though insisting on the Church's need to respect the autonomy of the temporal and political order, all major episcopal documents of recent years have emphasized that "the Church knows that the Kingdom begins here. We must work so that the people can live in a more human situation."[10] In this view, the Church's mission would be incomplete "if it did not take into consideration the real situation of people in their personal and social life because the person is the first and fundamental concern of the Church."[11]

Constructing this earthly ideal, as well as following Christ's message, involves a special concern for the poor. The preferential option for the poor, the outstanding theme that emerged at the Puebla meeting of the Latin American Bishops Conference in 1979, originated in the grass roots of the Brazilian Church (especially organizations like Catholic Youth Workers), was adopted by regional bishops' groups during the late 1960's, and, by the mid-1970's, had become a recurring theme in CNBB documents. For example, "God sent His son, Jesus, to be the hope and defense of the weak, the powerless, the oppressed. . . . The Church should follow Christ's example. It cannot exclude anybody and should offer the means of salvation it received from Christ to all, powerful and weak. But its option and its preferred people must be the weak and oppressed."[12]

Along with other changes in the Church's self-conception came a new emphasis on its prophetic mission in furthering the cause of justice. "The Church would fail in the historic use of its prophetic mission if it did not point out sin, the social inequity of our times, manifest in the exploitation of people that divides humanity into oppressed and oppressors; if it failed to denounce the abuses of authorities who place themselves above good and evil; if it did not cry out against the egotism of nations and people who sacrifice other countries and people for their own self-interest."[13]

It was not until 1976 that the bishops issued statements that went beyond the 1973 documents on human rights. But in the meantime, CNBB leaders became active in the campaign to defend human rights, and the Church in the Amazon, the Northeast, and São Paulo, as well as in some isolated dioceses, continued their human rights work. The most publicized work during this period came from the bishops of the state of São Paulo, where Dom Paulo Arns had become the outstanding leader. The 1975 document of the São Paulo bishops, "Don't Oppress Your Brother," appeared right after a repressive wave and was one of the strongest, most important episcopal statements against torture.

In the name of the Gospel of Jesus Christ, we, the bishops of the Church of this state of São Paulo, raise our voice against the wave of violence that manifests itself in assassinations, kidnappings, beatings. . . . We are witnessing flagrant disrespect for the human being, characterized by arbitrary imprisonments that usually involve kidnappings; the recrudescence of torture, including several deaths; and public and private threats, often stemming from the authorities.[14]

In response to the assassinations of two priests in the Amazon and the kidnapping and torturing of the bishop of Nova Iguaçu, Dom Adriano Hypólito, the CNBB's Central Commission issued a statement in November 1976 condemning the repression against the Church, the generalized violence, the injustices suffered by the popular classes, the impunity accorded right-wing violence, inequities in land distribution, the Indians' situation, and the national security doctrine. This document, "Pastoral Communication to the People of God," marked a new phase in the CNBB's development characterized by more incisive criticisms of authoritarianism. Months later, in March 1977, at the Fifteenth General Assembly of the CNBB, the bishops by a vote of 210 to 3 approved another major document, "Christian Requirements for the Political Order." Developing themes already present in the "Pastoral Communication," "Christian Requirements" insisted on the state's responsibility to defend human rights and promote the common good; sharply criticized the decision-making process, which excluded the majority of the population and led to mass marginalization; emphasized the importance of participation and democratic freedoms; and attacked the national security doctrine, which was the foundation of the military regime. It was the first time the bishops as a collective body had approved such a progressive document.

Documents written in subsequent years have followed the same line of analysis, in many cases going even further. Especially impressive was the degree of unanimity on progressive positions, beginning with the 1977 General Assembly and lasting until 1983. The most important progressive documents approved by the general assemblies, "Subsidies for Puebla" (1978), "The Church and Land Problems" (1980), and "Urban Land and Pastoral Action" (1982), passed with only one or two opposing votes.

Although directed toward different questions, these statements and other episcopal documents contain a fundamentally coherent vision of the Church and its relationship to politics. Based on the ecclesial emphasis on the common good and respect for the dignity of all people, the bishops have insisted on the importance of including everyone in the benefits of development. They are highly critical of development processes that exclude the masses. In contrast to progressive documents of the pre-1964 period, these statements reveal a recognition that conventional development does not necessarily resolve the basic problems of the majority of the population. The years of authoritarian rule and inegalitiarian development created an acute awareness that some paths to economic growth could exacerbate marginalization. For example, "The Church and Land Problems" argued that the problems of peasants and small farmers partly result from the dramatic expansion of agribusiness; although this expansion resulted in high growth rates, it also caused serious problems for a significant portion of the population. "Elements for a Social Policy" (1979) criticized development in which "the wealthy get wealthier at the expense of the poor, who are increasingly poorer."[15]

The bishops criticized authoritarianism, repression, and the national security doctrine. For example,

The security and the well-being of a nation are incompatible with the permanent insecurity of its people. This insecurity is created by arbitrary repressive measures with no possibility of self-defense, by compulsory internments, by unexplained disappearances, by degrading trials and legal proceedings, by acts of violence practiced by the clandestine terrorist groups, and by frequent and virtually absolute impunity granted these groups.[16]

The bishops have repeatedly emphasized democracy, human rights, and participation as ideals that just political systems must realize. "Democracy is one of the absolute requisites for freedom and for human dignity, as defended by Christian ethics."[17] The emphasis on participation has gone beyond a narrow juridical view to the right of all people to have real opportunities to participate. The bishops believe that the popular classes can contribute to resolving social problems if they are granted the right to participate. All major episcopal documents make clear that the Church is not satisfied with elitist, nonparticipatory, inegalitarian development models, even when they are legitimated by the electoral process and formally respect conventional civil liberties. The bishops see civil liberties as indispensable to a good political system, but not sufficient.[18] For this reason, they remained critical of the military regime for attempting to create an elitist system, largely closed to popular participation, even when this system attempted to legitimate itself through the electoral process in the early 1980's.

Another element in the bishops' thinking on politics is that the marginalized sectors of the population should receive special consideration. In its 1981 reflection on the political situation, the CNBB's Permanent Council stated that "no reforms will consolidate stable forms of democracy if they do not take into consideration the need to create room so that the workers and the unemployed, the *posseiros* expelled from their land and accused of subversion, the Indians, the malnourished, the masses who lack education, access to health facilities, decent housing, stable jobs, adequate wages, are finally recognized as citizens with full rights."[19]

The bishops' vision of the good society would require profound restructuring of the current order. Drawing on the view that God gave the earth and its resources to humanity as a collective resource, "The Church and Land Problems" argues that all people have a right to the land and that land should be used for the common good rather than as a speculative investment. It states that *posseiros* should have a right to otherwise idle land and calls for major reform of the society's agrarian structures. "The problems of rural and urban workers and the problems of the land can be resolved only if the mentalities and structures of our society are changed."[20] In a similar vein, the 1982 General Assembly document affirms the precedence of the poor's right to own the land they live on over the right to unlimited private property. The bishops have spoken out against police brutality against the poor,[21] and have criticized the emphasis on export agriculture, which has often exacerbated the impoverishment of the peasantry. They are aware that their vision of the just political order will not be implemented in the near future, but they have come to believe that, as the ultimate spokesmen of the Brazilian Church, they have an obligation to denounce social injustice and call for a new order.

Church-State Relations

Tensions between the Church and state remained high between 1974 and 1978. As a collective body, the bishops became more critical of the regime, and grass-roots Catholic organizations continued to clash with the state. Elements of the military gradually came to see the Church as one of the nation's principal enemies. A report by the Second Army written in 1974 declared that "the clergy are the most active of the enemies that threaten our national security. Through decidedly subversive processes, they are promoting the substitution of the political, social, and economic structures of Brazil by a new order, inspired by Marxian philosophy."[22]

One of the tensest periods in Church-state relations came in late 1976, when three spectacular incidents of repression against the Church occurred within a short time. The first incident took place in Merure, Mato Grosso, a conflict-prone region in the Amazon, in July 1976. On July 13, the government agency for dealing with the Indians, FUNAI, had set aside an area for them. On July 15, as the Indians began demarking the land, a group of sixty armed people including landowners and hired gunmen surrounded the parish house. One priest attempted to placate this group, but he was beaten. Shortly thereafter, Father Rodolfo Lunkenbein arrived with other Indians. He encouraged the armed men to take the matter to the courts, but they continued to harass both of the priests and the Indians. When the Indians attempted to intervene to protect Father Rodolfo, the landowners and gunmen opened fire. Two Indians and Lunkenbein were killed, and five other Indians were wounded. The Indians then retaliated and wounded a few of the aggressors.[23]

On September 22, 1976, five armed members of the paramilitary forces kidnapped Dom Adriano Hypólito, bishop of Nova Iguaçu, Rio de Janeiro. They bound and blindfolded the bishop and drove him to the opposite end of greater Rio, some 45 miles away, where they took off all his clothes and attempted to force alcohol down his throat. They painted him with red spray paint (the color was chosen because of his supposed sympathy for Communism), tied him, and abandoned him on a sidewalk.[24]

The third incident occurred in the town of Ribeirão Bonito, Mato Grosso, in the prelature of Dom Pedro Casaldáliga, where the level of violence and repression remained unabated (see Chapter 5). The first pastoral agents arrived in Ribeirão Bonito in 1973, and shortly thereafter a conflict arose between the Church and peasants and the police and latifundistas. In early October 1976, as the police were publicly torturing two brothers because of their involvement in efforts to organize the peasants, the police chief was assassinated in retaliation for ongoing brutality against the population. Days later, on October 5, their mother, who had had nothing to do with the assassination, was imprisoned, beaten, and tortured. The same day, the wife of one of the brothers was imprisoned and gang-raped by a group of soldiers, who also burned down their house and destroyed their crops. On October 11, 1976, because of the reports of generalized violence against the local population and the tortures of the two women, Father João Bosco Burnier and Dom Pedro stopped in Ribeirão Bonito as they were returning from a gathering of pastoral agents on the Indians' problems. The two went to the police station to complain about the imprisonments and tortures. The police were unwilling to listen and threatened to kill the priest and bishop if they made any denunciation. One of the soldiers hit Father Bosco with his rifle, then shot him in the head and killed him.[25]

These three incidents were the worst of a long series of repressive measures in the second half of 1976. In August, the governor of Mato Grosso charged that "there are two Communist plots in the country: one is in the Church, where some followers of Christ became radicalized and forgot God's word in order to preach Communism; the other is in politics."[26] In October, paramilitary forces made several threats on the life of Dom Waldir Calheiros, bishop of Volta Redonda. In November, an Italian priest working in the Amazon, Father Florentino Maboni, was tortured until he signed a confession stating that the Church was engaged in subversion. After his release, Maboni recanted the statement. When the Pastoral Land Commission (CPT) denounced the torture, the minister of justice, in an official note, accused the CPT of lying, even though Maboni had required medical treatment because of the beatings.[27] Also in November, the police in Pará interrogated Dom Estevão Cardoso, bishop of Conceição do Araguaia, and Dom Alano Pena, bishop of Marabá.

On December 13, another Italian missionary, Father Giuseppe Fontanella, was expelled for being a subversive after being imprisoned and pressured into signing a statement that Dom Estevão was a Communist.[28] On December 16, the secretary of security of the State of São Paulo, Colonel Erasmo Dias, accused Dom Tomás Balduino, bishop of Goiás Velho, of being a Communist. Dias revealed that he had systematically opened Balduino's mail and used the contents of a letter that criticized the use of torture to "prove" the accusation.[29] Within a week, other violations of the privacy of the mail were denounced by other bishops, including Dom Paulo Evaristo Arns. In December, days after Secretary of Security Dias had denounced the Church as a subversive institution, the minister of the interior threatened to expel missionaries working with the Indians. The minister stated, "The Church's position on the Indians is utopian, feudal, and backward. I do not believe in the good faith of the religious minority that claims to defend the poor. Many religious groups are acting in strange ways, supporting the subversives."[30]

After 1978, when the liberalization became more significant, Church-state relations gradually improved. Even though the CNBB was issuing its most progressive statements during this period, the intensity of state attacks upon the Church diminished. The João Figueiredo administration (1979-85) tried to create a more open regime and to avoid conflict with the Church. The reform of parties and other political institutions enabled the Church to concentrate on more specifically religious questions, reducing the arena of conflict with the state. As liberalization proceeded, the Church supported some government initiatives, especially the greater respect for basic civil liberties, the sharp decline in political imprisonments and torture, political amnesty, the party reform, and the 1982 elections for state governors, the first such elections since 1965.

Despite the general improvement in Church-state relations, conflict continued. While lauding improvements in human rights, the Church stressed the importance of a more open, participatory, egalitarian system. The August 1981 "Christian Reflection on the Political Situation," for example, praised the increase in political flexibility, but the bishops noted that the regime retained authoritarian, elitist elements. They asserted that democracy does not consist simply of preserving political freedoms, but must include the masses in the political process and the benefits of development. In the early 1980's, when the severe economic crisis set in, the bishops spoke out on behalf of the popular sectors. A July 1983 statement by the Executive of the CNBB insisted that the state deal with the crisis in a way that did not require disproportionate sacrifices by the masses. In August 1984, after the campaign for direct elections for president had been defeated earlier that year, the Permanent Council of the CNBB issued a public statement expressing concern about "the general situation of the people, especially the poorest. The serious economic crisis continues to erode wages, generate unemployment, destroy national wealth, and place an unbearable burden on the shoulders of the population. . . . Frustrated by a small political minority, the nation is transformed into a mere spectator of its own destiny."[31]

The regime conversely continued to criticize Church interventions in political and economic matters. For example, in 1980, Mobral, a government literacy agency, wrote a document that accused the base communities of acting outside of their proper sphere and charged the pastoral agents working with them of inculcating Marxist ideas.[32] Not only was this accusation far-fetched in light of the anti-Marxist biases of the great majority of the clergy, the idea that a significant part of the Brazilian popular sectors would be open to Marxism was out of the question, considering the complete absence of revolutionary conditions.

The more conservative regime leaders remained very critical of the Church. In 1980, during an auto workers' strike in Greater São Paulo supported by the Church, Jarbas Passarinho, government leader in the Senate, criticized the clergy who had "traded theology for sociology and Bible preaching for socialist indoctrination. . . . I consider the positions of the socialist clergy the greatest problem the Brazilian government faces. The socialist priests combat the government with a vigor that far exceeds that of the leaders of the opposition political parties."[33] Other government leaders accused the Church of leading the strike and of violating the limits indicated by Pope John Paul II. Minister of Social Communication Said Fahrat stated that "Some priests from São Paulo are leading the auto workers' strike, breaking canon law, and ignoring the recommendations of Pope John Paul II."[34] Even President João Figueiredo, who was generally diplomatic in his handling of Church-state relations, joined the chorus of criticisms, eliciting, in return, criticism and statements of solidarity for the São Paulo and Santo André Churches from even relatively conservative bishops like Dom Eugênio Sales and Dom Avelar Brandão.

Conflict was especially sharp in rural areas, particularly the Amazon, where there was still considerable repression against the peasants and the Church leaders working with them. The basic cause of these conflicts was that while the Church called for major agrarian reform and supported the peasants, the government continued to follow policies that encourage the expansion of agribusiness.* Gov-

---

*The regime unequivocally rejected agrarian reform. In April 1979, Delfim Netto, then minister of agriculture, argued that agrarian reform is "perfectly absurd" because it would cause a decline in agricultural productivity and, by enabling the peas-

ernment leaders continued to perceive the Amazon Church's work as subversive. In 1978, General Euclydes Figueiredo, a high-ranking officer and the brother of President Figueiredo, accused Amazon priests of being Communists who "act in insidious ways, injecting their poison."[35] In January 1979, the public prosecutor of the State of Pará denounced Dom Estevão Cardoso as the "head of the movement that encourages collective disobedience of the law, violent confrontation of the population with the authorities, and the violent struggle of the social classes."[36]

Rather than attempting to describe several of the more important Church-state conflicts of recent years, the following pages focus on the Araguaia-Tocantins region. Located in northern Goiás, southern Pará, and western Maranhão, the Araguaia-Tocantins region was the site of many conflicts beginning in the late 1960's, but the situation deteriorated in the second half of the 1970's. This exacerbation of already severe social tensions resulted from the continuation of the pattern of settling the Amazon. Large firms bought huge tracts of land and violently expelled the peasants. At the same time, the influx of peasants continued. After the CPT started to work in the region, some peasants with legal rights to the land resisted these expulsions.[37]

Despite the *abertura* in Brazil's urban centers, the repression continued in most of the Amazon. Peasant leaders remained the special targets of repression, and pastoral agents, although somewhat protected because of their connection to the Church, were the object of constant threats. In May 1980, the candidate of the opposition slate for president of the Union of Rural Workers of Conceição do Araguaia, Pará, was assassinated, and the vice-president of the CPT of Pará received death threats.[38] Between 1979 and 1981, 30 politically motivated assassinations were documented in the region.

The peasants' situation throughout the Araguaia-Tocantins region was complicated by the fact that the local judge, João Batista de Castro Neto, was notorious for his corruption and violence against the peasants. The CPT collected dozens of testimonies

---

ants to remain on their land, would eliminate the rural-urban migration that helps keep down wages, thereby adversely affecting industry. *O Estado de São Paulo*, Apr. 5, 1979. His words were echoed a year and a half later by the president of the National Institute for Agrarian Reform (INCRA, a government agency), Paulo Yokota, who stated that land redistribution is utopian. "The government is not proposing land redistribution, but rather increases in production and productivity." *Jornal do Brasil*, Aug. 31, 1980.

against Castro; the bishops in the region published a letter denouncing him; a letter from a U.S. firm offering him money and cattle in exchange for protection was published; and even a PDS politician denounced him for his corruption, frequent use of violence, systematic fraud on land titles, and widespread use of illegal methods.[39] He was finally removed in October 1981. Although this case is extreme, pastoral workers report that the courts throughout the Amazon have almost always supported the landowners, even when the peasants have a just legal claim.

Given the private and public repression and the judiciary's complicity in it, the peasants had difficulty in organizing a union to defend their rights. Consequently, the Church was the only institution capable of defending the peasants. The CPT provided legal protection for peasants and encouraged them to organize and fight for their rights. One of the CPT's most significant efforts involved obtaining land titles for peasants. A law passed in December 1976 gave *posseiros* the right to receive a title to the land they lived on if they did not own another plot and had cultivated and lived on their land for at least one year. However, almost no peasants knew about the law, the means of filing for ownership were complicated, and in most regions the judicial system supported the landowners. In 1979, the CPT began filing for legal titles on behalf of hundreds of peasant families, but the local judiciary proved unresponsive. When the peasants started to refuse to leave the land they were entitled to, local elites employed repressive tactics.

In such a conflict-ridden region, the CPT could not have worked effectively without the bishops' support. One bishop, Dom Celso Pereira de Almeida (Pôrto Nacional) was president of the Tocantins-Araguaia CPT. The other bishops, Dom Alano Pena (Marabá), Dom Patrick Hanahan (Conceição do Araguaia), and Dom Cornélio Chizzini (Tocantinópolis), actively supported its work. On August 20, 1980, Dom Celso and Dom Cornélio signed a letter denouncing the actions of local landowners, Castro Neto, and the police. "As pastors looking at the increasingly anguishing reality of our poor people, whose rights are disrespected, whose land is violently taken, whose houses are burned, whose children go hungry, we cannot remain silent. . . . We feel compelled to announce the Gospel and denounce the wave of injustice that defeats and humiliates our brothers."[40]

That same month, the secretary of security of the State of Goiás launched an extensive military operation in the northern part of the state designed to extirpate the "subversion." There were widespread imprisonments and countless cases of police and landowner brutality against the peasants. For example, on September 9, 1980, in Axixa, Goiás, a group of 20 to 30 soldiers kidnapped 25 peasants and took them to a landowner's house. The peasants' wives asked two local priests to help, and the priests, accompanied by another peasant, went to the landowner's house. The landowner threatened to kill the three of them, the police beat them, and the two priests were hauled off to army headquarters, where they were again tortured. From there they went to the local jail; but the police captain refused to imprison them because the judge's imprisonment order was illegal and they had done nothing to break the law.

During the following weeks, the CPT documented hundreds of violent expulsions of peasants from the land, in many cases accompanied by destruction of their crops and burning of their houses.[41] Entire villages were burned down. The Church was also affected by this repression. On February 6, 1981, a gunman hired by a local landowner attempted to kill a priest, but he was forcefully disarmed. On March 24, twelve heavily armed military police and local landowners invaded Centro dos Mulatos, terrorized the local population, beat the priest, and bound and gagged the priest and four nuns. On July 5, 1981, a group of fifty landowners, hired gunmen, and police invaded a Church in Santa Rita where peasant leaders were meeting. They fired weapons when the priest tried to read the Bible and told pastoral agents they should choose between leaving the region and death.

The situation came to a head between August and October 1981 in one of the major conflicts between the Church and state in those years. On August 13, thirteen peasant leaders who worked closely with the Church were walking to a meeting when a police vehicle with four heavily armed officials of the Executive Land Group of the Araguaia-Tocantins (GETAT) and two landowners notorious for their violence approached them. The two sides opened fire on each other. One of the GETAT men was killed, and four other people in the car, along with several peasants, were wounded. The police then imprisoned and tortured the thirteen peasants, burned down their houses, and accused them of ambushing them. The peasants were charged with violating the National Security Law.

That same month, the Church was involved in serious conflicts be-

tween urban squatters and the state in Belém (Pará) and São Paulo
and between peasants and the state in Ronda Alta, Rio Grande do
Sul. This series of conflicts prompted Jarbas Passarinho, senator
from Pará and the PDS head of the Senate, to attack the Church on
August 30. Passarinho, a longtime critic of the progressive Church,
charged that a significant part of the clergy were Marxist subversives attempting to undermine the capitalist order. He stated that
the Church was responsible for instigating the "ambush" in southern Pará on August 13 and the land invasions in the Araguaia-Tocantins region, São Paulo, and Ronda Alta. These invasions, he concluded, had been planned in advance and coordinated to occur at
the same time. On the same day, the head of military operations in
Ronda Alta denounced the Church along similar lines.

These denunciations triggered three reactions. First, many bishops spoke out against Passarinho and the military commander for
their intemperate remarks and supported the Church in the Amazon, São Paulo, and Ronda Alta. Second, the repression intensified.
The *Jornal do Brasil* reported that "helicopters and military planes
spend the whole day flying over vast extensions of the jungle, land-
ing wherever possible to take the peasants by surprise. They confis-
cate even the simplest guns for hunting small animals."[42] In Tocantins-Araguaia, on September 1, the police arrested two French
priests, Aristide Camio and François Gouriou, who had said a mass
on August 12 for the thirteen peasants imprisoned the following day
for violating the National Security Law. The priests were charged
with directing the peasants to ambush the police. They remained in
jail until late 1982, when they were expelled from the country.[43]

Third, a number of high-ranking government officials responded
favorably to Passarinho's speech. An official spokesperson from the
Government Palace stated that "Passarinho saw what was obvious
to everyone, the desire of a small minority to destroy the country.
These priests aren't progressives, but subversives."[44] The governor
of the state of Bahia, Antônio Carlos Magalhães, accused the clergy
of "provoking a climate of apprehension, especially in the interior of
the country. These men are not interested in serving God, but rather
the devil."[45] The vice-governor of the state of Pará, Gerson dos Santos Pérez, accused "revolutionary" priests of being responsible for
the problems in the Araguaia-Tocantins region.[46] The minister of
health, Jair Soares, stated that "there is no doubt that sectors of the

Catholic Church participated in these invasions. There is also no doubt that these invasions were coordinated."[47]

Local security forces coordinated a scheme to discredit the Church. The military police opened a chapel in the area and began holding masses against the Catholic radicals.[48] On one occasion, the military flew a North American who had been involved in contraband activities and was not even a priest from Belém to São Geraldo do Araguaia to celebrate a mass. The CNBB repeatedly denounced these masses, but the bishops' criticisms did nothing to stop the police. On October 18, the police imprisoned four nuns and imprisoned and tortured an Irish priest, Peter McCarthy, because they refused to attend one of the masses organized by the police.[49] The military also began a personal defamation campaign against one of the French priests and the widow of a peasant leader assassinated by the military in May 1980, by accusing the two of being lovers.

Although isolated clerical actions may have gone beyond what Church moderates considered acceptable, the Araguaia Church won the strong support of the national Church.[50] After November 1981, the area quieted down, but the Tocantins-Araguaia case underscored some of the limits of political liberalization. In rural regions, there was still a high level of repression against popular efforts to organize and demand their rights. The landowners, the police and military, and in most cases the judiciary remained unwilling to change the prevailing pattern of domination in rural Brazil. The federal government, even while promoting political liberalization, was unwilling to change the agricultural policies that exacerbated tensions or to force the rural elites to adhere to the spirit of the liberalization project. Rural elites were one of the main sources of the military regime's support, and it was unwilling to jeopardize that support.

The Araguaia-Tocantins case also underscored the limits on improvement of Church-state relations during the political liberalization. Liberalization eased tensions between the Church and state at the national level, but in rural areas where the Church allied itself with the peasantry and where the peasantry was still the object of ongoing repression, serious conflict continued to exist. However extreme the Araguaia-Tocantins case was, it was not unique. After 1978, Propriá, Sergipe; Goiás Velho, Goiás; Ronda Alta, Rio Grando do Sul; Juazeiro, Bahia; the interior of Pernambuco; and

João Pessoa, Paraíba, were sites of highly publicized conflicts between the state and Church. All of these conflicts arose because the
rapid modernization of the countryside or the installation of hy-
droelectric projects expelled peasants from the land and because the
Church intervened on their behalf.[51] One local government official
summarized the way some extremists perceived the solution to rural
problems: "Kill the president of the union, the representative of the
National Confederation of Rural Workers, and the priests who instigate the peasants."[52]

Limits of the Church's Political Activities

After the mid-1970's the progressive sectors in Brazil moved away
from turning the Church into a political institution. Ironically, this
move was one key to the Church's success as an institution committed to working for human rights and social justice.

In the early stages of the popular Church, some dioceses were so
involved in defending the poor that they neglected more specifically
religious concerns such as catechism and sacraments. Some of the
most politically involved lay leaders and pastoral agents felt that Bible groups were a waste of time. For some priests and nuns, this led
to an identity crisis: if the Church's mission were expressed principally through political involvement, why work within ecclesiastical
structures? The balance that later emerged between specifically religious work and politics had not yet developed.

As liberalization permitted the rebirth of political institutions, the
popular Church became critical of excessive involvement in politics.
Not only was this no longer necessary, most progressive bishops
came to believe it could threaten the Church's identity. The Church
as a whole adopted more progressive political positions, but toned
down the radical condemnations of capitalism. Pastoral agents
spent less time on political issues and more time on specifically religious issues. Bible groups, family groups, youth circles, catechism
groups multiplied, all within the context of a new vision of faith.

The emphasis on the Church's specifically religious character
started to pervade the most important theological writings. This is
not the place for a detailed treatment of the development of Brazilian theology, but, especially by the second half of the 1970's, progressive theologians were as concerned with delimiting the Church's
political involvement as with emphasizing social justice. The most

significant progressive theologians have dealt extensively with Biblical themes; the role of the laity—especially the popular classes—in the Church; the relationship between pastoral agents and the masses; and popular religion and culture.[53]

The most important progressive theologians rejected the reduction of religion to radical politics and insisted upon the fundamental primacy of the Church as an institution. Hugo Assmann was the only well-known Brazilian theologian who wrote extensively about dependency or revolution, and in Brazil he was never very influential.[54] In fact, the leading progressive theologians in Brazil are equivocal about the term "liberation theology" because it usually indicates a degree of politicization uncommon in Brazil.

The popular Church believes that the Church's mission is to work toward creating God's kingdom, even though this task cannot be completed on earth. This requires an effort to construct a just social order, with more egalitarian relations and a fundamental respect for all.[55] The popular Church believes it must contribute to this process. To the Boff brothers, who have greatly influenced the development of the popular Church, the Church "is certainly not a political institution, in the narrow sense, but it has an undeniable political impact, like all other social institutions. By virtue of being a faith, Christian faith aspires to provide unity to all human practices. It must, therefore, inspire political practice."[56]

But progressive Church leaders also believe the Church must limit its political involvement. To them the Church is fundamentally a religious institution, not a political movement or party. They recognize that the Church has no special competence to lead the process of social transformation and that, furthermore, it benefits by not doing so, for only then can it stand above political systems and exercise its function as an interpreter of God's will. The Church's function is to encourage change and participation, without assuming control of the processes of change or establishing the means of participating. It should inform praxis without dictating what that praxis should be. It should reveal the political aspects of Christ's message and encourage people to assume political responsibility, but it should not engage in political organizing.

In practice, encouraging political change while remaining a fundamentally religious institution raises some difficult issues. One of the most difficult has been elections. Most Church people agreed that priests and nuns should not run for political office, actively participate in a political party, lead a popular movement, or tell people how to vote.[57] In 1982, most bishops and Church intellectuals underscored the importance of the elections, but they also emphasized respect for individual choice. As the CNBB's Representative Commission stated in 1975, "The Church has strictly educative functions . . . to help enable citizens to exercise their democratic duty freely, conscientiously, and responsibly. The Church should not choose a political party or indicate candidates."[58] Similarly, in 1979, Dom Cândido Padim argued that even though the Church should play a major role in politics, "We must reject the temptation to form a Christian party or Catholic unions. The people must assume the responsibility for transforming the society."[59]

Although there has been a strong consensus that priests should not run for office and that the Church should not endorse certain parties or candidates, there has been no similar consensus about what the Church *should* do regarding elections. This was one of the most difficult dilemmas generated by political liberalization. Given the lengthy tradition of popular skepticism about elections and the importance of elections in encouraging political change, many dioceses felt the need to promote some kind of political education. Many published electoral pamphlets in popular language, explaining the significance of the elections and the proposals of the different parties. They saw these pamphlets as a means of enabling the Church to help with political education without imposing specific choices. The pamphlets were somewhat heterogeneous, with marked variations in how they described the parties, but all were concerned with providing criteria to select a party. The Archdiocese of São Paulo, for example, emphasized that the popular sectors should participate in a party and that that party should show an ongoing concern for their problems. The São Paulo pamphlet described the parties in a way that showed favoritism toward the PMDB, PT, and PDT and opposition to the government party. Other dioceses (Rio de Janeiro, for example) opted for election pamphlets that avoided any evaluation of the parties, and most moderate and conservative dioceses simply avoided pamphlets.[60]

The issue of limits on the Church's political activities has also been delicate with respect to the CEBs. Many people in the communities are politically active, but the CEBs themselves are communities of faith, where people come together to read the Bible, share a religious ceremony, and discuss their lives. Church intellectuals and bishops have resisted identifying the CEBs with the popular movement or with any specific political party. Frei Betto criticizes the temptation to turn CEBs into instruments of the popular movements and argues that the communities have a specifically religious rather than political function.

> The Church cannot attempt to replace political parties, unions, neighborhood associations, the mechanisms specific to the political struggle. . . . Asking the base communities to also become a union movement, a grassroots party organization, or a social center is a mistake. . . . The specificity of the base communities lies in their religious character. This is the center of their existence. The people who participate in these communities are not motivated by professional, educational, or political interests. They are there because of their faith. This faith in Jesus Christ, lived and made explicit in communion with the Church, impels the simple people to participate in the base communities.[61]

As I show in Chapter 8 in analyzing the case of Nova Iguaçu, the question of the autonomy of CEBs vis-à-vis the popular movement is not always as clear in practice as it is in theory. In Nova Iguaçu, as elsewhere, the communities are principally communities of faith, and many CEB participants are not involved in politics. However, many CEB members are concerned about the social and political dimensions of faith, and they frequently lead local struggles for urban services or for rights of workers or peasants. Furthermore, many CEB leaders have been active in the PMDB or PT. Yet Church leaders have distinguished the religious and political spheres, and the CEBs themselves are primarily oriented toward religious questions.

Another difficult issue involves the relationship between the popular movements and Church commissions such as the CPT and Workers Pastoral Commission. Again, the Church has insisted on observing the fundamentally religious character of the ecclesiastical institution and, therefore, on ensuring that these commissions do not replace unions or neighborhood associations. The commissions can help support political movements, principally by encouraging people to participate, but they should leave the primary responsibility to the unions and neighborhood associations. Even though the commissions are often involved in defending human rights, they stress their preference that unions and neighborhood associations do the political organizing and make the decisions regarding the popular struggle. The CPT states, "We cannot substitute ourselves for the organs that should defend rural workers. . . . The commission cannot inhibit popular initiatives, nor can it become an organ for dealing with the organizations or people involved in conflicts. It cannot be confused with a movement that competes with other Church activities and initiatives. The commission is an indirect and complementary service."[62]

Again, however, the distinction between the pastoral commissions and the popular movements is not always clear in practice. Earlier in this chapter I documented this point with respect to the CPT's role in defending peasants in the Amazon; similar examples could be multiplied. Nevertheless, the commissions are attempting to define their own function in such a way that they are not the principal means of political struggle.

This effort to define limits to the Church's political activity has been an important factor in the development of the popular Church. By developing a clear conception of the limits on its political involvement, the popular Church strengthened its position within the Brazilian and the international Church until 1982.

The likely consequences of what the moderate sectors perceive as excessive Church involvement in politics can be seen by comparing the fates of the progressive sectors in Brazil, Chile, and Argentina. The two strongest movements of radical priests in Latin America took place in the latter two countries. In Argentina the Movement of Priests for the Third World began in 1968 during a period of military rule. It gradually became more radical, more identified with the Peronist Left, and more critical of the hierarchy, but it was wiped out by the repression in the mid-1970's. The Christians for Socialism movement in Chile began in 1971 when Salvador Allende was president and virtually died out in 1973, the victim of the coup and of ecclesiastical discipline.[63]

Four features distinguished these movements from the progressive sectors in Brazil. First, they were organized as movements with a clear leadership structure and defined objectives. Second, part of their purpose was criticizing the institutional Church. They ultimately formed a parallel magisterium, a clerical movement that in practice challenged the bishops' authority. The Brazilian Catholic Left of the early 1960's took a similar path, but no clerical groups ever organized for the purpose of criticizing the hierarchy. This choice made Christians for Socialism and the Movement of Priests for the Third World highly vulnerable to attack by state security agencies and by the institutional Church. In theological terms, they were out of communion with the bishops. It is not surprising that the hierarchy, far from protecting them when the repression fell, as generally happened in Brazil, helped discipline them.

Third, they took definite political stances and saw part of their function as supporting revolution. Both movements, like the Catholic Left in Brazil after 1962, believed that the essence of faith was work toward political transformation. Christians for Socialism explicitly advocated socialism and, in most cases, supported the Movement of the Revolutionary Left, a splinter party to the left of the Allende government. Similarly, by the early 1970's, the Movement of Priests for the Third World became closely linked to the left wing of the Peronist movement and, during the 1973-76 period, became identified as a socialist organization.[64]

Both Christians for Socialism and the Movement of Priests for the Third World perceived socialism as the necessary option for Christians, though neither movement had a very sophisticated conception of socialism.[65] By contrast, even though many leading Brazilian theologians and bishops are socialists, none have affirmed that a Christian must be a socialist. They are more critical of socialism and feel that even though faith dictates a special concern for the poor, it does not dictate the means to arrive at a given political system.[66] They also recognize that faith does not dictate the choice of a political party.

Finally, both the Argentine and the Chilean movements were more prone to simplistic radical social analysis, which further distanced them from the hierarchy.[67] For example, the Movement of Priests for the Third World wrote in 1972 that the Argentine capitalist system was in crisis, that the country was in a potentially revolutionary situation, and that the "people" were leading the struggle for change.[68] None of these affirmations realistically analyzed the political situation.

This close identification between faith and a specific political option opened these movements to attack by the hierarchy, especially in Chile, where this identification was particularly strong. Even before the apogee of tensions between Christians for Socialism and the Chilean hierarchy, the moderate cardinal of Santiago, Raúl Silva Hernández, wrote that the movement "is completely lacking in references to the Bible and especially to the Church. . . . I believe your actions are destructive of the Church."[69] In April 1973, months before the coup, the bishops proscribed clerical participation in Christians for Socialism because of the movement's unwillingness to accept the authority of the Church and its identification of faith with socialism. The Christians for Socialism movement "takes positions so clearly and decidedly political that it is indistinguishable from political parties or similar currents of opinion and activity. . . . We see an obsessive and exaggerated emphasis on the sociopolitical realm and a strong tendency to reduce the whole dynamism of the Church to this one dimension."[70] Even ex-participants have agreed that members of Christians for Socialism "were impatient, eagerly seeking radical solutions. They sometimes made hasty judgments, issued unfair denunciations, and fell into errors of interpretation."[71]

The tensions between the radical clergy and hierarchy in Chile were magnified by the level of social polarization during the Allende period, but the politicization of faith in Christians for Socialism would have created tensions in any political context. Since the late 1950's, the Chilean hierarchy has been one of the most progressive in Latin America, but the explicit politicization of the Church that occurred in Christians for Socialism led the hierarchy to feel that the Church's religious identity and ability to appeal to different segments of the society were being threatened.

Cohesion and Conflict in the Church

One of the notable characteristics of the 1974-82 period was that the Church experienced far less internal conflict than during the 1964-70 period. The greater internal cohesion of the more recent period was, in large part, a function of the decreasing influence of the Catholic Right, some toning down of the most radical statements, and a concerted effort by the progressives to work within the institution.

The tensions within the Church were never worse than during the 1964-70 period. On the one hand, the Catholic Right continued to engage in polemics with the progressives. Right-wing Catholic intellectuals like Gustavo Corção frequently criticized progressive Catholics, with Dom Helder Câmara being a special object of attack. In isolated cases, conservative bishops issued polemical public statements criticizing the progressives. In 1968, during the CNBB General Assembly, seventeen bishops sent a letter to President Arthur Costa e Silva publicly stating their disagreement with the progressive bishops and affirming their support for the regime.

On the other hand, despite the CNBB's conservative orientation, progressive pastoral activities at the grass roots sprang up all over the country. In the Amazon and the Northeast, as well as isolated dioceses elsewhere, the bishops supported these progressive movements. In many places, however, there were tensions between progressive priests and the hierarchy. Symptomatic of these tensions were several important letters written between 1967 and 1970 by groups of progressive priests criticizing the hierarchy. The most publicized of these letters was signed by 264 priests from Rio, São Paulo, and Belo Horizonte on October 24, 1967. The letter denounced living conditions among the masses and sharply criticized the institutional Church. "The Church, in its practices, accepts the brutal exploitation of the population. It relies on the contributions of the wealthy, the favors of politicians and the government, and it loses its freedom. It is impossible to hide the exploitation of some popular devotions. . . . We wonder if this doesn't justify the accusation that religion is the opiate of the people."[72]

The dynamism at the grass roots, however, was not sufficient to push the Church into positions more critical of the regime. Equally important, the Church's ability to act cohesively was being undermined. In 1969, the Central Commission of the CNBB expressed concern over the "feeling of pervasive disunity. There is an increasing ill-will, which goes beyond simple mistrust. This feeling affects all levels of the people of God: bishops, clergy, religious, laity."[73]

One of the most important factors in reducing tensions after 1970 was the decline of the Catholic Integralists. In the early 1970's, Tradition, Family, and Property (TFP), the most virulent expression of the Catholic Right, experienced the same fate the Catholic Left had earlier: being marginalized because the bishops felt its presence and actions undermined the Church's cohesion. Dom Eugênio Sales, a key figure in the sanctions against Catholic University Youth and a bishop known for his close relations with the regime, criticized the movement in 1970, and Dom Ivo Lorscheiter, president of the CNBB, castigated it in 1971. In February 1972, in the statement "Unity and Plurality in the Church," the CNBB condemned the actions of TFP and other right-wing groups,[74] and at the 1973 General Assembly of the CNBB, the bishops stated that TFP destroyed ecclesiastical unity.[75] The demise of the Catholic Right was also a result of the retirement of the bishops who actively supported this ultra-conservative conception of Catholicism. The last two, Dom

Geraldo Sigaud de Proença (Diamantina, Minas Gerais) and Dom Antônio de Castro Mayer (Campos, Rio de Janeiro) retired in 1980 and 1981.

The tensions between the progressive base and the hierarchy attenuated as the popular Church matured. After the flurry of critical, contentious letters in the 1967-70 period, progressive priests directed their efforts toward grass-roots work and ceased criticizing the hierarchy and the institutional Church. In this regard, the Church progressives may have benefited not only from the support of a number of bishops, but also, paradoxically, from the timing of the repression. Whereas in Chile and Argentina political conditions allowed priests' movements to be visible and vocal, in Brazil the clergy faced enough repression by 1968 that it needed to rely on, rather than criticize, the bishops.

The progressive bishops also worked within the institution to transform it rather than forming a movement critical of the hierarchy. A group of progressive bishops began to meet regularly in 1967 and played a central role in the Church's development. They were responsible for several major documents ("Marginalization of a People," "I Heard the Cry of My People," and "Y Juca-Pirama. The Indians: A People Doomed to Die") and played an important role in creating the Indian Missionary Council (CIMI), the CPT, and the Workers Pastoral Commission. Yet these bishops never issued a document critical of the CNBB or even of the conservative and reactionary bishops. They saw their function as exchanging ideas, providing support, and occasionally writing statements about the Church and pastoral action. They also made a conscious choice to include as many bishops as possible so as to reduce the possibility of being seen as a splinter group. The group expanded from about fifteen in 1967 to about sixty in the 1980's and continued to play an important role in the development of the Church.[76]

This less confrontive strategy helped the Brazilian Church restore internal harmony by the late 1970's. Although it remained a highly heterogeneous institution, the level of internal conflict diminished considerably after the late 1960's. Beginning with "Christian Requirements for the Political Order" in 1977, the bishops developed an extraordinary degree of internal cohesion on episcopal documents, and CNBB leaders have underscored this fact.[77]

Even the conservatives supported most of the CNBB's platform. Right after the Puebla conference in 1979, Dom Vicente Scherer, archbishop of Pôrto Alegre and an outstanding spokesperson for the conservatives, stated that liberation theology has many positive elements and is justified when it does not reduce religion to political or material questions. Dom Vicente argued that the press has distorted liberation theology and the pope's positions and that the Church should be concerned with the material condition of the people. He unequivocally stated his support for the preferential option for the poor. "We have commitments and obligations toward all, rich and poor alike. But the poor have the right to preferential treatment." He also stated that the government should do more to help the poor.[78] These opinions could as easily have come from a progressive theologian as from a leading spokesperson for the conservative faction.

Equally significant, conflict between the grass roots and the hierarchy became unusual. One of the rare cases of serious tensions between base communities and the bishop occurred in Rio de Janeiro, where Archbishop Eugênio Sales took a series of measures that debilitated an extensive community movement in the poor western zone of the city. The most significant cleavages, however, are horizontal—bishops, pastoral agents, and lay groups with competing conceptions of faith—rather than vertical (base versus hierarchy).

Perhaps more than any other characteristic, this harmony between the base and the hierarchy has made the Brazilian Church unique in Latin America. Because the progressives avoided sectarianism, they were not cut off from the rest of the institution. At times, they had to accept the limits the institution imposed; yet opting for ecclesiastical obedience and for slower change enabled the progressives to win increasing influence within the Church. Whereas the more political choices of Christians for Socialism received greater short-term publicity, the patience of the popular sectors in Brazil—in part imposed by the repression—gave them a greater capacity to transform the national Church.

The importance of good relations between the base and the hierarchy can be seen by comparison to other situations. In Chapter 4 I showed how the Catholic Left of the early 1960's was marginalized, and earlier in this chapter I indicated how the conflict between radical priests' movements and the hierarchy in Chile and Argentina led to the destruction of the former. In revolutionary situations in Central America, the Catholic base is an important political actor, but the Church lacks cohesion because of the tensions between the base and the hierarchy. This makes the base vulnerable to the same ecclesiastical sanctions that have occurred elsewhere and ultimately makes the Church's role in Nicaragua and El Salvador unstable and ambiguous.

Changing Attitudes Toward Popular Catholicism

One of the most important elements in the development of the popular Church was a new attitude toward popular Catholicism. The efforts to respect popular religion created a more fertile dialogue between the Church and the masses. When the Church espoused a politicized, secularized faith, distant from traditional Catholicism, the people often rejected it, but its later approach, less political and more supportive of the deep sense of popular devotion, enabled the Brazilian Church to enhance its effectiveness in working with the masses.

Popular Catholicism is a set of widespread traditional religious practices and beliefs that emphasize the devotional elements of faith, such as paying tributes to the saints; asking for favors and paying thanks through material means; using private symbols, devotions, and extra-official rites. The sacramental elements of faith controlled by the institutional Church are de-emphasized. These popular religious practices are found outside of and often in opposition to the institutional Church. The relations between the individual and God (or a saint) are direct rather than mediated by the clergy; in this sense, popular Catholicism is a somewhat private faith. These popular practices have generally been associated with passive, fatalistic political views and, as a result, have often been seen as alienated.[79]

To appreciate the importance of the re-evaluation of popular Catholicism, it is necessary to understand some of the failures of the popular Church in its early phases. The Second Vatican Council so strongly emphasized reform that there was an initial tendency to reject traditional popular Catholicism. This rejection was nothing new, but the Second Vatican Council imparted a sense of urgency that frequently intensified these critical attitudes. In many progressive dioceses, the clergy removed traditional images from the churches and discourged traditional practices such as processions. They viewed these practices as alienated expressions of a traditional faith that had to be eradicated before a politically liberating faith could be cultivated.[80]

Because of this, the Church had trouble expressing its message in ways accessible to the popular sectors. The masses found the new evangelization difficult to understand because the old symbols and images were not part of it and its language was sometimes inaccessible. The Church failed to capitalize on the rich popular tradition of involvement in religious customs. Progressive priests often failed to respect popular religiosity. One priest who played a major role in stimulating more positive attitudes toward popular religiosity wrote in 1969 that "the renovative Church seems incapable of producing popular books or images that effectively express the current renovation. Books of devotion and images become symbols of backwardness and obscurantism. We no longer know how to evangelize through images. The current religious symbols, images of saints, gestures, and sacraments no longer have that transparent capacity to reveal the true God."[81]

The politicization of the religious message reinforced the tensions created by the negative attitude toward popular religion. Most Catholics were not interested in a politicized, secularized faith and rejected what they perceived as political efforts not linked to their faith.* As one priest stated, "I have frequently seen the popular sectors reject a political discourse by a priest. In these cases, the political discourse is unconnected to the religious discourse, at times even violently replacing a religious discourse. The population rejects the message because it does not see the connection between this discourse and its faith."[82]

Even though most pastoral agents were critical toward popular religiosity, as early as the mid-1960's some progressive priests were reflecting about the need to value some aspects of popular religious

---

*The notion of a "secularized" faith refers to religious beliefs and practices that strive to be part of contemporary urban society. Beginning with German Lutheran Dietrich Bonhoeffer, and in Catholic theology with figures like Friedrich Gogarten, Western theology made secularization a leading issue. One of my main points in this section is that the popular Church in Latin America has rejected more secularized faith, but, in contrast to Europe, where only conservatives have rejected the more secularized beliefs, has done so in a politically progressive way. In fact, one of the primary criticisms Latin American theologians direct at progressive European theologians is that their concern with secularization is not very relevant to the Third World, where the masses still have a deep traditional religiosity. This argument is developed at length by Gutiérrez in *Força Histórica*, pp. 61-74, 86-92, 129-34, 243-328.

practices. Like many other innovations, these efforts were initiated by pastoral agents working at the grass roots,[83] were incorporated into theological discussions, and eventually became a matter of concern to the bishops. The most renowned figure in the early efforts to systematize the new reflections on popular religiosity was Joseph Comblin, a Belgian priest and theologian working in Recife. Comblin was convinced that popular religious practices had deficiencies.[84] But he and other pastoral agents who were re-evaluating popular religion also felt that the Church must respect popular practices. The Church could not simply attack popular religion, as was occurring in some dioceses. "It is clear that we should not brutally destroy traditional religion. We should establish a fraternal dialogue between the catechist and the catechizer."[85] For Comblin, popular religion was "a sign of autonomy of a people who no longer accept a prefabricated and imported religion. Therefore it is a sign of popular emancipation. . . . For the first time, the popular classes have a religion not controlled by the upper classes. . . . The popular religions are a sign of religious democratization."[86]

In an important article written in 1968, Comblin argued that there is no pure Catholicism, thereby challenging attitudes that saw anything outside the official teachings as superstition, ignorance, or even heresy. For Comblin, there was no clear hierarchy of truth between official and popular Catholicism. The principal difference is that the clergy imagines its Catholicism is "pure" and the popular classes are unconcerned with orthodoxy.[87]

In the next several years, more people reflected on popular culture and popular religion. In 1968, another Belgian priest-theologian who played a major role in the development of the popular Church, Eduardo Hoornaert, wrote the first of several influential studies that stressed an appreciation for some aspects of popular religion.[88] Others soon followed suit.[89]

This discussion, still embryonic in 1968, received an impetus from the Medellín conference. Though critical of some aspects of popular religion, the Latin American bishops nonetheless recognized in popular Catholicism "an enormous reserve of authentically Christian virtues, especially in the line of charity."[90] They also urged that the phenomenon be studied throughout the continent and devoted some of CELAM's resources to doing so.

Despite the increasing concern about popular religiosity, the political situation led many progressive dioceses into secularized, politicized conceptions of faith until around 1974, when the combination of the failures of this approach and the political liberalization caused the Church to rethink its own role and its practices regarding popular religiosity. Most dioceses began to understand that the politicized approach to religion was alienating to the laity and unnecessary. There were more effective ways of communicating religion's liberating message. Pastoral agents came to feel that religion did not have to be dry, intellectualized, or secularized to be a liberating force. Incorporating popular festivals and traditional devotions could generate an even stronger liberating thrust. Rather than attack popular religion, the Church had to build upon it. The re-evaluation of the problem was general, though particularly pronounced in the progressive dioceses. A number of voices were critical of the "phase of liturgic pureness of the European renovation," with its attack on popular religion, and insisted that popular religion is "a legitimate and original expression of the Mystery."[91]

Stimulated by innovative pastoral experiences at the base and the reflections on these experiences, the Church has generally expressed support for the positions on popular religiosity developed by liberation theologians. The final document of Puebla devoted considerable attention to the problem. It noted that popular Catholicism lacks adequate doctrinal awareness, but praised the "profound feeling of transcendence and, at the same time, of proximity to God. This feeling translates into a popular sagacity with contemplative expressions that guide the way Latin Americans experience their relationship with nature and with other people, in a sense of work and festivity, of solidarity, friendship, and kinship."[92]

The faith that has emerged in the popular Church contains many traditional elements alongside a politically progressive message. In some ways, this faith is closer to traditional popular religiosity than to the progressive, secularized world view that inspired most of the popular Church's predecessors, especially the Catholic Left of the early 1960's. Without understanding this rich combination of old and new, of traditional symbols linked to new meanings, it is impossible to comprehend the contemporary Church.

None of this means that the issue of how to deal with popular Catholicism has been definitively resolved. There are still different views about what practices are acceptable, and there is a gap between the Church's discourse and its pastoral practices. Yet one of the popular Church's most important successes has been in building upon the strong sense of religiosity. In doing so, the popular Church has appropriated many symbols and customs traditionally associated with "alienated" religious practices and has given these symbols a new meaning. Processions, long associated with traditional and politically conservative Catholic practices, have taken hold in many of the country's most progressive dioceses. These processions mobilize large numbers of people and present a curious mixture of old and new symbols, with new meanings attached to old symbols. For example, in Volta Redonda, Rio de Janeiro, 25,000 people (the city's population is 193,000) participated in the Easter procession of 1982. Many participants carried traditional symbols of the Cross, the Virgin, or saints; others carried banners demanding better wages, living conditions, and employment security; still others crossed the two symbolic worlds with banners hailing Jesus as "King of the Poor." The participants occasionally exchanged banners, illustrating the extraordinary crossing of symbolic worlds that has become common in the popular Church.

The Consolidation of New Ecclesial Structures

The late 1970's and early 1980's witnessed the consolidation of several important innovations in Church structures. These new ecclesial structures have given the popular sectors a dynamism that far exceeds their numerical representation among the bishops. About 20 percent of the bishops are committed to the popular Church model; yet, partially because of dynamic grass-roots activities, between 1976 and 1982 the popular sectors shared dominance within the Brazilian Church with the reformists. Among the most important of these new structures have been the CEBs, CPT, and CIMI.

Although first created around 1963, given a formal name by the General Pastoral Plan of 1965, and legitimated by Medellín, it was not until the early 1970's that the CEBs really started to grow. They became a new form of the Church, with more popular lay leadership than ever before, within a structure created and supported by the hierarchy. They also became clearly defined as an ecclesial structure found among the popular sectors and, during the early years, were particularly prevalent in rural areas. In their short history, CEBs have become one of the most important structures in the recent history of the Catholic Church, so much so that Brazil's most famous theologian speaks of them as "reinventing the Church."[93]

Through the base communities, the Brazilian Church has developed a structure that effectively reaches the masses. Considering the weak ecclesial links to the masses during the preceding four centuries, the number of participants and level of commitment are noteworthy. In the communities, new approaches to catechism, liturgy, community building, and theology have emerged.[94] These innovations have affected the Church in several Latin American countries, especially Chile, Peru, Nicaragua, and El Salvador. In this sense, the Brazilian Church began to export its transformation to other Latin American nations. At Puebla, the Latin American bishops stated that CEBs "create better interpersonal relationships, acceptance of God's Word, reflection about life and reality in light of the Bible; in the communities, the commitment to family, work, the neighborhood, and the local community are strengthened."[95]

Although the communities are primarily devotional groups, they have also been politically significant. As the state repressed unions and neighborhood associations, CEBs became virtually the only popular organizations that allowed people to organize to discuss their daily lives, their values, and their political needs. Despite the limited political consciousness of most members, CEBs represent a relative novelty in Brazilian political culture.[96] Most prior popular organizations were closely linked to—and ultimately susceptible to control by—the state.[97] By contrast, CEBs are autonomous of the state and political parties. They were—and still are—concerned more with their own development than with creating linkages in the traditional populist style to politicians who could obtain favors for them. CEBs have emphasized popular benefits and participation above all else—sometimes to the neglect of party politics. During the repressive years, this autonomy made them more difficult to control. Enthusiasts have often exaggerated their political impact, but in a traditionally elitist society, their emphasis on participatory, egalitarian values is significant.

Despite the attention they have received, CEBs are not the only important structure in the popular Church. Another important one is the CPT, which, like the CEBs, was originally a product of pastoral agents working at the grass roots. In response to the repression and other pastoral dilemmas in the Amazon, pastoral agents started to meet in the late 1960's. In 1972, when they had sufficient episcopal support, they created the precursor to the CPT at an Amazon regional encounter. Officially established in the Amazon in 1975 in

its present form, the CPT quickly became active in many dioceses in
the Northeast and, during the rest of the decade, began to work in
other parts of the country as well. The CPT offers legal services, de-
nounces injustices, encourages the creation of rural unions, urges
pastoral renovation, and offers courses on faith and politics. Although it has set limits on its political involvement, in many parts
of the Amazon where the peasants are unable to form unions because of the repression, the CPT continues to be the most important
institution defending human rights. By the late 1970's and early
1980's, as political liberalization advanced in urban centers, the
CPT became the Church institution most involved in conflict with
the state.

Much of its fame and notoriety come from defending peasants,
but the CPT has been active in other ways. The commission played
a major role in elaborating the CNBB's 1980 statement "The
Church and Land Problems." It has also been actively involved in
producing popular publications that link the Church's social and
political positions to the Bible.[98]

CIMI, created in April 1972, was also originally a product of Amazon pastoral agents concerned with the plight of the people they
worked with. Starting from a small nucleus, these agents helped
turn the Indian question into a national issue and encouraged the
Church to assume the defense of the Indian peoples. CIMI's positive
appraisal of Indian culture and its attempts to avoid indoctrinating
the Indians represent a radical departure from most earlier work.
One document stated, "The Indians already live the Good Word in-
tensely. Therefore, we should see in them, following Saint Paul, the
active 'Unknown God.' The missionary should avoid colonialist and
domineering attitudes. Our mission is not to maintain or change,
but to respect the Indians."[99]

CIMI does not attempt to convert the Indians to Catholicism, but
rather works as a service for them, defending their legal rights and
publicizing their situation. Another major CIMI function is facilitating contact among different Indian groups and among pastoral
agents working with the Indians. In isolated cases, it has also
worked to influence government legislation related to the Indians.
CIMI believes that the integration of the Indians into Brazilian society should be gradual and harmonious, respecting their pace in
cultural adjustment. It argues that the Indians have a right to their
land, even when this means rejecting modern development projects.

Concluding Remarks

The Brazilian Church continued its rapid transformation during the 1974-82 period. Despite all the changes before 1974, it was not until this period that the Church acquired its significance as the most progressive Catholic Church in the world and as an institution with a major impact on Brazilian politics. The 1974-82 period brought little that was absolutely new compared to the 1964-73 period, when the base communities first emerged and when radical bishops issued statements supporting major social transformation, or even compared to 1959-64, when the Catholic Left made its mark on the Church, integrating, for the first time in Brazil, radical political choices and Christian faith. What characterized the 1974-82 period was a stability and maturity that earlier years lacked. Through a more cautious understanding of the relationship between politics and religion, a more developed appreciation of how to work with the popular classes and of their cultural and religious values, a more harmonious relationship between the grass roots and the hierarchy, and the consolidation of new ecclesial structures, the Church was able to act cohesively despite internal differences, to make strong statements about Brazilian society and politics, and to acquire an unprecedented importance in international Catholicism.

CHAPTER 8

The Church and the Popular Movement: Nova Iguaçu, 1974-1985

NOVA IGUAÇU is a large (about 1.5 million inhabitants), working-class city thirty kilometers north of Rio de Janeiro. The neighborhood movement in Nova Iguaçu is interesting because of its importance and dynamic growth and its strong ties to the Church. After 1974, the limited and dispersed efforts of the local population to obtain better urban services were gradually transformed into one of the best-known and best-organized movements in the state of Rio de Janeiro, and the Catholic Church played an important role in the movement. Through the bishop's legitimation, the leadership of Catholic activists, and the presence of a Catholic base that bolsters the grass roots, progressive dioceses have strengthened popular movements. The case is also highly suggestive of the way the Church's role has changed during the process of political liberalization, which began around 1974—the same year when the work that led to Nova Iguaçu's neighborhood movement began—and of the way the Church contributed to democratization. Finally, the Nova Iguaçu example illustrates some dilemmas confronting both the popular Church and the popular movements, as well as the alliances and tensions that exist between the Church and these movements.[1]

This chapter continues the analysis of grass-roots organizations and of Church–civil society relationships. The Church's political significance in Nova Iguaçu cannot be comprehended through an exclusive focus on the hierarchy and on Church-state relations. Although the bishop's support for progressive grass-roots activities has been critical, it is the grass-roots organizations rather than the bishop that have been most important in supporting the popular movements. Furthermore, it has been the Church's role in empowering civil society (especially the popular movements) rather than its negotiations with the local political elite that has been most significant.

The Socioeconomic, Political, and Ecclesial Context

Located in the Baixada Fluminense, a large lowland with a hot climate, Nova Iguaçu became one of the most important orange-producing regions in the country around the turn of the century. The orange crop declined after 1926, when diseases started to kill the trees in parts of the Baixada. The municipality's population grew from 33,396 in 1920 to 105,809 in 1940,[2] but the population was still predominantly rural. By the end of World War II, orange production had dropped dramatically.[3]

After 1945, Nova Iguaçu began a new phase. As Greater Rio grew, real estate prices pushed the popular classes into favelas or outlying peripheral areas like Nova Iguaçu.[4] From 145,649 inhabitants in 1950, the population increased to 359,364 in 1960 and to 727,140 in 1970, making Nova Iguaçu the fastest growing major city in the country. In 1950 46.60 percent of the municipality's population still resided in rural areas, but by 1980 this figure had dropped to 0.29 percent. Growth slowed during the 1970's, but the population had increased to 1,094,805 by 1980, making Nova Iguaçu the seventh largest city in the country (see the accompanying table).

Nova Iguaçu is predominantly a working-class city (generally un-

	Population of Nova Iguaçu	
Year	Population	Percentage of population in rural areas
1920	33,396	
1940	105,809	
1950	145,649	46.60%
1960	359,364	28.34
1970	727,140	0.39
1980	1,094,805	0.29

SOURCE: Instituto Brasileiro de Geografia e Estatística, *Censo*, various years.

skilled labor), with a high percentage of migrants. In 1980, 55.5 percent of the total population were migrants. Of 374,000 people in the work force, 76,000 were involved in industry; 155,000 in services; 54,000 in construction; 48,000 in commerce and 19,000 in public sector jobs.[5]

The expansion of social services lagged far behind the city's growth. In 1980, only 37.7 percent of the municipality's population had running water, and only 30.3 percent had sewers; sewage is disposed through open canals and rivers, which severely damages the local ecology and contributes to the bad health conditions. The city had only 265 doctors, 27 dentists, and 961 hospital beds, in all cases approximately one-eighth Rio's per capita level.[6] Between 1968 and 1972, the mortality rate for children in their first four years of life was 39 percent.[7] Partially because of a shortage of schools, in 1978, according to the mayor's estimate, 150,000 school-aged children were not enrolled,[8] and most schools were in poor condition and seriously deficient in supplies. The illiteracy rate for people over ten years old was 17 percent in 1980, and only 3 percent of the population had completed high school. As of 1978, only about 15 percent of the municipality's garbage was collected, leaving some 500 tons of garbage per day in open sewers and on unoccupied land. Inadequate police facilities have led to one of the highest crime rates in the country. Less than 10 percent of the municipality's roads are paved, creating major transportation problems in rainy weather. A 1980 estimate showed that if the city administration continued to pave roads at the pace of the preceding decade, it would take 250 years to pave the existing streets.[9]

The chronic shortage of social services is a result of limited local resources and of state policies that have favored productive investments and services in wealthier residential districts. Coupled with the population's inability to compensate for the lack of these services, the shortage has generated extreme hardships for most of the population.

The population of Nova Iguaçu has a tradition of battling to obtain better social services.[10] As early as 1945, there were isolated attempts to organize the population for this purpose. In 1950, the first neighborhood associations (associações de bairro) were formed. As the national and local climate of the late populist years (1958-64) stimulated a rich political debate throughout the society, the neighborhood movement expanded.* In 1960, the leaders organized the First Congress of the Commissions for Urban Improvements of the Neighborhoods of Nova Iguaçu. The congress mobilized many neighborhood associations and obtained some concessions from the city administration. The pre-coup years saw other instances of popular mobilization in the Baixada Fluminense, including an important labor movement and occasional movements among peasants and rural workers. The post-1974 neighborhood movement would draw upon this history, several leaders in the post-1974 movement had actively participated in these earlier struggles.

The coup wiped out the most important popular movements. Key leaders of the neighborhood movement were imprisoned, and the repression prevented efforts to coordinate the movement among different neighborhoods, reducing it to isolated efforts. The surviving associations and commissions articulated their demands individually, and there was little governmental sensitivity to them. The repression and the dismembering of local opposition forces made any popular organizing outside the Church almost impossible.

The years following the coup were difficult for much of the local population. The city continued to grow at a rapid pace, bringing new social tensions. Real wages declined for most workers until around 1976, and municipal services failed to keep pace with the population growth. Politically, too, things were difficult. In addition to the official repressive apparatus, the infamous Death Squad was very active in the Baixada. By 1979, it had executed some 2,000 people in Nova Iguaçu; another paramilitary organization executed 764 in the first half of 1980 alone.[11] The progressive local leaders of the Brazilian Democratic Movement (MDB), the official opposition party, were imprisoned, and by 1970, the party had entered a deep crisis. Statewide, the MDB fell into the hands of a conservative

---

*I use the term "neighborhood movement" rather than the more common "urban social movement" because it is more specific. Urban social movements encompass a wide range of middle-class movements, such as ecological movements, efforts to obtain better services from the state, and attempts to develop community resources such as athletic facilities. Some intellectuals who have studied urban social movements (Castells, Borja) have emphasized their potential for transforming society. Although there is some possibility that the demands of the middle and the popular sectors will lead them to join together to confront the state, in the Third World context it is equally likely that their interests in terms of obtaining urban services will be contradictory. Since the masses' needs differ radically from those of the middle strata, to discuss urban social movements as a whole suggests an illusory unity of goals.

group closely linked to the military regime and noted for its corruption.[12] The local branch of the government party, the National Renovative Alliance (ARENA), was conservative even in comparison to its counterparts in other major cities. It, too, was notoriously corrupt and was largely uninterested in resolving the problems confronting the population. Despite its problems, the MDB defeated ARENA in 1974 and subsequent elections.*

Meanwhile, the Church was undergoing the changes that would make it the bulwark of popular movements. The diocese of Nova Iguaçu was created in 1960 and was relatively conservative until 1966. That year, Dom Adriano Hypólito was named bishop and began to encourage the changes that have closely identified the Church with the popular classes.[13] In 1968, at the first diocesan assembly, the diocese voted to make base communities (CEBs) one of its principal priorities.[14] Coinciding with the constriction of civil society, the Church began to create community groups—Bible circles, mothers' clubs, youth groups, catechism clubs—that discussed faith and social reality. During the most repressive years, the CEBs were virtually the only popular organizations that promoted critical political perspectives. Although these communities were involved only in rudimentary political actions, such as signing petitions for urban services, their existence would prove important for the development of popular movements, facilitating more extensive organization and mobilization when the repression relaxed. Many leaders and participants in the neighborhood movement were motivated by their experiences in the CEBs.

The only attempt between 1964 and 1974 to organize the local population on a more ongoing basis was the Movement of Community Integration, created by the diocese in 1968. This movement hoped to organize Catholics to lobby for better urban services, but in 1970 the state dissolved it. The neighborhood movement was reduced to isolated efforts to obtain immediate and limited material benefits, with no articulation between neighborhoods and no attempt to link these efforts to broader issues.

*In 1974, the top MDB candidate for federal deputy had 47,929 votes compared with 22,862 for the top ARENA candidate; the top MDB candidate for state deputy had 19,917 votes, compared with 9,974 for the top ARENA candidate; and the MDB candidate for federal senator outpolled the ARENA candidate, 99,628 to 43,352. For election coverage and data, see *Correio da Lavoura*, 2299 (Nov. 16-17, 1974). In 1978, the MDB won 118,774 votes for federal senator; ARENA got 72,942. *Jornal do Brasil*, May 16, 1982.

This picture changed with the beginning of political liberalization in 1974. Political liberalization followed the same general contours in Nova Iguaçu as nationally, with a gradual easing of repression, especially after 1978. However, some features of the liberalization process in Nova Iguaçu were distinctive. The city administration and the local branch of ARENA were particularly discredited, especially by the late 1970's—partially because of the neighborhood movement. The city administration remained unresponsive to popular demands, even though the easing of the repression allowed more freedom to organize the population. The MDB was in a deep crisis that began around 1970 and lasted through 1985. In contrast to some cities, where MDB politicians supported the popular movements, the neighborhood movement remained relatively isolated, with the Church its most significant ally.

Moreover, the paramilitary Right remained active. The systematic repression of the Médici years had disappeared, but terrorism by the far Right included many incidents against the Nova Iguaçu Church and members of the neighborhood movement. The most spectacular incidents involved the kidnapping and torturing of Dom Adriano Hypólito in 1976 and the bombing of the cathedral in 1979.[15] The specter of repression conditioned the development of the neighborhood movement after 1974.

The Neighborhood Movement, 1974-1985

In the second half of the 1970's, there was an unprecedented growth of popular movements in urban areas, especially neighborhood movements.[16] The origins of the Nova Iguaçu movement date to 1974, when two young doctors committed to the poor started to work in one of Nova Iguaçu's outlying neighborhoods. Initially they attended the population almost gratuitously and offered courses on health, but they gradually became aware of the limitations of such work. Medical treatment had only palliative effects in a region with widespread malnutrition, open sewers, no garbage collection, and other health problems, and they began to consider organizing the population to change those conditions.[17]

In 1975, the diocesan branch of Caritas, an international organ of the Catholic Church for serving the poor, hired these doctors and two others to start a health program. These four were responsible for transforming the previously isolated neighborhood efforts into a coherent popular movement. Committed to working with the poor and mobilizing them, the doctors made it clear that they were not Catholics and that their contributions would be medical and political, not religious. This frankness led to good relations with Dom Adriano and the progressive clergy, including the director of Caritas, but from the beginning the conservative clergy had reservations about their work.

In November 1975, the diocese held the first health discussion, led by the four doctors. Beginning with the second meeting, in March 1976, Caritas issued reports as a means of publicizing the meetings and disseminating ideas. At the second meeting, the group set forth its fundamental orientation.

The solution of health problems depends more on the population's unity and action than on the presence of a doctor. Having a health post is important, but it does not resolve health problems. Therefore, all the forms the population has of uniting to reflect on its problems and develop its consciousness and unity are important. Actions that are purely palliative, that are not concerned with the population's *conscientização*, discourage true learning and do not resolve health problems.[18]

In this early phase, the majority of people attending the courses worked at health posts. The doctors were satisfied with these courses, but they were also interested in reaching a different public, the poor themselves. In 1976, they gave health courses in six different neighborhoods throughout the municipality, usually visiting already established groups, most of which were connected to the diocese: Bible groups, mothers' clubs, youth groups. These visits often strengthened existing organizations or led to new organizations. The doctors emphasized awareness about the causes of health problems rather than medical treatment.

Immersion in the neighborhoods represented an important step for the young movement. The kind of participants changed. Fewer people in health care but more workers attended the meetings. The discussions started to include all problems faced by the population rather than just health issues. Simultaneously, the population began to organize neighborhood associations to address these needs. From the beginning, these efforts emphasized the concrete needs of the local population rather than the more theoretical discussions characteristic of the Church's conscientization work.

In May 1977, the movement began to call itself *Amigos de Bairro* (Friends of the Neighborhood), and assumed responsibility for publishing the newspaper, previously issued by Caritas. At the eleventh health encounter, in November 1977, the movement explicitly stated its objectives. "Friends of the Neighborhood is a movement concerned with the good of all people, with a better and more dignified existence." At this same meeting, the movement expressed its goal of expanding beyond the Church and becoming a mass movement: "Friends of the Neighborhood cannot be closed, it must communicate with all people and encourage all to participate."[19]

The movement continued to expand throughout 1976 and 1977 and involved a growing number of neighborhoods. This expansion brought a need for more formal leadership structures, and at the thirteenth meeting, in March 1978, the movement voted to create a Coordinating Commission whose functions would be to:

orient the movement, attempting to encourage the groups, but without dominating them; encourage the exchange of experiences; visit the neighborhoods; do a summary of the meetings; encourage the formation of new neighborhood associations; represent the movement whenever necessary; publish a newspaper about the problems and struggles of the neighborhoods; organize a central archive that includes the experiences of all the groups, important addresses, and other information for whomever needs it; offer mini-courses.[20]

Establishing a leadership structure was an important step in expanding beyond isolated material needs to develop a mass movement with broad political horizons. Another important step in this same direction came when the health newspaper became a newspaper for the movement. The movement had entered a period of consolidation and rapid expansion.

By May 1978, the bimonthly meetings involved people from eighteen different neighborhoods. At that time, the movement adopted its definitive name, *Movimento de Amigos de Bairro* (Friends of the Neighborhood Movement; MAB). The local associations continued to be the primary instrument for organizing the neighborhoods. MAB coordinated their efforts, turning them into a cohesive project capable of pressuring the state into greater responsiveness to local needs.

In May 1978, two issues affected the movement's development. One of the most active associations took a petition with 1,500 signatures to the city administration, but the mayor refused to receive it, stating that he would accept demands only from people who had paid their property tax. The residents wrote to several city council members (*vereadores*) protesting this policy, and the movement interested the local press in the issue. These pressures from different segments of the society forced the mayor to partially retract his initial statement. On July 25, he stated his willingness to receive all petitions but declared that in allocating public resources, he would give priority to those who paid their taxes. This was MAB's first major victory in pressuring the city administration to re-evaluate its policies toward the popular sectors. Equally important, it was the first time MAB received considerable press attention and won allies among local politicians. Another serious conflict between MAB and the city administration occurred when the mayor agreed to attend a meeting with residents of one neighborhood but without advance notice sent a representative instead.[21]

To protest this cavalier treatment, MAB held an assembly on October 14, 1978, to discuss the administration's irresponsibility. Some 700 participants representing 38 neighborhoods attended; of these, 34 associations had signed a letter to the mayor protesting the municipality's failure to attend to the population's needs. The assembly began a new period in MAB's development, marked by more extensive participation and by stronger links to local politicians and the press, which increased the movement's impact.[22]

Organizational and political changes accompanied the movement's expansion and the parallel changes in the national political situation. In January 1979, MAB elected its first formal Coordinating Council, which met every week rather than every two months. The movement divided into five regional groups to attempt to ensure greater sensitivity to grass-roots needs.

Even though MAB was evolving into a mass movement, it was still almost exclusively concerned with immediate material needs. This began to change in late 1978 and early 1979 as the leadership addressed local and national issues. MAB participated in the solidarity movement with the 1979 ABC strike and with a teachers' strike in Rio, sent representatives to local demonstrations, and supported party reform, political amnesty, and local government reform.

MAB's dynamism created a new problem for a city administration accustomed to ignoring popular demands. During MAB's early phases (1975-78), the administration, headed by a notoriously conservative and corrupt branch of the government party, treated MAB leaders with disrespect. MAB participants were consistently told to meet with a city representative at a given time and place, only to arrive and find that the official was engaged elsewhere. After agreeing to hold bimonthly hearings to listen to the population's demands, the administration attempted to renege on the commitment.

MAB used the administration's unresponsiveness as a means of further delegitimating the city government. The movement publicized the government's repeated failures to meet promises, its disrespect for MAB participants, the financial scandals that surrounded the administration, and its failures to attend to the needs of the local population. Largely in response to these failings, MAB held a second major assembly on July 15, 1979. The assembly had 3,000 participants, representing 60 neighborhoods. The growing importance of the movement was visible in the publicity the assembly received and in the presence of important political figures, including one of the state's federal senators. The meeting was also successful in forcing the administration to agree to weekly meetings with representatives from different neighborhoods. MAB, by now the most important popular movement in Nova Iguaçu, had entered a new, more mature phase.

The party reform initiated in 1979 was one of the most important steps in the *abertura*. It deeply affected the entire political struggle, including the popular movements and the Church, and in this specific case, MAB. MAB's leaders had always experienced some internal divisions, but the party reform accentuated these divisions. Most MAB leaders opted for the Party of the Brazilian Democratic Movement (PMDB) or the Workers Party (PT); a few eventually joined the PDT. Among the members of the original Coordinating Council, eleven opted for the former and eight for the latter. The party issue would have been less significant if it had not paralleled other differences regarding the leadership of popular movements. Some people (mostly members of the PT) were more concerned about grass-roots discussions and ensuring that the common people led the process; others (mostly in the PMDB) emphasized creating a mass movement that would participate in the democratization process. Ironically, then, the *abertura*, which facilitated the growth of the movement, also created internal competition and division.

A demonstration at the Government Palace in Rio on June 13, 1980, with 700 participants, was the first time MAB went to the state government to demand urban improvements. This move marked an important step in MAB's visibility and ability to negotiate with the state. It meant dealing with a higher level of the state and initiated a strategy of forcing the Democratic Social Party (PDS) and the now extinct Popular Party (PP) to compete in providing services. The PDS governed Nova Iguaçu, and the PP the state of Rio. The governor of Rio, the only opposition governor in the country, was a conservative figure within the most conservative opposition party and had strong links to the federal government, but his strategy for dealing with the popular movements was less confrontational and repressive than that of the PDS administration of Nova Iguaçu.

Until December 1981, despite tensions between PT and PMDB leaders, the existence of competing conceptions helped MAB articulate a balance between grass-roots work and broader political action that made it one of the more successful neighborhood movements in the country. By late 1981, almost a hundred neighborhood associations were participating.

Despite MAB's successes, its tasks became more complicated with greater maturity. Mobilizing the local population remained difficult, given the region's security problems, the poor and (relatively) expensive transportation, and the limited time available to many people. Financial problems continued to plague the movement. The repression relaxed, but the stability of the *abertura* remained in doubt. Until the November 1982 elections, the city administration was fairly unresponsive to MAB and to popular demands; the normally cautious *Jornal do Brasil* reported that "nowhere in the state of Rio is the government party so discredited as in Nova Iguaçu."[23]

In December 1981, the movement began a period of greater internal conflict at the leadership level and some demobilization of the grass roots. The most important problem was the accentuation of internal tensions in the movement, principally stemming from partisan disputes. In December 1981, MAB held the Second Congress of Neighborhood Associations of Nova Iguaçu (the first had been held in 1960), became a federation, and held elections for a new Coordinating Council. The elections for the Coordinating Council led to sharp and unforeseen disputes. Many of the original leaders, including the four doctors, lost out. Twelve of the nineteen original members remained, but the overall composition of the Coordinating Council changed. There were tensions between the new leaders and some of those who left, and charges of manipulation were made on both sides. Never before had MAB experienced such deep internal disputes. These tensions within the movement played into the government's hands. The regime fared relatively well, until 1982, at institutionalizing an elitist system within the bounds of electoral politics, while the opposition was somewhat disarticulated. Popular movements lacked the dynamic growth that had characterized the 1974-80 period.

The 1982 elections for governor, the federal and state congresses, and local government stimulated many debates and conflicts within the movement. Officially, MAB adopted a position of autonomy vis-à-vis political parties. This meant that as a movement, MAB did not opt for any particular party, and that it was open to all individuals, regardless of party affiliation. At the same time, however, many MAB leaders recognized the importance of electing individuals more sympathetic to the movement. Approximately a dozen MAB leaders ran for office, all but one on the PMDB or the PT tickets.

The election results proved a major disappointment to the movement's leaders, most of whom had worked for the PMDB and the PT. None of the popular candidates of Nova Iguaçu were elected. Leonel Brizola won by a large plurality in Nova Iguaçu, and the PDT easily won the municipal elections. In the dispute for mayor, the election yielded the following results: PDT, 129,789; PDS, 67,484; PMDB, 66,252; PTB, 20,084; PT, 7,262.[24]

In Nova Iguaçu, a relatively conservative faction of the PDT came to power. Although less repressive and more open than past local governments, it also faced problems of corruption and responsiveness. Statewide, Brizola implemented populist practices aimed at developing popular support. Faced with the severe economic crisis, the federal government's strategy of reducing resources to opposition governors, and a PDT minority in the state parliament, Brizola had difficulties in effecting major changes. At both the municipal and state levels, the fact that the opposition had won free, competitive elections but could not introduce substantial improvements in popular living conditions created new problems for MAB. As one movement leader stated, "When the PDS was in power, everyone knew that the government was against the people. With Brizola, with the PDT, it is harder. Brizola says he is your friend, but in practice he is not much better than the PDS. But most people don't see this."[25]

Despite these new challenges and a temporary demobilization of the grass roots, MAB continued to be one of the most important popular movements in the state. In December 1983, the movement held new elections for the Coordinating Council, and the different factions once again improved their relations, beginning another phase of growth. In early 1984, the movement participated extensively in the campaign for direct elections. In November 1984, it held its largest demonstration ever, with about 4,000 people, around issues of public health. By January 1985, when Tancredo Neves was elected president, MAB represented 120 neighborhood associations in the Baixada Fluminense.

The Church and MAB

During MAB's early development, the movement was highly dependent on the Church. As the regime liberalized, the popular movements acquired more autonomy toward the Church for two principal reasons. First, as the regime opened up, the dynamics of the social process allowed the popular movements more liberty to mobilize, and there was less need to organize within the Church. The Church's politically limited organizations were unable to satisfy the more complex strategic, organizational, and financial demands of popular movements. As political organizations reactivated and challenged the Church's dominance of the popular movements, conflicting ideas emerged on how the movements should be led. The Church lagged behind in its political formulations, strengthening the tendency of other groups to assume the leadership of the most important movements. This non-Church leadership materialized in Nova Iguaçu through the role played by the four medical doctors and several persons associated with the Left.

Second, Dom Adriano and most other Church leaders consciously decided to encourage the autonomy of popular movements. They perceived this option as a means of strengthening the movements by opening them to non-Catholics. The diocese recognized its lack of competence in the political decisions that popular movements now faced. It also perceived this option as a means of reaffirming its identity as a religious institution. Even though MAB sprang from work supported by Caritas, Dom Adriano wholly supported MAB's autonomy vis-à-vis the Church.

The movement needed to be autonomous with respect to the Church to be able to include people from other religions or people who do not practice any religion. A political movement should not go through the Church because it has to be broader than the Church. It is also advantageous for pastoral work that the movement be autonomous. That way, pastoral work can concentrate on the religious sphere, on the Bible Circles, religious ceremonies, base communities. The communities can continue focusing on the Bible and the social concerns that emerge from their faith.[26]

Even though more Catholic activists assumed leadership positions, MAB's dependence on the Church diminished as it focused more on popular mobilization and less on medical work. As the movement became better known, it relied less on support from local parishes. Despite continued financial difficulties, it became more autonomous in this sphere after Caritas decided in 1978 to stop supporting the four doctors on the grounds that in the new political situation its limited financial resources should support work with the Catholic population.

The rank and file, too, gradually became less Catholic. As MAB became a mass movement and did less medical work, many CEB participants who had attended the health seminars dropped out. Members of other religious groups and those who did not actively participate in any Church joined the movement, as did leaders in the region's popular struggles, further diversifying the movement.

Nevertheless, the autonomy of the popular movements with respect to the Church should not be overstated. In Nova Iguaçu, as in many parts of the country, a strong connection between the popular movements and the Church continues to exist. It would be more accurate to say that the Church and the movement have sought a relationship of autonomy than to assert that this autonomy exists in an absolute form.[27] The institutional Church has continued to play an important role in MAB's development through several means.

First, until November 1982 it helped protect the movement from repression. At critical periods, it was still the diocese that could speak out against authoritarianism. When, for example, urban squatters were involved in a difficult struggle for land in 1981 and 1982, the Church defended them. MAB lacked the resources to handle such a difficult case.

Second, many neighborhood associations meet in local churches, which not only resolves their space problem but also serves as a sign of ecclesial support. Until October 1985, when MAB purchased its own headquarters, the diocese provided a space for MAB's office, where the Coordinating Council met weekly. Since one of MAB's outstanding problems has been a lack of funds to publicize meetings, distribute the newspaper, and underwrite travel to meetings or to support neighborhood associations in their struggles, the fact that the movement did not have to rent an office freed resources for other uses. The use of a diocesan building was also a source of legitimation and a means of avoiding repression.

Third, the diocese provides limited financial support, usually indirectly. It has helped finance the health program, loaned MAB a mimeograph machine, does not charge the movement for the use of electricity or water, and occasionally gives MAB small financial donations to support its work to promote social justice.

Finally, the diocese provides a moral legitimacy that encourages Catholics to participate. The Church enjoys greater legitimacy than any other institution in Nova Iguaçu. Much of the population views the Church as the only reliable institution and the only institution willing to set aside its own self-interest. The clergy are usually the only educated people who have ongoing contact with the population and hence have unparalleled credibility. Consequently, the support of the majority of clergy has been very helpful to the movement.

The key to the close connection between MAB and the diocese has been Dom Adriano. From the beginning, he fully supported MAB. In an interview, he stated, "We have an evangelical commitment to make a preferential option for the poor. So how are we going to realize this option? It's not enough to just talk and pray. As a Christian and as a pastor, I feel I have a duty to support movements that work for the good of the people."[28]

The diocese's most important organizations have also supported MAB. Caritas, for example, made possible the health work that led to MAB's creation. Caritas lets MAB use a mimeograph machine and has hired three MAB leaders, two of whom spend their salaried time in popular organizing, the other of whom works in the Caritas office. The Justice and Peace Commission and the diocese's Workers Pastoral Commission (CPO) have generally backed MAB, although there have been some tensions between the CPO and MAB.[29]

Most of the clergy have supported MAB, principally through promoting a vision of faith among the laity that emphasizes social justice and political participation. Some priests have encouraged people to participate in MAB or to form neighborhood associations, and many let the associations use the local church for meetings. Characteristic of the progressive clergy's support of the popular movement were the activities of a foreign priest who arrived in Nova Iguaçu in 1978. From the beginning his attitude was that the Church should back the popular movements but respect their autonomy. "The Church has the grass roots, but it doesn't have many people who know what to do politically. It doesn't have people who can lead the grass roots. Therefore we must support the people who can. Also, it is not the Church's role to lead the movement. What projects should be undertaken? How should the struggle be realized? These questions go beyond the Church's domain."[30]

When this priest arrived in 1978, one of his first steps was to encourage the creation of more base communities and to develop a vision of faith linked to social justice. After several months of working in this direction, several lay people and he prepared and distributed a questionnaire on the neighborhood's major problems. They invited all residents —not just Catholics—to participate in the survey. At this point, an active participant in the region's popular struggles until the early 1970's, who had been jailed 32 times for political reasons under the military regime, became involved. He had long ceased being an active Catholic, but the priest's attitude and willingness to work with non-Catholics encouraged him to attend the meetings.

For many years, even though I am a Catholic, I didn't have much to do with the Church. The Church felt it didn't need the poor. The priests didn't baptize our children, they didn't say funeral masses for peasants, they didn't give us any support. This bothered me. . . . The Church was against the common people and for the wealthy. . . . In 1978, seeing that the Church was helping the people, I began to participate again. It wasn't that I stayed away from the Church for all those years, but rather that the Church was removed from the people.[31]

After the Church helped create the neighborhood association, its role started to change. The population assumed control of the association, and the old popular leader became its outstanding leader. This association quickly became one of the best organized in Nova Iguaçu. Even though the movement had established its autonomy, Church support did not cease. The priest encouraged CEB participants to join the association by stressing the value of political participation, and the association still meets in the Church.

In addition to the support of the bishop, priests, and diocesan organizations, grass-roots Church movements have contributed (and continue to contribute) to MAB's growth, even though the base communities in Nova Iguaçu are primarily dedicated to evangelization and are not politically sophisticated.[32] MAB and other movements are responsible for political organizing; the diocese focuses on evangelization, which includes encouraging people to observe the social and political dimensions of faith. Yet by encouraging a large number of people to think more critically about politics, CEBs have helped encourage political participation. The CEBs gave many people experience in organization and participation and a disposition to fight for urban improvements. Significantly, the neighborhood associations are generally strongest in areas where the Church has encouraged the creation of CEBs. A MAB leader who was a longtime activist in the area's popular struggles reflected on how the grass-roots Church work has strengthened the popular struggles.

The people who participated before 1964 were directed from above, by the parties and politicians of the period. The movement grew a lot but didn't have much substance. It made a lot of noise but lacked continuity. Before elections, it grew rapidly, but after the elections, it gradually faded. Today's movements are different. Today, the work is more politically conscious. The participants know why they are there, they discuss more, participate more actively. Today they aren't just dragged along. That's what the difference is, that today the movement has a firm base. This difference is largely because of the Church's work.[33]

In addition to creating a grass-roots constituency that has bolstered the base of the popular movements, the diocese has encouraged the development of popular leaders. Eight of the nineteen members of the initial Coordinating Council received their political education principally through the Church, and six more had strong ties to the Church. Nine members of the second Coordinating Council developed political consciousness through their work in the Church. At the neighborhood level, the predominance of Catholic activists is greater. A woman who first participated in the local CEB, then joined the Workers Pastoral Commission and her local neighborhood association, and was eventually a member of MAB's first Coordinating Council explained her own political evolution.

My political consciousness grew through the Church. I was always a very religious person and was active in the Church. But before coming to Nova Iguaçu, I had experienced only the closed Church of Rio. It didn't get involved in politics, or if it did, it was on the government's side. For them, the Bible isn't linked to life. Seven years ago, we moved to Nova Iguaçu. That's when I started to develop a political consciousness. I participated in the base community and learned a different understanding of the Bible, committed to the poor and to social justice.[34]

MAB, the Left, and the Church

Between the early 1970's and about 1978, a historically unprecedented alliance existed between the popular Church and the Marxist Left, which had traditionally seen the Church as one of its principal enemies. After the terrible defeat suffered between 1968 and 1974, significant parts of the Left rejected vanguard approaches and became more concerned about basic civil liberties, more willing to work with democratic opposition forces, and more interested in grass-roots work. And even though they disagreed with many political conceptions of the Left, some progressive dioceses provided room for people committed to social transformation to work with the popular classes. In Nova Iguaçu, without the diocese's financial support, legitimation, and help in contacting organized Catholic groups, the doctors whose work led to MAB would have encountered many difficulties. Given the repression and popular fear of participating in politics, doing anything more than palliative medical work would have been almost impossible.

This alliance between the Left and the Church was important in the development of the neighborhood movement in Nova Iguaçu. Even though the population of Nova Iguaçu has a history of popular resistance and organization, it was not until a stable, politically aware leadership emerged that these efforts transcended immediate material perspectives. Before 1975, Catholics were organized in local ecclesial communities concerned with social reality, but there were no efforts to create a broad social movement that could change the way local government was run. It took the active involvement of four doctors committed to working with the popular classes to transform isolated petitions into a significant popular movement. Their presence was significant in helping the local population to organize. One MAB leader stated,

The population was still completely passive, and there was almost no organization. Then the doctor arrived and everyone woke up. It encourages the people to have a doctor who shows some interest in their problems. He encouraged the people to reflect about the causes of problems in the neighborhood. He asked, Why do these problems exist? Then the people started to say that it was because of the miserable wage levels, because the city administration never does anything it promises, and so forth. Some people started to see that things weren't going the way they should, that it is better for us to demand our rights than to pay for medications.[35]

The four doctors and others from the Left helped raise broader political issues and actively worked to coordinate efforts among neighborhoods. The evolution from a movement concerned solely with the population's immediate needs to one whose leaders attempted to relate these needs to broader political issues was important. Popular movements can create pressures that cause authoritarian regimes to open up, but to do so, they must go beyond immediate material benefits to broader political issues. Excessive focus on broader issues easily leads to gaps between the leaders, who in a movement like MAB are politically sophisticated, and the rank and file, who are seldom aware of the links between broader political issues and their immediate material needs. Yet exclusive concern with immediate material needs prevents a movement from contributing to broader social change and makes it susceptible to internal crisis once it obtains the benefits it seeks or, conversely, once it becomes frustrated from repeated failure.

The efforts to coordinate work among neighborhoods also gave a new character to the movement. The movement quickly became concerned about cooperation among the participating neighborhoods. This was in marked contrast to previous neighborhood movements in Nova Iguaçu, since only during the brief period before and after the 1960 congress had there been serious efforts to coordinate work among neighborhoods. It is also one of the characteristics that made MAB an unusually well-articulated movement. This coordination created the possibility of a mass movement, with greater chances of pressuring the state. The new movement consequently provided greater variation in political experiences that more local movements do not afford. Visitations between neighborhoods and exchanges of ideas encouraged other neighborhoods, expanding the movement.

The role of the doctors in organizing the local population is characteristic of most movements in Brazil. The popular classes have always organized to resist domination, but without the input of leaders generally drawn from outside circles, popular resistance has not led to political movements that could change the society. Even the post-1974 movements, which have been more autonomous with respect to political parties and intellectuals, have generally relied on outside support, especially in their early phases.

Despite the strong presence of the Catholic Left in the movement and the predominance of Catholic participants at the neighborhood level, the four doctors who began the movement were outstanding leaders until December 1981. This phenomenon of a predominantly Catholic base and non-Catholic leadership is common, but it has generated some tensions. Earlier I noted that Dom Adriano has fully supported MAB and its autonomy, but this perspective is far from uniform. In contrast to some popular dioceses where the clergy is overwhelmingly committed to the popular cause, the Nova Iguaçu diocese is somewhat divided, with a number of moderate and some conservative priests who openly and sharply disagree with the bishop.

Within the diocese there are many competing conceptions of the Church's role, its relationship to politics, and consequently its relationship to popular movements. Although the predominant tendency has been to support MAB, some clergy have opposed the movement. Even some progressive Catholics have felt that the Left has done little grass-roots organizing and therefore should not lead the movement. In their view, the masses, not intellectuals, should lead popular movements. They argue that MAB's leadership is an elite with a limited understanding of "real" popular needs and values and that the movement has promoted broader political issues at the expense of grass-roots work. Even though most of the diocese's priests and religious workers verbally eschew organizing the population for political purposes, some clergy delegitimize the efforts of "outsiders" who do so. Others criticize MAB for not developing more effective popular participation.

In MAB's case it is not clear that these criticisms are justified. Over half of the members of both coordinating councils have been workers, and the rest live simply in Nova Iguaçu and have shown a long-term commitment to working with the popular classes. Furthermore, the movement's success in mobilizing the local population, obtaining material improvements, and fighting for a more responsive local government suggests that it has articulated popular needs and channeled them effectively. These facts, however, do not eliminate tensions between some Church people and MAB.

More important than these occasional tensions between progres-

sive Catholics and MAB have been the conflicts between conservative clergy and the movement. One example of how the conservative
clergy view MAB and especially the four doctors and other Leftists
in the movement will suffice to indicate the kinds of criticism they
voice. One priest who verbally espouses a moderate line but has authoritarian practices and paternalistic attitudes discouraged people
in his parish and in the mothers' clubs from participating in MAB.

> MAB was started by outsiders. It started here, in my parish, but escaped
> from my hands. They were doctors from Rio who wanted to do something
> about the misery of the Baixada. We didn't support them because they were
> outsiders. I didn't know why they were here. They were taking advantage
> of the grass-roots work I had done. I feel suspicious about MAB. I see in it
> an ideology that I don't completely share, and the workers don't have a
> means of defending themselves against this ideology, they don't have a way
> of understanding it. MAB takes Church people and makes them think
> things they might not want to. . . . It is impossible to defend the workers
> against this ideology.[36]

These criticisms reflect the tensions and debates found throughout the Brazilian and Latin American Church. This priest's views
about avoiding Church participation in politics and encouraging
clerical control of the popular sectors are common among conservatives. His words reveal a competition for popular sympathies
(and control) that is also widespread. His opposition to MAB
shows that even in progressive dioceses, the Church often has a contradictory political impact. Although the diocese has generally
strengthened MAB, some clerics attempt to control or even delegitimize the movement.

Equally striking is this priest's attitude that MAB could make
people believe things that "they might not want to." His attitude
that the masses' limited critical abilities can easily lead them into
participating in movements whose objectives they do not understand is questionable. The popular classes may not understand the
sophisticated political debates at the leadership level of popular
movements, but it is difficult to manipulate them into participating
in a movement. On the contrary, they are usually suspicious of outsiders interested in organizing the population. The experience of
needing to offer concrete benefits to work successfully with the popular classes is widespread; they participate only if they get something out of the "deal."[37]

For its part, the Left is sometimes critical of the Church. Although the doctors who helped start MAB appreciate the support of Dom Adriano, Caritas, and the progressive clergy, their vision of how to lead the popular movement differs from that of most progressive Catholics. One of them said,

> The Church has the idiosyncrasy, the internal contradiction, of not admitting how it works. It leads the popular process, but then it claims that this process is spontaneous, that it is the popular classes who are directing their own process. It delegitimizes the kind of leadership, of vanguard, needed to develop effective popular movements. For us, the leaders must elaborate a project according to their ability to understand popular demands. The challenge is in being able to capture and channel those demands. The Church delegitimizes that step.[38]

Notwithstanding these tensions, one of the factors that has helped make MAB so dynamic has been the combination of the leadership from the Left and the strength of the popular Church. Indeed, the ability of the non-Catholic Left and Catholics to work together in Nova Iguaçu stands out in comparison with many regions of the country where that relationship has been strained. A harmonious relationship with the diocese will be a key factor in MAB's future.

Conclusions

Throughout this book I have underscored the importance of paying more attention to grass-roots Catholic organizations, especially CEBs. These communities are a significant force, both in the Catholic Church and in Brazilian politics. Brazilian CEBs are distinctive for their number, age, and close links to the hierarchy, but base communities have become an important source of Church change in several Latin American countries. Not without reason have all parts of the ecclesiastical spectrum shown a keen interest in CEBs.

In terms of political consciousness, action, and impact, Brazilian CEBs are remarkably heterogeneous. Brazil is a vast country, with enormous regional differences. The way local populations have organized and the problems they have encountered parallel these regional differences. The local Church response to popular movements also varies greatly, according to how the bishop, clergy, and laity view the Church's function and relationship to politics, and how they regard a particular popular movement.[39]

The links between CEBs, popular movements, and political par-

ties are very complex, far more so than most analyses have suggested. CEBs in major industrialized areas such as São Paulo and
Nova Iguaçu have the most sophisticated political consciousness;
yet even here this consciousness is quite rudimentary among the majority of participants.

Despite the presence of some left-wing leaders and its success,
MAB's objectives and its ability to effect political change are relatively limited in the short run. In fact, by 1982 MAB faced serious
difficulties, underscoring the fact that even well-organized movements can be somewhat fragile and cyclical.[40] On the other hand,
CEBs have helped introduce new social practices with an emphasis
on participation and democratic methods and have strengthened
popular movements throughout many parts of the country. The
charge of conservatives that the CEBs are deeply political has little
to do with the reality of the vast majority of base communities in
Brazil, but their perception that CEBs affect political life is clearly correct. This impact is even greater in Central America, where
many CEB members have actively participated in the revolutionary
process.

In this chapter I have called attention to the importance of not
restricting analysis of the Church's political impact to Church-state
relations. Political life includes a vast network of nonstate activities
that can bolster different sectors of civil society. Despite infrequent
interactions with the political elite, the Church has been one of the
most important political forces in the region and has helped empower Nova Iguaçu's popular movements. I have also called attention to the limits on the Church's involvement in popular movements; the competition between the Church, political parties, and
popular movements that frequently exists at the grass-roots level;
the tensions and debates that exist within the Church concerning its
proper political role; and the kinds of dilemmas the popular movements have faced.

The chapter also indicates how the Church's political role
changed during the process of political liberalization. Even progressive Church leaders felt that the Church's work must change as civil
society developed the capacity to articulate its own political mechanisms. During the period under consideration, the Nova Iguaçu
Church changed from being the only institution capable of defending human rights to one among many forces interested in promoting
social change. Yet, as I have suggested, the Church continued to

have an important political function in developing a vision of faith that encourages political participation. Characteristic of progressive Church leaders who defend the view that the Church should continue its politically relevant work under the democratic regime was Dom Adriano. Opposing the ecclesiastical tendencies that promoted a greater separation between religion and politics, in December 1984 he wrote that the Church must continue to "defend the weak and the fragile, unmask social injustices, and announce the hope of the Kingdom of God." He insisted that the Church's nature is essentially prophetic and that the "redemocratization of our country . . . in no way restricts the prophetic mission of our Church."[41]

Finally, the partial decline of MAB after 1982 helps underscore a major dilemma in the political struggle in Brazil: constructing a democracy that involves the masses in significant ways. During much of the 1970's, the proliferation and creativity of grass-roots movements generated considerable hope. Political leaders and social scientists saw these movements as a way of challenging Brazil's traditional authoritarian political culture and of creating a more dynamic democracy. Since 1982, however, these movements have tended to decline. The increasing importance of electoral politics, the fundamentally cautious character of the main parties, the economic crisis, and the reversion to the traditional politics of elite accommodation all contributed to this tendency.[42] If a more participatory and less elitist democracy is to be constructed, grass-roots movements—of which the Church helped engender so many—will surely play a leading role.

CHAPTER 9

The Church, Popular Classes, and Democracy

BETWEEN APPROXIMATELY 1968 and 1976, the progressive sectors of the Catholic Church had a virtual monopoly of political work with the popular classes. As the *abertura* advanced, this situation changed as political parties and social movements sought popular support. After 1978 the rebirth of political society posed new questions for progressive Catholics regarding ways of promoting democracy. The political situation raised dilemmas regarding the way the Church should work with the popular sectors, the relationship between Catholic groups (especially CEBs) and popular movements, and the relationship between these groups and political parties.

In this chapter I examine the political contributions and limitations of the progressive Church's work in the post-1979 period. My primary argument is that despite important innovations in the Church's work, *basista* tendencies limited its contributions to creating a "liberating" vision of faith or supporting popular struggles. By *basista* and the noun form, *basismo*, I refer to a somewhat naive belief in the capacity of the base (grass-roots) to resolve its problems without the assistance of intellectuals,* political parties, or other outside support.

It is important to note three caveats. First, I do not attempt to assess the Church's political impact as a whole, but rather limit myself to the progressive (popular) sectors, particularly the political poten-

---

*As used here, "intellectual," following the usage of many Latin American social scientists, refers not only to university scholars, but also to other educated people engaged in formulating or teaching ideas or policies that affect the political struggle. In this sense, the category includes pastoral agents involved in conscientizing the masses.

tial and limits of work with the base communities. Second, within the popular Church there is significant heterogeneity that I do not pretend to capture. Some sectors of the popular Church dealt well with the problems I raise. However, at all levels of the popular Church—bishops, theologians and social scientists, and particularly grass-roots pastoral agents—the *basista* tendency was pronounced. Finally, I focus on the strengths and weaknesses of the Church's political work. These strengths and weaknesses are an important component in determining the opposition's capacity to change the society, but in the context of a society where elites continue to be so powerful, political change depends more on actors such as the military and the dominant sectors than on the Church.

Conceptions of Grass-roots Practices in the Popular Church

Perhaps the outstanding characteristic of the popular Church between 1964 and 1973 was the effort to reach the popular sectors in a new way. Even before the popular Church was deeply involved in politics, progressive pastoral agents were committed to developing closer ties to the poor, to sharing their suffering and joys in deeper ways.

These agents began to question their own role and traditional forms of work with the people. They became critical of past clerical attitudes and viewed them as authoritarian, paternalistic, and distant from the popular situation. A working group on presbyteries noted in 1969, "Often the priest is seen by the popular sectors as wealthy, someone who understands everything, different. The priest, at times, fails to present himself as a bearer of God's word. There is complacency, paternalism, a failure to confide in the laity."[1] The group concluded that the Church had no real understanding of the masses' material situation, much less their values.

Progressive pastoral agents felt that they could not expect the popular sectors to understand erudite religious practices. In their view, pastoral work was excessively geared toward the sacraments, with little concern about deeper human contact and deeper forms of evangelization. They felt that the Church had been too concerned with external appearances—attendance at mass, the number of people who met the formal requirements of the Church—and had neglected other forms of evangelization. One person criticized the predominant pastoral approach for turning the priest into "a distributor of benevolent rites. The predominance of rites suffocates the transmission of the religious message. The concern with external celebrations, cultivation of the saints, and private devotions comes first, and true evangelization is neglected."[2]

Progressive priests felt that they had to assume a new role and develop a new attitude. They had to become facilitators for the community and to discuss problems with the popular classes, with respect for their values and culture. They emphasized service to the community and avoidance of authoritarian practices. A young theologian who subsequently became a prominent bishop wrote in 1966 that the priest should be the "servant of the Word and a man who worships God, a brother of all people who is at their service, a Christian distant from the structures of domination so he can identify with the popular classes. . . . The priest today must be accessible, equal to others."[3]

This new role meant developing confidence in the laity and encouraging them to assume greater initiative. There was an emphasis that "the priest must believe in the laity. Confide in lay leaders, give them freedom of initiative and coresponsibility. The priest should not exercise direct, but rather indirect, leadership."[4] In this view, the Church should be an organization for and of the people, not a self-serving institution.

The popular Church emphasizes the dialectical character of the learning relationship and the abilities of all people. Characteristic of this view is a document affirming that "nobody knows everything and nobody knows nothing. Everybody has something to learn and something to teach. The dialogue between teachers and learners [formadores and formandos] will be the basic method."[5] In this conception, sensitive and effective pastoral work requires an attitude of patience and service and an attempt to conduct a dialogue with the popular classes.[6] This perspective argues that without listening, the pastoral agent cannot understand popular values and needs.

This pedagogy emphasizes that to be effective the educator must penetrate the world view of the popular classes. This process is not easy, nor does it occur overnight. The middle-class intellectual generally learns through theoretical concepts, but the popular classes, given their lack of formal education and their difficult living conditions, which dictate pragmatism and an "immediatist" perspective, learn most effectively through concrete experiences. Nothing makes this clearer than the masses' rejection of intellectual discussions that have no bearing on the immediate situation.[7]

The progressive clergy emphasize becoming as much like the poor as possible. The popular Church has developed the notion of changing one's social position (*lugares sociais*) to express this attempt to identify with the popular classes.[8] This effort is captured in an Indian Missionary Council document that calls for pastoral agents to "opt, as humans and as the Church, for a realistic incarnation, committed to life with the indigenous people, living with them, researching, discovering, appreciating them, adopting their culture and assuming their culture and their cause."[9] The emphasis on living with and like the people stems partially from the evangelical stand on poverty as a value. It also facilitates pastoral work. Pastoral agents frequently renounce privileges that the poor do not have, such as automobiles or telephones. They believe in living with the people in material conditions that do not sharply distinguish their life from the people's.

Influenced by the Christian humanist conception that all people are the children of God and have a right to material and personal dignity, the popular Church attempts to value the life experiences of the popular classes. Many pastoral agents speak of how much they have learned from the masses and of the positive human values found among the people. They strongly emphasize respect for popular beliefs and practices, including popular religiosity.[10]

The popular Church stresses the wisdom manifested in day-to-day survival techniques in the face of oppression.[11] To the progressives, the popular classes are not inept; they are the victims of oppressive social structures. If pastoral agents work effectively with the people, they can help them develop a critical capacity. Instead of passively accepting what happens, the people can learn to reflect on society and make choices about changing that society.[12]

Because of these views, the Church emphasizes that the popular sectors should play a major role within it. At a landmark regional gathering, pastoral agents from the Amazon concluded that "the training of pastoral agents should emphasize the local, autochthonous elements. Nobody can exercise leadership in a community as well as the people themselves."[13] The emphasis on lay participation has modified traditionally hierarchical ecclesial structures and decision-making processes in many popular dioceses. These dioceses rely on assemblies, with lay majorities, to determine diocesan priorities and means of working toward Church objectives. Even though the bishop retains ultimate formal authority, in practice he functions as an *animador*, a pastoral agent whose primary purpose is to visit and encourage communities throughout the diocese, coordinate pastoral efforts, and represent the diocese in dealings with the national Church. Most popular bishops play down their authority and encourage democracy within the Church. This internal democracy is limited by class and educational differences—knowledge and status are sources of power—and by the lack of change in formal authority relations, but the effort to achieve more democratic structures is noteworthy.[14]

The Church's Contributions to the Popular Process

In assessing the Church's grass-roots practices, it is important to emphasize that many tensions remained unresolved.[15] There is often a gap between discourse and practice. The discourse of allowing the popular classes to make their own decisions is often accompanied by guidance or control. For example, popular Catholicism is rarely as accepted in practice as it is on paper. Often the tradition of clericalism is so strong that priests dominate discussions or community lay leaders become domineering mini-priests.[16] In some cases, pastoral agents have difficulty in encouraging participation among people who are accustomed to a more passive role in the Church.[17] The issue of encouraging change while respecting popular values is complex and is often simplified in the Church's discourse. Finally, the success of the base communities varies from case to case; not all have functioned smoothly. Nevertheless, the Church has made some important contributions to the popular process.

The emphasis on promoting popular participation in leadership has been pronounced in the base communities.[18] A 1978 report of a community in the prelature of Diamantino, Mato Grosso, is indicative of the participatory character of many base communities. "In the Bible Circles, everyone has the chance to participate and give an opinion. The people of the communities have a voice and place within that vital space called the community. . . . The meetings are led by lay people who encourage everyone to speak. Everyone has a chance to speak, and her or his opinion is respected."[19]

This participatory experience is novel in light of the traditional authoritarianism and elitism in Brazil's political institutions and of the relative difficulty the popular classes have had in achieving political unity. The more democratic, participatory activities of the popular classes—football, Carnaval, the Afro-Brazilian religions, the beach—have always been relatively distant from the political sphere.[20] Popular participation in politics has been limited. Politicians and the major political parties traditionally went into neighborhoods at election time, made promises, and then disappeared until the next election. Even within the unions, participation has been limited. Although the unions mobilized large numbers of people during events such as strikes, until the emergence of the "new syndicalism" in the second half of the 1970's, they were notorious for reproducing much of the authoritarianism and elitism found in other institutions.[21]

The Church's contributions to creating more democratic, participatory practices at the grass roots could help challenge one source of authoritarianism in the political order. The state is not the only authoritarian institution in Brazilian society. Authoritarianism characterizes most major social institutions and relationships, from the education system to relationships between men and women to practices within the Leninist parties.[22] Development of democratic social practices can lead to challenges to authoritarian political structures, as indicated by the many CEB participants who are actively involved in popular movements and political parties.

Another contribution by the Church to the popular process is the creation of strong human bonds within the CEBs, even in cases where political consciousness is limited. The reports of CEBs are replete with mentions of friendships, the discovery of personal worth, the sense of community and fraternity, and democratic practices. The report of a community on the periphery of São Paulo, for example, noted that "in the CEB there is an effective communion of people and a sense of fraternity, even a true sharing of material goods. People get to know each other, they love each other and work together. The CEB is an instrument for listening to the desires and needs of the people. It produces a transformation from individualistic lives to community life."[23]

This sense of community is important in human terms and potentially at the political level as well. There is no necessary dichotomy between community and political organization; on the contrary, community solidarity may facilitate political organization. Even Bible groups that do not act on social problems provide a rudimentary experience of popular organization. This is an important step in a society where the popular strata have most often sought individualistic solutions to their problems. The intellectuals of the popular Church view this sense of community and fraternity as one of the major contributions of the base communities to the Brazilian Church and Brazilian society.[24]

The Church's work with the masses has helped many discover a sense of human worth. Self-confidence and dignity are intrinsically important, and the process of personal self-discovery can lead to more critical political participation. Through CEBs and other Catholic organizations, many people have had their first experience of popular discussion and organization. Participation in CEBs can demystify the political process and help people see that it is possible to participate in and contribute to change. It can help challenge the passivity and fatalism that are part of popular political consciousness. The Left often criticizes the Church for being too concerned with personal issues and community at the expense of political work, but there is no inherent contradiction between personal discovery or community and more specifically political efforts.

In Brazil, no institution has so strongly underscored the importance of respecting popular values as the Church. In doing so, it has called attention to an important objective usually overlooked by policymaking elites.[25] Although recognizing that development policies must address the fundamental material needs of the population, Church progressives insist that they respect human values.

While recognizing the potential the Church's community work may have in changing the political order, we must avoid excessive optimism on this score. The link between more democratic social practices and a more democratic political order is not automatic. Democratization of social relations (however important at the human level) does not inherently produce democratization of the political order. In a society with such a centralized power structure, the extent to which changes in social relations can effect changes in the political realm remains to be seen.* Furthermore, even though

*The complex relationship between the democratization of social relationships and democratization of the political order requires considerably more thought, both among political theorists and among social scientists writing on social movements. One contribution of feminist political theory has been to underscore the political aspects of social relations. However, most feminist theory has overstated the extent to which political change can be realized by changing social relations. In *The Mermaid and the Minotaur*, for example, Dorothy Dinnerstein essentially traces political dom-

CEBs have been important to the participants, the problem of *basismo* may limit the contributions grass-roots Catholic organizations can make in changing the society.

The Role of the Pastoral Agent

The Church's pedagogical statements encompass a wide range of pedagogical and political positions. They always criticize the elitism, authoritarianism, and paternalism that traditionally characterized the Church's work with the popular classes. They also unequivocally rule out the vanguard attitudes that continue to characterize some of the Left. But they say little about the pastoral agent's positive contributions to the pedagogical process.

At the opposite extreme from Leninism, many pastoral agents deny that outsiders can contribute significantly to the popular process. Some agents feel that the workers must do everything themselves. One expression of this view is that the intellectual should become as much like the people as possible. One important Church intellectual writes: "The mistake of educated people is believing they can really know something without feeling and without becoming deeply involved in life, in the struggle for a better world. If educated people are distant from the people, if they do not feel the hopes and fears of the people, they will not be able to explain life. . . . The intellectual must join the people, must unite with them, must become one with the people."[26] In the name of expressing solidarity with the popular classes, some pastoral agents virtually deny their differences from the people.

Such denials are far from uncommon, sometimes even in cases of relatively authoritarian practices. Linked to this is often an anti-intellectualism that denies that non-church agents can help the masses. This attitude overlooks the contributions social scientists, pedagogues, and other intellectuals have made to the popular Church.[27]

Today many pastoral agents opt to live with the poor in conditions somewhat similar to theirs. This is a value choice that can fa-

ination to forms of domination and inegalitarianism in personal relationships. Implicitly, the way to create a more democratic political order would be by changing child-rearing practices. Among the writings on social movements, several important articles deal with the subject tangentially. See F.H. Cardoso, "Regime Político"; Singer, "Movimentos de Bairros"; Singer, "Movimentos Sociais"; and Souza Lima, "Notas."

cilitate communication between the agent and the masses. It gives them greater confidence in the agent, and, equally important, it gives the agent greater insight into their life. But living with the people is not the same as becoming one of them.

Even if a pastoral agent attempts to become a member of the masses, they never really accept the agent as being an equal. Given the difference in cultural backgrounds and the fact that living in a popular class area is a choice for the agent and a necessity for the people, this perception is accurate. There are vast differences in class background, education, access to knowledge, and material security. The popular sectors are not so naive that they overlook these differences or pretend they do not exist.[28] Furthermore, unity between the intellectual and the worker is illusory and negates the role the intellectual can play in education. An agent who wishes to help develop critical abilities must assume the role of someone who has something to offer—information, skills, and knowledge—that the people do not have.

Even a more moderate version of this negation of the intellectual's role is still questionable. This version does not insist that the educator renounce his or her role, but it does argue that the relationship between the intellectual and the people should be one of exchange. To teach effectively, the educator must establish a relationship of equality with the people, learn from them, and respect their values.

This perspective offers many valid contributions. Education at its best *is* an exchange; the educator *can* learn from students; and effective work with the popular classes *does* require the educator to overcome certain practices and values. But the exchange is not between equals. The intellectual has skills and knowledge needed by the masses if they are to change their situation. The intellectual has more access to power, more formal education, and a greater ability to understand the mechanisms of power in the society. And, in the final analysis, the educator chooses where and how to live whereas the popular sectors are forced to live in difficult conditions. As a result, the relationship between the people and the agent is never one of equality; it is always an authority relationship. The question is *how* that authority is used. Does the priest or nun provide an effective political education for the masses? Are they sensitive to popular values and do they allow participatory, democratic practices? Do they encourage the development of leaders within popular ranks?

Veneration of Popular Consciousness and Practices

A related problem is the tendency to venerate popular consciousness and practices. This perspective sees the popular classes as shrewdly resisting the dominant culture. They are aware of their exploitation and are continuously developing responses to it. The problem is not that they are alienated, but that they are not aware of how to use the knowledge they have.[29]

This perspective contains a half-truth: the masses are aware of their oppression and do have means of resisting it.[30] However, popular practices are not always unequivocally sagacious. It is difficult to agree, for example, with one author who considers that popular medicine has the same claim to legitimacy as elite medicine.[31] In some cases, popular medicine has *better* answers, but in many others, it is simply bad medicine. And while popular Catholicism certainly contains positive values, it is not the panacea that some Church intellectuals have suggested.[32] Similarly, it is difficult to believe that "the popular classes elaborate a *theory* to accompany their struggles,"[33] or that these ideas are always appropriate for fighting to change the society.

In some cases, the veneration of popular practices goes so far as to legitimate barroom conversations, soccer, and popular theater as sufficient forms of popular organization.[34] This overlooks that these forms of organization do little to challenge the oppression of the masses. To change this situation, the old forms of organization—unions, neighborhood associations, social movements, and political parties—remain as indispensable as ever. The popular sectors have often been manipulated politically,[35] but the answer to that problem is not to flee from political organization but rather to change the nature of that organization.

In all its manifestations, veneration of popular consciousness can discourage pastoral agents from helping the popular sectors develop a more critical faith and political vision. Popular consciousness contains many elements of the dominant culture, including some forms of fatalism and submissiveness.[36] These passive attitudes outweigh more active elements that might lead to social change. The move from largely accepting oppression to challenging it does not occur spontaneously. It involves an experience that can come from discussing politics or from actual political practice. But in either case

there will be leaders, intellectuals, and political parties who promote *conscientização*.

Even more unlikely than spontaneous *conscientização* is spontaneous political organization. The popular classes may organize on
their own in certain ways, usually defensive, such as to resist a favela removal or a land expulsion. But popular organization is seldom
sustained in the absence of an immediate threat. The process of developing ongoing popular organizations has consistently involved
the participation of external agents, especially during the initial
phases.[37] The question is not whether these agents are present, but
rather how they function.

Many pastoral agents justify a failure to promote *conscientização*
or organization on the grounds that this constitutes interference
with the popular process. They fail to see that despite all their efforts not to interfere, their presence is as much an interference as
that of other external agents. Again, the question is not whether
there is interference, it is *how* the agent interferes. Unless pastoral
agents assume some responsibility for stimulating change, they cannot help the popular classes overcome elements of passivity and
domination.

Grass-roots Education and Popular Movements

Many pastoral agents have the attitude that only grass-roots
work is valid. They believe that successful education of the popular
classes and respect for their values dictate small movements that allow for group discussion. They allege that larger movements manipulate the people, do not allow true popular participation, do not
respect the popular process, and do not provide good learning
opportunities. These agents encourage the popular sectors to participate in small, relatively closed movements, with more limited perspectives.

Small group discussions have an invaluable role in the popular
process, especially considering the lengthy tradition of authoritarianism in the society. It is an old and well-established principle that
the larger the movement, the more difficult it becomes to establish
participatory democratic practices.[38] However, mass movements
and political parties afford a different and equally important experience. Local movements are less likely to confront different levels
of the state, they do not provide the experience of mass organiza-

tion, and they rarely go beyond discussing immediate material benefits, which makes them vulnerable to disappearing once they have achieved their immediate objectives or once they have become frustrated by repeated failures. Mass movements may not allow the popular classes to discuss politics frequently, but the Church can provide this opportunity. And mass movements do allow the popular classes to experience unity with a large number of people, to clash more directly with the state, and to confront an important range of broader political questions that more isolated, local movements usually do not consider. Broader popular movements almost invariably face issues such as relations with other popular movements, the state, and political parties or the proper response to major political events. Broader movements also stand better chances of pressuring the state into making material concessions.

Mass movements or parties cannot possibly function in the same way that a small community group does, but this does not make them "manipulative." Some leaders may engage in manipulative or undemocratic practices, but underlying the charge of manipulation is often a skepticism on the part of the pastoral agent regarding the popular ability to discern political realities. The question for a mass movement is not whether every participant in a meeting can express an opinion. Demands of political efficacy do not permit this. The question is whether the movement successfully encourages participation, helps generate discussions at the grass roots, articulates the most important popular demands, and mobilizes the population. It is important to keep in touch with the grass roots, encourage participation, and develop leadership within the popular classes, but it is also important for the movement to expand as much as possible.

Work in small movements also fails to confront the reality of the political system. The concern with *conscientização* and internally democratic and participatory practices is important in an elitist society, but grass-roots work is limited if it never expands beyond small groups. In fact, one of the most important goals of grass-roots work should be enabling the popular classes to expand their political horizons and move beyond a perspective limited to their immediate needs.

Social change requires effective popular movements and political parties that can contest the state's power. Local movements may successfully obtain some material benefits, but they will never generate the pressures needed to cause any significant social change. As

Fernando Henrique Cardoso writes, "Any efforts at social transformation that do not deal with the question of the state are theoretically unsatisfactory and politically inefficacious."[39] The emphasis on grass-roots participation, democratic practices, and community cannot serve as a substitute for mass movements and political parties.

Another controversial issue in popular organizing regards the pace of popular movements. During the 1968-76 period, efforts at popular organizing were so repressed that the movements were necessarily limited in their scope. As political liberalization advanced during the late 1970's, the popular Church faced new questions regarding the principle of respecting the popular movements. What was the right speed for *conscientização*? On the one hand there was the principle of respecting the learning pace of the popular classes. On the other hand, the exigencies of the political situation demanded a faster pace on the part of popular movements. A discussion group can take a year, or five years if need be, to attain a minimal advance in political consciousness. By contrast, a strike requires immediate decisions that depend on a correct assessment of the political situation.

The political liberalization meant that the slower pedagogical pace of the most repressive years was no longer appropriate. If pastoral agents did not help Catholic groups understand the changing political scenario, these groups would lag behind the national situation and the popular movements. The party reform, for example, dictated the need for quick discussion; otherwise, Catholics would have faced a de facto situation of choosing between alternatives without having much hope of contributing to creating those alternatives. Pastoral agents had to decide whether to wait for the base communities to take the initiative in discussing the party reform or to introduce that question themselves. Political efficacy dictated one strategy, and attempting to follow the popular class's learning pace dictated another.

As with other problems, the popular Church responded to this dilemma in a variety of ways. Many agents recognized the importance of encouraging the base communities to discuss the political changes. Others, however, have continued to promote a relatively slow learning pace and theoretical discussions. They are less inclined to urge the people to participate in broader popular movements, and they feel it is better to promote a slow pace of *conscientização* than to push people into positions they are "not ready to accept."[40] One study commissioned by the CNBB stated, "It is important and necessary that the natural stages of development of the people and communities are respected. We must respect the slow process of conscientization of the people. Burning stages is a serious danger of impatient pastoral vanguardism. Rushing too much can be worse than not intervening."[41]

Yet the people do not have a "natural" pace of *conscientização* or organization. Intellectuals usually play some role in helping determine the pace of a movement. A failure to grow reflects in part the inability of the leadership to understand the best pace. But this might be because the pace is too slow; it is not necessarily the result of vanguardism. Just as the popular classes will not follow movements that are radical from the outset and have little to do with their concrete material needs, so, too, they are likely to abandon a movement that never goes anywhere.

Grass-roots Work and Political Parties

One of the most important steps in the political liberalization was the party reform initiated in 1979.[42] For years party reform had been a fundamental demand of sectors of the opposition, but when it finally came, it did as much to divide the opposition as to give it an authentic voice. The party reform and the issue of elections were troublesome to the popular Church, which, like the opposition at large, has suffered some internal divisions. The most politically active members of the base communities opted for the PT or PMDB. Part of the popular Church, however, adopted the attitude that the political parties were too distant from the people to merit participation.

It probably was true that the parties did not develop the popular sensitivity of parts of the Church. They continued to be concerned with coming to power, and their technocratic language was difficult for the popular sectors to understand. Nevertheless, to state that the parties are not interested in the popular cause, that they manipulate the people to obtain votes, or that they do not support the popular movements overlooked the dynamism of parties in the past several years.[43] The PT and sectors of the PMDB represented new experiences in Brazilian history in that they attempted to develop pedagogically sensitive practices and to support the popular movements. The PT was more concerned about *conscientização* and supporting popular movements than about coming to power in the short run.[44]

Many people overlooked the parties' attempts to support the base and failed to understand the importance of the party question to the popular movements. They believed that the popular movements were what really mattered and that the party question was secondary. This view failed to understand that the development of the popular movements depended on a broader political struggle. Without the support of mass political parties, the conquests that the popular movements can win are limited. Ultimately, it is the parties that are able to deal directly with the question of the state, and it is through the state that major social changes are effected. Grass-roots work will bring limited benefits to the majority of the people unless the state changes.

The party question is crucial for the popular movements. The influence the popular classes conquer in the society depends on the broader political struggle, not just grass-roots organizing. Even rudimentary grass-roots organizing is dependent on the state. In this regard, the contrast between the PMDB and the PDS is more significant than many elements of the opposition understood. Even PMDB candidates somewhat distant from the popular classes were more responsive to popular demands.

While the *basista* elements within the Church and the society as a whole insisted that they were not interested in the short-term power struggle, that struggle was determining Brazil's future. Political purists felt that they should concentrate on grass-roots work and popular movements and that only tomorrow should they deal with the question of the state. But not only did the question of the state affect the popular movements, it was also a chimera to believe that the much-awaited tomorrow might arrive if the opposition did not act.

The link between social movements and political parties is critical to the future of Brazilian democracy. In the absence of dynamic social movements, Brazilian democracy will almost surely be characterized by elitism, by the relative political weakness of the popular classes, and by sharp socioeconomic inequalities, for it is the social movements that have most consistently and clearly raised the banner of a more participatory democracy, a less elitist society, and more balanced development.

From 1980 until the movement for direct elections in 1984, social movements tended to decline. As electoral politics became more important, some leaders of movements concentrated on parties. In these cases, electoral politics tended to absorb the movements.

In other cases, movements tended toward greater isolation from partisan politics, but in doing so sometimes failed to address issues that deeply affected their own future.[45] Nowhere was this gap between social movements and political parties so evident as in the response to the November 1981 "electoral package," a series of electoral reforms imposed by the military government in an attempt to ensure victory in the November 1982 elections. Even though the electoral package was a singularly important measure, civil society did not respond until late December. The social movements failed to respond at all, and there were no mass demonstrations for several weeks following the measure. The social movements failed to understand how deeply the measure would influence the subsequent political struggle.

The movement for direct elections in early 1984 closed this gap between social movements and parties. The most important movements and the opposition parties joined to demand the direct elections that would have sharply curtailed the military's control of the transition to democracy. However, after the movement for direct elections was defeated, social movements again declined.

None of this should be construed as support for parties that are constructed from above or for subordinating social movements to the parties. Emphasizing the links between party politics and popular movements is not tantamount to arguing that only political parties can resolve the issues that concern social movements. The society has become far too heterogeneous for a party to address completely the needs of the major social movements.[46] In addition, the tradition of party elitism is so strong that the parties would be less responsive to popular needs were it not for the presence of the popular movements. There is a need for autonomous popular movements—but movements should not confuse autonomy with aloofness.

The question of how to develop a party more sensitive to the base remains an important and difficult question. However, it is clear that ignoring the party question because the parties are too distant from the people is an inadequate response. A perfect political party will never exist. In fact, the parties will probably prove responsive to the popular movements only to the extent that these movements force them to be so. If the popular movements let the political parties deal with "political" questions and assume for themselves the task of fighting for popular benefits, these movements are not only failing to understand the deep links between the party struggle and the popular struggle, they are also failing to contribute to creating more responsive parties precisely when this is a real possibility.

Final Observations

The progressive Church has stimulated some of the most creative innovations in the past two decades of Brazilian politics. Its ability to continue doing so will depend partly on how well it addresses the issue of *basismo*. Any institution can pronounce itself in favor of social justice. What is at stake is not so much whether the Church calls for justice, but whether it is capable of encouraging movements that work toward changing the society.

The struggle to respect the learning pace, values, and culture of the popular classes is difficult, given the immense gulf that separates their world from that of the middle-class intellectual. But if the popular Church is to make significant political contributions, it must encourage a concern with political efficacy and realism. This does not mean that the Church itself must become a political vehicle, but at the very least pastoral agents cannot delegitimate political institutions and retain a de facto control of popular sympathies.

Many of the Church's best intellectuals are aware of the importance of these issues. Clodovis Boff has sharply criticized the veneration of popular consciousness for leading to *basista* attitudes that can produce only uncritical or ineffective political attitudes and practices.

We should not serve the people and then close our eyes to their subjugation and the negative effects this subjugation has for popular consciousness. The situation in which they live, or more accurately, the situation in which they are kept by the dominant classes, is pathological. . . . The fear of interfering in the development of popular consciousness cannot be justified on the pretense of respect. . . . The question is not whether to influence the people. It is rather how to influence them. . . . Fetishism of the people is a sign of ignorance and represents a disservice to them.[47]

A majority of the Church's 1982 election pamphlets showed some awareness of the importance of the party question. The most publicized and influential pamphlet, from the Archdiocese of São Paulo, stated, "The distance that separates the popular sectors from the state cannot be overcome just through the dynamic of the popular movements. The living and working conditions of the great majority of the exploited and marginalized population can be transformed only if the popular classes are capable of influencing the centers of decisions and power."[48]

But at the base, even though there were signs of progress, pastoral agents often lagged behind. There was still considerable confusion over such issues as how to encourage popular movements and how to address the party question. Veneration of popular consciousness and rejection of outside elements were still common. The difficulties the popular sectors faced were compounded by external pressures against the progressive Church. Rome, the Latin American Bishops Conference, and the Brazilian state wanted to see the Church further removed from politics. By allowing the rebirth of more specifically political institutions, political liberalization generated pressures against the popular groups within the Church and reinforced *basista* tendencies.

CHAPTER 10

The Politics of the Popular Church

DURING THE LIBERALIZATION period, the Catholic Church made many contributions to democratization, ranging from the defense of human rights to criticisms of authoritarian abuses to support for popular movements. After the party reorganization in 1979, the Church's political importance declined somewhat. Yet one of its contributions—the vision of development proposed by the Catholic Left—influenced some important political actors, including significant parts of the Left, the Workers Party, the new union movement, and many peasant leagues, labor unions, and neighborhood associations. The popular Church was not directly responsible for these movements, but through its vision of society and leadership in different organizations, it had a major impact.

A relatively small number of Church leaders and think tanks have been primarily responsible for formulating the political views of the popular Church. Even though grass-roots pastoral workers created many significant innovations, these leading intellectuals and institutes played the predominant role in systematizing and diffusing ideas. Through literature written for pastoral agents and base communities, through work with progressive bishops, and through courses given in different parts of the country, these leaders of the popular Church have played a major role in shaping the political vision of the Church as a whole.

Whatever one's opinion of the contributions, contradictions, and weaknesses of the popular Church's political views, it is difficult to deny their importance or relative originality.[1] Yet despite the importance of the progressive Church's views on development, little has been written on the subject. In previous chapters I discussed some basic concerns of the popular Church regarding development—the emphasis on democracy, the criticisms of elitist and authoritarian development, the insistence that the popular sectors receive special consideration, the respect for popular values, and the call for rural and urban land reform. In this chapter I discuss its analysis of capitalism, socialism, and social relations; and its emphasis on participation. In both areas popular Church leaders have contributed prominently to the political debate.

Capitalism, Socialism, and Social Relations

Criticisms of liberal capitalism are nothing new in the Brazilian Church. As early as the 1950's, bishops criticized the egotism of capitalism. Yet between then and the 1970's, a major change occurred in the hierarchy's attitudes toward capitalism. Before the coup, even the reformist bishops believed that economic growth would resolve major social problems such as marginalization and poverty. They had no perception that some models of development could exacerbate the living conditions of a large part of the population. The reformist bishops made critical statements about liberal capitalism, but they were criticizing what they perceived as excesses in the system and not its core. They did not see social problems as intrinsic to capitalism, but as having an individual (egotism, corruption) rather than a systemic origin. Their solution was to call for the state to regulate capitalism to make it more humane.

The functioning of Brazilian capitalism after 1964 and the changes in the Church's institutional identity led many ecclesiastical leaders to question their assumptions. Among the progressive bishops, disillusionment led to calls for radical change. The criticisms of capitalism became so widespread that the Medellín and Puebla meetings of the Latin American Bishops Conferences incorporated them in their conclusions.[2]

Although anticapitalism is strong in the popular Church, the alternative to capitalism is not as clear. The Church disclaims responsibility for devising the means of effecting social change and feels that it would be internally divisive to debate approaches to change. The vast majority of leaders believe that the Church should focus on pastoral problems and the needs of the population rather than engage in debates on how to construct a new society.

Popular Church leaders who have reflected about the issues view socialism, Communism, and Marxism in varied ways. Most radical Catholics share many of the same ideals as other leftists, and many consider themselves socialists or Marxists. The emphasis in progressive Catholic thought on egalitarianism coincides with objectives of the non-Catholic Left. Like most Marxists and socialists, popular Church intellectuals believe that structural transformations are required to create a just society, and they are critical of dependent authoritarian capitalism. Progressive Catholics in Europe and Latin America have also been attracted to the ideals (which do not always correspond to the reality) of participatory socialist regimes.

Although the theoretical debate about Christianity and Marxism originated in Europe,[3] the most significant alliances between Catholics and socialists or Communists occurred in Latin America, especially Brazil, Chile (1970-73), Nicaragua (mid-1970's to the present), and El Salvador (late 1970's to the present). In Chile, the Catholic Left was an important element in the Allende government, and the efforts to construct a harmonious relationship between a democratically elected Marxist president and the hierarchy drew the attention of the Catholic world. In both Nicaragua and El Salvador, Catholics formed alliances with revolutionary forces to attempt to overthrow highly repressive authoritarian regimes.[4]

In these three other cases, Catholics committed to radical change established a working relationship with other forces on the Left. Often, however, the relationship has been strained. In the Brazilian case, although the Marxist Left has influenced the Catholic Left, after 1964 progressive Catholicism developed partly as a reaction against the Marxist Left. The group of Catholic intellectuals that emerged after the coup was critical of the traditional Marxist Left. Responding in part to the terrible fate of clandestine organizations between 1968 and 1976, Church intellectuals, some of whom had personally experienced imprisonment and torture,[5] felt the need to create new approaches to working with the popular sectors and new paths to social change. Even with the acceptance by the Marxist Left of more democratic values, conflict between radical Catholics and Marxists has continued. Since the *abertura*, progressive pastoral agents and most of the non-Catholic Left have differed over work with the popular classes, particularly over the issue of respecting popular values versus giving strong direction to popular movements. They also have different views on the process of social transformation and the nature of the good society.

The more cautious popular bishops like Dom Paulo Evaristo Arns speak of a third system, neither capitalist nor socialist, without specifying the features of that system. Dom Cláudio Hummes, bishop of Brazil's most industrialized region, the ABC area in greater São Paulo, states a preference for a more socialized society without opting unequivocally for socialism. Most of the popular Church's leading theologians, social scientists, and bishops are critically (and often vaguely) sympathetic toward socialism. Those favorable to socialism include Dom José Maria Pires, Dom Helder Câmara, Dom Tomás Balduino, Dom Pedro Casaldáliga, Dom Antônio Fragoso, and theologian Clodovis Boff.[6]

Although the popular Church is critical of capitalism, even the bishops and Church intellectuals who consider themselves socialists condemn Leninism and most socialist models. Their opposition stems partially from the Christian humanist tradition, which eschews violence as a means of realizing change and places a greater emphasis on democratic liberties and respect for the individual than does the Leninist model.

According to progressive Church leaders, the Leninist model lacks cogency because it supposes a revolutionary situation that does not exist in Brazil. The vanguard party is a dangerous chimera because it can so easily be isolated and repressed by a well-organized regime enjoying considerable support in civil society. In contrast to the Leninist parties, the Church has emphasized that liberation of the popular classes is a long-term project.[7] Not only is this a more realistic assessment of the current situation, it could also help avoid the utopian radicalization characteristic of parts of the Left throughout Latin America, which frequently had tragic consequences.[8]

The progressive Church's view that the popular sectors can assume leadership of the liberation process clashes with Lenin's conception of popular consciousness and emphasis on the vanguard. Lenin dismissed popular practices and consciousness as inevitably limited to a reformist perspective. He argued that a vanguard party must create the conditions for revolution and lead the masses into rebellion.[9] The Church sees this as an authoritarian conception that does not respect the masses' abilities, learning pace, or values. Frei Betto, for example, sharply criticizes the vanguard conception.

The vanguard's manipulation is characterized by the group's claim that it is the only interpreter of what the people need. All initiatives spring from the interior of this group and not from forms of popular organization. Imbibed with a self-legitimating ideology, the group goes to the grass roots, not to serve and accompany the workers, but to co-opt new members for their party. The group always comes first, the masses come second. . . . Reality is understood not through experience, but through "rigorous" analyses that reveal the dogmatic character of the concepts more than the real contradictions.[10]

Church intellectuals criticize socialist societies for their suppression of individual liberties, their authoritarianism, the excessive power of the state bureaucracy, and elitism. They feel that authoritarian socialism may address the material needs of the population, but that it fails to represent a desirable alternative social order.[11] In their view, most socialist countries exclude the masses from the decision-making process. The system is still elitist, but the state replaces the bourgeoisie as the primary oppressor.[12] Popular Church intellectuals recognize that there is no perfect social system and are critical of the utopian character of most Marxian thought.[13] These views are in contrast to the frequently less critical views on socialism of progressive Catholics in other Latin American countries, again underscoring the more cautious character of Brazil's Catholic Left.

One of the most important and innovative aspects of the popular Church in Brazil is its emphasis on the affective dimensions of life. The traditional Marxian Left focused almost exclusively on socioeconomic needs. Concerns such as friendship, community, and interpersonal relations were never part of its discourse, and it generally assumed that revolution would satisfy the most important human needs. Following a well-established line of Catholic thought, the contemporary popular Church places great value on interpersonal relations, which it perceives as a fundamental human need partially autonomous of the socioeconomic sphere. Though attributing many problems of the masses to poverty, the Catholic Left is critical of the view that revolution would resolve affective questions. This emphasis on affective questions also differs from liberal conceptions, which focus largely on the need for freedom. Progressive Catholic intellectuals generally believe that in the absence of mechanisms that fulfill basic socioeconomic and emotional needs, liberal freedoms lose some of their importance. They also question the common liberal assumption that a vast majority of the population will be able to satisfy these needs if basic civil freedoms are ensured.

Despite these criticisms of socialism and capitalism, the popular Church has not conceptualized a model of the way to promote social change. The nebulous character of pronouncements in favor of a "third path" is noteworthy. It is not clear what, if any, existing societies could be considered a third path. Ideologues of very different beliefs, ranging from conservatives to radical Catholic thinkers and from populists (Juan Perón) to authoritarian corporatists (President Juan Onganía of Argentina, 1966-70), have long espoused a third path.[14] Ever since *Rerum Novarum* (1891), Catholic thought of widely different political tendencies has condemned "selfish capitalism" and "atheistic Marxism." Although there are many differences between conservative ideologies and those of Brazil's Catholic Left, the vagueness of the notion of a third path makes it impossible to assess what it means. Only a minority of the Catholic Left explicitly subscribes to a third path ideology, but the problem of lack of clarity about a different society is common to a majority.

Compounding this lack of clarity is the belief of all sectors of the Church that a religious institution should not engage in formulating specific solutions, but rather should be a nonpartisan critic of society. As a result, progressive Catholics have generally not dealt with important questions implicit in their vision, such as the viability and means of constructing a more democratic socialist system—admittedly a remote problem in the Brazilian context—or even concrete strategies for change. Furthermore, popular Church thought sometimes has a utopian character—for example, discussion of popular liberation fails to acknowledge that the popular classes are unlikely to obtain political or socioeconomic liberation, whatever that means, in the foreseeable future.

The views of progressive Church leaders do, however, serve as a check on facile socialist and capitalist ideologies. This is particularly true of the Church's attempt to posit human relationships and felicity as the ultimate objective of any political change. The insight progressive Catholics offer is that although a given social system or political regime may further the values of community, respect for the individual and for civil liberties and participation, they do not inhere in any particular system. Popular Church leaders emphasize the political element in creating a better society, but they also feel that this task is more than a political one.[15] Political transformation and economic development are necessary, but they are not sufficient to realize the kind of society and human relationships called for in Church doctrine.*

Political Participation and the Catholic Left

The Catholic Left's emphasis on participation is one of the outstanding traits of its views on development. Popular Church intellectuals see participation as valuable in its own right. All persons have the right to help make the decisions that shape a society's future, and exercising that right is a means of realizing oneself. They also see participation as a means of promoting social justice by ensuring that all social classes and groups are represented in the state. The political system should create mechanisms that encourage policymakers to respond to the needs of different sectors of society. Formal channels for participation are insufficient because they do not deal with the structural roots of authoritarianism. Consequently, it is necessary to provide the citizens with the tools (especially education) that enable them to participate more effectively.

Church progressives feel that participation is a prerequisite to adequate solutions to the problems of the popular classes. They believe that the popular classes can develop creative solutions to their own problems.[16] Participation is a necessary means of relaying information to the ultimate decision-makers about what the society's most important needs are and how they can be met. By listening to popular needs, the state could develop more effective solutions to problems. Popular Church leaders emphasize that more so than any technocrats, the popular sectors are aware of their own needs and have ideas on meeting those needs. This belief was underscored by

*The relationship between political change and a good social order is one of the great questions in the classical sociological tradition, addressed at length by Marx, Durkheim, and Weber, among others. In contrast to what he called the utopian socialists, Marx argued that political change (through revolution) was essential to resolve major social problems. He was less clear about how socialism would resolve social problems. This continues to be a major lacuna in most Marxist theory. Weber emphasized that many problems in contemporary society are products of the modern world, and not only of capitalism. But he was unduly pessimistic about the possibility that political change could resolve any major social problems. Durkheim felt that the state could improve the quality of human relations by creating community groups, but he did not adequately address the issue of how to democratize the state in such a way that it would be willing to do so; see *Suicide*, pp. 361-92.

Dom Moacyr Grechi, bishop of Acre and Purus and at the time national president of the Pastoral Land Commission, in a deposition to the Federal Congress in May 1977.

The Church has insisted that only an effective agrarian reform could resolve the conflicts found all over the country. We have also insisted that the success of agrarian reform depends on a widespread national debate, with the privileged participation of the people affected, the peasants. . . . Our contact and experiences with the rural people suggest that the common allegation that the peasants are incapable of suggesting and making the needed changes is false and tendentious.[17]

Out of this emphasis on popular participation has come a belief in the importance of grass-roots organizations. Church leaders see these organizations as the principal channel for articulating popular needs and believe that they should play an important role in any society. They have affirmed the importance of the autonomy of popular movements with respect to political parties.

The concern with popular participation also shaped the popular Church's discussion of political parties. In 1982, the major election pamphlets called on the parties to promote popular participation, and some Church people and groups went so far as to assert that workers and peasants should construct the parties. For example, a 1980 document by Catholic Workers Action stated, "The Brazilian working class needs a political party. To be authentic, this party should be constructed from below, by people who are participating in the struggles of the working class, and, above all, it should have a majority of workers."[18]

This particular document captures the flavor of many *basista* Church discussions concerning parties. The concern with popular participation in parties is important, but the concept of a party of workers ignores the need for parties to bring together people according to political view and not just social class. This emphasis on popular participation and control of parties led to an affinity between base communities and the Workers Party (PT) in some parts of the country, especially Greater São Paulo.[19] Even though the link was weaker outside Greater São Paulo, a good part of the party's limited success resulted from it.

As a corollary to the emphasis on participation, popular Church leaders criticize the belief that technicians and planners can resolve major social problems in a closed system. They believe that planners cannot understand the needs of the masses, nor can they know the

best way of implementing a program. They argue that technical solutions, whether in capitalist or socialist societies, may appear to be
rational, well planned, and well conceived, but they ignore the complex reality of the society and tend to impose a solution upon the
population.[20]

In this emphasis on participation, there is a tendency to simplify
complex issues. To project what works in a community or a diocese
as a model for a society, as some pastoral agents implicitly do, dis-
torts social reality—and consequently the kinds of political answers
one proposes. It is easier to encourage participation in a diocese
than in the state, and the decisions involved in resolving diocesan
priorities are simpler than those related to the foreign debt and
other economic and technological questions.[21] The developmental
process is complex and ofen requires technical knowledge that only
elites possess. Participation often involves trade-offs; it can take
longer to find a solution when it is based on extensive efforts to respond to popular needs. Nor is it always clear what kind of institutional structures could permit effective participation. Church
leaders have not addressed the issue of how to ensure that people
will participate when appropriate structures exist. Finally, the emphasis on grass-roots participation sometimes results in a rejection
of institutions with limited local-level participation. Since this attitude can lead to ignoring political parties and the state, it can be
politically inefficacious. For all these reasons, the Catholic Left's
emphasis on participation is not an adequate conception of how to
change society.

Nevertheless, the discussion of participation underscores elements of the development process that are often neglected. Participation is not a panacea to all the ills of underdevelopment and authoritarianism, but it can give people a sense of worth and help
ensure that different sectors of society are represented. High levels
of participation are not needed in a liberal democracy, but they can
help promote an expansion of democratic rights.[22] Participation is
also a way of generating collective responsibility for decisions. Furthermore, popular participation can contribute to creative solutions
to social problems. The people have a deeper experiential knowledge of the problems they face than technicians do. They may not
be able to resolve a problem without technical assistance, but conversely, it is unlikely that any technician, regardless of intentions,

can devise satisfactory solutions for the popular classes in the absence of channels of participation and communication.

The Catholic Left's confidence that the popular sectors can contribute to resolving developmental problems is not wholly unfounded, even though it is usually exaggerated. In their daily contact with the popular sectors, pastoral agents have witnessed the people's ability to respond creatively to problems such as how to use land or other resources and how to respond to outside threats. CEBs in urban areas often work collectively to build houses, community buildings, or health posts and even to install water and sewer lines; in rural areas, they have formed cooperatives of producers and consumers. The ability of such measures to change inegalitarian social structures is limited; yet they have helped the population resolve some basic material needs, have generated a sense of community, and have shown the popular capacity to work together.*

The belief that the popular classes can contribute has been incorporated into the theory of "community development," which grew up around a belief that local communities contain latent resources that, if mobilized, can help solve some of the community's problems. Many advocates of local approaches to development overstate their potential, but local government based on extensive popular participation has registered some successes. In Brazil, the most significant successes in recent years have occurred in Boa Esperança in Espírito Santo (1971 to 1982) and Lages in Santa Catarina (1976 to 1982). Both municipalities experienced dramatic increases in local participation in government; rapid growth in economic production, especially among small farmers; improvements in the school system; and implementation of alternative technologies.[23] On the other hand, the fragility and limits of these experiences were manifested in the decline of both municipalities.

Although the Catholic Left underestimates the complexities in creating a highly participatory system, its criticisms of the technocratic, authoritarian model offer some insights. Skilled technocrats

---

*During the late 1970's, the significance of these community practices was an important subject of debate. Much of the Left felt that these practices could demobilize the population by discouraging it from confronting the state; others emphasized their positive aspects. One of the main published forums of this debate was the journal *Proposta.*

with specialized knowledge are essential in any modern society, but technocrats can further the interests of dominant sectors in the name of technical competence, and their models of formal rationality can create extremely irrational consequences for large parts of the population.[24]

Even in Brazil, where the military regime could claim greater success than its counterparts in Argentina, Chile, or Uruguay, the problems of authoritarian development are obvious. The military was able to promote rapid economic growth for a prolonged period, but it did little to meet the needs of large sectors of the population.

The Church called attention to the need to question those, either on the Right or on the Left, who believe that technicians offer the best solutions for social problems and that political participation and political efficiency are antagonistic goals.[25] Without providing solutions to the questions it poses, the Church has underscored the importance of thinking about development in new ways and has particularly emphasized efforts to create more participatory patterns that address basic human needs. Resolving the dilemmas of development requires some political, economic, and social stability, and at times, there can be tension between this need and more participatory forms of government. In the long run, however, finding adequate solutions to the dilemmas of development also requires the creative potential of as much of the population as possible.[26] This potential can exist in intellectuals and elites of all political tendencies, and, as the Church has underscored, it can also exist among the masses.

Conclusions

The Church neither has nor claims to have a clear, cohesive conception of the development process. Few pastoral agents at the grass roots are politically sophisticated, and even the bishops do not have a strong grasp of the difficult dilemmas of development. There are nebulous points, weaknesses, and naiveté in the Church's views on development. Many pastoral agents make the facile assumption that if the popular classes organize themselves well enough, they will change the society. Many overestimate the capacity of grass-roots democratization to transform society. Few have thought about what the profile of a new society should be or how to arrive at that society, and few have addressed the question of promoting participation in complex societies.

The opposite side of the overestimation of the strength of popular organizations was a generalized underestimation of the importance of political institutions, especially the state and parties. Most popular Church leaders expected that political liberalization would allow popular organizations to become increasingly dynamic. In fact the opposite happened after 1982, as traditional political institutions competed with, and to some extent replaced, grass-roots organizations. Although there were important exceptions, the majority of radical Catholic activists failed to grasp this possibility. This failure was not the main factor behind the decline of the popular Church (see Chapter 11), but it certainly contributed.

This is not, however, to understate the Church's political impact during an important period of Brazilian history. The Church helped to promote a more critical consciousness, encouraged political participation, and criticized development choices. And although the Church lacks a development model, Church thought encouraged reflection about the development process. Its emphasis on popular values, on participation, on democratic practices, on a just economic system, and on fraternity and community provides principles that should be observed in all societies.

The Catholic Left's discussion of these questions helped shape the political debate for an extended period of time. Paradoxically, however, as democratization proceeded, the influence of the popular Church declined, especially after 1982. The popular Church fought to promote democracy, but when it came, it brought more dilemmas than answers. This was particularly noticeable in states like Rio and São Paulo, where opposition governments co-opted popular movements in an effort to control mobilization. But the gradual decline in the importance of the popular Church after 1982 does not detract from the impact it had in fighting the military regime. And the conflict between the Church and many of the movements and persons influenced by Catholic practice and thought should not obscure the significant imprint of progressive Catholicism.

Even though it would be unfair to expect the Church to be the primary agent of social change, it is reasonable to expect it to develop practices consistent with its discourse. Despite ambiguities, contradictions, and conflicts, the Brazilian Church has done so more successfully than any other Church in Latin America. Not-withstanding the limited political vision of many Catholic activists, the Church had a major impact in empowering civil society through grass-roots Catholic organizations, through bishops' denunciations, and through calls for a more democratic order.[27] And although the popular Church itself declined, many of the important experiments it encouraged promise to continue to affect Brazilian politics in the foreseeable future.

CHAPTER 11

The Decline of the Popular Church, 1982-1985

IN PREVIOUS chapters I have argued that by about 1976, the Brazilian Church was probably the most progressive in the world. It continued evolving in a generally progressive direction over the next six years. By about 1982, however, conservative pressures against the Brazilian Church mounted, and it began to move in a more cautious direction, becoming a less important political actor.[1]

This concluding chapter explores the nature and causes of this more cautious trend. As of early 1985, it was impossible to tell how far this trend would go, but it appeared that it would at least prevent further evolution of the Brazilian Church along increasingly progressive lines. Two primary factors were responsible for the more cautious approach: the democratization process and a significant challenge from the neo-conservative ecclesiastical sectors. First, however, I want to briefly address the issue of *why* the Brazilian Church became progressive while many Latin American Churches did not.

The Distinctive Character of the Brazilian Church

One of the underlying themes of this book, through my explicit emphasis on the distinctive character of the Church in Brazil, has been the significant differences among the Catholic Churches in different Latin American countries. Four factors help explain these differences across countries. First, the nature of the linkages of the national Church to the Vatican varies, particularly (although not exclusively) because of different orientations of the papal nuncio.

Second, the ecclesiastical situation proper varies according to country. For example, the Church's orientation is affected by whether there is a shortage of priests, by whether it holds a religious monopoly, and by other factors. Third, variables such as effective leadership and the nature of the strategy of different factions within the Church are important. Finally, to return to a theme running throughout the book, the differing national political situations also affect the Church's orientation. All four of these factors help explain the unique development of the Brazilian Church.

At least since the early 1950's, the Brazilian Church has established a progressive tradition that has few counterparts elsewhere in Latin America. At least three factors contributed to the strength of progressive tendencies in Brazil before 1964. First, by the early 1950's, Brazil's Church had unusually strong links to progressive sectors of the Vatican. Throughout the 1950's, the Vatican consistently supported Dom Helder Câmara, whose importance in the development of progressive Catholicism is unquestionable. Dom Armando Lombardi, the papal nuncio between 1952 and 1964, nominated as bishops a number of progressive priests who had worked with Catholic Action. These bishops were instrumental in encouraging progressive change during the 1960's.

Second, in contrast to the Church in some Spanish American countries, the Brazilian Church has a history of relative institutional weakness, one manifestation of which has been a constant shortage of priests. In response, the Brazilian Church has long encouraged greater lay leadership than its counterparts in most of Spanish America. The cadre of lay leaders that assembled around the Centro Dom Vital in the 1920's and 1930's, the Catholic Left of the 1958-64 period, and the base communities are salient examples. Despite differences, these movements were alike in giving the laity a more prominent role. This fact helped make possible greater innovation at the grass roots than occurred in most other countries.

Third, the Brazilian Church has a limited history of persecution by liberal forces. Between 1889 and 1964, there were few major Church-state conflicts. In societies where anticlericalism loomed large as an issue, the Church generally responded defensively, closing itself to the modern world. In Mexico, Spain, and elsewhere, conservative responses to liberal persecution affected the Church for many decades.

In addition, after 1964 progressive Church leaders in Brazil made choices that increased their chances of changing the institution and avoiding isolation. The effort to work with rather than against the bishops and the emphasis on defining limits to the Church's political role stand out as particularly important in this regard. The emphasis on respecting popular religiosity also contributed to ecclesial effectiveness and made it harder to challenge the progressives.

The nature of political change in Brazil also contributed to the distinctive character of the Church. Comparative analysis of bureaucratic-authoritarian regimes in Latin America has underscored the relatively low level of "threat" that existed prior to the 1964 coup.[2] This low level meant that most Church leaders, especially after 1968, did not anticipate a Communist takeover or a socioeconomic collapse that would adversely affect the institution. Where Church leaders perceived a high possibility of radical socioeconomic change or breakdown, they (like leaders in other institutions) have tended to take sharply defined positions in recent decades. In situations of revolution (Cuba and Nicaragua) or of a very high perceived threat (Chile and Uruguay in 1973, Argentina in 1976), a majority of bishops responded defensively, even though a minority of priests and lay leaders opted for revolution. The Church has a long history of difficulty in coexisting with Communist regimes; so this defensive response is not surprising. Indeed, in the aftermath of the 1964 coup in Brazil, a majority of bishops did react defensively, but over time the perception of a threat from the Left eroded and the perception of a threat from the Right increased.

Conversely, situations of stable, elitist democracy (Colombia, Mexico, Venezuela) have encouraged conservative responses by Church leaders and a goal of integrating the institution into the society. The Churches in these societies have not faced the challenges the Brazilian Church has. In terms of the hierarchy's response, the situation in Brazil—a relatively low level of threat, coupled with the closing of liberal channels of dissent—was the most favorable to progressive change. The timing of Church change and state repression also favored progressive innovation in Brazil. Because the repression came before the proliferation of movements of radical priests, the progressive clergy were forced to work within the institution. As a result, there was less internal conflict and greater episcopal support for grass-roots innovations.

Alone, neither the historical development of the Brazilian Church nor Brazil's political and socioeconomic changes explain the distinctive character of the Church in the world's largest Catholic nation. But together, they contributed to a unique set of circumstances generally propitious to progressive change, which was further facilitated by the outstanding leadership of the progressive sectors.

The Church's Role in a Period of Political Transition

The Brazilian *abertura* was singularly protracted, and at least until the 1982 elections it was not clear that there would be a return to democracy. Gradually, however, democratization permitted the rebirth of civil society, and as a result, the Church no longer felt compelled to speak for civil society in the same way. Because other institutions could once again assume political tasks, some Church moderates who had earlier supported deeper political involvement favored greater caution. Whereas a majority of prelates had opposed the human rights abuses of the military government, only a minority—the popular bishops—were equally concerned about socioeconomic problems in a liberal democracy. The return to democracy therefore reduced the incentive many bishops had to comment on politics. Conservatives seized on the new political situation as a means of insisting that the Church change its political involvement. The leader of this movement was D. Eugênio Sales, who stated, "A new period for the Brazilian Church is beginning. The Church had a very active role in the period when Brazil was becoming a closed society. It was the 'voice of those who had no voice.' Today, the parliament, press, and parties are functioning fully. They should speak, and the Church should take care of its own affairs."[3]

Some leaders of the progressive sectors partially agreed with this perspective. Dom Ivo Lorscheiter stated in December 1984 that "in the last twenty years, the Church hierarchy often had to speak about political, social, and economic problems because the laity could not do so. From now on, in a situation of greater freedom and popular organization, although the hierarchy will not become silent, it wants the laity to speak more."[4]

After 1982, the conservative tendencies of the opposition parties also diminished the prominence of the progressive sectors of the Church. During most of the 1970's, there was an unstated alliance between liberal opposition forces and the progressive Church. This alliance eroded over time, and by March 1985, with the exception of the temporary joining of forces during the campaign for direct elections in 1984, the divisions between liberals and popular Church leaders were pronounced. The latter were generally disgruntled with the basically cautious, elitist, nonparticipatory character of the opposition parties, especially the PMDB; the former often dismissed the Catholic Left as politically naive or irrelevant.

Although democratization led to some diminishing of the Church's political role, there were some countervailing factors. The Church's increasing commitment to progressive religious principles during the 1974-82 period showed that its positions toward the regime were not simply an immediate response to a sense of threat but that its conception of its mission had changed during the years of authoritarian rule. Most moderates believe that the Church should take social positions and assume a preferential option for the poor. There is a consensus among the bishops that the Church should call for social justice and for a more open, participatory, and egalitarian system. These concerns are pronounced in regions of the country where democratization had limited impact, especially in rural areas of the Amazon and the Northeast. In many rural areas, the forms of domination continued to be unsophisticated and repressive, and the Church often played a key role in defending peasants.

The strengthening of political parties led the Church to be less active on many issues, but the progressive sectors continued to be concerned about the popular classes. The care with which the progressives delimited the Church's institutional role was, in part, an attempt to ensure that they would have something to say in the new political situation. The strengthening of political society did not completely change the Church's role because it sought a unique role. In one regard, the Church in Nova Iguaçu is typical of popular dioceses: even though the relationship between the Church and the popular movements has changed, the Church is still an important force.

The Church's political relevance is strengthened by popular attitudes toward religion and politics. The Church enjoys greater legitimacy in popular circles than do most politicians or political movements. The great majority of the people are skeptical about politics and politicians. They tend to view politicians as self-interested[5] and politics as something for the powerful. Religion has a significant capacity to mobilize the popular classes and continues to be a major factor in the daily lives of many people.

In addition, because the Church does not worry about coming to power, it can remain more concerned with pedagogical issues than can popular movements or political parties. Popular movements and parties face complex issues, and even when they are concerned about grass-roots participation and democratic practices, they cannot always provide the same room for discussion that the ecclesial communities do. Furthermore, party politicians often speak a technocratic language, creating a need for an institution committed specifically to grass-roots work.[6]

The Neo-Conservative Challenge

The most significant pressure for the Church to play a less important political role came not from the liberalization process but from neo-conservative sectors within the Church. The neo-conservative reaction to Church innovation began in Europe and some Latin American countries in the early 1970's, and by 1982 it had also expanded in Brazil.

In this century, the Church has gone through periods of significant innovation (especially 1958 to the mid-1970's) and of conservative reaction to innovation (for example, 1903-22). Despite the profound changes of the past three decades, the conservative forces in the Church never disappeared. The result has been a series of intricate struggles in one of the most complex institutions in the world. The same institution that produced Camilo Torres (the Colombian priest-guerrilla) continues to reject birth control, and the same institution that remains closed to ordaining women as priests or to altering formal hierarchical structures has given rise to the most progressive theologians among the major Christian churches.

The past two decades have seen ongoing struggles between conservatives, moderates, and radicals, both in Europe and Latin America, with no unilinear direction in terms of Church change. Vatican II brought major innovations in European Catholicism, but then in the late 1960's and early 1970's, these thrusts for change were partially enervated. A similar pattern emerged later in Latin America; from the early 1960's to the early 1970's, the Church changed rapidly, but since about 1972 in most countries the reforms have been more cautious, and in some they have been reversed. Since the accession of John Paul II, a conservative pattern has been consolidated. Institutional leaders felt that change—especially in Latin America—had either gone too far or threatened to do so.[7]

The earlier Dutch case provides little room for optimism among those who would like to see Brazil's Church continue evolving in a progressive direction. From the early 1960's until about 1972, the Dutch Church was the most progressive in the world, adopting a series of innovations, particularly in terms of authority relations in the Church. After a series of minor "disciplinary" measures, beginning in 1970 the Vatican thwarted the further development of the Dutch Church along progressive, more democratic lines. In November 1970, the Vatican Congregation for the Clergy vetoed a Dutch Pastoral Council plan to give the laity a deciding voice on most issues of pastoral policy. In 1970 and 1972, Rome named two conservative bishops to what had been a coherent bloc of seven progressive prelates. The new bishops were chosen despite strong opposition by local laity, priests, brothers, nuns, and the Dutch bishops. Coupled with other measures, such as an investigation against leading Dutch theologian Edward Schillebeecx, a Vatican veto of a new catechism for adults in 1966, refusals to approve changes, rejections of Dutch documents as "unorthodox," and concerted efforts to isolate the Dutch bishops from the world episcopacy, the nominations seriously weakened the Dutch Church's ability to promote internal change.[8]

The neo-conservative reaction to change in the Latin American Church began in 1972, with the election of Alfonso López Trujillo as secretary general of the Latin American Bishops Conference (CELAM). After several years of progressive advances in the Latin American Church, the moderate and conservative sectors regained control of CELAM, and a period of greater conservatism began in several national churches.[9] Under the auspices of López Trujillo and close associate Belgian theologian Roger Vekemans (who lives in Colombia), the conservatives articulated a counterproposal to the liberationists. They used the language of the liberationists, but depoliticized it. For example, they adopted the notion of liberation but de-emphasized its political aspects and gave it a more spiritual turn, focusing on liberation from sin. They argued that the liberationists had reduced faith to politics, turned the Church into a political organization, and threatened the Church's unity.[10]

The conservatives attempted to use the third meeting of the Latin American bishops, at Puebla in 1979, as a way of isolating the progressive sectors. They controlled the preparation for the Puebla conference, which was billed as an attempt to harness liberation theol-

ogy. The CELAM secretariat's working document for the Puebla
conference reversed many themes of the Medellín conference and
virtually reinstituted a neo-Christendom model of the Church. According to the document, the major problem of Latin America was
secularization. Structural problems and social injustice received secondary treatment. The secretariat then handpicked the theologians
and social scientists who would attend the conference, systematically excluding even the most respected liberationists. In a letter,
which was accidentally discovered by the press, to the conservative
archbishop of Aracaju, Brazil, López Trujillo insisted that the conservatives had to prepare an ideological platform before coming to
Puebla and exhorted, "Prepare your bombers, get some of your de-
licious venom ready. . . . May your blows be on the mark."[11]

This particular attempt to curb the popular Church was largely
unsuccessful, especially in Brazil. López Trujillo was personally discredited for his practices. More important, progressives and moderates criticized the working document for its view that secularization is the fundamental pastoral problem confronting the Latin
American Church, its conservative outlook on the the meaning of
Christ's life and message, its argument that cultural and not political and economic issues are the major problems in Latin America,
its weak discussion of political reality, and its tendency to legitimate
military regimes. The Brazilian Church essentially rejected the
working document. Theologians, social scientists, regional episcopal groups, pastoral commissions, and eventually the CNBB implicitly or explicitly called for a radically different analysis and pastoral
options.[12] In large part because of the input of the Brazilians, Puebla
ended as a stalemate between conservatives, reformists, and liberationists.[13] Since the conference, however, CELAM has continued to
bolster the conservatives. Even though this attempt to discredit the
popular model of the Church failed, CELAM's capacity to impose
conservative Church patterns is significant.

The neo-conservative movement remained relatively weak in Brazil throughout the 1970's. However, as the Brazilian Church became
one of the most important and progressive in the world, its relationship to Rome changed. Some divergences emerged, and, in contrast
to the 1958-70 period of encouragement of Church reform in Brazil,
the Vatican began to limit innovation. The first conflict arose in
1969, on a strictly ecclesiastical rather than a political issue. During
the late 1960s, the Brazilian Church faced a serious vocations crisis

as a large number of men and women left the priesthood and religious orders. At the annual assembly of the CNBB in 1969, the bishops approved the ordination of married men and increased opportunities for ex-priests and former member of religious orders to play active roles. Rome sharply opposed this proposal.[14]

By 1975, conflict between the Brazilian Church and Rome over issues of national church autonomy and politics had begun. By then, the CNBB had become involved in the human rights issue, and it began to promote an International Tribunal of Human Rights. Rome responded that such an initiative should come from the Vatican, not from the Brazilian episcopacy, even though many other national conferences warmly welcomed the idea. In 1977, after ten years of reflecting a religious ceremony consistent with some basic elements of popular culture, values, and religion, the CNBB published a guide for masses for popular groups. Even though the guide was relatively conventional, the initiative went beyond what Rome found acceptable, and in late 1979, the Vatican vetoed it. In 1982, the Vatican also rejected two other Brazilian proposals for popular masses, the "Mass of the Earth Without Evil" and the "Quilombo Mass."*

Despite these minor conflicts, the Vatican generally did little to rein in the Brazilian Church until after 1980. In some respects, Pope John Paul II even supported the progressive Church. In 1980 in Brazil, he supported the preferential option for the poor, emphasized social justice and participation, criticized unjust social structures, supported the base communities, and praised the Brazilian bishops. In one of his most publicized speeches in Brazil, the pope stated,

Throughout the world, the Church wants to be of the poor. In Brazil, it also wants to be a Church of the poor. . . . The Church tells the poor—those who live in misery—that they are particularly close to God and His Kingdom. The only struggle, the only battle, in which the Church wishes to serve, is the noble struggle for truth and justice and the battle for the true good. . . . Only a just society, which attempts to become ever more just, has a reason for existing.[15]

After 1980, however, the pope and the Vatican took measures to limit further change in the Brazilian Church. One significant step was a papal letter to the Brazilian bishops in December 1980 affirm-

---

* *Quilombo* is the Brazilian word for hiding places for bands of runaway slaves. The term conjures up the image of the black quest for freedom. The Quilombo Mass played on this theme.

ing that the Church should not become involved in social questions
to the detriment of its specifically religious mission. The letter was
not particularly critical, but it indicated some tendency to attempt
to limit the popular Church.[16]

In 1980, the pope requested Dom Paulo Arns to write a report explaining (and defending) the Church's role in the auto workers'
strike.[17] In 1981, he requested a Vatican representative to keep close
watch on the seminary in São Paulo. These measures were warning
signs to the archdiocese, probably the most important in the country because of its size and dynamic leadership. The pope has supported the pastoral line of Dom Eugênio Sales, archbishop of Rio de
Janeiro and the leader of the neo-conservative sectors, and has invited Sales to Rome to represent the Brazilian hierarchy on several
occasions.[18] The pope's concern about the political activities of the
Jesuits in Latin America led to a special meeting of the order in February 1982 at which the pope imposed unprecedented controls. Although the measure did not directly affect the Brazilian Church, it
was a clear sign of the pope's willingness to use unusual measures
to retain control over the flock.[19] In March 1982, the Vatican Congregation of the Clergy issued a document prohibiting clerical involvement in political associations or unions.[20] Even though few if
any progressive clerics in Brazil are members of unions or political
associations, the document was clearly aimed at the liberationist
sectors of the Latin American Church.

By 1982, the sharp deterioration in relations between the Vatican
and the Nicaraguan government was causing deep concern among
progressive Catholics throughout Latin America. Nicaragua seemed
to offer the Church some possibilities of coexisting with a revolutionary regime. In contrast to most great revolutions of this century,
which were markedly anticlerical,* the Nicaraguan revolution enjoyed the strong support of a large part of the active Catholic population, and the bishops' document justifying tyrannicide, published in early 1979, condemned the Somoza regime and implicitly

---

*The revolutions in China, the Soviet Union, Cuba, and Mexico were all mark-
edly anticlerical and led to significant repression of the Catholic Church. On the
Chinese case, see Hanson. The documentation on the Soviet case is extensive, even
though often marked by cold war ideology; see Galter. There continues to be conflict
between Church and state in the Soviet Union and much of Eastern Europe. Overviews of the situation are Simon; Jancar; and Kolarz, pp. 176-217. A good history of
Church-state conflict during the Mexican revolution is Olivera Sedano. On Cuba, see
Dewart, pp. 92-185; and Crahan, "Salvation."

supported the revolution. In terms of regime attitudes toward the Church, initial Church support for the regime, and some regime policies, there was common ground. However, since early 1980, most of the Nicaraguan bishops have increasingly opposed the regime and the popular Church as it exists in Nicaragua. The bishops favor pluralistic liberalism, which they believe is threatened in Nicaragua. Furthermore, they fear that the revolution could encroach upon Church autonomy, especially in the area of education, and that the Nicaraguan Church radicals have reduced religion to politics. Many observers perceived the pope's June 1982 letter condemning the popular Church as an absurdity and his reiterations of this theme during his March 1983 visit to Nicaragua as a warning sign to progressive Church leaders throughout Latin America.[21] In late 1984 and early 1985, the pope took disciplinary measures against the four priests who held cabinet positions in the Nicaraguan government.

The tensions between the Vatican and Nicaragua affected progressive sectors throughout Latin America, and Vatican and CELAM criticisms of Church progressives aided the renaissance of the conservatives in Brazil. In 1982 the conservatives made their first major attempt to lead the Church in a different direction. After having acquiesced in the progressive movement of the preceding decade, they began to try to delegitimate the popular Church and construct an alternative agenda. Bishops with strong links to the Vatican and CELAM led these efforts, but they also involved a number of middle-class lay movements with a traditional conception of faith.[22]

Especially since the election of John Paul II, liberation theology has come under attack from CELAM and Rome.[23] In 1977, the International Theological Commission of the Vatican issued a cautious statement critical of reductionistic versions of liberation theology.[24] In addition, Rome pressured some progressive bishops into not attending the Third International Ecumenical Congress on Theology, held in São Paulo in February 1980. The real attack against liberation theology in Brazil began in 1982, with the publication of several works sharply critical of Leonardo Boff.[25] Since the mid-1970's the Vatican has been investigating the works of Boff, the best-known Brazilian theologian, on the grounds that his views stray too far from Catholic orthodoxy.[26]

These attacks pushed the investigation of Boff's work into a new phase, and in September 1984, the theologian was called to Rome to defend his writings. After several months of deliberation, the Vatican formally condemned Boff in May 1985, imposing an indefinite silence. Since Boff has been Brazil's most prominent theologian since the early 1970's, this action was perceived as a warning to the entire progressive sector in Latin America. The investigation and condemnation helped fuel attacks against him and the progressives in Brazil. Clodovis Boff, Leonardo's younger brother and also one of the outstanding theologians in Brazil, was also punished. On February 24, 1984, Dom Eugênio Sales removed him from the Catholic University of Rio, and on December 12, 1984, the Vatican prohibited him from teaching in Rome.[27] In September 1984, the Vatican Congregation for the Doctrine of the Faith, headed by Cardinal Joseph Ratzinger, issued an important report that, without condemning liberation theology, was quite critical. Then in October 1984, during his trip to the Caribbean, John Paul II condemned the Marxist elements in liberation theology. In April 1985, Vatican official Agnelo Rossi, ex-archbishop of São Paulo (1964-70), published a document highly critical of liberation theology.

The attacks on Leonardo Boff in 1982 marked the most significant conflict the Brazilian Church had experienced in years. It was followed by the re-emergence of other conflicts in 1983 and 1984, when the conservatives stepped up their criticisms. In April 1983, the conservatives nominated a slate of officers for the CNBB. Although defeated, they fared better than any conservative slate since the early 1970's, indicating the conservatives' considerable success in reaffirming their agenda. At the same time, Dom Luciano Duarte, a leader of the conservative movement, accused the progressives of disobedience to the pope and invited papal intervention.[28]

With the important exception of the condemnation of Leonardo Boff, the Vatican opted for an essentially nonconfrontive strategy with the Brazilian Church. While attempting to avert open conflict and condemnation, it nevertheless sought to limit change in a progressive direction. The Vatican has sent a number of warnings without explicitly criticizing the Brazilian Church. Vatican control over episcopal nominations has played an integral part in this strategy. The CNBB has pushed for greater national and local say in the nomination of new bishops, but the Vatican has insisted on retaining control of this prerogative, which is one of the Vatican's most important means of affecting the Brazilian Church. The key individual in episcopal nominations is the papal nuncio, and Rome generally accepts his recommendations. In some cases, he consults local priests, members of religious orders, and lay leaders, but this consultation has no authority.

In recent years, the nuncio has used his authority to bolster the conservative sectors of the Church. In several cases, the papal nuncio requested a diocese to submit suggestions but then completely ignored them and imposed a conservative figure. Two examples of conservative episcopal nominations occurred in 1981 in the archdioceses of Pôrto Alegre and Brasília. The outgoing archbishops were both conservatives, and in the case of Brasília observers assumed that the incoming archbishop would also be conservative to avoid serious Church-state conflict in the nation's capital. However, in the case of Pôrto Alegre, Dom Ivo Lorscheiter was believed favored because he is so highly respected by his episcopal counterparts. From 1971 until the present, Dom Ivo has been either secretary general or president of the CNBB. Despite this, he was bypassed, and Dom Cláudio Collings, a conservative bishop of a small town in Rio Grande, was named. The nomination was an apparent setback for the progressives since the archbishop of Pôrto Alegre is the natural spokesman for the southern Church. In October 1984, the Vatican named a conservative (Dom Clóvis Frainer) as the new archbishop of Manaus, and in April 1985, it named an unknown moderate (Dom José Cardoso Sobrinho) as Dom Helder Câmara's replacement in Recife.

Other nominations have followed a similar pattern, in some cases being imposed from above despite widespread local opposition. The most dramatic cases occurred in Viana in Maranhão in 1975, and Vitória in Espírito Santo in 1982. Both dioceses played leading roles in the early development of the popular Church, and in both cases, when the bishop retired, the nuncio named a conservative replacement, setting off a lengthy and bitter dispute that led to the dismantling of existing ecclesial networks. In Viana, after the death of Dom Hélio Campos in 1975, Dom Adalberto Paulo da Silva was appointed bishop despite strong local opposition. By firing several paid lay leaders, transferring a large number of clergy out of the diocese, one of whom he even excommunicated, and prohibiting involvement in opposition political activity, the new bishop dismantled the pastoral programs established by his predecessor.[29]

The neo-conservative movement has criticized many aspects of the progressive Church, including liberation theology, ecclesial practices, and the role of base communities. There is considerable heterogeneity in conservative viewpoints, but criticisms overlap somewhat. In general terms, the neo-conservative critique of the popular Church has focused on the relationship between faith and politics and on authority lines within the Church. More specifically, the neo-conservatives have focused on several issues.[30]

First, the neo-conservatives criticize the progressives for de-emphasizing spirituality. In the neo-conservative conception of faith, the essence of spirituality is one's personal relationship to God. The main problem in the world is sin, conceived of as distance from God. Socioeconomic injustice is subordinate to the more important question of a personal relationship to God. The most important liberation is from sin, not from socioeconomic or political injustice.

Second, the neo-conservatives criticize the progressives for their understanding of the preferential option for the poor. They charge that the progressives focus exclusively on this option to the neglect of other social classes. For the neo-conservatives, the progressive emphasis on the poor has led to an obscuring of the true source of faith, Jesus Christ. Some neo-conservatives argue that the preferential option refers to those who are poor not in a material sense but rather in a spiritual sense. As Archbishop Sales stated, "The option for the poor should be an evangelical option that includes all the poor in any sense of poverty, including material and spiritual. The poor are all those who need God's greatness."[31]

Third, the neo-conservatives argue for a more hierarchical Church. They believe that Christ gave authority to the pope and bishops to be leaders of the Church and that the laity has the obligation to follow the teachings of the hierarchy. They charge that the progressive Church has obfuscated authority lines with its emphasis on lay participation and internal democracy. Diocesan assemblies with a lay majority have final authority in many popular dioceses; such a practice is not only an anomaly, but also actively criticized by leaders of neo-conservative dioceses. For example, Dom Manoel Pedro da Cunha Cintra, bishop of Petrópolis in Rio de Janeiro, stated that "listening to the base should not mean letting the people make the decisions. The Church should not be democratic because the quality of opinions is more important than the number of opinions."[32]

The neo-conservatives also criticize the base communities as they have evolved. Though not opposed to the notion of small ecclesial groups, they believe that CEBs are first and foremost ecclesial organizations. The Church and not the popular classes should determine the basic orientation of CEBs. As Archbishop Sales stated, "The CEBs are Church and therefore are born from Christ; their mission is not determined by the people."[33] Base communities should be oriented toward evangelization, understood in the traditional way of "improving" popular religiosity.

At least in their discourse, the neo-conservatives do not attack the notion of the Church's social mission. However, they argue that the objective of CEBs should not be linked to worldly liberation or to party options. Furthermore, they believe that CEBs should be open to all social classes, not just the popular sectors. In practice, though not on paper, the neo-conservatives de-emphasize the notion of the Church as the people of God.

Further, the neo-conservatives feel that the progressives are excessively critical of the Church. In their perspective, the Church is a perfect institution born of Christ. They return to conventional themes of unquestioning obedience to papal and episcopal authority. They argue that the progressives are divisive of the Church's unity because they criticize the Church's past actions and present structures. The neo-conservatives deny that the Church was traditionally aligned with the dominant classes and had a weak presence among the popular sectors.

Perhaps most important, the neo-conservatives criticize Church progressives for being too close to Marxism and too uncritical of socialism. The neo-conservatives see liberation theology as inspired by Marxist analysis of reality, which, they argue, is antagonistic to the nature of the Church. Although recognizing that capitalism is not perfect, they clearly feel a predilection for capitalist systems and criticize the progressives' affinity for socialism.

In return, the progressives believe that the conservatives misrepresent their positions. For example, by the early 1980's, the great majority of Church progressives were emphasizing spirituality.[34] Progressives argue that the question is one of different approaches to spirituality: they believe that spirituality must be linked to doing Christ's will, which, in turn, they see as linked to justice. Although progressives would not disagree that the main issue is sin, they would place greater emphasis on the sinfulness of unjust structures. Notwithstanding the serious tensions between the dominant classes and the progressive Church in some areas, the progressives accept in principle the importance of working with all social classes. However, they argue that the Church's message must be addressed preferentially to the economically deprived. The progressives address the theme of the Church's universality differently and argue that the conservatives sacrifice the institution's true purpose in maintaining close relations with the dominant sectors. They also believe that the neo-conservatives are as politically involved as they themselves, but are unwilling to recognize this fact. Finally, they dispute the neo-conservative charges about the proximity of liberation theology to Marxist analysis.[35]

Given the conservative pressures from the Vatican and CELAM, the progressives find themselves in a difficult situation. On the one hand, they realize that they must continue to work within the institution as a whole if they are to avoid suffering the fate of the radical clerical movements of the 1970's. On the other hand, working within the institution will probably entail making increasing concessions to conservative viewpoints that are antithetical to the progressives' understanding of the Church's mission.

Although the trend toward a more hierarchical, politically cautious Church under the leadership of John Paul II seems clear, several factors may mitigate the force of that trend in Brazil. Although the Brazilian Church is second only to the Nicaraguan in terms of being controversial, the pope's perception of the Brazilian Church apparently differs from his view of the Nicaraguan Church. This difference may stem from the pope's experiences in Poland, where the Church has had to combat an oppressive authoritarian socialist state,[36] as well as from the relative separation of the popular Church in Nicaragua from the institutional Church. The strong links between the base communities and the institutional Church in Brazil help defend the popular sectors against the charge of being anti-institutional or constituting a parallel magisterium. Furthermore, much as the pope has, the Brazilian Church has insisted on the specifically religious character of the Church. There is no radical conflict on this point, even though the progressives take the political aspects of faith further than the pope. Finally, even though CELAM continues to be in the hands of conservative leaders, a similar orientation among CELAM leaders did not prevent the Brazilian Church from being progressive during the 1972-82 period. In fact, it was during this period that the Brazilian Church became the most progressive national church in Latin America and was able to defeat the conservative program at the Puebla conference in 1979.

The Vatican is surely aware of the high cost of actively confronting the Church that represents the world's largest Catholic population. It also recognizes the vitality of the progressive sectors of the Latin American Church in the past two decades. The Vatican seems willing to reassert a conception of faith that makes the middle classes and Europe and the United States the dominant center of Catholicism, but it would also like to preserve some of the positive effects of Church innovation in Latin America.

The outstanding leadership among progressive theologians, social scientists, and bishops may also help offset conservative tendencies. The majority of the strong leaders in the Brazilian Church are committed to the popular cause. Even though the popular bishops are a minority (roughly 20 percent of the episcopacy), they have arguably been the most dynamic in terms of creating new structures, developing new theologies, and reaching large numbers of people. They are also the bishops with most pastoral experience on issues such as the use of urban land, popular religion, and popular values and needs. The leadership of the progressives is also shown in their predominance in the major Church institutes and commissions.

Despite these mitigating factors, it seems likely that the conservative movement will expand. The international and institutional character of the Church, coupled with the transition to democracy, will exercise some constraining force on the popular sectors of the Brazilian Church. They will continue to be stronger in Brazil than elsewhere, but it would be surprising if they expanded. Nevertheless, many, both in the international Church and in Brazilian society, will continue to watch the Brazilian Church closely. Regardless of its future, it has already stimulated innovations that have changed the Latin American Church and had a significant impact on Brazilian politics.

Reference Matter

Notes

Complete authors' names, dates, and publication data are given in the Select References, pp. 297-319. I have used the following abbreviations in the Notes and Select References.

REB   *Revista Eclesiástica Brasileira*
RCRB *Revista da Conferência dos Religiosos do Brazil*

Preface

1. Feuerbach, *Essence*; Marx and Engels, *Religion*, p. 42; Nietzsche, *Zarathustra*; Freud, *Future*; Weber, *Sociology*.

2. Gramsci's studies of the way religion reinforced the system of domination in nineteenth- and early twentieth-century Italy are suggestive; see *Prison Notebooks*, pp. 325-43, 396-99. Also interesting in this vein are studies of the political context of popular religious practices; see Brandão, *Deuses do Povo*; and R. C. Fernandes.

Chapter 1

1. The classic study in this regard is Michels, *Political Parties*. Michels studied power relations within European Socialist parties and noted that despite their commitment to democratic, egalitarian methods, they employed authoritarian means of developing the resources needed to come to power. This point has also been well established by sociologists working on institutions and bureaucracy; see, for example, Blau.

2. Niebuhr, *Denominationalism*, p. 3.

3. See Levine and Wilde on the Colombian hierarchy's attitudes toward revolution involving violence.

4. On this point, see Smith, "Religion and Social Change." He extends this analysis in his excellent *Church and Politics in Chile*, especially pp. 3-64.

5. The most important case was the Christians for Socialism movement in Chile, where the hierarchy ultimately banned clerical participation. See Smith, *Church and Politics in Chile*, pp. 230-80; McGovern, "Chile Under Allende and Christians for Socialism," in McGovern, pp. 210-42; and Ro-

jas and Vanderschueren. For an interpretation by a priest who was a leader in Christians for Socialism, see Arroyo. A valuable collection of documents, including the text of the hierarchy's proscription of clerical participation in Christians for Socialism, can be found in Eagleson.

6. See, for example, Romano; Velho; Márcio Moreira Alves, *Igreja*, especially pp. 41-56, 247-50; Bresser Pereira, pp. 13-80; and Paiva, "Igreja Moderna."

7. Some Latin American scholars influenced by Marxism have criticized institutional analysis of the Church. Significant contributions include Gómez de Souza, "Igreja e Sociedade" and *JUC*; Souza Lima, *Evolução*; and Palácios. For a similar approach to understanding change in the Church throughout Latin America, see Richards. For an influential attempt to combine elements of Marxian and institutional analysis, see Maduro.

8. Bruneau, *Political Transformation*, p. 4. Elsewhere Bruneau notes that "obviously mass attendance is not the greatest indicator of Church influence" (p. 62, *n*21), but he tends to identify influence with an institutional conception of the Church's mission. Although Bruneau focuses primarily on influence, his book (pp.229-36) contains a good discussion of prophecy (in the sense of the Church's function of announcing God's will) within the Church, indicating an awareness that the motivations of some sectors might escape the logic of institutional influence. See also Bruneau, *Church in Brazil*. In response to criticism, Bruneau wrote a recent clarification that develops a notion of institutional interests compatible with my own approach; see "Issues."

9. The argument here follows Weber's insistence that interest be conceptualized as a subjective phenomenon; see *Theory*, pp. 87-115.

10. "Mensagem da Igreja de Goiás" (mimeo., ca. 1976), p. 12; and "Relatório da Diocese de Goiás," in Mesters et al., p. 70.

11. Philip Selznick emphasizes this point in "Foundations" and *Leadership*. Alvin Gouldner ("Organizational Analysis") and Peter Blau (*Bureaucracy*) emphasize the rational elements in most organizations, but still underscore that organizations contain internal tensions over goals and means.

12. Among the extensive literature on the expansion of Pentecostalism, see F. Rolim, *Religião*; and Willems.

13. For an extensive discussion of the concept of models of the Church, see Dulles. Dulles was inspired by Niebuhr's classic *Christ and Culture*. Without using the term "models of the Church," Niebuhr develops five typical visions of the relationship between faith and human society. Leonardo Boff also discusses different models of the Church in *Igreja*, pp. 15-41. Gustavo Gutiérrez discusses different conceptions of salvation and of the Church's mission in *Teologia*, pp. 49-72, 125-56, 209-33. See also Levine, *Religion and Politics*, pp. 41-53.

14. For a similar view, see Levine, *Religion and Politics*, pp. 3-17, 290-312; Romano, pp. 11-44; and Geertz, pp. 87-141.

15. Weber, *Theory*, p. 364. This crucial point is developed at length in Eisenstadt's introduction to Weber, *Max Weber on Charisma*.

16. See Weber, *Sociology*, pp. 46-59.

17. The discussion follows the classic distinction between church and sect developed by Weber, "The Protestant Sects and the Spirit of Capitalism," in *From Max Weber*, pp. 302-22; and especially Troeltsch, pp. 330-43, 993-1001. This distinction has undergone many refinements since Troeltsch. Yinger (pp. 142-55) develops the distinction into a sixfold typology. An important historical and theoretical study of the transformation of a sect into a church, focusing on North Carolina, is L. Pope, pp. 117-40. Another useful discussion on the transformation of sects into churches is Moberg, pp. 73-126. An interesting adaptation to the Latin American context is Comblin, *Futuro*.

18. Troeltsch, p. 1007.

19. Ibid., pp. 69-164, 331-43, 993-1001; Maduro, pp. 123-41.

20. L. Pope, pp. 117-40; Niebuhr, *Denominationalism*, pp. 26-76.

21. See, for example, Linz; Glock and Stark, pp. 185-229; and McHale.

22. On this point, see Lorscheider; and Dulles.

23. See Sanks.

24. The encyclical is reproduced in Gremillion, pp. 387-416.

25. These constraints and limitations have been emphasized by Smith, *Church and Politics in Chile*, pp. 3-64; O'Dea; Hebblethwaite, *Runaway Church*; Vaillancourt; and Sanks. On the measures against the Dutch Church, see Coleman, pp. 179-296; and Goddijn, pp. 99-139.

26. As Warwick argues in "Effectiveness," whereas a business can claim success if it turns a good profit, a Church may even see acquiring wealth as a negative sign. Goddijn's study of the Dutch Church, pp. 16-49, also emphasizes the unique character of the Church as a social organization and the potential conflict between excessive institutionalization and development of a sense of community.

27. Weber, *From Max Weber*, p. 262.

28. Weber argues in his comparison of Confucianism and Protestantism that Protestantism had some magical elements; see *Religion of China*, pp. 226-49. He develops the argument that religion has become a distinctive realm of nonrationality in *Sociology*, pp. 20-31; and *From Max Weber*, pp. 267-301.

29. It is, however, necessary to qualify the observation since history is also replete with religious movements, frequently of a messianic nature, that sought to alter the social order, sometimes in radical ways. See Lanternari.

30. On the early history of Christianity as a radical, lower-middle-class movement, see Troeltsch, pp. 39-69; and Engels, "On the Early History of Christianity," in Feuer, *Marx and Engels*, pp. 168-93. Significantly, the early Church has received considerable attention from the contemporary popular Church. Among other works, see Lesbaupin, *Bem-Aventurança*.

31. The essays by F. H. Cardoso in *Ideías e Seu Lugar* provide a fine introduction, focusing on changing ideas in the social sciences, to the way social conflict gives rise to new ideas.

32. On this point, see Souza Lima, *Evolução Política*.

33. Several studies have made this point with respect to Western industrial societies. See, for example, Lenski; Hazelrigg; and Linz.

34. For a similar view, with respect to the military, see Stepan, *Military in Politics*.

35. On the difficulties Catholic lay movements have had in gaining more autonomy in Europe, see Vaillancourt; and Poggi.

36. See L. Boff's comments in Salem, p. 39; and Gutiérrez, *Força Histórica*, pp. 114, 129, 279, 293, 311.

37. In emphasizing change from below, I diverge from Weber's premises. Despite his many rich observations on change in institutions, Weber underestimates the extent to which change can come from the grass roots as well as from leaders. He sees institutional change as a result of elite action; I am equally concerned about the role of lay movements and grass-roots pastoral agents in molding the popular Church. There is a need to examine the role lay and grass-roots movements have played in transforming the Church in other national situations. In his fine study of the Dutch Church, Coleman (especially pp. 88-119) makes an argument similar to that presented here for the Brazilian case.

38. Among recent studies on popular religious beliefs, the works of Brandão are a good starting point; see *Deuses do Povo* and *Sacerdotes de Viola*. Hoornaert traces the early history of popular religious beliefs in his seminal work *Formação*. A recent two-volume history of the Church in Brazil calls attention to the importance of focusing on popular beliefs as well as institutional practices; see Hauck et al. Azzi traces the history of some popular religious customs in *Catolicismo Popular*. I discuss the way the institutional Church has viewed popular religious customs in Chapters 2 and 7.

39. *Conscientização* can be roughly translated as "consciousness raising," but *conscientização* always includes a component of consciousness raising toward political action.

40. Clodovis Boff argues that it is precisely in shaping the consciousness of the different classes that the Church has the greatest political impact; see *Comunidade Eclesial*, pp. 85-112.

41. This point has been emphasized by such diverse figures as Brazilian theologian Clodovis Boff, North American anthropologist Shepard Forman, and Peruvian theologian Gustavo Gutiérrez. See C. Boff, "Influência Política," especially pp. 106-10; Forman, pp. 203-43; and Gutiérrez, *Força Histórica*, pp. 136-39.

42. Bruneau deftly describes the major features of this crisis in *Political Transformation*. He correctly underscores the profound impact of the need to defend certain interests on causing the Church to open. In this sense, I place more emphasis on institutional elements than Souza Lima does in his interpretation in *Evolução*. Souza Lima downplays the importance of the expansion of Protestantism, the development of European theology, the threat from the Left, and the changes introduced by Vatican II.

43. The theme of a poor Church became so widely accepted that it was incorporated into the conclusions of the Medellín and Puebla meetings of CELAM. From Medellín, see Conselho Episcopal Latinoamericano (CELAM), para. 14. From Puebla, see CELAM, *Evangelização*, paras. 1148-59.

44. Gutiérrez, *Teologia*, pp. 125-29.

45. One of the few published Leninist critiques of the Church is Abramovay. Romano provides an important Marxian critique of the Church in *Brasil*. The Church's criticisms of the Leninist Left are made explicit in Betto, "Educação"; and Gómez de Souza, "Movimento Popular, Igreja e Política," in his *Classes Populares*. It is impossible to make any universally valid statements about the relationship between the Marxian Left and the popular Church, given the wide range of positions within both groups.

46. L. Boff, *Teologia do Cativeiro*, p. 213.

47. This point has been made in two important articles by Della Cava, "Política," and "Catholicism and Society." Most popular Church intellectuals have underestimated the impact of the Church's commitment to appeal to all classes.

Chapter 2

1. Leme, *Carta Pastoral a Olinda*.

2. On the Brazilian Church in the nineteenth century, see Hauck et al.; Souza Montenegro, pp. 43-134; Bruneau, *Political Transformation*, pp. 11-37; and Boehrer. On the decline of the religious orders, see Muller, pp. 59-153. Specifically on the Church in São Paulo, see Silveira Camargo, vols. 6-7. A good introduction to the European Church during this same period is Droulers.

3. On this issue, see Villaça; Bruneau, *Political Transformation*, pp. 25-30; Souza Montenegro, pp. 79-134; Harring; Hugo Fragoso, "A Igreja na Formação do Estado Liberal, 1840-1875," in Hauck et al., pp. 186-92; Pereira; and Thornton.

4. An excellent discussion of the Church's general situation, the reform movement, and the conflicts generated by that movement is Della Cava, *Miracle at Joaseiro*, pp. 20-26, 32-51, 68-80. An interesting discussion of Romanization is Ribeiro de Oliveira, "Religião e Dominação de Classe." On Romanization, see also Bastide. A statement on the Church's weaknesses and flaws and a prescription for change by one of the leading progressive clerics of the period is Maria, *Igreja*, originally published in 1900 under the title *Memória sobre a Religião, Ordens Religiosas, Instituições Pias e Beneficentes no Brasil*, and republished in 1950 under the title *O Catolicismo no Brasil* (Rio de Janeiro). An overview of the reform movements is Hauck et al., pp. 83-85, 103-4, 112-19, 182-86, 192-200. On reforms in the state of São Paulo, see Silveira Camargo, vol. 7; and Azzi, "Dom Antônio Joaquim de Melo."

5. On the revitalization of religious orders, see Muller, pp. 59-153. On the acceptance of legal disestablishment, see Azzi, "D. Antônio de Macedo Costa." Mecham, in his classic *Church and State*, emphasizes that religious issues did not provoke as much political conflict in Brazil as in most other Latin American nations.

6. On Pius XI and the early development of Catholic Action, see Poggi, pp. 14-29. On the growth of Catholic Action in Western Europe, see Fogarty, pp. 186-293. A good discussion of Catholic attempts at modernization during this period is O'Dea, pp. 38-89. On the attempts to mobilize

the laity, see Vaillancourt, pp. 19-59. Rhodes provides a balanced discussion of the papacy of Pius XI, especially the Vatican's relations with the Fascist countries. On the Vatican's orientation to major international events and its overall strategy, see also Holmes, pp. 1-118; and Murphy, pp. 24-57.

7. For the encyclical, *Divini Redemptoris*, see Fremantle, pp. 255-62.

8. On the persecution of the Church in the Soviet Union, see Galter. On Church-state conflict during the early years (1910-29) of the Mexican revolution, see Quirk; and Olivera Sedano. On the 1931-36 period in Spain, see Sánchez. For a general overview of Church-state relations in Latin America, see Mecham.

9. Silvano de Souza, "A Santidade Sacerdotal," *REB*, 11 (1951): 534. Among other articles expressing the view that secularization was eroding the basis for Catholic faith and morality, see Odorico Durieux, "Os Perigos do Cinema," *REB*, 1 (1941): 236-40; and "Pastoral Coletiva do Episcopado Paulista sobre Alguns Erros contra a Fé e a Moral," *REB*, 1 (1941): 889-901.

10. Frederico Didonet, "Cruzes e Consolações do Sacerdote," *REB*, 4 (1944): 261. See also Antônio d'Almeida Moraes Júnior, "Torturas do Padre do Seculo XX," *REB*, 1 (1941): 709-11.

11. Othon Motta, "Santificação do Clero," *REB*, 10 (1950): 302.

12. Gutiérrez, *Teologia*, pp. 55-74, discusses this conception of salvation at length.

13. Several works have dealt with the efforts to construct a more dynamic Catholic presence in social and political life. The most comprehensive is Todaro, "Pastors, Priests." An important overview of the 1916-64 period is Della Cava, "Catholicism and Society." See also Bruneau, *Political Transformation*, pp. 38-51. Several articles by Azzi deal with the same subject; see "O Início da Restauração Católica no Brasil, 1920-1930"; "Episcopado Brasileiro"; "O Início da Restauração Católica em Minas Gerais, 1920-1930"; "Fortalecimento"; and "Igreja Católica."

14. Soares d'Azevedo, *Vozes* (January 1940): 47, quoted in Azzi, "Igreja Católica," p. 62.

15. "Carta Pastoral do Arcebispo de Belo Horizonte," *REB*, 3 (1943): 518.

16. Wirth, pp. 90-93, 109, 114, 124-26, 144, 198-99, is strong on the revitalization of the Church in Minas. See also Azzi, "O Início da Restauração Católica em Minas Gerais, 1920-1930."

17. On Jackson de Figueiredo and the Centro Dom Vital, see Todaro, "Pastors, Priests," pp. 183-272. One of the most surprising lacunae in the history of recent Brazilian Catholicism is the absence of a good biography of Amoroso Lima. For his early thought, see the apologetic work by O'Neill. An unpublished memorandum by Sanders, "Evolution of a Catholic Intellectual," briefly traces his evolution to the mid-1960's. On the connections between the Centro and the radical Catholic Right of the 1960's, see Antoine, *Integrismo Brasileiro*, pp. 15-26, 42-46. For short intellectual biographies of some Catholic leaders of this period, see Villaça, *Pensamento Católico*, pp. 78-180; and Oliveira Torres, pp. 182-210.

18. On Amélia Rodrigues, leader of the League of Brazilian Catholic

Women and the Feminine Alliance, see Borges. On the Workers' Circles, see Wiarda, "Brazilian Catholic Labor Movement." On the early history of Catholic University Youth, see Gómez de Souza, *JUC.* On Brazilian Catholic Action, see Todaro, "Pastors, Priests," pp. 429-54.

19. On this point, see Azzi, "O Início da Restauração Católica no Brasil, 1920-1930," part 2, pp. 83-89.

20. This support has been documented by Azzi, "Igreja Católica"; and Todaro, "Pastors, Priests," pp. 454-86.

21. *Circular Coletivo do Episcopado Brasileiro ao Clero e aos Fieis* (Rio de Janeiro, 1942), p. 4. Signed by D. Leme, D. João Becker (Pôrto Alegre), and the archbishops of Bahia, Cuiaba, and Olinda and Recife.

22. On Leme's actions and beliefs, see the biography by Raja Gabáglia; Todaro, "Pastors, Priests," pp. 425-90; and Amoroso Lima, *Cardeal Leme.*

23. In his first major encyclical, *Ubi Arcano Dei,* Pius XI stated that the Church is teacher and head of all other institutions. Segments of the encyclical are published in Fremantle, pp. 222-24. *Quas Primas* (1925) affirmed that only the Church can provide the principles for a just resolution of social problems. Pius's somewhat triumphal attitudes are highlighted by Murphy, pp. 39-57.

24. "Manifesto do Episcopado Brasileiro," *REB,* 5 (1945): 422. In a similar vein, see also Amoroso Lima, "Limites do Nacionalismo"; and Becker, *Decadência da Civilização.*

25. Agnelo Rossi, "Religião e História do Brasil," *Vozes* (November 1942): 773-74, quoted in Azzi, "Igreja Católica," p. 57.

26. See the 1949 letter from the bishops of the state of São Paulo to President Dutra, criticizing the "campaign of the immoral and corrupt cinema, the corrupt radio, and the debauched, destructive press and literature," in *REB,* 9 (1949): 533. See also the *Pastoral Coletiva dos Cardeais, Arcebispos, Bispos e Prelados Residenciais do Brasil* (Petrópolis, 1951).

27. On LEC, see Todaro, "Pastors, Priests," pp. 273-345; and Todaro Williams, "Politicization of the Brazilian Catholic Church."

28. Soares d'Azevedo, *Vozes* (January 1940): 47; and Mário Couto, *Vozes* (January 1938): p. 20; quoted in Azzi, "Igreja Católica," p. 67. Along these lines, also see Becker, *Comunismo Russo.*

29. *Carta Pastoral e Mandamento do Episcopado Brasileiro sobre o Comunismo Ateu* (Rio de Janeiro, 1937).

30. "Manifesto do Episcopado Brasileiro sobre a Ação Social," *REB,* 6 (1946): 482.

31. On the links between Catholics and Integralists, see Todaro, "Pastors, Priests," pp. 346-424; and Figueiredo Lustosa. Indispensable reading on the Integralist movement is Trindade. Trindade does not address the relationship between Catholics and Integralists at length, but he does note an ideological affinity. For Amoroso Lima's views on Integralism, see his *Indicações Políticas,* pp. 187-220.

32. "Manifesto do Episcopado Brasileiro sobre a Ação Social," *REB,* 6 (1946): 482.

33. *Carta Pastoral e Mandamento do Episcopado Brasileiro sobre o Comunismo Ateu* (Rio de Janeiro, 1937).

34. "Manifesto do Episcopado Brasileiro sobre a Ação Social," *REB*, 6 (1946): 479.

35. For an excellent discussion of the notion of the political and its relationship to the state, see Reis.

36. Frederico Didonet, "Pastoral de Evangelização," *REB*, 23 (1963): 5.

37. "Conclusões do I Congresso Nacional da Ação Católica Brasileira," *REB*, 6 (1946): 942. Other works that express a concern with popular religious ignorance include Álvaro Negromonte, "Sobre a Pregacão," *REB*, 5 (1945): 639-42; Frederico Didonet, "Nós e o Povo Cristão," *REB*, 8 (1948): 822-30; Gorgulino Garcia, "A Catequese dos Adultos," *REB*, 15 (1955): 93-95; and Feliz Morlion, "Realismo no Apostolado de Penetração no Brasil," *REB*, 12 (1952): 1-8.

38. Álvaro Negromonte, "Melhoremos os Catecismos Paroquiais," *REB*, 1 (1941): 125. Works on catechism or religious education include Rossi, "Uma Experiência," p. 732; Álvaro Negromonte, "Um Texto Novo de Catecismo," *REB*, 2 (1942): 77-82; Rossi, "Primeiros Manuais"; Geraldo van Rooijen, "A Posição da Igreja nos Bairros Operários de São Paulo," *REB*, 17 (1957): 149-60; and Luis Mousinho, "Formar Catequistas," *REB*, 11 (1951): 232-40.

39. See the conclusions of the first CELAM meeting, held in Rio in 1955, *REB*, 15 (1955): 1036; and of the Fourth General Assembly of the Brazilian Bishops Conference (CNBB), *REB*, 18 (1958): 641. See also Gil Bonfim, "A Falta de Seleção dos Candidatos ao Seminário," *REB*, 18 (1958): 743-49; Laacroix; "O Problema Sacerdotal no Brasil," *REB*, 3 (1943): 232-33; José Locks, "Indice de Perseverança nos Seminários," *REB*, 17 (1957): 351-60; Guilherme Barauna, "O Problema da Falta de Sacerdotes na América Latina," *REB*, 13 (1953): 667-69; and A. Ferraz, "Recrutamento Sacerdotal," *REB*, 5 (1945): 426-34. The Vatican's deep concern with the shortage of priests in Latin America is visible in an article by Vatican theologian Mons. Mário Ginetti, "O Problema das Vocações Sacerdotais na América Latina," *REB*, 12 (1952): 374-81.

40. Álvaro Negromonte, "A Salvação do Brasil Depende do Clero," *REB*, 19 (1959): 1-7.

41. Adalberto de Paula Nunes, "Por um Clero Numeroso e Santo," *REB*, 6 (1946): 902.

42. Othon Motta, "Santificação do Clero," *REB*, 10 (1950): 297-303. See also "Sacerdos Alter Christus," *REB*, 1 (1941): 8; Silvano de Souza, "A Santidade Sacerdotal," *REB*, 11 (1951): 529-34; and Adalberto de Paula Nunes, "Por um Clero Numeroso e Santo," *REB*, 6 (1946), especially pp. 901-2.

43. Frederico Didonet, "Nós e o Povo Cristão," *REB*, 8 (1948): 822, 826.

44. Ibid., p. 829; "Pastoral Coletiva do Episcopado Paulista," *REB*, 1 (1941): 299-300, 304.

45. Maria, pp. 119, 120-21.

46. This is one of the main arguments in Hauck et al.

47. Among the many works on the expansion of Protestantism, see Willems's classic *Followers*; Cesar et al.; and Read.

48. On this subject, see Ribeiro de Oliveira, "Coexistência das Religiões."

49. Boaventura Kloppenburg, "Padres, Igrejas e Laicato," *REB*, 16 (1956): 962. During the 1950's, *REB* published a vast number of articles on Masons, Protestants, and Spiritists.

50. This argument was put forward by the conservative D. Agnelo Rossi, among others. Rossi wrote a plethora of articles on the subject, including "Por que Missões Protestantes na América Latina?" *REB*, 6 (1946): 610-22; and "A Ação Bíblica Protestante no Brasil," *REB*, 7 (1947): 45-56. D. Leme shared this view, seeing the Protestant expansion as a plot by millionaire North Americans; see his *Ação Católica*, p. 100.

51. *REB*, 13 (1953): 762, 763.

52. Azevedo.

53. Kloppenburg, *Espiritismo no Brasil*, p. 5.

54. See Marshall. For further development of this concept in the Brazilian context, see W. G. dos Santos, *Cidadania e Justiça*.

55. For the traditionalist argument against agrarian reform, see Castro Mayer et al.

56. "Mensagem da Comissão Central da Conferência Nacional dos Bispos do Brasil," *RCRB*, 88 (1962): 618.

57. For examples of more progressive religious thought during the 1940-55 period, see Luis do Amaral Mousinho, "Propriedade Privada e Justiça Social," *REB*, 6 (1946): 814-28; Fernando Gomes, "A Ordem Social nos Documentos Pontifícios," *REB*, 7 (1947): 31-45; Kovecses Geza, "Formação do Clero Adaptada à Época," *REB*, 14 (1954): 274-84; Carlos Leôncio da Silva, "Linhas Fundamentais para uma Teologia da Educação," *REB*, 10 (1950): 352-69; Carlos Carmelo de Vasconcelos Mota, "Carta Pastoral de Saudação," *REB*, 4 (1944): 971-86; and Romeu Dale, "A Posição do Leigo no Corpo Místico de Cristo," *REB*, 13 (1953): 14-25.

Chapter 3

1. For both encyclicals, along with many other documents of the 1961-75 period, see Gremillion, pp. 143-242.

2. For a complete collection of conciliar documents, see Flannery. On the Church's mission in the modern world and its social mission, see especially *Gaudium et Spes*, pp. 903-1001. On the laity and changing authority relations, see *Lumen Gentium*, pp. 350-426; paras. 21-22 of *Ad Gentes Divinitas*, pp. 838-40; and *Apostolicam Actuositatem*, pp. 766-98. On ecumenism, see *Unitatis Redintegratio*, pp. 452-70; and on liturgy, *Sacrosanctum Concilium*, pp. 11-40. Among the best works on Vatican II, its impact on the Church, and its contradictions are Hebblethwaite; and O'Dea. Characteristic of those who felt the Church had gone too far is Hitchcock.

3. These movements and their ultimate failure to change the Church have been analyzed in depth. Among other sources, see O'Dea, pp. 38-89, and Vaillancourt, pp. 19-59.

4. Interviewed in Salem, p. 38. In interviews I conducted, D. Paulo Evaristo Arns, D. Adriano Hypólito, D. Waldir Calheiros, D. José Maria Pires,

D. Tomás Balduino, and D. Mauro Morelli underscored the importance of Vatican II or the PPC in promoting change in the Church. The council's impact on theological thought in Brazil is indicated by the vast number of articles on the council in *REB* and *RCRB*.

5. There is a rich literature on these movements. See Brandão, "Educação Fundamental"; Paiva, *Educação Popular*; and Aida Bezerra. By Paulo Freire, see especially *Educação* and *Pedagogy*. A critical work that places Freire's work and writings in historical perspective is Paiva, *Paulo Freire*.

6. Good introductions to the abundant literature on the late populist period include Skidmore; Flynn, pp. 190-309; and Maranhão, *Governo Kubitschek*.

7. On the Church and the state in Cuba, see Crahan, "Salvation"; and Dewart.

8. On the Catholic Right of the 1960's, see Antoine, *Integrismo Brasileiro*; and Márcio Moreira Alves, *Igreja e a Política*, pp. 221-39.

9. Other relevant discussions of Church ideology and development during these years are Della Cava, "Catholicism and Society"; Bruneau, *Political Transformation*, pp. 68-126; and Ferreira de Camargo, *Igreja e Desenvolvimento*.

10. On the creation, history, and importance of the CNBB, see Bruneau, *Political Transformation*, pp. 107-26; and M. Martins. For a lengthy history of the CNBB's formal authority structures, see Queiroga.

11. These movements are discussed in Couto Teixeira. In my view, Couto Teixeira overstates the links between these relatively conservative movements and the base communities, but his thesis is still a significant contribution. For greater historical detail on the liturgical movement, see Botte. On the ideology behind the Barra do Piraí experience, see Rossi, "Experiência" and "Primeiros Manuais." The Christian Family Movement is a very important movement, about which almost nothing has been written. Limited information is available in Lucas Moreira Neves, "O Movimento Familiar Cristão a Serviço da Igreja," *REB*, 20 (1960): 888-99.

12. The best work on the Natal Movement is Ferreira de Camargo, *Igreja e Desenvolvimento*. Also see Ferrari. On the Leo XIII Foundation and the São Sebastião Crusade, see Valla et al., pp. 65-110; and Parisse. Although MMM was one of the most important precursors to the base communities, little has been written about it. Couto Teixeira, pp. 62-67, provides some information. See also Frederico Didonet, "Movimento por um Mundo Melhor no Brasil," *REB*, 21 (1961): 400-403; Frederico Didonet, "A Linha do Mundo Melhor no Brasil," *REB*, 22 (1962): 672-75; and Caramuru de Barros, *Brasil*, pp. 22-23. For typical expressions of the ideology and concerns of the movement, see Frederico Didonet, "Pastoral de Evangelização," *REB*, 23 (1963): 3-12; Marins, *Problema Religioso*; Marins, *Curso do Mundo Melhor*; and Marins, *Renovação da Paróquia*.

13. Frederico Didonet, "Pastoral de Evangelização," *REB*, 23 (1963): 10. Didonet was a leader in MMM.

14. Constantino Koser, "Perfeição Cristã no Mundo e Fuga do Mundo," *REB*, 23 (1963): 890. In a similar vein, see Romeu Dale, "A Igreja Católica

às Vésperas do Concílio," *REB*, 21 (1961): 593-600; A. Rolim, "Culto Dominical"; and Vaz, "Consciência Histórica."

15. Constantino Koser, "Perfeição Cristã no Mundo e Fuga do Mundo," *REB*, 23 (1963): 890. See also Boaventura Kloppenburg, "Às Portas do XXI Concílio Ecumênico," *REB*, 21 (1961): 561-92. On this topic, the works of Harvey Cox and Friedrich Gogarten were influential throughout the Catholic world. By Cox, see especially *Secular City*. Gogarten's most important book on secularization, *Despair and Hope for Our Time*, was published in German in 1953, but not until 1970 in English. Around the time of Vatican II, a prolific literature emerged on this subject; for examples, see *Concilium* 19, *Spirituality in the Secular City* (New York, 1966).

16. Lorscheider, p. 871. See also Constantino Koser, "Após a Primeira Sessão do Concílio," *REB*, 22 (1962): 825-29.

17. On this theme, see Guilherme Barauna, "O Concílio: Representação da Igreja em Diálogo com o Evangelho," *REB*, 23 (1963): 917-42; and Romeu Dale, "Os Leigos e o Concílio," *REB*, 23 (1963): 903-16.

18. Eduardo Hoornaert, "A Igreja e a Pobreza," *REB*, 23 (1963): 577-82; Constantino Koser, "Os Grandes Temas da Constituição Dogmática Lumen Gentium," *REB*, 24 (1964), especially p. 961.

19. Tiago Cloin, "Problemas de Atualização da Pastoral," *RCRB*, 50 (1959): 466.

20. See Padim, *Educar*; Gómez de Souza, *Cristianismo Hoje*; and Caramuru de Barros, *Perspectivas Pastorais*.

21. One of the foremost spokespeople for the progressive reformists was Alceu Amoroso Lima, who published prolifically. Representative of his work during this period are two sets of essays written between 1958 and 1964, *Revolução, Reação ou Reforma* and *Pelo Humanismo Ameaçado*. The influential Father Fernando Bastos de Ávila argued for a third position, critical of both socialism and capitalism; see *Neo-capitalismo, Socialismo, Solidarismo*. One important journal of the most progressive Catholics was *Brasil Urgente*. Also representative of this faction were Gómez de Souza, *Cristianismo Hoje*; Josaphat, *Evangelho e Revolução Social*; Andrade; Tarso; and *Atitude Cristã*.

22. CNBB, *Plano de Pastoral de Conjunto*, p. 30. See also pp. 41 and 81 and the "Mensagem dos Bispos do Brasil sobre o Concílio," *RCRB*, 116 (1965): 65-70. For a detailed discussion of the two plans, see Queiroga, pp. 351-406; and Couto Teixeira, pp. 140-58.

23. On this point, see Vaillancourt; and Poggi.

24. The most important theologian writing on this subject was Yves Congar, who played an important role at Vatican II; see his *Lay People in the Church* and *Laity, Church, and World*.

25. On the change in authority patterns, see Sanks. On the emergence of new concepts of the Church that emphasized coresponsibility, see Dulles.

26. See, for example, the comments by JUC leader Gómez de Souza, *Cristão e o Mundo*, p. 25.

27. Marins, *Comunidade Eclesial de Base*, p. 30. For other works that called for strong lay participation, see Constantino Koser, "A Situação do

Laicato Católico nos Albores do Vaticano II," *REB*, 22 (1962): 886-904; Romeu Dale, "Os Leigos e o Concílio," *REB*, 23 (1963): 903-16; José Locks, "O Diácano Não-Sacerdote," *REB*, 23 (1963): 612-22; and Caramuru de Barros, *Perspectivas Pastorais*.

28. Agnelo Rossi, "As Atribuições dos Leigos na Atual Ação Católica Brasileira e a Formação que Supõe," *REB*, 13 (1953): 68.

29. Vaillancourt, pp. 1-59, emphasizes this point.

30. With the exception of Howard Wiarda's study on the Bible Circles, these movements have not received much attention; see "Catholic Labor Movement." For a brief discussion of the Christian mini-courses, see Márcio Moreira Alves, *Igreja e a Política*, pp. 114-21.

31. CNBB, *Plano de Emergência*, p. 10.

32. *Plano de Pastoral de Conjunto*, p. 41.

33. *Plano de Emergência*, pp. 7, 17-18.

34. Among other works that call for a more important lay role in the Church in response to the lack of priests, see Irany Vidal Bastos, "Paróquias sem Padre: Solução de uma Necessidade Urgente," in Gregory, pp. 135-52; Schooyans, chaps. 6, 8; Tito Buss, "Perservança e Desistência nos Seminários," *REB*, 22 (1962): 50-64; and Mário Gurgel, "Causas Agravantes da Crise Sacerdotal no Brasil," *REB*, 25 (1965): 263-68.

35. Among the reformists who related parish renewal to community, see Marins, *Comunidade Eclesial de Base*; Josaphat, *Estruturas a Serviço do Espírito*; Schooyans, chaps. 6, 8; Caramuru de Barros, *Comunidade Eclesial de Base*, chaps. 2, 3; Comblin, "Comunidades Eclesiais"; Marins, *Renovação da Paróquia*; Leão Douven, "Como Organizar uma Paróquia," *RCRB*, 44 (1959): 90-95; Godofredo Deelen, "O Contato entre Clero e Fieís Deve Tornar-se Mais Funcional," *RCRB*, 119 (1965): 291-96; and the series of articles by Leão Douven, "A Comunidade Paroquial," *RCRB*, 87-95 (1962-63).

36. CNBB, *Pastoral da Terra*, pp. 44, 50.

37. "A Igreja e o Vale do São Francisco," in ibid., pp. 72, 74.

38. *Pastoral de Terra*, p. 78.

39. See the speech by D. Inocêncio Engelke, in ibid., p. 48.

40. "Pastoral sobre o Problema Agrário," letter by three bishops of Rio Grande do Norte, *Pastoral da Terra*, p. 59.

41. The conclusions of the Second General Assembly of the CNBB (1954) stated, "Private property should be consecrated as the basic principle of agrarian reform." *Pastoral da Terra*, p. 84.

42. Ibid., p. 85.

43. "Pastoral sobre o Problema Rural," by the three bishops of Rio Grande do Norte, 1951, *Pastoral da Terra*, pp. 56, 57.

44. *Pastoral da Terra*, p. 102; see also p. 92.

45. Ibid., p. 128.

46. Ibid., pp. 96-98.

47. "Encontro dos Bispos do Vale do Rio Doce," 1961, in ibid., pp. 113-21.

48. "Declaração dos Bispos do Nordeste," 1956, *Pastoral da Terra*, p. 93.

49. *Pastoral da Terra*, p. 101.

50. On educational issues, the CNBB maintained traditional, conservative positions, defending the Church's position as the primary educator in the society and criticizing efforts to improve public education. For the bishops' position, see "Declaração dos Cardeais, Arcebispos e Bispos do Brasil," *REB*, 18 (1958): 815-18. The Brazilian edition of Bruneau's *Political Transformation, O Catolicismo Brasileiro em Época de Transição* (São Paulo, 1974), includes a chapter on the subject.

51. "Declaração dos Cardeais, Arcebispos e Bispos do Brasil," *REB*, 18 (1958): 819. Along these lines, other important documents are "Mensagem da Comissão Central da CNBB," *RCRB*, 88 (1962): 618-20; and "Declaração dos Cardeais, Arcebispos e Bispos do Brasil," *REB*, 22 (1962): 485-90.

52. "Declaração dos Cardeais, Arcebispos e Bispos do Brasil," *REB*, 22 (1962): 488.

53. *Pastoral da Terra*, p. 122. Also see "Conclusões do Seminário de Estudos sobre a Educação Brasileira e o Desenvolvimento Brasileiro," *RCRB*, 71 (1961): 305-10.

54. On the Church's role in the peasant unions, see Bruneau, *Political Transformation*, pp. 83-94; Hewitt; and de Kadt, pp. 109-21.

55. *Pastoral da Terra*, pp. 46-48, 53.

56. Ibid., p. 83.

57. See, for example, "Declaração dos Cardeais, Arcebispos e Bispos do Brasil," *REB*, 22 (1962): 488; "Mensagem da Comissão Central da CNBB," *RCRB*, 88 (1962): 620.

58. On the bishops' nationalistic views, see the "Declaração dos Cardeais, Arcebispos e Bispos do Brasil," *REB*, 18 (1958): 821.

59. *Pastoral da Terra*, p. 127.

60. Ibid., p. 50; see also pp. 45-46.

61. Ibid., p. 111. See also the 1961 statement of the Central Commission of the CNBB, in ibid., p. 127; and Vicente Scherer, "Nossos Problemas Agrários e Rurais," *REB*, 22 (1962): 234-36. In addition to the statements on agrarian problems, other episcopal documents were fiercely anti-Communist. Virtually every major episcopal document on social problems contained some negative references to Communists. Particularly strong statements in this regard include "Manifesto do Episcopado Fluminense sobre a Situação Nacional," *RCRB*, 36 (1958): 341-43; "Declarações de Arcebispos, Bispos e Sacerdotes do Nordeste," *RCRB*, 89 (1962): 681-83; and "Declarações do Episcopado do Rio Grande do Sul," *REB*, 19 (1959): 991-92. Even one of the most progressive documents referred to the threat of "atheistic Communism, which destroys the most authentic human values." "Declaração dos Cardeais, Arcebispos e Bispos do Brasil," *REB*, 22 (1962): 488. The *REB*, at the time an organ for reformist Church thought, ran many anti-Communist articles in the early 1960's.

Chapter 4

1. See Poggi.

2. *REB*, 6 (1946): 940.

3. João Batista Portocarrero Costa, "A Ação Católica na Esperança do

Episcopado," *REB*, 6 (1946): 562. See also Carlos Carmelo de Vasconcelos Mota (archbishop of São Paulo), "Carta Pastoral de Saudação," *REB*, 4 (1944): 979. On the clergy's attitudes toward Catholic Action, see Mateus Hoepers, "Necessidade da Ação Católica," *REB*, 13 (1953): 143-45; José Fernandes Veloso, "Variedades de Formas e Métodos da Ação Católica," *REB*, 13 (1953): 49-61; Féliz Morlion, "Realismo no Apostolado de Penetração no Brasil," *REB*, 12 (1952): 1-9; D. Rafael Hooij, "A Obrigatoriedade da Ação Católica," *REB*, 13 (1953): 282-93; Domingos Gugliemelli, "Responsabilidade do Clero perante à Ação Católica," *REB*, 7 (1947): 76-88; "Carta Pastoral do Arcebispo de Belo Horizonte," *REB*, 3 (1943): 502-26; and Agnelo Rossi, "As Atribuições dos Leigos na Atual Ação Católica Brasileira e a Formação Que Supõem," *REB*, 13 (1953): 62-71. For a more progressive view of the relationship between hierarchy and laity in Catholic Action, see Luiz Vítor Sartori, "O Papel do Assistente Eclesiástico da Ação Católica," *REB*, 1 (1941): 321-25.

4. My discussion of JUC focuses principally on its ideology and relationship to the hierarchy. For information on the movement's history, the best works are Gómez de Souza, *JUC*; and Beozzo, *Cristãos*. On the reciprocal influences between ISEB, European progressive Catholicism, and Catholic radicals in Brazil, see Paiva, *Paulo Freire*. De Kadt, pp. 58-101, is strong on the intellectual influences behind the Catholic Left. Also see the fine article by Sanders, "Catholicism and Development."

5. Quoted in Souza Lima, *Evolução Política*, pp. 87, 89.

6. There is an extensive literature on the Communist party during the 1958-64 period, even though little has been written about the relationship of the party to the Catholic Left. A short history of the party, focusing on its attitude toward bourgeois democratic rights, is Konder. An interesting account is provided by the party's leader in the interviews collected by Moraes and Viana. Another important account by a party leader is Vinhas. A good collection of documents is *PCB: Vinte Anos de Política*; or for the 1922-82 period, Edgard Carone, ed., *O PCB* (São Paulo, 1982), 3 vols. On the development of the PC do B, see the narrative and documents in Pomar.

7. "Manifesto do Diretório Central dos Estudantes da Pontifícia Universidade Católica do Rio de Janeiro," in Souza Lima, *Evolução Política*, pp. 98-107.

8. Vaz, "Jovens Cristãos."

9. For the hierarchy's document outlining measures against JUC, see *REB*, 21 (1961): 947. For subsequent criticisms of and measures against JUC and the Catholic Left, see *REB*, 22 (1962): 234-36, 496-98, 764; *REB*, 23 (1963): 315-32, 498-500, 687-700, 786-87; and *REB*, 24 (1964): 207-11, 493-97. For further detail, see Gómez de Souza, *JUC*; de Kadt; and Beozzo, *Cristãos*.

10. This account focuses principally on AP's ideology and its role as a precursor to the popular Church. The most extensive account is provided by Lima and Arantes. De Kadt, pp. 81-101, 118-21, gives a good account of AP's development until the coup. See also Souza Lima, *Evolução Política*, pp. 43-51; and Márcio Moreira Alves, *Grain of Mustard Seed*, pp. 117-40. For a critical view of the Catholic Left as a whole, see Oliveira

Torres, pp. 226-78. For a sympathetic discussion, focusing on AP, see Mendes de Almeida.

11. The estimate comes from Sanders, "Catholicism and Development," p. 96.

12. See "Ação Popular," *REB*, 22 (1962): 129-32.

13. Significant in this regard is that Cândido Mendes de Almeida (*Memento dos Vivos*) considers AP the primary expression of the Catholic Left.

14. Ação Popular, p. 124.

15. On Catholic influences, see de Kadt, pp. 90-94.

16. Ação Popular, p. 137.

17. Ibid., p. 126.

18. On AP's development after the coup, see the moving personal reflection "Betinho" by H. J. de Souza. Souza was a leader in JUC, left the Church to create AP, and spent seven years underground before finally leaving Brazil as an exile. See also Lima and Arantes; and Floridi, pp. 234-61.

19. The most comprehensive work on MEB is de Kadt. For a shorter discussion, see Pereira Peixoto.

20. De Kadt's survey (p. 141) revealed that 73 percent of the highest-level and 59 percent of mid-level MEB leaders had participated in ACB.

21. Movimento de Educação de Base, *MEB em Cinco Anos*, p. 16.

22. Ibid., p. 34.

23. Ibid., p. 41.

24. One of the most proficient studies of Freire, focusing on the intellectual roots of his work, is Paiva, *Paulo Freire*. In recent years, a vast literature in English, Portuguese, and Spanish has emerged. Among other works, see Barreto; Jannuzzi, and Collins.

25. Freire, *Educação*, p. 105. 26. Ibid., p. 111.

27. Ibid., p. 59. 28. Ibid., p. 35.

29. Berryman, "Liberation Theology," p. 77, n. 42.

30. Gutiérrez, *Teologia*, p. 88. See also the comments by theologian Leonardo Boff in *Teologia do Cativeiro*, p. 18.

31. The intraclass nature of Italian Catholic Action prevented it from developing a stronger connection to the social movements in the society at large. There were no groups that identified themselves by class; the hierarchy suppressed efforts to organize along occupational lines precisely because they were seen as threatening the movement's allegiance to the Church. On this point, see Poggi, pp. 109-24.

32. See the comments by D. Cândido Padim in Regis de Morais, p. 43.

33. On the role Brazil's Catholic Left had in formulating a Latin American theology, see García Rubio.

34. D. Waldir Calheiros made this point in an interview, Mar. 24, 1982. See also the comments by D. Helder Câmara in an interview in Salem, p. 108.

Chapter 5

1. The term comes from Skidmore's book, *Politics in Brazil, 1930-1964: An Experiment in Democracy*. Skidmore has been justly criticized by

Schmitter for understating the authoritarian elements present in the 1945-64 period; see "The 'Portugalization' of Brazil?" Schmitter's article makes many contributions, but it may obfuscate more than it elucidates to call the 1945-64 period one of authoritarian rule.

2. There is an extensive literature on this period of military rule. A good introductory overview is Flynn. Important collections of different interpretations are Stepan, *Authoritarian Brazil*; and Bruneau and Faucher. On the role of the military, see Stepan, *Military in Politics*. For a recent interpretation of the coup and the forces behind it, see Dreifuss. Wanderley Guilherme dos Santos focuses more on political institutions and parties in his analysis of the coup; see "Calculus of Conflict." A comprehensive overview of the development of the regime and the opposition is M. H. Moreira Alves.

3. "Declaração da CNBB sobre a Situação Nacional," in Souza Lima, *Evolução Política*, p. 147.

4. "Manifestos e Denúncias contra a Ação do Comunismo no Brasil," *REB*, 24 (1964): 207. In a similar vein, see Augusto Álvares da Silva, "Carta Pastoral," *Vozes*, 58 (1964): 63-68; and João Rezende Costa, *REB*, 24 (1964): 209-10.

5. On the CNBB's move to the right in 1963-64, see Krischke, "Populism and the Catholic Church." For useful documentary material on the positions of different lay groups and bishops toward the "revolution," see Centro de Pastoral Vergueiro, pt. 1, pp. 11-20.

6. On the pre-coup climate and fears, see Stepan, *Military in Politics*, pp. 134-71.

7. Ibid., p. 148.

8. Many aspects of the CNBB's history, including its gradual turn toward the right in the 1963-68 period, have been documented. See Bruneau, *Political Transformation*, pp. 107-44; Antoine, *Church and Power*, pp. 205-75; Queiroga; and M. Martins.

9. "Nossas Responsabilidades em Face da 'Populorum Progressio' e das Conclusões de Mar del Plata," *REB*, 27 (1967): 472. These were the conclusions of the CNBB's Thirteenth General Assembly, held in May 1967. Three years after the coup, the CNBB was still more cautious about stating concrete positions than it was during the pre-coup years. The tenth assembly of CELAM, at Mar del Plata, Argentina, in October 1966, was a major event in the development of the Latin American Church. It anticipated some of the conclusions of Medellín.

10. *SEDOC*, 1 (1968-69): 986.

11. Secretariado Geral da CNBB, "Brasil 1969," Aug. 1969.

12. There is an extensive literature on developments in the Amazon. A good overview is Pompermayer. For a history of the regime's policies, see CNBB, *Pastoral da Terra: Posse e Conflitos*, pp. 51-141, 159-206. An important study of economic aspects is Mahar, *Frontier Development Policy*. Ianni, *Ditadura e Agricultura*, focuses on economic, social, and political considerations. See also Ianni's history of economic development and land struggles in the Araguaia region in southern Pará, 1917-77, *Luta pela Terra*. F. H. Cardoso and Muller; and José Marcelino Monteiro da Costa, ed.,

Amazônia: Desenvolvimento e Ocupação (Rio de Janeiro, 1979), provide useful information.

13. Fundação IBGE, *Censo Agrícola*, 1960, 1970, 1975.

14. Ibid., 1950, 1975.

15. On the struggles of the *posseiros* and other peasants, see the fine works by J. de Souza Martins, *Expropriação e Violência*, and *Camponeses*, pp. 103-50. A major work on the peasant struggles in Alto Sorocabana, São Paulo, which have some parallels to the Amazon struggles, is d'Incão.

16. A fine introduction to the problems of the Indians in the post-1964 period is Davis. For an evaluation by the bishop most closely linked to the Indian Missionary Council, see Tomás Balduino, "O CIMI e a Terra dos Índios," deposition to the Parliamentary Commission to Investigate Land Problems (Brasília, Mar. 23, 1977).

17. The conclusions of this meeting are published in *SEDOC*, 1 (1968-69): 60.

18. Ibid., p. 49.

19. Ibid., p. 983.

20. Ibid., 3 (1970-71): 1380-81.

21. Ibid., p. 1374, from the 1970 Assembly of Regional North II, Nov. 24-27, 1970.

22. Ibid., 4 (1971-72): 605.

23. Casaldáliga, *Igreja da Amazônia*.

24. For text of document, see *SEDOC*, 2 (1969-70): 1561-65.

25. Ibid., 4 (1971-72): 987-88.

26. Ibid., p. 1195.

27. Ibid., 5 (1972-73): 112.

28. For a summary of the conclusions of this encounter, see *REB*, 32 (1972): 703-4.

29. Documentation on the São Félix case comes from a number of sources. The most complete for the period up to 1971 is Casaldáliga's first pastoral letter, *Igreja da Amazônia*. Other useful writings by D. Pedro are *Creio na Justiça* and "Visão da Igreja a Partir da Periferia," *REB*, 38 (1978): 579-605. See Pompermayer, pp. 315-32, for the background and some description of the Church's attempts to defend the peasantry. Salem, pp. 190 200, has a brief description of the Church's development. Márcio Moreira Alves, *Igreja e a Política*, pp. 193-97; and Lernoux, pp. 268-77, describe the conflict with Father Francisco Jentel. Three journalistic accounts, including lengthy interviews are E. Martins; Cabestrero, *Iglesia Que Lucha*; and Cabestrero, *Diálogos em Mato Grosso*. Centro de Pastoral Vergueiro, pt. 4, pp. 40, 68-71, has information on several conflicts. Among the many journal and newspaper accounts, see *SEDOC*, 6 (1973-74): 340-41; *REB*, 33 (1973): 734, 983-84; *Los Angeles Times*, June 17, 1973; *Brazilian Information Bulletin* (Berkeley, Calif.), Fall 1973; *Latin America Press*, June 25, 1974.

30. *O Estado de São Paulo*, May 5, 1972, quoted in Centro de Pastoral Vergueiro, pt. 4, p. 69.

31. Part of the text is quoted by Pompermayer, p. 325.

32. Ianni, *Luta pela Terra*, pp. 99, 122. This study is a fine introduction

to the transformation of the Araguaia region and the violence between landowners and peasants.

33. On the armed movement in Araguaia, see the account and documents by sympathizer Pomar.

34. *SEDOC*, 5 (1972-73): 576.

35. Interview with author, Nov. 1981.

36. Centro de Pastoral Vergueiro, pt. 5, pp. 34-35.

37. Souza Lima, *Evolução Política*, p. 222.

38. Ibid., p. 227.   39. Ibid., p. 235.

40. Ibid., p. 237.   41. *SEDOC*, 7 (1974-75): 98, 99.

42. My data are taken from the fine overview by Cavalcanti, "Tristes Processos Econômicos"; and from Cavalcanti, "Dimensões de Marginalização do Nordeste." For overviews of the Northeast's development, see Cavalcanti de Albuquerque and Cavalcanti; Oliveira.

43. As Cohn (p. 64) writes, "The Northeast acquired national importance because of the magnitude of the social tensions and political problems in the region. It became a national problem that required more effective and systematic federal intervention because of the exacerbation of social and political tensions during the 1950's." See also Oliveira, especially pp. 45-58, 99-133.

44. On the peasant mobilization and the general political context of Northeastern Brazil during this period, see J. de Souza Martins, *Camponeses*, pp. 62-92; Hewitt; Alcântara de Camargo; and C. Moraes.

45. On the coup and its effects in the region, see Paiva, "Pedagogia e Luta Social."

46. Câmara, *Revolution Through Peace*, p. 3.

47. For some journalistic reflections and interviews with D. Helder, see Broucker. A shorter account is Gómez de Souza, "D. Helder, Irmão dos Pobres," in his collection, *Classes Populares*, pp. 289-95. Gómez de Souza worked closely with D. Helder for several years. A more recent theological statement by D. Helder is *The Desert Is Fertile*.

48. Several of D. Fragoso's essays and speeches are collected in *Evangile et révolution sociale*. On D. Fragoso, also see Salem, pp. 110-14, 180-90. Many of D. José Maria Pires's essays are collected in his *Do Centro para a Margem*.

49. *REB*, 25 (1965): 131.

50. *Notícias de Igreja Universal*, 46/47 (Feb. 1-15, 1968).

51. Centro de Pastoral Vergueiro, pt. 1, p. 33.

52. Ibid., pt. 2, p. 17. Another conflict between the auxiliary bishop and the regime occurred in May 1968. See Bruneau, *Political Transformation*, pp. 197-98.

53. *SEDOC*, 1 (1968-69): 53.

54. Ibid., 2 (1969-70): 59-61.

55. Quoted in Dussel, pt. 1, pp. 192-93.

56. *SEDOC*, 3 (1970-71): 489.

57. See Bruneau, *Political Transformation*, pp. 212-13.

58. For these statements of solidarity, see *SEDOC*, 3 (1970-71): 635-43, 987-99.

59. For text of statement, see ibid., pp. 759-61.

60. For text of note, see *REB*, 31 (1971): 1012.

61. On this incident, see *Informationes Catholiques Internationales*, 400, 402, and 406 (1972); *NADOC*, 260 (1972); and *Notícias Aliadas*, 23 (Mar. 1972).

62. On this earlier controversy, see Bruneau, *Political Transformation*, pp. 198-99.

63. Centro de Pastoral Vergueiro, pt. 4, p. 42.

64. O'Donnell, "Tensions," p. 294. For a progressive bishop's perspective on bureaucratic-authoritarian regimes and their attempts to control civil society, see Padim, "Doutrina da Segurança Nacional."

65. Souza Lima, *Evolução Política*, pp. 168, 197.

66. Ibid., pp. 196, 198.

67. On the history of base communities in São Paulo, see Ferreira de Camargo, "Comunidades Eclesiais de Base," especially pp. 62-68. On the development of the archdiocese as a whole, see Bruneau, *Church in Brazil*, chap. 5. For an analysis of the development of base communities in one particular region of the archdiocese, see Souto.

68. For text of speech, see Centro de Pastoral Vergueiro, pt. 1, pp. 23-24.

69. Ibid., pt. 2, p. 50.

70. Interview with author, Oct. 1, 1981.

71. An interesting collection of interviews with D. Paulo, which covers his views on a wide range of issues, is Arns, *Em Defesa dos Direitos Humanos*.

72. On the Death Squad, see Bicudo. Bicudo was a member of São Paulo's Justice and Peace Commission.

73. Interview with author, Oct. 1, 1981.

74. A valuable study of the commission is C. Pope.

75. Centro de Pastoral Vergueiro, pt. 4, p. 64.

76. For detailed data on these problems, see Ferreira de Camargo et al. On problems of development in São Paulo, see also Berlinck; and Kowarick.

77. Ferreira de Camargo et al., pp. 8, 9.

78. *SEDOC*, 5 (1972-73): 108-9.

79. These observations are based on extensive interviews in dioceses throughout the country. Little has been published about the early development of the popular Church. On the emergence of the base communities, the reports by the communities and the pastoral agents working with them provide useful information. See Mesters et al.; *SEDOC* 9 (Oct. and Nov. 1976 issues); and *SEDOC* 11 (1978-79): 258-448, 705-862. See also Conferência Nacional dos Bispos do Brasil (CNBB), *Comunidades*.

80. This point has been emphasized in Vanilda Paiva's work. On the links between CEBs and the Church in Central America, see Cáceres et al., pp. 47-160; Cáceres; Montgomery; and Berryman, *Religious Roots*.

81. Despite the importance of the CEBs, the social science literature about them is weak. On their origins, see Couto Teixeira; or, from the viewpoint of a bishop who helped encourage the early CEBs, L. G. Fernandes. A good introductory discussion is Bruneau, "Basic Christian Communi-

ties." See also the interesting assessment by Ireland. For a reflection by sympathizers, see Torres and Eagleson, *Challenge of Basic Christian Communities*. A forthcoming work on grass-roots innovations throughout the continent is Levine, *Popular Religion*. The reports from the first three national encounters of CEBs are published in *SEDOC* 7 (May 1975), 9 (July 1976), and 11 (Oct. 1978 and Jan./Feb. 1979).

82. See Marins, *Comunidade Eclesial de Base*, pp. 58-59; Affonso Felipe Gregory, "As Paróquias Urbanas Querem Ser Verdadeiras Comunidades," in Gregory, pp. 89-102; CNBB, *Plano de Pastoral de Conjunto*, p. 39; Caramuru de Barros, *Comunidade Eclesial de Base*, chaps. 2-3; and Comblin, "Comunidades Eclesiais."

83. Mesters, "Futuro do Nosso Passado," p. 126.

84. See José Marins, "Experiências Novas em Paróquias," in Gregory, pp. 119-33; Caramuru de Barros, *Comunidade Eclesial de Base*, chap. 4; Caramuru de Barros, *Perspectivas Pastorais*; and Barbé and Retumba.

85. See Caramuru de Barros, *Comunidade Eclesial de Base*; and Marins, *Comunidade Eclesial de Base*. For Caramuru de Barros, the most important aspects of the base communities involved developing better human relations, more effective lay participation, more effective religious education, and a new Church presence in the society; see especially pp. 50-53. For Marins, the notion of *base*, which later came to be identified with the lower classes, simply meant "the lowest level of the Church as community" (p. 94).

86. For a similar point, see Souza Netto, pp. 17-31.

87. "A Experiência da Paróquia do Alto do Pascoal (Recife)," in Mesters et al., p. 63.

88. Interview, Oct. 20, 1981.

89. Interview, Oct. 1, 1981.

90. My argument differs from the interpretations of Souza Lima and Gómez de Souza, both of whom attribute a decisive role to the Catholic Left. See Chapters 4 and 6 for further information on the differences between the Catholic Left and the popular Church.

91. Document of the CNBB's Ninth General Assembly, *Comunicado Mensal da CNBB*, 191 (1968): 33, 34.

92. Statement of the CNBB's Central Commission, in ibid., 196/198 (1969): 11-15.

93. Document of the CNBB's Eleventh General Assembly, *SEDOC*, 3 (1970-71): 85-86.

94. Ibid., p. 86.

95. See, for example, the document published by the Diocese of Crateús, in CNBB, *Pastoral da Terra*, pp. 135-52. Crateús and João Pessoa are two of the dioceses that have most focused on the notion of human rights. On João Pessoa, see Paiva, "Pedagogia e Luta Social."

96. Statement of the CNBB's Thirteenth General Assembly, *SEDOC*, 5 (1972-73): 1383-84.

97. Statement of the CNBB's Central Commission, *REB*, 33 (1973): 444.

98. On the Spanish Church, see Gómez Pérez; Fernández Areal; and Cooper. For an interpretation of the relationship between state enterprises, transnational corporations, and the industrial bourgeoisie, see Evans.

99. For the encyclical, see Gremillion, pp. 387-416.

100. Ibid., p. 514.

101. There is extensive literature on the background, conclusions, and significance of Medellín. See Oliveros, pp. 74-129; Dussel, pp. 52-78; Muñoz; and Libânio, *Grandes Rupturas*, pp. 121-90.

102. Conselho Episcopal Latino-Americano (CELAM), *Igreja*, sections 1.20 and 6.13.

Chapter 6

1. A lengthier version of this chapter was published in *REB*, 43 (1983): 29-92. Despite its importance, little has been written about JOC. Márcio Moreira Alves has a short discussion of JOC and Catholic Workers Action (ACO) in *Igreja e a Política*, pp. 152-57. In 1981, the archdiocesan newspaper *O São Paulo* ran a series of brief articles on JOC's history. On JOC's history in the 1930's, see Todaro, "Pastors, Priests," pp. 441-45.

2. See Bedoyere for a brief biography.

3. "Situação da Juventude Trabalhadora," 1950. Many of the documents cited here can be located at the CNBB library in Brasília.

4. "Conferência Nacional," May 5-13, 1951.

5. On the Bible Circles, see Wiarda, "Catholic Labor Movement."

6. "Situação da Juventude Trabalhadora," 1950.

7. François Rioux, "A Técnica Jocista e o Assistente," Primeira Semana Nacional de Assistentes, Rio de Janeiro, Jan. 19-24, 1948.

8. Ibid.

9. "Situação da Juventude Trabalhadora," 1950.

10. "Relatório da Situação Atual da Juventude Trabalhadora e da JOC no Brasil," 1956.

11. *O São Paulo*, Mar. 13-19, 1981.

12. "II Congresso Mundial da JOC," Rio de Janeiro, Nov. 1961.

13. Untitled document, 1961.

14. "I Congresso Nacional de Jovens Trabalhadores," Nov. 1961.

15. "Segunda Semana Nacional dos Assistentes," Feb. 1959.

16. "Inquérito Anual," 1960-61.

17. Interview, Sept. 4, 1981.

18. Interview, June 22, 1981.

19. "Segunda Semana Nacional dos Assistentes," Feb. 1959.

20. "I Congresso Nacional de Jovens Trabalhadores," Nov. 1961.

21. Interviews, Sept. 4, 1981.

22. "Declaração dos Cardeais, Arcebispos e Bispos do Brasil," *REB*, 22 (1962): 488.

23. CNBB, *Pastoral da Terra*, pp. 128-29.

24. "Evolução do Movimento," 1964. Although it is not dated, the document was clearly written before the coup.

25. Ibid.

26. "Colaboração da JOC e da ACO para uma Pastoral Operária," 1963.

27. "Dez Anos de Ação Católica Operária," SEDOC, 6 (1973-74): 314. This statement was part of the original 1962 statement of objectives.

28. Carta aos Dirigentes, 16 (1962).

29. Interview, Sept. 4, 1981.

30. Ferreira de Camargo et al., p. 67.

31. Sylvia Ann Hewlett, "Poverty and Inequality in Brazil," in Sylvia Ann Hewlett and Richard Weinert, eds., Brazil and Mexico: Patterns in Late Development (Philadelphia, 1982), p. 320.

32. Given the tremendous fragmentation of the Left after 1964, these generalizations must be made cautiously. Popular Action entered a process of rapid radicalization described in the moving personal statement by H. J. de Souza in Uchoa Cavalcanti and Ramos, pp. 67-112. The Brazilian Communist Party was the only major Marxist group not to follow this extreme radicalization; see Vinhas, pp. 235-53; and D. Moraes and Viana, pp. 175-96. There is an extensive literature on the trajectories of other leftist groups.

33. Particularly noteworthy in this regard is the impact of dependency theory on the early stages of the development of liberation theology. On this point, see Gutiérrez, Teologia, pp. 75-88; and Silva Gotay, pp. 203-32.

34. "A JOC diante dos Acontecimentos de Primeiro de Abril," 1964.

35. Interview, July 13, 1981.

36. Quoted in Márcio Moreira Alves, Igreja e a Política, p. 154.

37. Unfortunately, the military confiscated the Recife document and burned all but a few copies. For excerpts, see ibid.

38. "O Documento Amarelo," July 1969.

39. "Manifesto da JOC," Sept. 29, 1967.

40. On this conflict, see Márcio Moreira Alves, O Cristo do Povo, pp. 58-63; Bruneau, Political Transformation, pp. 182-87; and Antoine, Church and Power, pp. 84-89. Indicative of the importance of JOC and ACO in generating Church-state conflict is that Bruneau devotes 14 of 27 pages on Church-state conflicts between 1966 and 1968 to ACO and JOC. Centro de Pastoral Vergueiro, Relações Igreja-Estado, includes nine cases of conflict between JOC or ACO and the state, of which six developed into major confrontations.

41. On the Contagem and Osasco strikes, see the fine study by Weffort, "Participação e Conflito Industrial." Weffort provides significant information on the role of Catholics at Osasco but does not mention their role at Contagem. On the Church-state conflict at Osasco, see SEDOC, 1 (1968-69): 815-37; Bruneau, Political Transformation, pp. 199-202; Márcio Moreira Alves, Igreja e a Política, pp. 203-4; and Antoine, Church and Power, pp. 187-94. On the development of the Church's pastoral work at Osasco, 1964-70, see Barbé and Retumba. My information on JOC's role at Contagem came principally from an interview with an ex-participant.

42. For text of document, see Marins, Práxis, pp. 69-71. For details, see SEDOC, 1 (1968-69): 1207-56; Bruneau, Political Transformation, pp. 203-9; and Antoine, Church and Power, pp. 195-202.

43. On the death of Father Henrique, see *SEDOC*, 2 (1969-70): 143-48.
44. Interview, Sept. 4, 1981.
45. Interview, June 22, 1981.
46. This chapter in JOC's history is described by Antoine, *Church and Power*, pp. 182-87.
47. On the Volta Redonda incident, see Centro de Pastoral Vergueiro, pt. 3, pp. 13-21.
48. For text of document, see *SEDOC*, 3 (1970-71): 648-50. On the invasion in Rio, see Centro de Pastoral Vergueiro, pt. 4, pp. 18-20.
49. Interview, June 25, 1981.
50. Márcio Moreira Alves, *Igreja e a Política*, p. 153.
51. Interview, June 25, 1981.
52. On factory-level repression, see Frederico; and the personal reflections of labor leaders in Frente Nacional do Trabalho, "Vinte Anos de Luta," pt. 5 (São Paulo, 1980).
53. Interview, June 25, 1981.
54. "Resumo do Conselho Nacional," 1970.
55. "O Documento Amarelo," July 1969.
56. "Encontro da Pastoral Operária," Jan. 9-12, 1961.
57. "Pastoral da Igreja no Meio Operário," 1964.
58. "Encontro Nacional de Assistentes," June 1964.
59. "Colaboração da JOC e da ACO para uma Pastoral Operária," 1963.
60. "Encontro Nacional de Padres no Meio Operário," JOC/ACO, May 1966.
61. "Encontro Nacional de Assistentes," June 1964.
62. Interview, July 9, 1981.
63. *O São Paulo*, Feb. 10-16, 1979.
64. Early base communities in Osasco, São Paulo, and rural Maranhão were initiated by JOC advisors and Jocistas. See Barbé and Retumba on early base communities in Osasco; and "Relatório do Maranhão," in Mesters et al., pp. 98-105.
65. On regime ideology and legitimation attempts, see Lamounier.
66. This point has been amply documented by Antoine, *Church and Power*; Márcio Moreira Alves, *Igreja e a Política*; Bruneau, *Political Transformation*; and Centro de Pastoral Vergueiro, *Relações Igreja-Estado*.
67. Interview, June 10, 1981.
68. Libânio, "Uma Comunidade," p. 305.

Chapter 7

1. Although I do not explicitly address the development or major themes of liberation theology, Chapters 7, 9, and 10 deal extensively with some of its major ideas. A fine introduction to the development and major functions of liberation theology in Brazil is García Rubio. Other histories trace the development of liberation theology throughout the continent. See Oliveros; Mondin; Kirk; and Míguez Bonino, pp. 21-84. A good synthetic introduction to liberation theology's major themes by one of its most important ex-

ponents is Galilea, *Teología*. A good English-language introduction is McGovern, pp. 172-209. Most North American introductions do not sufficiently emphasize that many leading progressive theologians insist on the specifically religious character of the Church and have devoted more attention to Biblical themes, popular religiosity, and pastoral problems than to political questions. Despite this caveat, Berryman, "Liberation Theology"; Sanks and Smith; and Levine, *Religion and Politics*, pp. 43-49, are helpful discussions. Two books by Gustavo Gutiérrez are important, both as key statements by one of the leading liberation theologians and also for their incisive observations on how liberation theology purports to differ from its predecessors, including progressive and radical European theology. See *Teologia* and *Força Histórica*. Among those critical of liberation theology, the history and exposition by Vekemans, *Teología*, is particularly important. For a criticism of the efforts to synthesize Christianity and Marxism, see Hebblethwaite, *Christian-Marxist Dialogue*. In Brazil, the most publicized critique has been Kloppenburg, *Igreja Popular*.

2. Robert McAfee Brown, one of the leading contemporary North American Protestant theologians, writes, "I do not think there are any issues on the theological or human scene more important than the ones liberation theologians are addressing" (p. 11). Representative of the vast amalgam of people and movements influenced by liberation theology is the volume edited by Torres and Eagleson, *Theology in the Americas*.

3. My views of the liberalization process are developed in greater detail in two collaborative articles. See (with Donald Share) "Transitions Through Transaction" and (with Eduardo Viola) "Transitions to Democracy." There is an extensive bibliography on the subject; the most important sources are indicated in these two articles.

4. On the Cost of Living Movement, see Tilman Evers, "Os Movimentos Sociais Urbanos: O Caso do 'Movimento Custo de Vida,'" in Moisés et al., pp. 73-98. There is a large literature on the new labor movement. Among the best works are Moisés, "Qual É a Estratégia"; Moisés, "Current Issues"; Humphrey; Tavares de Almeida, "Tendências"; and Tavares de Almeida, "Novas Demandas." For a fine overview of a number of social movements in São Paulo, see Singer and Brant.

5. "A Pastoral Social," *Estudos da CNBB*, 10 (1976): 36.

6. Ibid., pp. 47-48. Along these lines, see the CNBB's criticisms of the Puebla Consultation Document, "Subsídios para Puebla," *REB*, 38 (1978): 327-41; and the incisive criticisms by the bishops of Regional Northeast II, "A Caminhada do Povo de Deus na América Latina," *REB*, 38 (1978): 300-326. Both documents criticize the view that secularization is one of the major problems the Latin American Church faces.

7. CNBB, Representative Commission, "Comunicação Pastoral ao Povo de Deus," in Souza Lima, *Evolução Política*, p. 252.

8. CNBB, "Diretrizes Gerais da Ação Pastoral da Igreja no Brasil," *Documentos da CNBB*, 4 (1975): 78-79.

9. CNBB, "Igreja e Problemas da Terra" (São Paulo, 1980), p. 24. Document of the Eighteenth General Assembly, Feb. 14, 1980.

10. "Comunicação Pastoral ao Povo de Deus," in Souza Lima, *Evolução Política*, p. 252. Written in Oct. 1976 and published in Nov. 1976.

11. CNBB, "Solo Urbano e Ação Pastoral," *Documentos da CNBB*, 23 (1982): 37. Document of the Twentieth General Assembly, Feb. 18, 1982.

12. "Comunicação Pastoral ao Povo de Deus," in Souza Lima, *Evolução Política*, p. 250.

13. CNBB, "A Pastoral Social," p. 49.

14. *SEDOC*, 8 (1975-76): 729. See also the denunciation by the Justice and Peace Commission of São Paulo issued at the same time, published in *SEDOC*, 9 (1976-77): 118-19.

15. "Subsídios para uma Política Social," *Estudos da CNBB*, 24 (1979): 10.

16. "Exigências Cristãs de uma Ordem Política," p. 263. See also "Diretrizes Gerais para a Ação Pastoral da Igreja no Brasil," in *SEDOC*, 8 (1975-76): 582-616.

17. "Reflexão Cristã sobre a Conjuntura Política," *Documentos da CNBB*, 22 (1981): 4. Document approved by the CNBB's Permanent Council, Aug. 29, 1981.

18. See particularly ibid.

19. Ibid., p. 11.

20. "A Igreja e Problemas da Terra," p. 37.

21. See especially the statement by the Comissão Pastoral dos Direitos Humanos e dos Marginalizados da Arquidiocese de São Paulo, "Violência contra os Humildes," *SEDOC*, 10 (1977-78): 961-64.

22. The report was not released until 1979, when it caused a big uproar. See the *Jornal do Brasil*, Apr. 9, 1979.

23. See "Comunicação Pastoral ao Povo de Deus," in Souza Lima, *Evolução Política*, p. 241.

24. For information on this kidnapping, see *SEDOC*, 97 (Dec. 1976): 661-73.

25. On Bosco's death, see ibid., pp. 673-94. See also "Ribeirão Bonito: A Caminhada de um Povo," in *Cadernos do CEAS*, 57 (Sept.-Oct. 1978): 37-42.

26. *Jornal do Brasil*, Aug. 17, 1976.

27. *O Estado de São Paulo*, Nov. 9 and Dec. 9, 1976.

28. *Jornal do Brasil*, Dec. 13, 1976.

29. Ibid., Dec. 18 and 21, 1976.

30. *O Estado de São Paulo*, Dec. 28, 1976.

31. "Mensagem do Conselho Permanente da CNBB," *SEDOC*, 17 (1984-85): 484.

32. Mobral. This document is somewhat difficult to obtain, but a synopsis was published in *IstoÉ*, Dec. 3, 1980.

33. *SEDOC*, 13 (1980-81): 253-55.

34. *Jornal do Brasil*, Apr. 23, 1980.

35. *Jornal do Brasil*, Mar. 10, 1978.

36. *O Liberal* (Belém de Pará), June 9, 1979.

37. For extensive documentation on the conflicts, see Comissão Pastoral da Terra (CPT), *Denúncia*.

282 Notes to Pages 159-65

38. See *Jornal do Brasil*, Feb. 10 and June 28, 1980.
39. CPT, *Denúncia*, 1: 31-35, 69-83.
40. Ibid., 1: 49.
41. See ibid., vol. 2.
42. *Jornal do Brasil*, Sept. 6, 1981.
43. For further information, see *REB*, 41 (1981): 826-31; *REB*, 42 (1982): 602-11; *SEDOC*, 14 (1981-82): 667-700; *SEDOC*, 15 (1982-83): 356-66.
44. *Jornal do Brasil*, Sept. 3, 1981. 45. Ibid.
46. Ibid., Sept. 7, 1981. 47. Ibid., Sept. 11, 1981.
48. Ibid., Sept. 11 and Oct. 19, 1981.
49. Ibid., Oct. 19, 1981.
50. See the preface by D. Luciano Mendes de Almeida, secretary general of the CNBB, to Chinem. See also the supportive comments by D. Luciano Mendes, D. Avelar Brandão, D. Vicente Scherer, D. Helder Câmara, D. Quirino Adolfo Schmitz, and D. Adriano Hypólito in *Jornal do Brasil*, Sept. 11, 1981; by Mons. Afonso Hammes, D. David Picão, D. Carlos Carmelo de Vasconcelos Motta, D. Alfredo Novak, and D. Aparecido José Dias in *Jornal do Brasil*, Sept. 1, 1981; and by D. Paulo Evaristo Arns, *New York Times*, Sept. 14, 1981.
51. The best documented case is that of Paraíba. On the transformation of the Paraíba countryside, see Paiva et al.; Paiva, "Pedagogia e Luta Social"; and Dulce Maria Barbosa Cartalice, "Penetração do Capitalismo no Campo: Um Estudo de Caso—Alagamar," in *Cadernos do CEAS*, 65 (1980): 33-45. For information on earlier conflicts, see *SEDOC*, 8 (1975-76): 829-30, and *SEDOC*, 9 (1976-77): 947-49.
52. Statement by the secretary of the Township of Xapuri, Acre, *Jornal do Brasil*, June 28, 1980.
53. References to all these themes except Bible interpretation are found elsewhere, especially in this chapter and the first half of Chapter 9. There is a vast literature on Bible interpretation. A good overview of the new Christology, with extensive bibliography, is L. Boff, "Jesus Cristo Libertador." This article builds on his seminal *Jesus Cristo, Libertador*. The writings of Carlos Mesters on the Old Testament also stand out; see, for example, *Palavra de Deus*.
54. Assmann's most important book, *Opresión-liberación*, came out in Spanish because of the censorship in Brazil.
55. The list of works on the Church's political responsibilities and limits is extensive. Among the most important are C. Boff, *Comunidade Eclesial*; C. Boff, *Teologia e Prática*; Libânio, "Teologia no Brasil"; L. Boff, *Igreja*; L. Boff, *Teologia do Cativeiro*, especially pp. 187-220; L. Boff, *A Fé na Periferia do Mundo*, pp. 57-75; C. Boff and L. Boff; L. Boff, *Caminhar da Igreja*, pp. 103-7, 113-16; Loureiro Botas; Betto, "Prática Pastoral"; Betto, "Da Prática"; Betto, "Oração"; Antônio Alves de Melo, "Fé em Jesus Cristo e Compromisso Político-Partidário," *REB*, 42 (1982): 551-56; and Rogério de Almeida Cunha, "Papel da Igreja na Luta Política," *REB*, 42 (1982): 562-87.
56. C. Boff and L. Boff, pp. 16-17.

57. See the 1976 election letter by D. Quirino Adolfo Schmitz, *SEDOC*, 9 (1976-77): 203-5. See also the letter by D. Romeu Alberti, bishop of Apucarana, Paraná, in *SEDOC*, 9 (1976-77): 205-8.

58. CNBB, "A Pastoral Social," p. 34.

59. *Folha de São Paulo*, Nov. 10, 1979. There have been few exceptions to the general trend away from indicating specific parties or candidates. In 1978, D. Tomás Balduino of Goiás Velho, Goiás, encouraged voting for the MDB. See the article in *Jornal do Brasil*, Oct. 21, 1978. In 1981, D. Pedro Casaldáliga affirmed that the PMDB, PT, and PDT were the only reliable opposition parties, and theologian Leonardo Boff argued that the PT came closest to realizing the Church's conception of the political order.

60. See Comissão Arquidiocesana de Pastoral dos Direitos Humanos e Marginalizados de São Paulo. Over the years, *SEDOC* has published a large number of diocesan and episcopal statements on parties and elections.

61. Betto, "Da Prática," pp. 95, 104. On this point, see also Betto, "Prática Pastoral"; L. Boff, "Teologia à Escuta"; L. Boff, *Teologia do Cativeiro*, pp. 10, 198, 217; and Jether Pereira Ramalho, "Há Outros Companheiros Nesta Caminhada," *REB*, 41 (1981): 681-85.

62. Conclusions of the meeting of the National CPT, *Boletim da CPT*, May–June 1975.

63. On the Movement of Priests for the Third World, see Dodson, "Religious Innovation." For a comparison of the two movements, see Dodson, "Christian Left." On the Christians for Socialism movement, see the sources mentioned in note 5 of Chapter 1.

64. On the close identification between the Peronist Left and the movement, see Gillespie, pp. 47-88; "Ante el Regreso de Perón," in Movimiento de los Sacerdotes para el Tercer Mundo, pp. 117-19, and Mugica, especially pp. 29-44.

65. See, for example, Movimiento de los Sacerdotes para el Tercer Mundo, pp. 108-9.

66. In this area, the works of C. Boff have been particularly important; see *Teologia e Prática*, and "Igreja."

67. On this point, see Dodson, "Religious Innovation," pp. 119-64.

68. Movimiento de los Sacerdotes para el Tercer Mundo, pp. 72, 102.

69. Raúl Silva Hernández, in Cristianos por el Socialismo, pp. 189, 194.

70. Eagleson, pp. 182, 189.

71. Written by an unidentified ex-leader of Christians for Socialism, in ibid., p. ix. Along similar lines, see the critical remarks by Arthur McGovern and Brian Smith, two North Americans basically sympathetic to the movement. For two very critical views, see Vekemans, *Teología*; and Teresa Donoso Loero, *Historia de los Cristianos por el Socialismo en Chile* (Santiago, 1975).

72. *Paz e Terra* 6 (1968): 229-43. Among other letters by critical priests, religious, and laity, see "Carta de 663 Sacerdotes aos Bispos em Medellín," July 27, 1968, signed by 235 Brazilians, in *Missão Operária*, vol. 2, no. 5 (Aug. 1968): 36-39; "Carta dos Padres," *REB*, 28 (1968): 366-71; "Padres Oblatos Denunciam Injustiças Sociais," *REB*, 28 (1976): 475-76; "Conflito de Botucatu," *SEDOC*, 1 (1968-69): 169-91; "Carta de Leigos, Reli-

giosos e Padres de Nova Friburgo," *SEDOC*, 1 (1968-69): 389-94; "Carta de 350 Padres de Volta Redonda, São Paulo e Rio de Janeiro aos Bispos," *SEDOC*, 1 (1968-69): 394-99; "Carta de 110 Padres de Guanabara," *SE-DOC*, 1 (1968-69): 399-401; "Carta dos Seminaristas aos Bispos," *SE-DOC*, 1 (1968-69): 539-41; "Carta do Clero de Volta Redonda," *SEDOC*, 1 (1968-69): 995-96; "Carta de Leigos, Religiosas e Padres," *SEDOC*, 3 (1970-71): 327-32; and "Carta dos Padres de São Paulo ao Arcebispo," in Centro de Pastoral Vergueiro, pt. 2, p. 34.

73. *Comunicado Mensal da CNBB*, 200 (1969): p. 7.

74. See Antoine, *Integrismo Brasileiro*, pp. 39-41, 73.

75. *SEDOC*, 5 (1972-73): 1386.

76. My information on this group came from interviews with two bishops who participated from the start, D. Tomás Balduino and D. Waldir Calheiros.

77. See, for example, the interview with D. Aloísio Lorscheider, at that time secretary general of the CNBB, in *SEDOC*, 9 (1976-77): 1056-59.

78. *Folha de São Paulo*, Feb. 20, 1979.

79. On the characteristics and definition of popular religiosity, see Ribeiro de Oliveira; Galilea, *Religiosidade Popular*, pp. 11-20; Cesar, "Catolicismo Popular"; Antoniazzi; and Ribeiro de Oliveira, *Catolicismo Popular*.

80. Typical of the attacks on popular religion by progressive reformists was Dorvalino Koch, *Fundamento Secular-Cristão do Desenvolvimento* (Petrópolis, 1971).

81. Hoornaert, "Distinção," p. 603. D. Waldir Calheiros of Volta Redonda stated in an interview with the author, "In the renovative fervor of the post-Concilium years, there was often a failure to respect popular Catholicism. Images were removed from the churches, devotion to the saints was discouraged. . . . We had not yet developed a liberating discourse within the traditional religious practices of the people." See also the reports of the base communities of Linhares and Vitória in Espírito Santo in Mesters et al., pp. 53, 14-15. On the early progressive rejection of popular religiosity and later re-evaluation of this subject, see the interview with Carlos Rodrigues Brandão in *SEDOC*, 12 (1979-80): 1115-16; Galilea, *Religiosidade Popular*, pp. 41-52; and Souza Netto.

82. Interview, Aug. 5, 1981.

83. Among the earliest works by progressive priests who proposed a reevaluation of popular religiosity were A. Rolim, "Em Torno"; and Leers, "Igreja."

84. "Popular religiosity does not satisfactorily correspond to the entirety of the Christian message. . . . The popular sectors live a religion that is not only insufficient, but also causes backwardness in temporal development. Fatalism and religious resignation generate inertia, discouragement, and indifference to earthly material problems." Comblin, *Sinais dos Tempos*, p. 15.

85. Comblin, "Prolegômenos," p. 851.

86. Comblin, *Sinais dos Tempos*, pp. 105-6.

87. Ibid., pp. 258-79.

88. Hoornaert, "Problemas," pp. 280-307.
89. See, for example, Schooyans, pp. 69-87; and Caramuru de Barros, *Perspectivas Pastorais*, pp. 25, 26. Even though Schooyans and Caramuru wrote in the Vatican II tradition, which usually scorned popular religiosity, they showed an appreciation for these traditional practices.
90. CELAM, *Igreja*, sect. 6.2.
91. Queiroz. Galilea makes this same criticism in *Religiosidade Popular*, pp. 41-52. Many theological statements and Church documents indicate the Church's positions. See Suess, "Pastoral Popular"; F. C. Rolim, "Religiosidade Popular"; Suess, *Catolicismo Popular*; Leers, *Cristãos*, pp. 13-42; Hoornaert, "Pressupostos Antropológicos"; Hoornaert, "Catolicismo Popular"; Brandão et al.; and L. Boff, "Catolicismo Popular." On the history of popular religiosity in Brazil, see Azzi, "Religiosidade Popular"; Azzi, "Elementos"; Hoornaert, *Formação*, pp. 98-136; Azzi, *Episcopado do Brasil*; and Azzi, *Catolicismo Popular*.
92. CELAM, *Evangelização*, para. 413. See also paras. 444-69.
93. L. Boff, *Eclesiogênese*.
94. On the theology and religious practices in the base communities, see L. Boff, "Eclesiologias"; Mesters, "Futuro do Nosso Passado"; Mesters, "Brisa Leve"; L. Boff, *Igreja*, pp. 196-212; Mesters, "Interpretação"; Marie-Dominique Chenu, "A Nova Consciência do Fundamento Trinitário da Igreja," *Concilium*, 166 (1981): 21-31; and Guimarães, pp. 34-39, 117-215.
95. CELAM, *Evangelização*, para. 629.
96. Eduardo Viola and I develop this argument and analyze some of the political impacts and limits of CEBs and other social movements in "New Social Movements."
97. The classic example is the corporatist labor structures, created by Vargas, which have served as a means of controlling the labor movement ever since. There is an extensive literature on these corporatist labor structures. On their origins and early history, see Werneck Vianni. H. H. de Souza Martins traces elements of change and continuity in the state's control of the labor movement in *Estado*, as does Erickson in *Sindicalismo*. Philippe Schmitter (*Interest Conflict*) discusses the state's control of associational life more broadly, but with some attention to labor. An important study of how these corporatist structures were used to control labor under the authoritarian regime is Mericle. An earlier study that also emphasizes the dependent character of the labor movement is J. A. Rodrigues.
98. For studies of the CPT, see Poletto; and Grzybowski.
99. CIMI, "Missões Indígenas de Mato Grosso Debatem Linha de Ação," mimeo., Nov. 1973. For further information on CIMI and its views, see Suess, "Caminhada"; and Ricardo. On the creation of CIMI, see *REB*, 32 (1972): 453-57. See also Bruneau, *Church in Brazil*, chap. 5; *SEDOC*, 9 (1976-77): 1181-85; and *SEDOC*, 12 (1979-80): 467-83.

Chapter 8

1. When I did my dissertation research, there was a dearth of good studies on the relationship between the Church and popular movements. More

286 Notes to Pages 183-87

recently, however, some important works have appeared. See Doimo; Paiva, *Igreja*; and Krischke and Mainwaring, *Igreja*. I discuss other aspects of the neighborhood movement of Nova Iguaçu in "Grass Roots Popular Movements."

2. Data are from the official census.

3. On the development of Nova Iguaçu, I relied on L. L. Queiroz, chap. 2; and Adão Bernardes.

4. The population of Rio was 1,157,873 in 1920; 1,764,141 in 1940; 3,281,908 in 1960; 4,251,918 in 1970; and 5,183,992 in 1980. Real estate prices in Rio increased 3.76 times in real terms between 1957 and 1976. "Solo Urbano e Ação Pastoral," *Documentos da CNBB*, 23 (1982): 8. The expansion of the favela population outpaced the overall population growth. According to one estimate, the favela population increased from 57,889 in 1933 to 965,000 in 1961. Fundação Leão XIII, *Favelas: Um Compromisso Que Vamos Resgatar* (Rio de Janeiro, 1962). Today there are about 1.8 million favela dwellers, according to estimates of the Archdiocese of Rio. The figures can be debated, but the trend they suggest is clear. On the expansion of favelas in Rio, see Valla et al.; and Parisse.

5. Instituto Brasileiro de Geografia e Estatística, *Censo 1970*. For a socioeconomic profile of the Baixada Fluminense's population, see Cristina Saliby et al., "A Política de Habitação Popular: Suas Consequências sobre a População Proletária do Grande Rio," unpublished manuscript, Rio de Janeiro, 1977; and Adão Bernardes, pp. 122-41.

6. Health information comes from Movimento dos Amigos do Bairro (MAB), "Primeiro Ciclo de Debates Populares do MAB," mimeo., Nov. 1980.

7. L. L. Queiroz, p. 79.

8. MAB, "Primeiro Ciclo."

9. Ibid.

10. See L. L. Queiroz, chap. 2, on pre-1974 popular mobilizations.

11. M. H. Moreira Alves, p. 500. On the Death Squad's activities in Nova Iguaçu, see *Jornal do Brasil*, Apr. 13, 1983.

12. On the MDB in Rio de Janeiro, see Diniz.

13. For an introduction to D. Adriano's perception of the Church and politics, see the "Entrevista com D. Adriano," *Vozes*, 75 (Jan.-Feb. 1981); and the interview with D. Adriano in *SEDOC*, 11 (1978-79): 496-511.

14. Information on the diocese's development came from interviews and from diocesan publications such as the annual *Plano Pastoral da Diocese de Nova Iguaçu* and *O Povo de Deus Assume a Caminhada* (Petrópolis, 1983). Interviews with D. Adriano Hypólito, the director of Caritas Diocesana, a member of the Justice and Peace Commission and a founder of and current advisor to the Workers Pastoral Commission, were especially helpful on this subject. Also see Ivo Lesbaupin, "Direitos Humanos e Classes Populares," M. A. thesis, Instituto Universitário de Pesquisas do Rio de Janeiro, 1982, pp. 16-19, on the Nova Iguaçu Church.

15. For the kidnapping and torturing of D. Adriano, see Chapter 7. See also the introduction to the "Entrevista com D. Adriano," *Vozes*, 75 (Jan.-Feb. 1981); and *REB*, 40 (1980): 177-82.

16. Since the late 1970's, these movements have received considerable attention. Although I disagree with many of their conclusions, the works of Manuel Castells, Jean Lojkine, and Jordi Borja were seminal in reassessing these movements. By Castells, see *Movimientos sociales urbanos* and *Cidade, Democracia e Socialismo*. Borja's most influential work is *Movimientos sociales urbanos*. By Lojkine, see *Marxisme* and *Politique urbaine*. A fine critique of Castells's work is Paul Singer, "Urbanização, Dependência e Marginalização na América Latina," in Singer, *Economica Política da Urbanização*. In this vein, see also Luiz Antônio Machado da Silva and Alícia Ziccardi, "Notas para uma Discussão sobre Movimentos Sociais Urbanos," *Cadernos do Centro de Estudos Rurais e Urbanos*, 1st series, 13 (1980): 79-95. Important Brazilian contributions include Boschi, *Movimentos Coletivos*; Moisés, "Classes Populares"; Moisés, "Experiências de Mobilização"; Singer, "Movimentos de Bairro"; Souto; Boschi, "Movimentos Sociais"; and R. Cardoso.

17. On the connection between this health work and the early development of the neighborhood movement, see Bohadana.

18. *Encontro*, 2 (Mar. 1976).   19. Ibid., 11 (Nov. 1977).

20. Ibid., 12 (Jan. 1978).   21. Ibid., 15 (July 1978).

22. On the assembly, see ibid., 16 (Oct. 1978).

23. *Jornal do Brasil*, Sept. 27, 1981.

24. *Correio da Lavoura*, 3432 (Dec. 24, 1982).

25. Interview, Jan. 21, 1985.

26. Interview, July 3, 1981.

27. One of the strongest statements that the popular movements are still dependent on Church support is Souza Lima, "Notas."

28. Interview, July 3, 1981.

29. On Nova Iguaçu's Justice and Peace Commission, see *SEDOC*, 15 (1982-83): 1243-51.

30. Interview, June 1, 1981.

31. Interview, June 2, 1981. He refers to peasants because he lived in a rural part of the municipality until 1974.

32. On the political limitations and religious primacy of Brazilian CEBs, see Libânio, "Uma Comunidade"; L. Boff, "Teologia à Escuta"; Betto, *Comunidade Eclesial de Base*; Libânio, "Igreja"; and Loureiro Botas.

33. Interview, June 26, 1981.   34. Interview, Mar. 27, 1981.

35. Interview, May 18, 1981.   36. Interview, Sept. 12, 1981.

37. On this point, see Carvalho; Camerman and Bohadana; and Leeds and Leeds, especially pp. 26-52, 264-88. This observation is not unique to the masses in Brazil. A classic tenet of some strains of liberal political theory is the difficulty of getting people to participate in collective movements; see Mancur Olson, *The Logic of Collective Action* (Cambridge, Mass., 1965).

38. Interview, Sept. 19, 1981. For similar criticisms, see L. L. Queiroz; Romano; Abramovay; Paiva, "Anotações"; and Velho.

39. Some of this diversity in the relationship between the Church and popular movements is apparent in the different studies in Boschi, *Movimentos Coletivos*.

40. Much of the literature on urban social movements has been exces-

sively optimistic about their capacity to promote social change. Recently a more critical literature has emphasized the limited nature and cyclical character of these movements. See Boschi, "Movimentos Sociais"; R. Cardoso; Renato Raul Boschi and Lícia do Prado Valladares, "Movimentos Associativos de Camadas Populares Urbanas: Análise Comparativa de Seis Casos," in Boschi, *Movimentos Coletivos*, pp. 103-43; Singer, "Movimentos de Bairros" and "Movimentos Sociais"; and F. H. Cardoso, "Regime Político."

41. *Boletim Diocesano* (Diocese of Nova Iguaçu), no. 191 (Dec. 1, 1984).

42. Much of the theoretical literature has noted the cyclical character of most social movements and the difficulty of maintaining ongoing mobilization; see, for instance, Hirschman; and Tilly.

Chapter 9

An earlier version of Chapter 9 appeared as "The Catholic Church, Popular Education, and Political Change in Brazil," in the *Journal of Inter-American Studies and World Affairs*, 26 (Feb. 1984): 97-124, copyright ©1984 by Sage Publications, Inc. I am grateful to Sage Publications, Inc., for permission to reuse this material.

1. CNBB, *Documentos dos Presbitérios*, pp. 9, 56.

2. A. Rolim, "Em Torno," p. 18. See also Hoornaert, "Distinção," p. 602.

3. Carvalheira, pp. 533, 536. See also Hoornaert, "Igreja"; and Comblin, *Futuro*.

4. CNBB, *Documentos dos Presbitérios*, p. 11.

5. Workers Pastoral Commission of Sao Pãulo, mimeo., Nov. 12, 1972.

6. The writings of Frei Betto on pedagogical work with the popular sectors have been especially influential. See, for example, "Educação." Paulo Freire's works also remain highly influential and also clearly express the views sketched here. See especially *Educação* and *Pedagogy*. Other important pedagogical statements by popular Church intellectuals include Wanderley; C. Boff, "Agente de Pastoral"; C. Boff, "Comunidades"; L. Boff, "Teologia à Escuta"; Fragoso, "Libertação"; and Lesbaupin, "Papel dos Intelectuais." In addition, there are a plethora of statements by different dioceses and pastoral commissions. I especially consulted documents of CPT, CPO, ACO, and the dioceses of Espírito Santo, São Mateus, and Goiás Velho.

7. This point is emphasized in Wanderley.

8. On this point, see C. Boff, *Teologia e Prática*, pp. 281-303; Libânio, *Discernimento e Política*, pp. 35-41; Betto, "Educação"; Libânio, *Problema da Salvação*, chap. 1; Hoornaert, "História da Igreja"; and Gómez de Souza, *Classes Populares*, pp. 63-71. Although he does not use the term "social position," José de Souza Martins discusses the same issue in *Camponeses*, pp. 9-19, and *Expropriação e Violência*, pp. 180-81.

9. "II National Assembly of CIMI," mimeo., 1975. See also Mesters, "Futuro do Nosso Passado," p. 123.

10. See C. Boff, "Agente de Pastoral," p. 229.

11. This emphasis on popular wisdom has been developed at length by a number of intellectuals. Among others, see Costa, "Para Analisar"; Weffort, "Nordestinos"; Rocha; Garcia, "Educação Popular"; Costa, "Pastoral Popular"; Leeds and Leeds; and C. Boff, "Agente de Pastoral."

12. See Fragoso, "Libertação." On this point, as well as with many other pedagogical issues, the similarity to MEB and Paulo Freire is remarkable.

13. "Linhas Prioritárias de Pastoral na Amazônia," *SEDOC*, 7 (1974-75): 783.

14. On this subject, see C. Boff, "Uma Igreja Popular."

15. More extensive, though at times excessively optimistic, discussions of the Church's contributions to the popular process can be found in the writings of popular Church intellectuals. See C. Boff, "Comunidades"; C. Boff, "Agente de Pastoral"; Betto, *Comunidade Eclesial de Base*; L. Boff, "Teologica à Escuta"; Pereira Ramalho, "CEBs"; and Libânio, "Igreja" and "Uma Comunidade."

16. On this point, see the provocative article by Costa, "Pastoral Popular." See also Hoornaert, "Comunidades"; Pereira Ramalho, "CEBs," especially pp. 272-74; Libânio, "Uma Comunidade," especially pp. 311-15; Affonso Gregory, "As Comunidades Eclesiais de Base: Chances e Desafios—Alguns Destaques Sociológicos," in Gregory and Ghisleni, especially pp. 38-39; Pereira Ramalho, "Algumas Notas"; and Lauro de Oliveira Lima, *Os Mecanismos da Liberdade* (São Paulo, 1980), pp. 362-64.

17. On this point, see Medina and Ribeiro de Oliveira, pp. 47-55, 61-71.

18. See Ribeiro de Oliveira, "Posição do Leigo." On the way the base communities have helped democratize Church structures, see Guimarães, pp. 34-39, 117-215. More broadly on the laity's role in the popular Church, see L. Boff, *Igreja*, pp. 58-81, 204-19.

19. *SEDOC*, 11 (1978-79): 313.

20. This does not mean that these activities are socially irrelevant, as Roberto Da Matta has underscored in his fine works on popular culture; see *Carnavais* and *Antropologia Estrutural* (Petrópolis, 1973), pp. 121-68.

21. On the authoritarian tendencies in the labor movement, see H. H. de Souza Martins, especially pp. 13-72; L. Rodrigues, pp. 188-91; and J. A. Rodrigues, pp. 123-42, 167-81. These authoritarian tendencies also coexisted with other moments when the unions were more democratic and participatory and mobilized large numbers of people. Weffort's "Sindicatos e Política" particularly emphasizes the periods of mobilizations and argues that the submissive character of the labor movement can be exaggerated. In a similar vein, see Maranhão, *Sindicatos e Democratização*; Moisés, *Greve de Masse*; and Gato.

22. This elitist political culture is discussed in O'Donnell, "A mi que me importa"; Schwartzman; and Faoro. Eduardo Viola and I discuss this subject in "New Social Movements." For an assessment of authoritarian patterns in the schools, the work place, and the home, which also calls attention to the Church's work as a democratizing force, see Fischer.

23. *SEDOC*, 11 (1978-79): 335. See also the description by the community of Santa Margarida, also on the periphery of São Paulo, in the same number of *SEDOC*, p. 354.

24. See, for example, Libânio, "Uma Comunidade," pp. 300-301; L. Boff, "Teologia à Escuta," p. 62; Pereira Ramalho, "CEBs," p. 266; Libânio, "Igreja"; C. Boff, "Comunidades"; Mesters, "Futuro do Nosso Passado"; Gregory and Ghisleni; and C. Boff, "Pedrinha Soltou-se."

25. On the importance of respecting traditional values in the development process, see Goulet, "Development Experts," and "Defense of Cultural Rights." On the same subject, from a conservative perspective, see Berger.

26. Lesbaupin, "Papel dos Intelectuais," pp. 17-18.

27. In a recent article, Vanilda Paiva discusses this anti-intellectualism at length; see "Anotações."

28. On this point, see Carvalho.

29. This is the perspective of Pedro Benjamin Garcia, among others; see "Educação Popular" and "Saber Popular."

30. Along these lines, some writings on the way favelas have resisted domination are particularly interesting; see Leeds and Leeds; Perlman; and Valladares.

31. Costa, "Para Analisar," p. 17.

32. For example, Hoornaert, *Formação*, pp. 99-104.

33. Costa, "Para Analisar," p. 19.

34. Bernard von der Weid, "Educação Popular: Um Depoimento," *Cadernos de Educação Popular*, 1 (1982): 56-57.

35. On this subject and popular attitudes toward politicians and elections, see Rio Caldeira.

36. Several outstanding Brazilian intellectuals have addressed the question of elements of resistance and submission in popular culture, religion, and consciousness. See Chaui, pp. 39-84; Ortiz; Brandão, *Deuses do Povo*; and Da Matta, *Carnavais*.

37. On this point, see J. de Souza Martins, *Camponeses*, pp. 9-19, 81-92; Leeds and Leeds; and Perlman. As they mature, popular movements can acquire far more autonomy with respect to external agents. On this point, see Camerman and Bohadana.

38. See Dahl, *After the Revolution?*, pp. 59-103.

39. Cardoso, "Regime Político." On this point, see also the fine article by Singer, "Movimentos Sociais."

40. On the notion of respecting each individual's development and not encouraging people to participate before they are ready, see the excellent article by Paiva, "Pedagogia e Luta Social."

41. CNBB, *Comunidades Eclesiais*, p. 71.

42. On the party reform, see Sanders, "Brazil in 1980."

43. One of the most *basista* popular bishops, D. José Maria Pires (João Pessoa), states that "at this time the parties have little to offer the people. . . . They arrived too early and their presence has reduced the force of the social movements." *Jornal do Brasil*, Mar. 1, 1982. See also *Jornal do Brasil*, Apr. 24, 1981.

44. On this point, see Moisés, "PT." For a detailed examination of the PT, see Keck.

45. Ingrid Andersen Sarti and Rubem Barbosa Filho address similar di-

lemmas in the labor movement in "Desafios e Desafinos nos Caminhos da Cidadania," *Dados*, 26 (1983): 315-34.

46. See F. H. Cardoso, *Democracia para Mudar*, pp. 17-36, 47-60; and F. H. Cardoso, "Regime Político." See also Gómez de Souza, *Classes Populares*, pp. 237-68.

47. C. Boff, "Agente de Pastoral," p. 225.

48. Comissão Arquidiocesana de Pastoral dos Direitos Humanos e Marginalizados de São Paulo, p. 29.

Chapter 10

1. Of course, there are some antecedents and prior influences, ranging from humanist Catholic existentialism to Russian populism.

2. See, for example, Conselho Episcopal Latino-Americano (CELAM), *Evangelização*, pp. 312, 495, 542, 550.

3. Among the most important works were Garaudy; Gerardi; and Aptheker. Good discussions are Hebblethwaite, *Christian-Marxist Dialogue*; and McGovern, pp. 90-134.

4. On the Nicaraguan case, see Dodson and Montgomery; Cáceres; and Cáceres et al.

5. The most famous case was that of Frei Betto and the Dominicans. See Betto's *Batismo*.

6. The positions of D. Paulo, D. Cláudio, and D. José Maria Pires are recorded in Salem, pp. 151, 132-34, 137. Although it is not the central theme of the article, Clodovis Boff makes a cautious statement essentially in favor of socialism in "Justiça na História."

7. See L. Boff, *Igreja*, p. 211; and L. Boff, *Teologia do Cativeiro*, p. 199.

8. Most of the Communist Left still diverges from the progressive Church on most issues, but several leading Marxist scholars have published statements that coincide in many ways with the Church's criticisms of Leninism. Carlos Nelson Coutinho and Leandro Konder have condemned the vanguardism that has historically characterized much of the Brazilian Left and have called for democratic practices in all systems, both as an objective and as a means. By Coutinho, see *Democracia*, especially pp. 17-42, 61-92, 112-18. By Konder, see *Democracia e os Comunistas*.

9. These views are expressed particularly strongly in *What Must Be Done?*, especially pp. 28-44, 78-93, 108-39. Some leading figures in the Marxist tradition placed a far greater emphasis on popular values and capacities. Rosa Luxemburg emphasized the creative capacity of the popular sectors and criticized the "despotic centralism" of Lenin's vanguard notion. See *Rosa Luxemburg Speaks*, pp. 112-30, 153-218. Although critical of what he called "commonsense" (popular) perspectives, Antonio Gramsci underscored some positive elements in popular consciousness. In contrast to Lenin, who sees the vanguard as a small elite group, Gramsci argues that "all men are intellectuals." *Prison Notebooks*, p. 9; see also pp. 5-14, 196-200, 323-43, 419-23. For a critique of the Leninist view that popular consciousness is necessarily "reformist," see Jelin.

10. Betto, "Educação," pp. 166-67. This article is a sharp critique of van-

guardism. Betto reiterates the criticisms in *Comunidade Eclesial de Base*, especially pp. 37, 43-44. See also Gómez de Souza, *Classes Populares*, pp. 55-92, 237-68; J. de Souza Martins, *Camponeses*, pp. 9-19, 87, 92-102; Wanderly; C. Boff, "Agente de Pastoral"; and L. Boff, "Teologia à Escuta" and *Caminhar da Igreja*, p. 141. For the views on the Left of D. Marcelo Cavalheira, D. Waldir Calheiros, and D. Cláudio Hummes, see Salem, pp. 117-18, 122, 132.

11. See L. Boff, *Caminhar da Igreja*, p. 201. For Boff's views on the importance of freedom in any system, see *Teologia do Cativeiro*, pp. 83-102.

12. C. Boff, "Agente de Pastoral."

13. See L. Boff, *Teologia do Cativeiro*, pp. 91-92, 103-6, 117-30; and Demo, especially pp. 85-104. Critics have often overlooked this critical edge of progressive Catholic thought. In "Theology of Liberation," Thomas Sanders accuses liberation theology of overlooking the fact that there is no perfect liberation and of venerating the accomplishments of revolutionary regimes. These criticisms are valid for some theologians, but the predominant thrust of progressive Catholic thought in Brazil is more critical than Sanders suggests. See the sharp reply to Sanders by Alves.

14. On this third path tradition, see Stepan, *State and Society*, pp. 26-45. The best statement of Perón's ideology is his book, *La comunidad organizada* (Buenos Aires, 1973). On the Onganía period, see O'Donnell, *Estado burocrático-autoritario*.

15. See L. Boff, *Teologia do Cativeiro*, pp. 19-26. For a similar point, see Galilea, *Teologia*, pp. 32-34.

16. See the comments by D. Tomás Balduino in Salem, p. 149.

17. *SEDOC*, 10 (1977-78): 323. See also his remarks in Salem, pp. 126-27. See also Leers, *Cristãos*, pp. 280-95; J. de Souza Martins, *Expropriação e Violência*, pp. 35-44; and J. de Souza Martins, *Camponeses*, pp. 9-19, 92-102, 127-37.

18. National Committee (Equipe) of ACO, Jan. 1980, mimeo.

19. On the relationship between the various parties and the CEBs, see Galleta; and Betto, "Comunidades."

20. Gómez de Souza, "Crisis del desarrollo." See also his *Classes Populares*, pp. 237-68.

21. On the difficulties of developing a more participatory system in large, complex societies and the need for elites to control some decisions, see Dahl, *After the Revolution?*, pp. 28-103, 140-66.

22. On this point, see MacPherson; Pateman; and Offe. For a compelling analysis of the unlikelihood of maintaining high levels of ongoing mobilization, see Hirschman.

23. On Boa Esperança, see H. J. de Souza, "Boa Esperança." On Lages, see Márcio Moreira Alves, *Força do Povo*. For a history of community development programs in Brazil, which sees them as a means of eliciting support for inegalitarian development projects, see Bezerra Ammann. For a statement by one of the Brazilian ideologues of these programs, see Baptista.

24. Marx's early work addressed at length the tendency of the state bu-

reaucracy to further some interests to the exclusion of others, and Max Weber called attention to the way the "efficient" planning model (bureaucracy) could develop formal rationality while impeding substantive rationality. See Marx, "Critique of Hegel's Philosophy of the State," in *Writings of the Young Marx*, pp. 151-202. By Weber, see *From Max Weber*, pp. 220-35. See also F. H. Cardoso, *Estado y Sociedad*, pp. 91-112. On the ways in which the technocratic discourse furthers the interests of dominant sectors, see Chaui, pp. 1-13, 39-60. Although written with the advanced industrial societies in mind, the works of Herbert Marcuse and Jürgen Habermas on rationality and domination are also apposite; see Marcuse; and Habermas, pp. 62-122.

25. Huntington's classic *Political Order* promoted the view that political participation and efficacy are generally contradictory objectives. Crozier, Huntington, and Watanuki continue this line of thought in *Crisis of Democracy*. See also Huntington and Nelson. Huntington was one of the most important foreign political advisors to Leitão de Abreu, chief of cabinet in the Médici and Figueiredo administrations.

26. For a critique of the technocratic, antiparticipatory, "efficient" approach to development, see Chaui, pp. 3-14, 39-60. For a discussion of the way authoritarianism inhibits creative solutions to the problems of development, see F. H. Cardoso, *Autoritarismo e Democratização*, pp. 223-40. For a critique of the view that authoritarianism is needed to promote con ditions for development, see F. H. Cardoso, *Estado y Sociedad*, pp. 11-36. From a different perspective, Dahl in *Polyarchy* shows sensitivity to the difficulties of creating open, participatory regimes in the Third World, yet criticizes the view that Third World conditions demand authoritarian solutions.

27. My argument here differs from that advanced by Brian Smith in "Churches and Human Rights." Smith argues that throughout Latin America the Church was not very effective in defending human rights. However, he focuses only on the direct impact of the Church's efforts to defend human rights and fails to perceive that through a variety of indirect means, the Church played a major role in empowering civil society.

Chapter 11

1. As this book was going to press, Ralph Della Cava wrote an important article on the decline of the popular Church. His arguments are basically similar to mine. See "The Church." I benefited from an earlier verbal presentation of the paper.

2. The notion of threat is developed in Guillermo O'Donnell's works on bureaucratic-authoritarianism; see *Estado burocrático-autoritario*.

3. *Jornal do Brasil*, July 7, 1983.

4. *Estado de São Paulo*, Dec. 30, 1984.

5. On the way the people in a working-class neighborhood of Sao Paulo perceive politicians, political parties, and political participation, see Rio Caldeira.

6. On this point, see Gómez de Souza, *Classes Populares*, pp. 237-46.
7. For an informative account of John Paul II's mission, written from a conservative viewpoint, see Johnson.
8. On these measures against the Dutch Church, see Coleman; and Goddijn. More broadly, on the post–Vatican II conservative character of Rome, see Hebblethwaite, *Runaway Church*; and Vaillancourt.
9. On Colombia and Venezuela, see Levine, *Religion and Politics*, pp. 69-96. The Peruvian Church began a period of mild retraction in the late 1970's; see Romero de Iguíñiz.
10. By Vekemans, see *Teología*; and "Unidad y pluralismo," which argues that the Church's unity is being threatened in contemporary Latin America. By López Trujillo, see "Compromiso político," "Análisis marxista," *Liberation*, and "Liberación." The best theologian working in Brazil who has written along these lines is Belgian Herbert Lepargneur; see especially *Teología*. See also Kloppenburg, *Igreja Popular*.
11. Quoted in Berryman's interesting account, "What Happened," p. 83. Some of the underhanded methods Vekemans and López Trujillo employed are described in a letter of protest written by over a hundred German theologians, including Jürgen Moltmann and Johannes Baptist Metz, published in *Religião e Sociedade*, 3 (1978): 209-14.
12. See L. Boff, "Teología da Libertação: O Mínimo do Mínimo," *REB*, 38 (1978): 696-705; C. Boff, "A Ilusão de uma Nova Cristandade," *REB*, 38 (1978): 5-17; Luiz Alberto Gómez de Souza, "Documento de Consulta: Críticas ao Diagnóstico da Realidade," *REB*, 38 (1978): 18-32; J. B. Libânio, "A Cristologia no Documento Preparatório para Puebla," *REB*, 38 (1978): 43-58; José Comblin, "Temas Doutrinais com Vistas à Conferência de Puebla," *REB*, 38 (1978): 195-207; José Oscar Beozzo, "A Evangelização na América Latina: Uma Visão Histórica com Vistas a Puebla," *REB*, 38 (1978): 208-43; Comissão Pastoral da Terra, "A CPT e Puebla," SEDOC, 10 (1977-78): 1089-1101; Regional Northeast II of the CNBB, "A Caminhada do Povo de Deus na América Latina," *REB*, 38 (1978): 300-326; CNBB, "Subsídios para Puebla," *REB*, 38 (1978): 327-42.
13. Good introductions to Puebla are Berryman, "What Happened"; and Wilde. For an interpretation of Puebla by two of Brazil's leading popular Church intellectuals, see Gómez de Souza, *Classes Populares*, pp. 170-223; and L. Boff, "Puebla."
14. This conflict and others are discussed in Beozzo, "Igreja do Brasil."
15. *Pronunciamentos do Papa no Brasil* (Petrópolis, 1980), pp. 55, 57, 58. Other speeches in this volume express the pope's support for the CEBs and praise the Brazilian bishops. On the pope's visit, see also Adair Leonardo Rocha and Luiz Alberto Gómez de Souza, eds., *O Povo e o Papa* (Rio de Janeiro, 1980), a collection of essays by theologians and social scientists supportive of the popular Church. The pope also gave a lengthy interview supportive of the Brazilian Church after returning to Rome; see *Jornal do Brasil*, Aug. 23, 1980.
16. "A Carta de João Paulo II aos Bispos do Brasil," *REB*, 41 (1981): 152-57.
17. On the Church's role in the auto workers' strikes of 1978-80, see *Re-*

ligião e Sociedade, 6 (1980): 7-68; Marcelino Fortes et al., "Contribuição para a Análise das Greves de Maio 78" (unpublished document, Jan. 1979); Centro Ecumênico de Documentação e Informação, "1980: ABC da Greve," *Aconteceu*, special edition, May 1980; Centro de Pastoral Vergueiro, "As Greves do ABC," *Cadernos de Documentação*, 3 (December 1980); and F. C. Rolim, "A Greve."

18. Dom Eugênio himself discusses the Vatican's support for his pastoral line in "O Apoio do Papa à Arquidiocese do Rio," *O Globo*, Oct. 27, 1984. On Dom Eugênio's role in the movement against liberation theology, see "D. Eugenio pode ter Deflagrado Movimento contra TL," *Folha de São Paulo*, Sept. 14, 1984.

19. *Jornal do Brasil*, Feb. 28, 1982.

20. Ibid., Mar. 9, 1982.

21. On the Nicaraguan situation, see Crahan, "Varieties of Faith"; Cáceres et al., pp. 17-46, 161-204; and Ezcurra. For an indication of the concern of Brazilian Church progressives, see Pedro Ribeiro de Oliveira, "O Papa na Nicaragua: Uma Análise dos Acontecimentos," *REB*, 43 (1983): 5-9.

22. On these movements, see José Comblin, "Os Movimentos e a Pastoral Latinoamericana," *REB*, 43 (1983): 227-62.

23. The movement against liberation theology is discussed by d'Ans; and Comblin, "América Latina."

24. Published in *SEDOC*, 10 (1977-78): 733-47.

25. See Kloppenburg, *Igreja Popular*, pp. 179-86; Karl Josef Romer, "Por Que o Livro de L. Boff, *Igreja, Carisma e Poder* não é Aceitável," *Boletim da Revista do Clero*, 19 (1982): 30-36; and Urbano Zilles, "Tréplica," *Boletim da Revista do Clero* 19 (1982): 27-29. For Boff's replies, see "Igreja, Carisma e Poder: Uma Justificação contra Falsas Leituras," *REB*, 42 (1982): 227-60; and "Resposta," *Boletim da Revista do Clero*, 19 (1982): 23-26.

26. On the controversy surrounding Boff, see *REB*, 40 (1980): 169-77; *Veja*, Sept. 5, 1983; and "A Punição de Boff," *Tempo e Presença*, 198 (1985): 3-17.

27. See *REB*, 44 (1984): 592-616; and "Frei Clodovis Boff é Impedido de dar Aulas em Universidade Romana," *Folha de São Paulo*, Dec. 13, 1984.

28. *Folha de São Paulo*, Apr. 12, 1983.

29. See "O Evangelho segundo Viana," mimeo., n.d. Part of this lengthy document is published in *Cadernos do CEAS*, 57 (1978): 24-28.

30. The international debate about liberation theology is too vast a subject to be considered in depth here. Because it expressed the Vatican's official position, the most important critique is Vatican, Congregation for the Doctrine of the Faith. See also Ratzinger. In addition to the Brazilian sources already cited, for critical views see Novak; Kloppenburg, *Temptations*; and Wagner. The most important journal that advocates the conservative positions is *Communio*.

31. *Estado de São Paulo*, Apr. 9, 1983. See also John Paul II's "Mensagem do Papa às CEBs do Brasil," *SEDOC*, 13 (1980-81): 270.

32. *SEDOC*, 15 (1982-83): 894.

33. "Comunidades Eclesiais de Base," p. 21.
34. A representative work is Gutiérrez, We Drink.
35. For the liberationists' response to the conservative criticisms, see the various articles in the Dec. 1984 issue of REB, responding to the Vatican's "Instruction." See also L. Boff and C. Boff, "Cinco Observações."
36. On the situation of the Church in Poland, see Rubem César Fernandes, "A Igreja na Polônia: Um Santuário da Oposição," Religião e Sociedade, 5 (1980): 7-28; and Adam Michnick, "A Esquerda, a Igreja e o Estado na Polônia," Religião e Sociedade 4 (1979): 61-94.

Select References

Abramovay, Ricardo. "Marxistas e Cristãos: Pontos para um Diálogo," *Proposta*, 16 (March 1981): 11-20.

Ação Popular. "Ação Popular: Documento-Base," in Luiz Gonzaga de Souza Lima, *Evolução Política dos Católicos e da Igreja no Brasil*. Petrópolis, 1979.

Adão Bernardes, Júlia. *Espaço e Movimentos Reivindicatónos: O Caso de Nova Iguaçu*. Rio de Janeiro, 1983.

Alcântara de Camargo, Aspásia. *Bresil nord-est: Mouvements paysans et crise populiste*. Paris, 1973.

Althusser, Louis. *Lenin and Philosophy and Other Essays*. New York, 1971.

Alves, Rubem. "Christian Realism: Ideology of the Establishment," *Christianity and Crisis*, 33 (1973): 173-76.

Amoroso Lima, Alceu. *O Cardeal Leme: Um Depoimento*. Rio de Janeiro, 1943.

———. *Indicações Políticas*. Rio de Janeiro, 1936.

———. *Pelo Humanismo Ameaçado*. Rio de Janeiro, 1965.

———. *Revolução, Reação ou Reforma*. Rio de Janeiro, 1964.

Andrade, Juracy. *A Igreja na Cidade*. Rio de Janeiro, 1965.

Antoine, Charles. *Church and Power in Brazil*. Maryknoll, N.Y., 1973.

———. *O Integrismo Brasileiro*. Rio de Janeiro, 1980.

Antoniazzi, Alberto. "Várias Interpretações do Catolicismo Popular no Brasil," *REB*, 36 (1976): 82-94.

Aptheker, Herbert. *The Urgency of Marxist-Christian Dialogue*. New York, 1970.

Arns, Paulo Evaristo. *Em Defesa dos Direitos Humanos: Encontro com o Repórter*. Rio de Janeiro, 1978.

Arroyo, Gonzalo. "Nota sobre la iglesia y los cristianos de izquierda a la hora del putsch en Chile," *Latin American Perspectives*, 2 (Spring 1975): 89-99.

Assmann, Hugo. *Opresión-liberación: Desafio a los Cristianos*. Montevideo, 1971.

Azevedo, Thales de. *O Catolicismo no Brasil*. Rio de Janeiro, 1955.

Azzi, Riolando. *O Catolicismo Popular no Brasil*. Petrópolis, 1978.

298   *Select References*

———. "D. Antônio de Macedo Costa e a Posição da Igreja do Brasil diante do Advento da República em 1889," *Síntese*, 8 (1976): 45-70.
———. "Dom Antônio Joaquim de Melo, Bispo de São Paulo (1851-1861), e o Movimento de Reforma Católica no Século XIX," *REB*, 35 (1975): 902-22.
———. "Elementos para a História do Catolicismo Popular," *REB*, 36 (1976): 95-130.
———. "O Episcopado Brasileiro frente à Revolução de 1930," *Síntese*, 12 (1977): 47-78.
———. *O Episcopado do Brasil frente ao Catolicismo Popular.* Petrópolis, 1972.
———. "O Fortalecimento da Restauração Católica em Minas Gerais, 1920-1930," *Síntese*, 17 (1979): 69-85.
———. "A Igreja Católica no Brasil durante o Estado Novo (1937-1945)," *Síntese*, 19 (1980): 49-71.
———. "O Início da Restauração Católica em Minas Gerais, 1920-1930," *Síntese* 14 (1978): 65-92.
———. "O Início da Restauração Católica no Brasil, 1920-1930," *Síntese*, 10 (1977): 61-90; 11 (1977): 73-102.
———. "Religiosidade Popular," *REB*, 38 (1978): 642-50.
Baptista, Myrian Veras. *Desenvolvimento de Comunidade: Estudo da Integração do Planejamento do Desenvolvimento de Comunidade no Planejamento do Desenvolvimento Global.* São Paulo, 1976.
Barbé, Domingos, and Emmanuel Retumba. *Retrato de uma Comunidade de Base.* Petrópolis, 1970.
Barreiro, Julio. *Educación popular y proceso de concientización.* Buenos Aires, 1974.
Bastide, Roger. "Religion and the Church in Brazil," in T. Lynn Smith and Alexander Marchant, eds., *Brazil: Portrait of Half a Continent.* New York, 1951, pp. 334-55.
Bastos de Avila, Fernando. *Neo-capitalismo, Socialismo, Solidarismo.* Rio de Janeiro, 1963.
Becker, João. *O Comunismo Russo e a Civilização Cristã.* Pôrto Alegre, 1930.
———. *A Decadência da Civilização.* Pôrto Alegre, 1940.
Bedoyere, Michael de la. *The Cardijn Story.* London, 1958.
Beozzo, José Oscar. *Cristãos na Universitade e na Política.* Petrópolis, 1984.
Berger, Peter. *Pyramids of Sacrifice: Political Ethics and Social Change.* Garden City, N.Y., 1974.
Berlinck, Manoel Tosta. *Marginalidade Social e Relações de Classe em São Paulo.* Petrópolis, 1975.
Berryman, Phillip. "Latin American Liberation Theology," in Sergio Torres and John Eagleson, eds., *Theology in the Americas.* Maryknoll, N.Y., 1976, pp. 20-83.
———. *The Religious Roots of Rebellion: Christians in Central American Revolutions.* Maryknoll, N.Y., 1984.
———. "What Happened at Puebla," in Daniel Levine, ed., *Churches and Politics in Latin America.* Beverly Hills, Calif., 1979, pp. 55-86.

Betto, Frei. *Batismo de Sangue*. Rio de Janeiro, 1982.
———. "As Comunidades Eclesiais de Base como Potencial de Transformação de Sociedade Brasileira," *REB*, 43 (1983): 494-503.
———. "Da Prática da Pastoral Popular," *Encontros com a Civilização Brasileira*, 2 (1978): 95-112.
———. "A Educação nas Classes Populares," *Encontros com a Civilização Brasileira*, 13 (1979): 162-73.
———. "Oração: Uma Exigência (Também) Política," *REB*, 42 (1982): 444-55.
———. "Prática Pastoral e Prática Política," *Tempo e Presença*, 26 (1980): 11-29.
———. *O Que É Comunidade Eclesial de Base*. São Paulo, 1981.
Bezerra, Aída. "As Atividades em Educação Popular," in Carlos Rodrigues Brandão, ed., *A Questão Política da Educação Popular*. São Paulo, 1980, pp. 16-39.
Bezerra, Almery. "Da Necessidade de um Ideal Histórico," in Luiz Gonzaga de Souza Lima, *Evolução Política dos Católicos e da Igreja no Brasil*. Petrópolis, 1979.
Bezerra Ammann, Safira. *Ideologia do Desenvolvimento de Comunidade no Brasil*. São Paulo, 1980.
Bicudo, Hélio. *Meu Depoimento sobre o Esquadrão da Morte*. São Paulo, 1976.
Blau, Peter. *Bureaucracy in Modern Society*. New York, 1956.
Boehrer, George. "The Church in the Second Reign, 1840-1889," in Henry H. Keith and S. F. Edwards, eds., *Conflict and Continuity in Brazilian Society*. Columbia, S.C., 1969.
Boff, Clodovis. "Agente de Pastoral e Povo," *REB*, 40 (1980): 216-42.
———. *Comunidade Eclesial, Comunidade Política*. Petrópolis, 1979.
———. "Comunidades Eclesiais de Base e Práticas de Libertação," *REB*, 40 (1980): 595-625.
———. "A Igreja, o Povo e o Poder," *REB*, 40 (1980): 11-47.
———. "Uma Igreja Popular: Impressões de uma Visita pela Igreja de Crateús," *REB*, 41 (1981): 728-44.
———. "A Influência Política das CEBs," *Religião e Sociedade*, 4 (1979): 95-119.
———. "A Justiça na História," *Vozes*, 72 (1978): 85-96.
———. "E uma Pedrinha Soltou-se: As Bases do Povo de Deus," *REB*, 42 (1982): 659-87.
———. *Teologia e Prática*. Petrópolis, 1978.
Boff, Clodovis, and Leonardo Boff. "Comunidades Cristãs e Política Partidária," *Encontros com a Civilização Brasileira*, 3 (1978): 11-25.
Boff, Leonardo. *O Caminhar da Igreja com os Oprimidos*. Rio de Janeiro, 1980.
———. "Catolicismo Popular: Que É Catolicismo?" *REB*, 36 (1976): 19-52.
———. *Eclesiogênese: As Comunidades Eclesiais de Base Reinventam a Igreja*. Petrópolis, 1977.
———. "As Eclesiologias Presentes nas Comunidades Eclesiais de Base," in Mesters et al. *Uma Igreja Que Nasce do Povo*. Petrópolis, 1975, pp. 201-9.

———. *A Fé na Periferia do Mundo*. Petrópolis, 1978.
———. *Igreja: Carisma e Poder*. Petrópolis, 1981.
———. *Jesus Cristo, Libertador*. Petrópolis, 1971.
———. "Jesus Cristo Libertador: Uma Visão Cristológica a Partir da Periferia," *REB*, 37 (1977): 501-24.
———. "Puebla: Ganhos, Avanços, Questões Emergentes," *REB*, 39 (1979): 43-63.
———. "Teologia à Escuta do Povo," *REB*, 41 (1981): 55-119.
———. *Teologia do Cativeiro e da Libertação*. Petrópolis, 1980.
Boff, Leonardo, and Clodovis Boff. "Cinco Observações de Fundo à Intervenção do Cardeal Ratzinger acerca da Teologia da Libertação," *REB*, 44 (1984): 115-20.
Bohadana, Estrella. "Experiências de Participação Popular em Ações de Saúde," in IBASE, ed., *Saúde e Trabalho no Brasil*. Petrópolis, 1982, pp. 107-28.
Borges, Dain. "Church, State, and Family," in "The Family in Bahia, Brazil, 1870-1945." Ph.D. dissertation, Stanford University, 1985.
Borja, Jordi. *Movimientos Sociales Urbanos*. Buenos Aires, 1975.
Boschi, Renato. "Movimentos Sociais e a Institucionalização de uma Ordem." Rio de Janeiro, 1983.
———, ed. *Movimentos Coletivos no Brasil Urbano*. Rio de Janeiro, 1983.
Botte, Bernard. *O Movimento Litúrgico*. São Paulo, 1978.
Brandão, Carlos Rodrigues. "Da Educação Fundamental ao Fundamental da Educação," *Proposta*, supplement, 1 (September 1977).
———. *Os Deuses do Povo*. São Paulo, 1980.
———. *Sacerdotes de Viola*. Petrópolis, 1981.
———, ed. *A Questão Política da Educação Popular*. São Paulo, 1980.
Brandão, Carlos Rodrigues, et al. *Religião e Catolicismo do Povo*. Curitiba, 1977.
Bresser Pereira, Luiz Carlos. *As Revoluções Utópicas*. Petrópolis, 1979.
Broucker, José de. *Dom Helder Camara*. Maryknoll, N.Y., 1970.
Brown, Robert McAfee. *Theology in a New Key*. Philadelphia, 1978.
Bruneau, Thomas. "Basic Christian Communities in Latin America: Their Nature and Significance (especially in Brazil)," in Daniel H. Levine, ed., *Churches and Politics in Latin America*. Beverly Hills, Calif., 1979, pp. 111-34.
———. *The Church in Brazil: The Politics of Religion*. Austin, Tex., 1982.
———. "Issues in the Study of the Church and Politics in Brazil." Forthcoming article.
———. *The Political Transformation of the Brazilian Catholic Church*. New York, 1974.
Bruneau, Thomas, and Philippe Faucher, eds. *Authoritarian Capitalism: Brazil's Contemporary Economic and Political Development*. Boulder, Colo., 1981.
Cabestrero, Teofilo. *Diálogos en Mato Grosso con Pedro Casaldáliga*. Salamanca, 1978.
———. *Una Iglesia Que Lucha contra la Injusticia*. Madrid, 1973.

Cáceres, Jorge. "Radicalización Política y Pastoral Popular en El Salvador," *Revista ECSA*, 33 (1982): 93-153.

Cáceres, Jorge, et al. *Iglesia, Política y Profecia*. San José, Costa Rica, 1983.

Câmara, Helder. *The Desert Is Fertile*. Maryknoll, N.Y., 1974.

———. *Revolution Through Peace*. New York, 1971.

Camerman, Cristiano, and Estrella Bohadana. "O Agente Externo na Favela." Unpublished paper, Rio de Janeiro, 1981.

Caramuru de Barros, Raimundo. *Brasil: Uma Igreja em Renovação*. Petrópolis, 1967.

———. *Comunidade Eclesial de Base: Uma Opção Pastoral Decisiva*. Petrópolis, 1968.

———. *Perspectivas Pastorais para o Brasil de Hoje*. Rio de Janeiro, 1964.

Cardoso, Fernando Henrique. *Autoritarismo e Democratização*. Rio de Janeiro, 1975.

———. *Democracia para Mudar*. Rio de Janeiro, 1978.

———. *Estado y Sociedad en América Latina*. Buenos Aires, 1972.

———. *As Ideías e Seu Lugar*. Petrópolis, 1980.

———. "Perspectivas de Desenvolvimento e Meio Ambiente: O Caso do Brasil," *Encontros com a Civilização Brasileira*, 20 (1980): 31-70.

———. "Regime Político e Mudança Social," *Revista de Cultura e Política*, 3 (Nov. 1980/Jan. 1981): 7-25.

Cardoso, Fernando Henrique, and Geraldo Muller. *Amazônia: Expansão do Capitalismo*. São Paulo, 1977.

Cardoso, Ruth. "Movimentos Sociais Urbanos: Balanço Crítico," in Sebastião Velasco e Cruz et al., *Sociedade e Política no Brasil pós-64*, São Paulo, 1983, pp. 215-39.

Carone, Edgard, ed. *O PCB*. 3 vols. São Paulo, 1982.

Carvalheira, Marcelo. "O Tipo de Padre Que a Igreja Espera após o Concílio Vaticano II," *REB*, 26 (1966): 529-51.

Carvalho, Ivo Antônio. "Saúde e Educação de Base: Algumas Notas," *Proposta*, 3 (1976): 19-33.

Casaldáliga, Pedro. *Eu Creio na Justiça e na Esperança*. Rio de Janeiro, 1978.

———. *Uma Igreja da Amazônia em Conflito com o Latifúndio e a Marginalização Social*. N.p., 1971.

Castells, Manuel. *Cidade, Democracia e Socialismo*. Rio de Janeiro, 1980.

———. *Movimentos Sociales Urbanos*. Mexico City, 1974.

Castro Mayer, Antônio, et al. *Reforma Agrária: Questão de Consciência*. São Paulo, 1961.

Cavalcanti, Clóvis. "Dimensões de Marginalização do Nordeste: O Caso Extremo do Vale do Parnaíba." Mimeographed, Recife, Oct. 1974.

———. "Tristes Processos Econômicos: O Padrão Recente de Desenvolvimento do Nordeste." Mimeographed, Recife, June 1979.

Cavalcanti de Albuquerque, Roberto, and Clóvis Cavalcanti. *Desenvolvimento Regional no Brasil*. Brasília, 1976.

Centro de Pastoral Vergueiro. *As Relações Igreja-Estado no Brasil, 1964/1978*. 5 vols. São Paulo, 1978-81.

César, Waldo. "O Que É 'Popular' no Catolicismo Popular?" *REB*, 36 (1976): 5-18.

César, Waldo, et al. *Protestantismo e Imperialismo na América Latina.* Petrópolis, 1968.

Chaui, Marilena. *Cultura e Democracia.* São Paulo, 1981.

Chinem, Rivaldo. *Sentença: Padres e Posseiros do Araguaia.* Rio de Janeiro, 1983.

Cohn, Amélia. *Crise Regional e Planejamento.* São Paulo, 1976.

Coleman, John. *The Evolution of Dutch Catholicism.* Berkeley, Calif., 1978.

Collins, Denis. *Paulo Freire: His Life, Works, and Thought.* New York, 1979.

Comblin, José. "A América Latina e o Presente Debate Teológico entre Neo-conservadores e Liberais," *REB*, 41 (1981): 790-816.

———. "Comunidades Eclesiais de Base e Pastoral Urbana," *REB*, 30 (1970): 783-828.

———. *O Futuro dos Ministérios na Igreja Latinoamericana.* Petrópolis, 1969.

———. "Os Movimentos e a Pastoral Latinoamericana," *REB*, 43 (1983): 227-62.

———. "Prolegômenos da Catequese no Brasil." *REB*, 27 (1967): 845-74.

———. *Os Sinais dos Tempos e a Evangelização.* São Paulo, 1968.

Comissão Arquidiocesana de Pastoral dos Direitos Humanos e Marginalizados de São Paulo. *Fé e Política.* Petrópolis, 1981.

Comissão Pastoral da Terra (CPT). *Denúncia: Caso Araguaia-Tocantins.* Goiânia, 1981.

———. *A Luta Pela Terra na Biblia.* Goiânia, 1981.

Conferência Nacional dos Bispos do Brasil (CNBB). *Comunidades Eclesiais de Base no Brasil.* São Paulo, 1979.

———. *Comunidades: Igreja na Base.* São Paulo, 1977.

———. *Documentos dos Presbitérios.* Rio de Janeiro, 1969.

———. *Pastoral da Terra.* São Paulo, 1977.

———. *Pastoral da Terra: Posse e Conflitos.* São Paulo, 1976.

———. *Plano de Emergência para a Igreja do Brasil.* Rio de Janeiro, 1963.

———. *Plano de Pastoral de Conjunto.* Rio de Janeiro, 1967.

Congar, Yves. *Laity, Church, and World.* Baltimore, 1961.

———. *Lay People in the Church: A Study for a Theology of the Laity.* Westminister, Md., 1957.

Conselho Episcopal Latinoamericano (CELAM). *A Evangelização no Presente e no Futuro da América Latina.* Petrópolis, 1980.

———. *A Igreja na Atual Transformação da América Latina à Luz do Concílio.* Petrópolis, 1969.

Cooper, Norman B. *Catholicism and the Franco Regime.* Beverly Hills, Calif., 1975.

Correia de Andrade, Manuel. "Ligas Camponesas e Sindicatos Rurais no Nordeste, 1957-1964," *Temas de Ciências Humanas,* 8 (1980): 115-32.

Costa, Beatriz da. "Para Analisar uma Prática de Educação Popular," *Cadernos de Educação Popular,* 1 (1981): 7-48.

————. "Pastoral Popular: Notas para um Debate," *Cadernos do CEDI*, 1 (n.d.).

Coutinho, Carlos Nelson. *A Democracia como Valor Universal*. São Paulo, 1980.

Couto Teixeira, Faustino Luiz. "Comunidade Eclesial de Base: Elementos Explicativos de Sua Gênese." Master's thesis, Pontifícia Universidade Católica, Rio de Janeiro, 1982.

Cox, Harvey. *The Secular City: Secularization and Urbanization in Theological Perspective*. New York, 1965.

Crahan, Margaret. "Salvation Through Christ or Marx: Religion in Revolutionary Cuba," in Daniel H. Levine, ed., *Churches and Politics in Latin America*. Beverly Hills, Calif., 1979, pp. 238-66.

————. "Varieties of Faith: Religion in Contemporary Nicaragua." Notre Dame, Ind., Dec. 1983. Kellogg Institute Working Paper no. 5.

Cristianos por el Socialismo. *Cristianos por el Socialismo*. Santiago, 1972.

Crozier, Michel, Samuel Huntington, and Joji Watanuki. *The Crisis of Democracy*. New York, 1975.

Dahl, Robert. *After the Revolution?* New Haven, 1970.

————. *Polyarchy: Participation and Opposition*. New Haven, 1971.

Da Matta, Roberto. *Carnavais, Malandros e Heróis: Para uma Sociologia do Dilema Brasileiro*. Rio de Janeiro, 1979.

————. *Ensaios de Antropologia Estrutural*. Petrópolis, 1973.

d'Ans, Hugues. "Teologia da Libertação e Libertação da Teologia," *REB*, 38 (1978): 402-45.

Dassin, Joan. "The Brazilian Press and the Politics of *Abertura*," *Journal of Interamerican Studies and World Affairs*, 26 (1984): 385-414.

Davis, Shelton. *Victims of the Miracle*. New York, 1977.

de Kadt, Emmanuel. *Catholic Radicals in Brazil*. New York, 1970.

Della Cava, Ralph. "Catholicism and Society in Twentieth Century Brazil," *Latin American Research Review*, 11 (1976): 7-50.

————. "The Church and the 'Abertura,' 1974-1985," in Alfred Stepan, ed., *Democratizing Brazil*. New Haven, forthcoming.

————. *Miracle at Joaseiro*. New York, 1970.

————. "Política a Curto Prazo e Religião a Longo Prazo," *Encontros com a Civilização Brasileira*, 1 (1978): 242-58.

Delzell, Charles F., ed. *The Papacy and Totalitarianism Between the Two Wars*. New York, 1974.

Demo, Pedro. "Problemas Sociológicos da Comunidade," in Conferência Nacional dos Bispos do Brasil, ed., *Comunidades: Igreja na Base*. São Paulo, 1977.

Dewart, Leslie. *Christianity and Revolution: The Lesson of Cuba*. New York, 1963.

d'Incão, Maria Conceição. *O Boia-Fria: Acumulação e Miséria*. Petrópolis, 1975.

Diniz, Eli. *Voto e Máquina Política: Patronagem e Clientelismo no Rio de Janeiro*. Rio de Janeiro, 1982.

Dinnerstein, Dorothy. *The Mermaid and the Minotaur*. New York, 1977.

Dodson, Michael. "The Christian Left in Latin American Politics," in Daniel H. Levine, ed., *Churches and Politics in Latin America*. Beverly Hills, Calif., 1980, pp. 111-34.

————. "Religious Innovation and the Politics of Argentina: A Study of the Movement of Priests for the Third World." Ph.D. dissertation, Indiana University, 1974.

Dodson, Michael, and Tommie Sue Montgomery. "The Churches in the Nicaraguan Revolution," in Thomas W. Walker, ed., *Nicaragua in Revolution*. New York, 1982, pp. 161-80.

Doimo, Ana Maria. *Movimento Social Urbano, Igreja e Participação Popular*. Petrópolis, 1984.

Dreifuss, Rene. *1964, a Conquista do Estado: Ação, Poder e Golpe de Classe*. Petrópolis, 1981.

Droulers, Paul. "Roman Catholicism," in Guy Métraux and Francçis Crouzet, eds., *The Nineteenth Century World*. New York, 1963, pp. 282-315.

Dulles, Avery. *Models of the Church*. Garden City, N.Y., 1974.

Durkheim, Émile. *Suicide*. New York, 1951.

Dussel, Enrique. *De Medellín a Puebla: Uma Década de Sangue e Esperança*. São Paulo, 1981.

Eagleson, John, ed. *Christians and Socialism: Documentation of the Christians for Socialism Movement in Latin America*. Maryknoll, N.Y., 1975.

Engels, Friedrich. "On the Early History of Christianity," in Lewis Feuer, ed., *Marx and Engels: Basic Writings on Politics and Philosophy*. Garden City, N.Y., 1959.

Erickson, Kenneth Paul. *Sindicalismo no Processo Político no Brasil*. São Paulo, 1979.

Evans, Peter. *Dependent Development: The Alliance of Multinational, State, and Local Capital in Brazil*. Princeton, 1979.

Ezcurra, Ana María. *La agresión ideológica contra la revolución sandinista*. Mexico City, 1983.

Faoro, Raimundo. *Os Donos do Poder*. Pôrto Alegre, 1958.

Fernandes, Luis Gonzaga. "Gênese, Dinâmica e Perspectiva das CEBs no Brasil," *REB*, 42 (1982): 456-64.

Fernandes, Rubem César. *Os Cavalheiros do Bom Jesus*. São Paulo, 1983.

Fernández Areal, Manuel. *Política Católica en España*. Barcelona, 1970.

Ferrari, Alceu. *Igreja e Desenvolvimento: O Movimento de Natal*. Natal, 1968.

Ferreira de Camargo, Cândido Procópio. *Católicos, Protestantes, Espíritas*. Petrópolis, 1973.

————. *Igreja e Desenvolvimento*. São Paulo, 1971.

Ferreira de Camargo, Cândido Procópio, et al. "Comunidades Eclesiais de Base," in Paul Singer and Vinícius Caldeira Brant, eds., *São Paulo: O Povo em Movimento*. Petrópolis, 1980.

————. *São Paulo 1975: Crescimento e Pobreza*. São Paulo, 1976.

Feuer, Lewis, ed. *Marx and Engels: Basic Writings on Politics and Philosophy*. Garden City, N.Y., 1959.

Feuerbach, Ludwig. *The Essence of Christianity*. New York, 1957.

Figueiredo Lustosa, Oscar de. "A Igreja e o Integralismo no Brasil." *Revista de História*, 108 (1976): 503-32.
Fischer, Nilton Bueno. "Working Class Culture: A Case Study of Authority in Brazil." Ph.D. dissertation, Stanford University, 1981.
Flannery, Austin P., ed. *Documents of Vatican II*. Grand Rapids, Mich., 1975.
Floridi, Ulisse Aleio. *Radicalismo Cattolico Brasiliano*. Rome, 1968.
Flynn, Peter. *Brazil: A Political Analysis*. Boulder, Colo., 1978.
Fogarty, Michael. *Christian Democracy in Western Europe, 1820-1953*. Notre Dame, Ind., 1957.
Forman, Shepard. *The Brazilian Peasantry*. New York, 1975.
Fragoso, Antônio. *Evangile et révolution sociale*. Paris, 1969.
———. "A Libertação do Homem." *SEDOC*, 5 (1973): 835-44.
Frederico, Celso. "Organização do Trabalho e Luta de Classes," *Temas de Ciências Humanas*, 6 (1979): 177-94.
Freire, Paulo. *A Educação como a Prática da Liberdade*. Rio de Janeiro, 1980.
———. *Pedagogy of the Oppressed*. New York, 1970.
Fremantle, Anne. *The Papal Encyclicals in Their Historical Context*. New York, 1956.
Freud, Sigmund. *The Future of an Illusion*. Garden City, N.Y., 1964.
Galilea, Segundo. *Religiosidade Popular e Pastoral*. São Paulo, 1978.
———. *Teología de la Liberación: Ensayo de Síntesis*. Bogotá, 1976.
Galletta, Ricardo. "Pastoral Popular e Política Partidária," *Communicações do ISER*, 5 (1983): 14-24.
Galter, Albert. *Le Communisme et l'église catholique: Le "Livre Rouge" de la persécution*. Paris, 1956.
Garaudy, Roger. *From Anathema to Dialogue: A Marxist Challenge to the Christian Churches*. New York, 1966.
Garcia, Pedro Benjamin. "Educação Popular: Algumas Reflexões em Torno da Questão do Saber," in Carlos Rodrigues Brandão, ed., *A Questão Política da Educação Popular*. São Paulo, 1980, pp. 88-121.
———. "Saber Popular / Educação Popular," *Cadernos de Educação Popular*, 3 (1982): 33-62.
García Rubio, Alfonso. *Teologia da Libertação: Política ou Profetismo?* São Paulo, 1977.
Gato, Marcelo. "Considerações sobre a Questão Sindical e a Democracia," *Temas de Ciências Humanas*, 5 (1979): 125-48.
Geertz, Clifford. *The Interpretation of Cultures*. New York, 1973.
Gerardi, Giulio. *Marxism and Christianity*. New York, 1968.
Gillespie, Richard. *Soldiers of Perón: Argentina's Montoneros*. Oxford, 1982.
Glock, Charles, and Rodney Stark. *Religion and Society in Tension*. Chicago, 1965.
Goddijn, Walter. *The Deferred Revolution*. New York, 1975.
Goertzel, Ted George. "Brazilian Student Attitudes Towards Politics and Education." Ph.D. dissertation, Washington University, 1970.

Gogarten, Friedrich. *Despair and Hope for Our Time.* Philadelphia, 1970.

Gómez de Souza, Luiz Alberto. *Classes Populares e Igreja nos Caminhos da História.* Petrópolis, 1981.

———. "La Crisis del desarrollo y la participación popular en América Latina." Paper for the Action for Development Project of the Food and Agriculture Organization. Dec. 1980.

———. *O Cristão e o Mundo.* Petrópolis, 1965.

———. "Igreja e Sociedade: Elementos para um Marco Teórico," *Síntese*, 13 (1978): 15-30.

———. *A JUC: Os Estudantes Católicos e a Política.* Petrópolis, 1984.

———, ed. *Cristianismo Hoje.* Rio de Janeiro, 1962.

Gómez Pérez, Rafael. *Política y Religión en el Régimen de Franco.* Barcelona, 1976.

Gouldner, Alvin. "Organizational Analysis," in Thomas Merton, et al., *Sociology Today: Problems and Prospects.* New York, 1959, pp. 400-420.

Goulet, Denis. "Development Experts: The One-Eyed Giants," *World Development,* 8 (1980): 481-90.

———. "In Defense of Cultural Rights: Technology, Tradition, and Conflicting Models of Rationality," *Human Rights Quarterly,* 3 (1981): 3-18.

Gramsci, Antonio. *Selections from the Prison Notebooks.* New York, 1971.

Gregory, Affonso Felippe, ed. *A Paróquia Ontem, Hoje e Amanhã.* Petrópolis, 1967.

Gregory, Affonso Felippe, and Maria Ghisleni. *Chances e Desafios das Comunidades Eclesiais de Base.* Petrópolis, 1979.

Gremillion, Joseph, ed. *The Gospel of Peace and Justice.* Maryknoll, N.Y., 1976.

Grzybowski, Cândido. "A Comissão Pastoral da Terra e os Colonos do Sul do Brasil," in Vanilda Paiva, ed., *Igreja e Questão Agrária.* São Paulo, 1985, pp. 248-73.

Guimarães, Almir Ribeiro. *Comunidades Eclesiais de Base no Brasil.* Petrópolis, 1978.

Gutiérrez, Gustavo. *A Força Histórica dos Pobres.* Petrópolis, 1981. Spanish original, 1979.

———. *Teologia da Libertação.* Petrópolis, 1975. Spanish original, 1971.

———. *We Drink from Our Own Wells.* Maryknoll, N.Y., 1984.

Habermas, Jürgen. *Toward a Rational Society.* Boston, 1970.

Hanson, Eric O. "The Chinese State and the Catholic Church." Ph.D. dissertation, Stanford University, 1976.

Harring, Clarence. "The Church-State Conflict in Brazil," in Frederick Pike, ed., *The Conflict Between Church and State in Latin America.* New York, 1967, pp. 154-63.

Hauck, João Fagundes, et al. *História da Igreja no Brasil.* II/2. Petrópolis, 1980.

Hazelrigg, Lawrence. "Religious and Class Bases of Political Conflict in Italy," *American Journal of Sociology,* 75 (1970): 496-511.

Hebblethwaite, Peter. *The Christian-Marxist Dialogue and Beyond.* London, 1977.

————. *The Runaway Church: Postconciliar Growth or Decline?* London, 1975.

Hebette, Jean, and Rosa E. Azevedo Marin. "Colonização Espontânea, Política Agrária e Grupos Sociais," in José Marcelino Monteiro da Costa, ed., *Amazônia: Desenvolvimento e Ocupação.* Rio de Janeiro, 1979, pp. 141-92.

Herz, John, ed., *From Dictatorship to Democracy.* Westport, Conn., 1982.

Hewitt, Cynthia. "Brazil: The Peasant Movement of Pernambuco, 1961-1964," in Henry Landsberger, ed., *Latin American Peasant Movements.* Ithaca, N.Y., 1969, pp. 374-98.

Hirschman, Albert. *Shifting Involvements: Private Interests and Public Action.* Princeton, 1982.

Hitchcock, James. *The Decline and Fall of Radical Catholicism.* New York, 1971.

Holmes, J. Derek. *The Papacy in the Modern World, 1914-1978.* London, 1981.

Hoornaert, Eduardo. "O Catolicismo Popular numa Perspectiva de Libertação: Pressupostos," *REB,* 36 (1976): 189-201.

————. "Comunidades de Base: Dez Anos de Experiência," *REB,* 38 (1978): 474-502.

————. "A Distinção entre 'Lei' e 'Religião' no Nordeste," *REB,* 29 (1969): 580-606.

————. *A Formação do Catolicismo Brasileiro, 1550-1800.* Petrópolis, 1974.

————. "A Igreja diante de uma Nova Situação," *REB,* 26 (1966): 872-84.

————. "Para uma História da Igreja no Brasil," *REB,* 37 (1977): 185-87.

————. "Pressupostos Antropológicos para a Compreensão do Sincretismo," *Vozes,* 71 (1977): 563-72.

————. "Problemas de Pastoral Popular no Brasil," *REB,* 28 (1968): 280-307.

Humphrey, John. *Capitalist Control and Workers' Struggle in the Brazilian Auto Industry.* Princeton, 1982.

Huntington, Samuel. *Political Order in Changing Societies.* New Haven, 1968.

Huntington, Samuel, and Joan Nelson. *No Easy Choice: Political Participation in Developing Countries.* Cambridge, Mass., 1976.

Ianni, Octávio. *Ditadura e Agricultura.* Rio de Janeiro, 1979.

————. *A Luta pela Terra.* Petrópolis, 1978.

Instituto Brasileiro de Análise Social e Econômica (IBASE). *Saúde e Trabalho no Brasil.* Petrópolis, 1982.

Ireland, Rowan. "Catholic Base Communities, Spiritist Groups, and the Deepening of Democracy." Wilson Center, Latin American Program, Working Paper no. 131, 1983.

Jancar, Barbara Wolfe. "Religious Dissent in the Soviet Union," in Rudolph Toekes, ed., *Dissent in the USSR,* Baltimore, 1975, pp. 191-230.

Jannuzzi, Gilberta Martino. *Confronto Pedagógico: Paulo Freire e Mobral.* São Paulo, 1979.

Jelin, Elizabeth. *La Protesta Obrera.* Buenos Aires, 1974.

Johnson, Paul. *Pope John Paul II and the Catholic Restoration.* New York, 1981.
Josaphat, Carlos. *Estruturas a Serviço do Espírito.* Petrópolis, 1968.
———. *Evangelho e Revolução Social.* São Paulo, 1963.
Keck, Margaret. "The Workers' Party and Democratization in Brazil." Ph.D. dissertation, Columbia University, 1986.
Kirk, J. Andrew. *Liberation Theology: An Evangelical View from the Third World.* Atlanta, 1979.
Kloppenburg, Boaventura. *O Espiritismo no Brasil: Orientação para os Católicos.* Petrópolis, 1960.
———. *Igreja Popular.* Rio de Janeiro, 1983.
———. *Temptations for Liberation Theology.* Chicago, 1974.
Kolarz, Walter. *Religion in the Soviet Union.* New York, 1961.
Konder, Leandro. *A Democracia e os Comunistas no Brasil.* Rio de Janeiro, 1980.
Kowarick, Lúcio. *A Espoliação Urbana.* Rio de Janeiro, 1980.
Krischke, Paulo. "Populism and the Catholic Church: The Crisis of Democracy in Brazil." Ph.D. dissertation, York University, 1983.
———, ed. *Brasil: Do Milagre à Abertura.* São Paulo, 1983.
Krischke, Paulo, and Scott Mainwaring, eds. *A Igreja na Base em Tempo de Transição.* Porto Alegre, forthcoming.
Laacroix, Pascoal. *O Mais Urgente Problema do Brasil: O Problema Sacerdotal e Sua Solução.* Petrópolis, 1936.
Lamounier, Bolívar. "O Discurso e o Processo: Da Distensão às Opções do Regime Brasileiro," in Henrique Rattner, ed., *Brasil 1990: Caminhos Alternativos do Desenvolvimento.* São Paulo, 1979, pp. 88-120.
Lamounier, Bolívar, and Fernando Henrique Cardoso, eds. *Os Partidos e as Eleições no Brasil.* Rio de Janeiro, 1978.
Lanternari, Vittorio. *The Religions of the Oppressed: A Study of Modern Messianic Cults.* New York, 1963.
Leeds, Anthony, and Elizabeth Leeds. *A Sociologia do Brasil Urbano.* Rio de Janeiro, 1978.
Leers, Bernardo. *Cristãos no Meio Rural.* Petrópolis, 1973.
———. "A Estrutura do Culto Dominical na Zona Rural," *RCRB,* 99 (1963): 521-34.
———. "Igreja e Desenvolvimento Rural," *REB,* 26 (1966): 331-42.
Leme, Sebastião. *A Ação Católica.* Rio de Janeiro, 1923.
———. *Carta Pastoral a Olinda.* Petrópolis, 1916.
Lenin, V. I. *What Must Be Done?* New York, 1969.
Lenski, Gerhard. *The Religious Factor.* Garden City, N.Y., 1961.
Lepargneur, Herbert. *Teologia da Libertação: Uma Avaliação.* São Paulo, 1979.
Lernoux, Penny. *The Cry of the People.* New York, 1982.
Lesbaupin, Ivo. *A Bem-Aventurança da Perseguição.* Petrópolis, 1975.
———. "O Papel dos Intelectuais junto às Classes Populares," *CEI,* 148 (1979): 16-19.
Levine, Daniel. *Religion and Politics in Latin America: The Catholic Church in Venezuela and Colombia.* Princeton, 1981.

―――, ed. *Churches and Politics in Latin America*. Beverly Hills, Calif., 1979.

―――. *Popular Religion, the Churches, and Political Conflict in Latin America*. Chapel Hill, N.C., 1986.

Levine, Daniel, and Alexander Wilde. "The Catholic Church, 'Politics,' and Violence: The Colombian Case," *Review of Politics*, 39 (1977): 220-49.

Libânio, João Baptista. "Uma Comunidade Que Se Redefine." *SEDOC*, 9 (1976-77): 295-326.

―――. *Discernimento e Política*. Petrópolis, 1977.

―――. *As Grandes Rupturas Sócio-Culturais e Eclesiais*. Petrópolis, 1980.

―――. "Igreja–Povo Oprimido Que Se Organiza para a Libertação," *REB*, 41 (1981): 279-311.

―――. *O Problema da Salvação no Catolicismo do Povo*. Petrópolis, 1977.

―――. "Teologia no Brasil: Reflexões Crítico-Metodológicas," *Perspectiva Teológica*, vol. 9, no. 17 (1977): 27-79.

Lima, Haroldo, and Aldo Arantes. *História da Ação Popular*. São Paulo, 1984.

Linz, Juan J. "Religion and Politics in Spain: From Conflict to Consensus Above Cleavage," *Social Compass*, 27 (1980): 255-77.

Lojkine, Jean. *Le Marxisme, l'état et la question urbaine*. Paris, 1977.

―――. *La Politique urbaine dans la région parisienne, 1945-1971*. Paris, 1972.

López Trujillo, Alfonso. "Análisis marxista y liberación cristiana," *Tierra Nueva*, 4 (1973): 5-43.

―――. "El Compromiso político del sacerdote," *Tierra Nueva*, 14 (1973): 17-53.

―――. "La Liberación y las liberaciones," *Tierra Nueva*, 1 (1972): 5-26.

―――. *Liberation or Revolution?* Huntington, Ind., 1977.

Lorscheider, Aloísio. "O Misterio da Igreja," *REB*, 23 (1963): 871-82.

Loureiro Botas, Paulo Cézar. "Aí! Que Saudades do Tempo em Que o Terço Resolvia Tudo!" *Tempo e Presença*, 26 (1980): 3-10.

Luxemburg, Rosa. *Rosa Luxemburg Speaks*. Edited by Mary-Alice Waters. New York, 1970.

MacPherson, C. B. *The Life and Times of Liberal Democracy*. New York, 1977.

Maduro, Otto. *Religião e Luta de Classes*. Petrópolis, 1981.

Mahar, Dennis. *Desenvolvimento Econômico de Amazônia: Uma Análise das Políticas Governamentais*. Rio de Janeiro, 1978.

―――. *Frontier Development Policy in Brazil: A Study of Amazonia*. New York, 1979.

Mainwaring, Scott. "Grass Roots Popular Movements and the Struggle for Democracy: Nova Iguaçu, 1974-1985," in Alfred Stepan, ed., *Democratizing Brazil*. New Haven, forthcoming.

―――. "A JOC e o Surgimento da Igreja na Base," *REB*, 43 (1983): 29-92.

Mainwaring, Scott, and Donald Share. "Transitions Through Transaction: Democratization in Brazil and Spain," in Wayne Selcher, ed., *Political*

310   *Select References*

Liberalization in Brazil: Dynamics, Dilemmas, and Future. Boulder, Colo., forthcoming.

Mainwaring, Scott, and Eduardo Viola. "New Social Movements, Political Culture, and Democracy: Brazil and Argentina in the 1980s," *Telos,* 61 (Fall 1984): 17-52.

———. "Transitions to Democracy: Brazil and Argentina in the 1980s." *Journal of International Affairs,* 38 (1985): 193-219.

Maranhão, Ricardo. *O Governo Kubitschek.* São Paulo, 1981.

———. *Sindicatos e Democratização.* São Paulo, 1979.

Marcuse, Herbert. *One Dimensional Man.* Boston, 1964.

Maria, Júlio. *A Igreja e a República.* Brasília, 1981.

Marins, José. *A Comunidade Eclesial de Base.* São Paulo, n.d. (ca. 1968).

———. "Comunidades Eclesiais de Base na América Latina," *Concilium,* 104 (1975): 404-13.

———. *Curso do Mundo Melhor.* São Paulo, 1962.

———. *O Problema Religioso.* São Paulo, 1964.

———. *Renovação da Paróquia.* São Paulo, 1964.

———, ed. *Práxis de los Padres de América Latina.* Bogotá, 1978.

Marshall, T. H. *Class, Citizenship, and Social Development.* Garden City, N.Y., 1965.

Martins, Edilson. *Nós do Araguaia.* Rio de Janeiro, 1979.

Martins, Margarita. Forthcoming Ph.D. dissertation on the CNBB, University of South Carolina.

Marx, Karl. *The German Ideology.* New York, 1947.

———. *Writings of the Young Marx on Philosophy and Society.* Edited by Loyd D. Easton and Kurt H. Guddat. Garden City, N.Y., 1967.

Marx, Karl, and Friedrich Engels. *On Religion.* Chico, Calif., 1982.

McGovern, Arthur. *Marxism: An American Christian Perspective.* Maryknoll, N.Y., 1980.

McHale, Vincent. "Religion and Electoral Politics in France: Some Recent Observations," *Canadian Journal of Political Science,* 2 (1969): 292-311.

Mecham, J. Lloyd. *Church and State in Latin America.* Chapel Hill, N.C., 1934.

Medina, Carlos Alberto, and Pedro Ribeiro de Oliveira. *Autoridade e Participação: Estudo Sociológico da Igreja Católica.* Petrópolis, 1973.

Mendes de Almeida, Cândido. *Memento dos Vivos: A Esquerda Católica no Brasil.* Rio de Janeiro, 1966.

Mericle, Kenneth. "Conflict Regulation in the Brazilian Industrial Relations System." Ph.D. dissertation, University of Wisconsin, 1974.

Mesters, Carlos. "A Brisa Leve, uma Nova Leitura da Bíblia," *SEDOC,* 11 (1978-79): 733-65.

———. "O Futuro do Nosso Passado," in Carlos Mesters et al., *Uma Igreja Que Nasce do Povo.* Petrópolis, 1975, pp. 120-200.

———. "Interpretação da Bíblia em Algumas Comunidades de Base no Brasil," *Concilium,* 158 (1980): 51-58.

———. *Palavra de Deus na História do Homem.* Petrópolis, 1971.

Mesters, Carlos, et al. *Uma Igreja Que Nasce do Povo.* Petrópolis, 1975.

Michels, Robert. *Political Parties.* New York, 1959.

Míguez Bonino, José. *Doing Theology in a Revolutionary Situation.* Philadelphia, 1975.
Moberg, David. *The Church as a Social Institution.* Englewood Cliffs, N.J., 1962.
Mobral. *O Problema das Comunidades Eclesiais de Base.* Rio de Janeiro, 1980.
Moisés, José Álvaro. "Classes Populares e Protesto Urbano." Ph.D. dissertation, University of São Paulo, 1978.
―――. "Crise Política e Democracia: A Transição Difícil," *Revista de Cultura e Política,* 2 (1980): 9-37.
―――. "Current Issues in the Labor Movement in Brazil," *Latin American Perspectives,* 6 (1979): 71-89.
―――. "Experiência de Mobilização Popular em São Paulo," *Contraponto,* vol. 3, no. 3 (1978): 69-86.
―――. *Greve de Massa e Crise Política.* São Paulo, 1978.
―――. "PT: Uma Novidade Histórica," in José Álvaro Moisés, *Lições de Liberdade e de Opressão,* Rio de Janeiro, 1982, pp. 205-20.
―――. "Qual É a Estratégia do Novo Sindicalismo?" in José Álvaro Moisés et al., *Alternativas Populares da Democracia.* Petrópolis, 1982, pp. 11-40.
Moisés, José Álvaro, et al. *Alternativas Populares da Democracia.* Petrópolis, 1982.
Mondin, Battista. *Os Teólogos da Libertação.* São Paulo, 1980.
Montero Moreno, Antonio. *Historia de la Persecución Religiosa en España, 1936-1939.* Madrid, 1961.
Montgomery, Tommie Sue. "Liberation and Revolution: Christianity as a Subversive Activity in Central America," in Martin Diskin, ed., *Trouble in Our Backyard: Central America and the United States in the Eighties.* New York, 1983, pp. 75-100.
Moraes, Clodomir. "Peasant Leagues in Brazil," in Rodolfo Stavenhagen, ed., *Agrarian Problems and Peasant Movements in Latin America.* Garden City, N.Y., 1970, pp. 453-502.
Moraes, Dênis de, and Francisco Viana, eds. *Prestes: Lutas e Autocríticas.* Petrópolis, 1982.
Moreira Alves, Márcio. *O Cristo do Povo.* Rio de Janeiro, 1968.
―――. *A Força do Povo: A Democracia Participativa em Lages.* Rio de Janeiro, 1980.
―――. *A Grain of Mustard Seed.* Garden City, N.Y., 1973.
―――. *A Igreja e a Política no Brasil.* Sao Paulo, 1979.
Moreira Alves, Maria Helena. "The Formation of the National Security State: The State and the Opposition in Military Brazil." Ph.D. dissertation, Massachusetts Institute of Technology, 1982.
―――. *The State and Opposition in Military Brazil.* Austin, Tex., forthcoming.
Movimento de Educacão de Base. *MEB em Cinco Anos, 1961-1966.* Rio de Janeiro, 1966.
Movimiento de los Sacerdotes para el Tercer Mundo. *Los Sacerdotes para el Tercer Mundo y la Actualidad Nacional.* Buenos Aires, 1973.

Mugica, Carlos. Peronismo y Cristianismo. Buenos Aires, 1973.

Muller, Christiano. Memória Histórica sobre a Religião na Bahia, 1823-1923. Bahia, 1923.

Muñoz, Ronaldo. Nueva Consciencia da la Iglesia en América Latina. Santiago, 1973.

Murphy, Francis X. The Papacy Today. New York, 1981.

Myhr, Robert. "Brazil," in Donald K. Emmerson, ed., Students and Politics in Developing Nations. New York, 1968.

———. "Student Activism and Development," in H. Jon Rosenbaum and William Tyler, eds., Contemporary Brazil: Issues in Economic and Political Development. New York, 1972, pp. 349-69.

Niebuhr, H. Richard. Christ and Culture. New York, 1951.

———. The Social Sources of Denominationalism. New York, 1929.

Nietzsche, Friedrich. Thus Spoke Zarathustra. Middlesex, Eng., 1961.

Novak, Michael. "Liberation Theology in Practice." Thought, 59 (1984): 136-48.

O'Dea, Thomas. The Catholic Crisis. Boston, 1968.

O'Donnell, Guillermo. El estado burocrático-autoritario, 1966-1973: Triunfos, derrotas, crisis. Buenos Aires, 1982.

———. "A mi que me importa: Notas sobre sociabilidad y política en Argentina y Brasil." Notre Dame, Ind., Jan. 1984. Kellogg Institute Working Paper no. 9.

———. "Notas para el estudio de procesos de democratización política a partir del estado burocrático-autoritario," Estudios CEDES, vol. 2, no. 5 (1979).

———. "Tensions in the Bureaucratic-Authoritarian State and the Question of Democracy," in David Collier, ed., The New Authoritarianism in Latin America. Princeton, 1979.

O'Donnell, Guillermo, Philippe Schmitter, and Laurence Whitehead, eds., Transitions from Authoritarian Rule: Southern Europe and Latin America. Forthcoming.

Offe, Claus. "New Social Movements as a Meta Political Challenge." Forthcoming.

Oliveira, Francisco de. Elegia para uma Re(li)gião. Rio de Janeiro, 1977.

Oliveira Torres, João Camilo de. História das Ideías Religiosas no Brasil. São Paulo, 1968.

Olivera Sedano, Alicia. Aspectos del Conflicto Religioso de 1926 a 1929: Sus Antecedentes y Consequencias. Mexico City, 1966.

Oliveros, Roberto. Liberación y Teología: Génesis y Crecimiento de una Reflexión. Lima, 1977.

O'Neill, M. Ancilla. Tristão de Athayde and the Catholic Social Movement in Brazil. Washington, D.C., 1939.

Ortiz, Renato. A Consciência Fragmentada. Rio de Janeiro, 1980.

Padim, Cândido. "A Doutrina da Segurança Nacional à Luz a Doutrina Social da Igreja," in Luiz Gonzaga de Souza Lima, ed., Evolução Política dos Católicos e da Igreja no Brasil. Petrópolis, 1979, pp. 150-67.

———. Educar para um Mundo Novo. Petrópolis, 1965.

Paiva, Vanilda. "Anotações para um Estudo sobre Populismo Católico e

Educação Popular," in Vanilda Paiva, ed., *Perspectivas y Dilemas da Educação Popular*. Rio de Janeiro, 1984, pp. 227-66.

———. *Educação Popular e Educação de Adultos*. Rio de Janeiro, 1972.

———. "A Igreja Moderna no Brasil," in Vanilda Paiva, ed., *Igreja e Questão Agrária*, São Paulo, 1985, pp. 52-67.

———. *Paulo Freire e o Nacionalismo-Desenvolvimentista*. Rio de Janeiro, 1980.

———. "Pedagogia e Luta Social no Campo Paraibano." *Síntese*, 29 (1983): 73-99; 30 (1984): 63-91.

———, ed. *Igreja e Questão Agrária*. São Paulo, 1985.

Paiva, Vanilda, et al. "Transformação Agrícola, Conflito Social e a Igreja na Mata Paraibana." Unpublished manuscript, Rio de Janeiro, 1979.

Palácios, Carlos. "Uma Consciência Histórica Irreversível, 1960-1979: Duas Décadas de História da Igreja no Brasil," *Síntese*, 17 (1979): 19-40.

Parisse, Luciano. *Favelas do Rio de Janeiro*. Rio de Janeiro, 1969.

Pateman, Carole. *Participation and Democratic Theory*. Cambridge, Eng., 1970.

PCB: Vinte Anos de Política, 1958-1979. São Paulo, 1980.

Pereira, Nilo. *Conflitos entre a Igreja e o Estado no Brasil*. Recife, 1970.

Pereira de Queiroz, Maria Isaura. *O Campesinato Brasileiro*. Petrópolis, 1973.

Pereira Peixoto, José. "Movimento de Educação de Base: Alguns Dados Históricos," *Proposta*, 3 (December 1976): 40-51.

Pereira Ramalho, Jether. "Algumas Notas sobre Duas Perspectivas de Pastoral Popular," *Cadernos do ISER*, 6 (1977): 31-39.

———. "CEBs: Nova Forma Participatória do Povo," *SEDOC*, 9 (1976): 264-75.

Perlman, Janice. *The Myth of Marginality: Urban Poverty and Politics in Rio de Janeiro*. Berkeley, Calif., 1976.

Pires, José Maria. *Do Centro para a Margem*. Petrópolis, 1980.

Poerner, Artur José. *O Poder Jovem: História da Participação Política dos Estudantes Brasileiros*. Rio de Janeiro, 1979.

Poggi, Gianfranco. *Catholic Action in Italy: The Sociology of a Sponsored Organization*. Stanford, 1967.

Poletto, Ivo. "As Contradições Sociais e a Pastoral da Terra," in Vanilda Paiva, ed., *Igreja e Questão Agrária*, São Paulo, 1985, pp. 129-48.

Pomar, Wladimir. *Araguaia: O Partido e a Guerrilha*. São Paulo, 1980.

Pompermayer, Malori José. "The State and the Frontier in Brazil: A Case Study of the Amazon." Ph.D. dissertation, Stanford University, 1979.

Pope, Clara. "Human Rights and the Catholic Church in Brazil, 1970-1983: The Pontifical Justice and Peace Commission of the Sao Paulo Archdiocese." Forthcoming article.

Pope, Liston. *Millhands and Preachers*. New Haven, 1942.

Portelli, Hugues. *Gramsci et la question religieuse*. Paris, 1974.

Queiroga, Gervásio Fernandes de. *CNBB: Comunhão e Corresponsabilidade*. São Paulo, 1977.

Queiroz, Antônio Celso. "A Religiosidade Popular," *RCRB*, 1977, pp. 14-15.

Queiroz, Leda Lúcia. "Movimentos Sociais Urbanos: O Movimento Amigos de Bairro de Nova Iguaçu." M.A. thesis, COPPE, Rio de Janeiro, 1981.

Quirk, Robert. *The Mexican Revolution and the Catholic Church, 1910-1929.* Bloomington, Ind., 1973.

Raja Gabáglia, Laurita Pessoa. *O Cardeal Leme.* Rio de Janeiro, 1962.

Ratzinger, Josef. "Explico-vos a Teologia da Libertação," *REB*, 44 (1984): 108-15.

Read, William. *New Patterns of Church Growth in Brazil.* Grand Rapids, Mich., 1965.

Regis de Morais, J. F. *Os Bispos e a Política no Brasil.* São Paulo, 1982.

Reis, Fábio Wanderley. "Mudança Política no Brasil: Aberturas, Perspectivas e Miragens." Forthcoming article.

———. "Strategy, Institutions, and the Autonomy of the Political." Notre Dame, Ind., Dec. 1983. Kellogg Institute Working Paper no. 3.

"Relatório da Diocese de Goiás," in Carlos Mesters et al., *Uma Igreja Que Nasce do Povo.* Petrópolis, 1975.

Rhodes, Anthony. *The Vatican in the Age of the Dictators.* London, 1973.

Ribeiro de Oliveira, Pedro. *O Catolicismo Popular no Brasil.* Rio de Janeiro, 1970.

———. "Coexistência das Religiões no Brasil," *Vozes*, 71 (1977): 555-62.

———. "A Posição do Leigo nas CEBs," *SEDOC*, 9 (1976): 286-95.

———. "Religião e Dominação de Classe: O Caso da Romanização," *Religião e Sociedade*, 6 (1980): 167-88.

———. "Religiosidade Popular na América Latina," *REB*, 32 (1972): 354-64.

Ricardo, Fany. *O Conselho Indigenista Missionário, 1965-1979.* Rio de Janeiro, 1980. Cadernos do ISER, no. 10.

Richards, Pablo. *Morte das Cristandades e Nascimento da Igreja.* São Paulo, 1982.

Rio Caldeira, Teresa Pires do. "Para Que Serve o Voto? As Eleições e o Cotidiano na Periferia de São Paulo," in Bolívar Lamounier, ed., *Voto de Desconfiança: Eleições e Mudança Política no Brasil, 1970-1979.* Petrópolis, 1980, pp. 81-116.

Rocha, Regina. "Educação Popular e Poder," *Cadernos do CEDI*, 6 (1980): 29-37.

Rodrigues, José Albertino. *Sindicato e Desenvolvimento no Brasil.* São Paulo, 1968.

Rodrigues, Leôncio. *Conflito Industrial e Sindicalismo no Brasil.* São Paulo, 1966.

Rojas, Jaime, and Franz Vanderschueren. "The Catholic Church of Chile: From 'Social Christianity' to 'Christians for Socialism.'" *The Church and Politics in Latin America*, Latin American Research Unit, Toronto, vol. 1, no. 2 (Feb. 1977).

Rolim, Antônio. "O Culto Dominical e os Religiosos," *RCRB*, 100 (1963): 631-36.

———. "Em Torno da Religiosidade no Brasil," *REB*, 25 (1965): 11-27.

Rolim, Francisco Cartaxo. "A Greve do ABC e a Igreja," *REB*, 44 (1984): 131-51.

———. *Religião e Classes Populares*. Petrópolis, 1980.
———. "Religiosidade Popular," in Cândido Padim et al., *Missão da Igreja no Brasil*. São Paulo, 1979, pp. 79-94.
Romano, Roberto. *Brasil: Igreja contra Estado*. São Paulo, 1979.
Romero de Iguiñiz, Catalina. "Cambios en la relación iglesia-sociedad en el Perú," *Revista Debates en Sociologia*, 7 (n.d.): 115-41.
Rossi, Agnelo. "Uma Experiência de Catequese Popular," *REB*, 17 (1957): 731-37.
———. "Os Primeiros Manuais da Catequese Popular," *REB*, 18 (1958): 463-64.
Salem, Helena, ed. *A Igreja dos Oprimidos*. São Paulo, 1981.
Sánchez, José M. *Reform and Reaction: The Politico-Religious Background of the Spanish Civil War*. Chapel Hill, N.C., 1963.
Sanders, Thomas. "Brazil in 1980: The Emerging Political Model," in Thomas Bruneau and Philippe Faucher, eds., *Authoritarian Capitalism: Brazil's Contemporary Economic and Political Development*. Boulder, Colo., 1981, pp. 193-218.
———. "Catholicism and Development: The Catholic Left in Brazil," in Kalman Silvert, ed., *Churches and States: The Religious Institution and Modernization*. New York, 1967, pp. 81-99.
———. "The Evolution of a Catholic Intellectual." Field letter to Richard H. Nolte, Institute of Current World Affairs, October 1967.
———. "The Theology of Liberation: Christian Utopianism," *Christianity and Crisis*, 33 (1973): 167-73.
Sanks, T. Howland. *Authority in the Church: A Study in Changing Paradigms*. Missoula, Mont., 1974.
Sanks, T. Howland, and Brian Smith. "Liberation Ecclesiology: Praxis, Theory, Praxis." *Theological Studies*, 38 (1977). 3-38.
Santos, Roberto. "Para Deter a Calamidade ou uma Alternativa ao Projeto Oficial sobre a Floresta Amazonia," *Encontros com a Civilização Brasileira*, 23 (1980): 65-86.
Santos, Wanderley Guilherme dos. "The Calculus of Conflict: Impasse in Brazilian Politics and the Crisis of 1964." Ph.D. dissertation, Stanford University, 1979.
———. *Cidadania e Justiça: A Política Social na Ordem Brasileira*. Rio de Janeiro, 1979.
———. *Poder e Política: Crônica do Autoritarismo Brasileiro*. Rio de Janeiro, 1978.
Schmitter, Philippe. *Interest Conflict and Political Change in Brazil*. Stanford, 1971.
———. "The 'Portugalization' of Brazil?" in Alfred Stepan, ed., *Authoritarian Brazil: Origins, Policies, and Future*. New Haven, 1973, pp. 179-232.
Schooyans, Michel. *O Desafio da Secularização*. São Paulo, 1968.
Schwartzman, Simon. *Bases do Autoritarismo no Brasil*. Rio de Janeiro, 1982.
Seganfreddo, Sônia. *UNE: Instrumento de Subversão*. Rio de Janeiro, 1963.
Selznick, Philip. "Foundations of the Theory of Organization," in Amitai

Etzioni, ed., *A Sociological Reader of Complex Organizations.* New York, 1969, pp. 19-32.
——. *Leadership in Administration.* Evanston, Ill., 1957.
Silva Gotay, Samuel. *El Pensamiento Cristiano Revolucionario en América Latina y el Cáribe.* Salamanca, 1981.
Silveira Camargo, Paulo Florêncio da. *A Igreja na História de São Paulo.* São Paulo, 1953.
Simon, Gerhard. "The Catholic Church and the Communist State in the Soviet Union and Eastern Europe," in Bohdan Bociurkiw and John Strong, eds., *Religion and Atheism in the U.S.S.R. and Eastern Europe,* Toronto, 1975, pp. 190-221.
Singer, Paul. *Economia Política da Urbanização.* São Paulo, 1977.
——. "Movimentos de Bairros," in Paul Singer and Vinícius Caldeira Brant, eds., *São Paulo: O Povo em Movimento.* Petrópolis, 1980, pp. 83-108.
——. "Movimentos Sociais em São Paulo: Traços Comuns e Perspectivas," in Paul Singer and Vinícius Caldeira Brant, eds., *São Paulo: O Povo em Movimento.* Petrópolis, 1980, pp. 207-30.
Singer, Paul, and Vinícius Caldeira Brant, eds. *São Paulo: O Povo em Movimento.* Petrópolis, 1980.
Skidmore, Thomas. *Politics in Brazil, 1930-1964: An Experiment in Democracy.* New York, 1967.
Smith, Brian. *The Church and Politics in Chile: Challenges to Modern Catholicism.* Princeton, 1982.
——. "Churches and Human Rights in Latin America: Recent Trends on the Subcontinent," in Daniel Levine, ed., *Churches and Politics in Latin America.* Beverly Hills, Calif., 1979, pp. 155-93.
——. "Religion and Social Change: Classical Theories and New Formulations in the Context of Recent Developments in Latin America," *Latin American Research Review,* 10 (1975): 3-34.
Sorj, Bernardo. "Agrarian Structure and Politics in Present Day Brazil," *Latin American Perspectives,* 24 (1980): 23-34.
Souto, Anna Luiza. "Movimentos Populares Urbanos e Suas Formas de Organização Ligadas à Igreja," in ANPOCS, *Ciências Sociais Hoje,* 2 (Brasília, 1983): 63-95.
Souza, Amaury de, and Bolívar Lamounier. "Governo e Sindicatos no Brasil: A Perspectiva dos Anos 80," *Dados,* 24 (1981): 139-59.
Souza, Herbet José de. "Betinho," in Pedro Celso Uchoa Cavalcanti and Jovelino Ramos, eds., *Memórias do Exílio: Brasil 1964 / 19??.* São Paulo, 1978, pp. 67-112.
——. "Juventude Cristã Hoje," in Luiz Gonzaga de Souza Lima, *Evolução Política dos Católicos e da Igreja no Brasil.* Petrópolis, 1979.
——. "Município de Boa Esperança: Participação Popular e Poder Local," in José Álvaro Moisés et al., *Alternativas Populares da Democracia.* Petrópolis, 1982, pp. 99-120.
Souza Lima, Luiz Gonzaga de. *Evolução Política dos Católicos e da Igreja no Brasil.* Petrópolis, 1979.

————. "Notas sobre as Comunidades Eclesiais de Base e a Organização Política," in José Álvaro Moisés et al., *Alternativas Populares da Democracia*. Petrópolis, 1982, pp. 41-72.

Souza Martins, Heloisa Helena Teixeira de. *O Estado e a Burocratização do Sindicato no Brasil*. São Paulo, 1979.

Souza Martins, José de. *Os Camponeses e a Política no Brasil*. Petrópolis, 1981.

————. *Expropriação e Violência: A Questão Política no Campo*. São Paulo, 1980.

Souza Montenegro, João Alfredo. *Evolução do Catolicismo no Brasil*. Petrópolis, 1972.

Souza Netto, Benjamin. *Tendências Atuais do Catolicismo no Brasil*. Rio de Janeiro, 1979. Cadernos do ISER no. 12.

Stepan, Alfred. *The Military in Politics: Changing Patterns in Brazil*. Princeton, 1971.

————. *The State and Society: Peru in Comparative Perspective*. Princeton, 1978.

————. "State Power and the Strength of Civil Society in the Southern Cone of Latin America," in Peter Evans et al., eds., *Bringing the State Back In*. New York, 1985, pp. 317–43.

————, ed. *Authoritarian Brazil: Origins, Policies, and Future*. New Haven, 1973.

Suess, Paulo. "A Caminhada do Conselho Indigenista Missionário, 1972-1984," *REB*, 44 (1984): 501-33.

————. *O Catolicismo Popular no Brasil*. São Paulo, 1979.

————. "Pastoral Popular: Discurso Teológico e Práxis Eclesial," *REB*, 38 (1978): 269-90.

Tarso, Paulo de. *Os Cristãos e a Revolução Social*. Rio de Janeiro, 1963.

Tavares de Almeida, Maria Hermínia. "Novas Demandas, Novos Direitos: Experiências do Sindicalismo Paulista na Última Década," *Dados*, 26 (1983): 243-64.

————. "Tendências Recentes de Negociação Coletiva no Brasil," *Dados*, 24 (1981): 161-89.

Therry, Leonard. "Dominant Power Components in the Brazilian Students' Movement," *Journal of Interamerican Studies and World Affairs*, 7 (1965): 27-48.

Thornton, Mary Crescentia. *The Church and Freemasonry in Brazil, 1872-1875: A Study in Regalism*. Washington, D.C., 1948.

Tilly, Charles. *From Mobilization to Revolution*. Reading, Mass., 1978.

Todaro, Margaret. "Pastors, Priests, and Politicians: A Study of the Brazilian Catholic Church, 1916-1945." Ph.D. dissertation, Columbia University, 1971.

Todaro Williams, Margaret. "The Politicization of the Brazilian Catholic Church: The Catholic Electoral League," *Journal of Interamerican Studies and World Affairs*, 16 (1974): 301-25.

Torres, Sergio, and John Eagleson, eds. *The Challenge of Basic Christian Communities*. Maryknoll, N.Y., 1981.

————. *Theology in the Americas*. Maryknoll, N.Y., 1976.

Trinidade, Hélio. *Integralismo: O Fascismo Brasileiro na Década de 30*. São Paulo, 1974.

Troeltsch, Ernst. *The Social Teachings of the Christian Churches*. New York, 1931.

Vaillancourt, Jean-Guy. *Papal Power: A Study of Vatican Control over Catholic Lay Groups*. Berkeley, Calif., 1980.

Valla, Victor, et al. *Para uma Formulação de uma Teoria de Educação Extra-escolar no Brasil: Ideologia, Educação e as Favelas do Rio de Janeiro, 1880-1980*. Rio de Janeiro, 1981.

Valladares, Lícia. *Passa-se uma Casa*. Rio de Janeiro, 1978.

Vallier, Ivan. *Catholicism, Social Control, and Modernization in Latin America*. Englewood Cliffs, N.J., 1970.

Vatican Congregation for the Doctrine of the Faith. "Instruction on Certain Aspects of the 'Theology of Liberation,'" *Origins*, Sept. 13, 1984.

Vaz, Henrique. "Consciência Histórica e Responsabilidade Histórica," in Luiz Alberto Gómez de Souza, ed., *Cristianismo Hoje*. Rio de Janeiro, 1962, pp. 69-82.

————. "Jovens Cristãos em Luta por uma História sem Servidões," in Luiz Alberto Gómez de Souza, ed., *Cristianismo Hoje*. Rio de Janeiro, 1962, pp. 53-68.

Vekemans, Roger. *Teología de la liberación y Cristianos por el socialismo*. Bogotá, 1976.

————. "Unidad y pluralismo en la iglesia," *Tierra Nueva*, 5 (1973): 45-50.

Velasco e Cruz, Sebastião, et al. *Sociedade e Política no Brasil Pós-64*. São Paulo, 1983.

Velho, Otávio Guilherme. "A Propósito de Terra e Igreja," *Encontros com a Civilização Brasileira*, 22 (1980): 157-68.

Vilela, Orlando. *Atitude Cristã em Face da Política*. Belo Horizonte, 1963.

Villaça, Antônio Carlos. *História da Questão Religiosa*. Rio de Janeiro, 1974.

————. *O Pensamento Católico no Brasil*. Rio de Janeiro, 1975.

Vinhas, Moisés. *O Partidão*. São Paulo, 1982.

Wagner, Peter. *Latin American Theology*. Grand Rapids, Mich., 1970.

Wanderley, Luiz Eduardo. "Comunidades Eclesiais de Base e Educação Popular," *REB*, 41 (1981): 686-707.

Warwick, Donald. "Personal and Organizational Effectiveness in the Roman Catholic Church," *Cross Currents*, 17 (1967): 401-17.

Weber, Max. *From Max Weber*. Edited by Hans Gerth and C. Wright Mills. New York, 1946.

————. *Max Weber on Charisma and Institution Building*. Edited by S. N. Eisenstadt. Chicago, 1968.

————. *The Religion of China*. New York, 1951.

————. *The Sociology of Religion*. Boston, 1963.

————. *The Theory of Social and Economic Organization*. New York, 1964.

Weffort, Francisco. "Nordestinos em São Paulo: Notas para um Estudo sobre Cultura Nacional e Cultura Popular," in *A Cultura do Povo*. São Paulo, 1979, pp. 13-23.

―――. *Participação e Conflito Industrial: Contagem e Osasco, 1968*. São Paulo, 1972. Cadernos CEBRAP no. 5.

―――. "Sindicatos e Política." Ph.D. dissertation, University of São Paulo, 1972.

Werneck Vianni, Luiz. *Liberalismo e Sindicato no Brasil*. Rio de Janeiro, 1976.

Wiarda, Howard. *The Brazilian Catholic Labor Movement*. Amherst, Mass., 1969.

―――. "The Catholic Labor Movement," in H. Jon Rosenbaum and William Tyler, eds., *Contemporary Brazil: Issues in Economic and Political Development*. New York, 1972, pp. 323-47.

Wilde, Alexander. "Ten Years of Change in the Church: Puebla and the Future," in Daniel Levine, ed., *Churches and Politics in Latin America*, Beverly Hills, Calif., 1979, pp. 267-80.

Willems, Emilio. *Followers of the New Faith*. Nashville, 1967.

Wirth, John. *Minas Gerais in the Brazilian Federation, 1889-1937*. Stanford, 1977.

Yinger, J. Milton. *Religion, Society, and the Individual*. New York, 1957.

Index